Russian Tactics

February 2024

United States Government
US Army

Contents

DISTRIBUTION STATEMENT: Approved for public release, distribution is unlimited.

Figures

Tables

This page intentionally left blank.

Preface

ATP 7-100.1 describes Russian tactics for use in Army training, professional education, and leader development. This document is part of the ATP 7-100 series that addresses a nation-state's military doctrine with a focus on army ground forces and tactical operations in offense, defense, and related mission sets. Other foundational topics include task organization, capabilities, and limitations related to military mission and support functions. ATP 7-100.1 serves as a foundation for understanding how Russian ground forces think and act in tactical operations. This publication presents multiple examples of functional tactics in dynamic operational environment conditions. The tactics in this ATP are descriptive and provide an orientation to tactics gathered from Russian doctrine, translated literature, and observations from recent historical events.

The principal audience for ATP 7-100.1 is all members of the profession of arms. Commanders and staffs of Army headquarters serving as joint task force or multinational headquarters should also refer to applicable joint or multinational doctrine concerning the range of military operations and joint or multinational forces. Trainers and educators throughout the Army will also use this publication.

Commanders, staffs, and subordinates ensure that their decisions and actions comply with applicable United States, international, and in some cases host-nation laws and regulations. Commanders at all levels ensure that their Soldiers operate in accordance with the law of war and the rules of engagement. (See FM 6-27.)

To compare information in this ATP with other Army doctrine, the reader must first understand the fundamentals of land operations in FM 3-0 and the Army's supporting ADPs and ATPs that describe military operations and the application of combat power. Joint and multinational application will require comparison to and contrast with relevant joint and multinational doctrine.

ATP 7-100.1 uses joint terms where applicable. Selected joint and Army terms and definitions appear in both the glossary and the text. For definitions shown in the text, the term is italicized, and the number of the proponent publication follows the definition. This publication is not the proponent for any Army terms.

Russian concepts and publications are mentioned throughout this publication. The former are underlined upon either first or second appearance, and the latter appear in italics. When a United States (U.S.) term—either joint or Army—has the same name as a Russian concept and the U.S. term is being referenced, it appears in italics.

ATP 7-100.1 applies to the Active Army, Army National Guard/Army National Guard of the United States, and United States Army Reserve unless otherwise stated.

The proponent of ATP 7-100.1 is the United States Army Combined Arms Center. The preparing agency is the Combined Arms Doctrine Directorate, United States Army Combined Arms Center. The lead agency tasked with developing this ATP is the United States Army Training and Doctrine Command G-2, Analysis and Control Element, Operational Environment and Threat Analysis Directorate. Send comments and recommendations on DA Form 2028 (*Recommended Changes to Publications and Blank Forms*) to Commander, United States Army Combined Arms Center and Fort Leavenworth, ATZL-MCD (ATP 7-100.1), 300 McPherson Avenue, Fort Leavenworth, KS 66027-2337; by email to usarmy.leavenworth.mccoe.mbx.cadd-org-mailbox@army.mil; or submit an electronic DA Form 2028.

This page intentionally left blank.

Introduction

ATP 7-100.1, as part of the U.S. Army 7-100 series and in support of AR 350-2, addresses the tactics, organization, and activities Russian military. This ATP describes how Russia would fight according to its doctrine. It uses Russian tactical concepts employed in training and exercises, primarily for large-scale combat operations (LSCO).

This ATP is not meant to represent how the Russians are currently fighting in Ukraine. Many insights and observations can be collected daily to either affirm or refute Russian doctrinal strategies and tactics, but it's far too early to acknowledge any definitive changes in doctrine. The Military District and unit diagrams in this ATP may be affected based on early observations of the conflict in Ukraine. With so many Russian units now in Ukraine, it will take some time to determine a new laydown of forces if that becomes necessary. Furthermore, with the losses Russia has suffered, it is too early to assess the structure and equipping of any Russian unit for the next 5 to 10 years.

We are still studying the conflict in Ukraine and continuing to revise our assessments. Therefore, the ATP is not the correct medium for publication of our initial observations nor potential future changes for the Russian Army. Instead, this type of information will be available at https://oe.tradoc.army.mil/how-russia-fights .

PART ONE – RUSSIAN FUNDAMENTALS

Chapter 1 describes the strategic overview, the Russian Federation in competition, strategic objectives and setting finishing with Russia's operational environment.

Chapter 2 describes the overview of the Russian military including its role and National support. Additionally, the development of the modern Russian military and the doctrine and thought of the military forces.

Chapter 3 describes the Russian ground forces organization, battle management and the organization into districts.

PART TWO – TACTICAL ACTIONS

Chapter 4 describes the Russian reconnaissance and security fundamentals and formations, how the integrated air defense system role in security and the concepts of electromagnetic warfare reconnaissance and security actions.

Chapter 5 describes the doctrinal concept of fires and the Russian strike complex which includes indirect fires, antitank, radio electromagnetic battle, aerospace and missiles and rockets.

Chapter 6 describes the Russian forces defense including the purpose, goals, and requirements with an in-depth breakdown of the types of defenses.

Chapter 7 describes the Russian forces offense including the principles, planning organization and how to execute the offensive. Additionally, tactical offensive actions for battalions, detachments and subunits are described.

APPENDIXES

Appendix A describes the Russian fires complex and doctrinal capabilities and application of missile and artillery forces.

Appendix B describes the ground forces tanks, infantry fighting vehicles and airborne vehicles capabilities and limitations.

Appendix C describes the aerospace support and the consolidation of space operations, medium to high level air defense, fixed and rotary wing aircraft and transport under one service branch.

Appendix D describes the air defense support and the majority of the Russian air defense forces is under the Russian Federation air defense forces and the capabilities and limitations of those forces.

Appendix E describes the antitank support equipment overview.

Appendix F describes the electromagnetic warfare tactical level capabilities and equipment.

Appendix G describes the engineer support for defensive and offensive engineering tasks, support actions and equipment.

Appendix H describes the material technical services and support units, requirements, equipment, and the integration in Russian combined arms.

Appendix I describes the nuclear, chemical, and biological protection operations, units and an equipment overview.

Appendix J describes the automated command and communication complexes, provides a functional overview of tactical level command and control, and radio equipment and integration in combined arms.

Appendix K describes the special operations forces doctrinally and organized with capabilities and integrated into combined arms national/strategic echelons.

PART ONE

Russian Fundamentals

Part One addresses four primary areas that set the context for Russian tactical actions. Chapter 1 presents Russia's strategic setting and introduces national capabilities that impact the tactical fight to help set the context for actions of the Ground Forces of the Russian Federation (Сухопутные войска Российской Федерации— Sukhoputnyye voyska Rossiyskoy Federatsii— SVRF shortened to SV in this document), discussed in subsequent chapters. Chapter 2 describes the historical basis of the current Russian military: its doctrine and concepts, current structure, and integration of joint capabilities. Chapter 3 focuses on battlefield task organization for defensive and offensive actions using "New Look" formations to perform standardized battle drills.

Chapter 1

Russian Strategic Overview

This chapter is an overview of the fundamental conditions that contextualize the Russian Federation, its military, and its actions in an operational environment (OE). It examines Russia's relations with the United States and projects Russia's approach to exploiting conditions of the environment to yield a strategic advantage. It also introduces national capabilities that support military operations, both during competition and conflict.

RUSSIA IN COMPETITION

1-1.   From the time of Peter the Great in the 17th and early 18th centuries to the present day, Russia has sought what it perceives is its rightful place as a world power. This drive is a result of Russia's geopolitical insecurity and a strategic culture and worldview influenced by the size of its territory, length of its borders, and a perception of military encirclement. As a major European power starting in the 18th century and for nearly three hundred years afterward, Russia was a dominant regional and global power. In 1991, with the collapse of the Soviet Union, Russia experienced a significant setback and has struggled with finding its new role in the international community.

1-2.   Russia's policy statements, including the 2021 National Security Strategy, provide a glimpse into Russian leader's vision for its role. While the Security Strategy is like the one announced in 2015, the tenor of the revised document is stronger, revealing Russia's view of deteriorating relations with the West. For the foreseeable future, this position sets the tone for all Russian national actions and for any interaction with the United States, NATO, and the West.

1-3.   Russia's relations with the United States are defined by a perpetual state of competition and self-interest. While there are instances of positive interaction on discrete programs, the relations between Russia and the United States remain predominantly competitive. Today's rivalry can be traced back as far as the 1918–1920 Allied invasion of Russia at Archangel and Vladivostok, which included U.S. troops, during the

Russian Revolution. Even after the U.S. alliance with the Soviet Union during the Second World War, both countries quickly returned to a competitive stance during the Cold War. Actions during the Cold War up to the present set an enduring tone of competition and confrontation between Russia and the United States.

1-4. During the Cold War, the rivalry between the United States and Soviet Union escalated and ultimately resulted in massive efforts to undermine and compete with one another. The eventual breakup of the Soviet Union and a turn toward democracy did not resolve this, but rather it paved the way for a new phase of competition and conflict that provides fodder for negative Russian narratives about the United States' role on the international stage. Today, substantial sectors of the Russian population and political structure consider the United States to be the primary cause of the dissolution of the Soviet Union. This inherent distrust of the United States and Russia's expanding rivalry with other European countries have exacerbated Russia's distrust of the U.S.-led liberal world order that embraces collective security, economic openness, and social progress.

1-5. Russia's 2021 National Security Strategy holds that Russia's policy pursuits are being restrained by a Western containment strategy via diplomatic, informational, military, and economic methods meant to continue Western dominance. The Security Strategy is complemented by its Information Security Doctrine, and a military doctrine that tasks its armed forces and other security services with defeating aggression against Russia and creating conditions favorable to Russian interests.

> ***Note***. The Russian National Security Strategy and other military publications serve as the basis for use of the term "aggressor" throughout this ATP. While Russia does use other terms such as "enemy" or "threat," its underlying security vision sees aggressors using direct and indirect methods to undermine and destroy the nation.

RUSSIAN STRATEGIC OBJECTIVES

1-6. Russia pursues a global strategy driven by a desire to once again be recognized as a world power. Its foreign policy stratagems will endure beyond the current leaders, and it is highly likely that future Russian leaders will pursue these policies for the foreseeable future, given its institutionalization throughout the Kremlin and other bureaucracies. As a world power, Russia believes it can provide stability for countries on its periphery, particularly the former Soviet states, and influence international policy and law away from the liberal international system of the West. To achieve this end state, Russia will give priority to the following strategic objectives: maintaining regional dominance, ensuring protection and security of its national interests as well as the current regime, countering foreign interference, and recognition as a global power.

REGIONAL DOMINANCE

1-7. Russia's quest for regional dominance is a longstanding characteristic of its foreign policy and directly related to its perception of encirclement and containment efforts from the West. Russia believes that maintaining regional dominance will preserve its ability to exert influence in its "near-abroad"—Russia's term for former Soviet states and other nearby countries. Russia views influence in this region as an effective buffer against potential aggressors and justifies any associated military engagements as purely strategic defensive actions, designed to maintain its bulwark against aggressors.

PROTECTION AND SECURITY

1-8. Russia's aspirations to have a more significant role on both regional and global stages are underpinned by an essential requirement to ensure protection and security of national interests. Policy and doctrine documents highlight domestic and foreign concerns, and the Russian military is tasked with ensuring these concerns do not impact the country's desired end state. As an element of national power, Russia openly modernizes and wields its military and nuclear capabilities as a deterrent to aggressors. Russia is emphasizing the development of structure, composition, and size, as well as improved technologies for these capabilities to engage anticipated internal and external threats.

COUNTERING FOREIGN INTERFERENCE

1-9. Russia's entire approach to international affairs is driven by the perspective that others are deliberately working to counter its efforts. It views NATO and the United States as the worst perpetrators of this interference and plans for the inevitable requirement to counter that interference. Notably, Russian policy and doctrine allow for both reactionary and preemptive actions, across all elements of national power, to protect its national interests.

RECOGNITION AS A WORLD POWER

1-10. All these objectives contribute to Russia's drive to achieve world power status, an end-state it views as necessary to shape the global environment and shift international policy and law away from the current U.S.-led system. To achieve this objective, Russia will continue its efforts to grow its international standing as a foil to the United States, NATO, and the liberal international system. These include forging key strategic partnerships in regions of the world where the United States lacks a strong foothold and providing political, economic, and military support to regimes friendly to Russia, all the while exploiting and manipulating the information environment to its advantage.

1-11. Russia's national policy statements and doctrine indicate a readiness and willingness to intervene in any international crisis it sees as relevant to its national interests. Russia emphasizes the importance of the diplomatic, informational, and economic elements of national power in recognition of its limited military power projection capabilities. Russia's sophistication in the application of soft power, particularly in the area of information, allows it to seize opportunities to gain strategic objectives. It does use its military capabilities to support sophisticated information operations that focus engagements with the West. Russia continues making progress in upgrading and reforming its military power to expand deterrence and security, however its nuclear arsenal remains its essential military guarantor in safeguarding the nation.

STRATEGIC SETTING

1-12. Russia approaches international relations in a deliberate and opportunistic manner. It perceives that the United States is weakening and forecasts a shift in power distribution that would result in more equal power sharing between the United States and rising powers like China and Russia. To capitalize on this perception, Russia, for the foreseeable future, will continue to seize on global opportunities to achieve situational advantage to further its strategic objectives and to confront the United States in the diplomatic, military, economic, and information domains. Russia will combine this approach with its long-established stratagem of competition and confrontation with the United States and NATO in the states on the periphery of its borders.

1-13. Conditions will enable Russia to compete with the United States and other Western nations, as well as to create opportunities for Russia to achieve a competitive advantage against its rivals. Paragraphs 1-17 through 1-25 describe key considerations about Russia's influence and exploitation of the future environment:

1-14. Russia's analysis of how the United States fights and its own experience in recent conflicts lead it to the understanding that information management is critical for successful actions. Russia uses information manipulation, deceptions, and disruption to achieve information dominance during competition and conflict. It also continues enhancement of automation of the command and control (C2) process coupled with integration of its military complexes to provide real-time battlefield visibility and awareness.

1-15. Russia will manipulate the objective reality favorable to its opponents to create a subjective reality favorable to itself. To accomplish this, it will employ reflexive control methods and use deception and influence to manipulate the perceptions of an "aggressor." Reflexive control is a methodology initiated by the Soviets in the 1960s. In plain terms, it is a process of transmitting cunningly designed information to the aggressor which will cause it to willingly make decisions beneficial to the Russians. Russia sees its actions as successful when it achieves cognitive dominance over its targets and leaders of aggressor states voluntarily make decisions favorable to Russia.

1-16. Russia will actively challenge the relative position of U.S. influence in the global order while avoiding direct confrontation with the U.S. military. Russia seeks to integrate its military, technological, information, diplomatic, economic, cultural, and other powers to achieve its strategic goals. Through integration of these methods and collaboration with its regional partners, Russia will create situations in which U.S. power is severely constrained. By using nonmilitary elements of power short of armed conflict during competition with the West it will avoid direct conflict with the United States but will still act to counter U.S. interests whenever it is to Russia's advantage to do so. This approach will be constrained by Russia's economic, demographic, and technical limitations.

1-17. An expanding spectrum of contentious issues will continue fueling future competition and conflict between Russia and the West. The number and intensity of friction points—some enduring and others new—will increase competition between Russia and the West and possibly bring them closer to overt conflict. Russia will continue to compete with the West for nuclear and missile supremacy, while newer theaters of competition open or intensify in the Arctic. That competition and conflict will take new and very different forms involving all domains and elements of national power.

1-18. Russia will continue to fight while maintaining deniability. Russia gains plausible deniability and a degree of diplomatic cover in carrying out proxy wars using criminal and militant groups, or special operations troops and other military or paramilitary forces (such as the Wagner Group and other aligned private military contractors). Russia will continue to use these proxies with covert conventional forces to achieve outcomes that would otherwise be untenable in the strategic arena. These actions allow Russia to further its objective of improving its world power status while avoiding direct military conflict with U.S. and NATO military forces.

1-19. Scientific and technological progress will provide Russia and its surrogates' militaries with increased precision, speed, range, adaptability, survivability, and effectiveness. Russia will continue to seek technologies that improve these characteristics to achieve overmatch using both developments from the civilian sector as well as direct military advances. It will continue using specific niche weapons systems, such as hypersonic missiles; unmanned aerial vehicles; precision-guided artillery; electromagnetic warfare; directed-energy weapons; and unmanned aircraft, vehicles, marine craft, and systems, directed at perceived U.S. vulnerabilities.

1-20. Russia will expand its capabilities to operate in and influence urban environments that are increasingly interconnected. The rapidly growing interconnection of economic and information systems will link populations at the individual level. Russia's use of information warfare (IV) will allow it to exploit these conditions.

1-21. Russia has less restrictive rules of engagement regulating competition and conflict than does the United States. Using unconventional methods, it will avoid condemnation and sanction by other nations during competition. As a result, use of proxy forces, information confrontation (IPb), or cyber-attacks in the competitive domains of land, air, maritime, space, and information will be more common than open military confrontation. In military conflicts, Russia actively plans for and practices the use of nuclear, chemical, and flame weapon fires at the strategic to tactical levels.

> ***Note.*** Distinctions between the Russian categories of information confrontation (информационное противоборство— *informatsionnye protivoborstvo— IPb)* and information warfare (информационная война—informatsionnaya voyna—IV) are debated within official Russian references. Information confrontation is presented in this ATP but the primary focus for tactical actions will be on information warfare.

1-22. Russia will exploit trends such as its youth, increased urbanization along major bodies of water, and technological advancements. While these trends do not define the entire list, their convergence will result in regional and international turbulence that Russia will likely exploit to its advantage. Other naturally occurring conditions, such as natural disasters, extreme weather events, and their second- and third-order effects will have significant impacts on an OE due to resulting competition and conflict between Russia and other nations.

1-23. Russia likely will target vulnerable countries or regions strategically important to achieving its objectives. Such areas with divided populations, especially those with ethnic Russians living in them, are the most vulnerable to Russian exploitation. Other areas with critical natural resources or those considered locations of strategic importance will also be of interest to Russia.

1-24. Russia will seek to contest the global commons. The global commons—the Earth's domains or areas that no one state controls, but on which all rely, such as oceans, atmosphere, and orbital space—will be increasingly contested in the future. Land, air, maritime, space, and cyberspace domains will continue to be targeted by Russia to achieve its objectives.

1-25. All these factors will create conditions U.S. forces must be prepared to encounter when conducting multi-domain operations against Russia or a Russian proxy force. Russia will use all its instruments of national power in an integrated campaign to further its strategic goals and objectives. It will direct, control, and integrate the actors and actions that impact tactical-level U.S. forces from the Russian national strategic level.

RUSSIA'S OPERATIONAL ENVIRONMENT

1-26. Russia's perception of an OE is characterized by a sense of strategic vulnerability and a desperate desire for great power status. It harbors concerns about its population over the potential for unrest caused by the general dissatisfaction with the standard of living and is entirely untrusting of the United States and its Western European allies. Russia seeks to insulate itself from the United States and its allies by creating a sphere of influence in its near-abroad in the former Soviet states and is working to become more cooperative with countries outside of Europe. The following conditions are presented using eight interrelated operational variables which are political, military, economic, social, information, infrastructure, physical environment, and time, collectively referred to as PMESII-PT serve as a descriptive overview of Russia's understanding of its OE.

POLITICAL

1-27. To maintain the current operational environment, current Russian leaders in power must continue to achieve the nations' strategic goals:

- Integration of all elements of national power-political, cultural, economic (including energy), military, diplomatic, and IV are necessary to succeed in competition and conflicts.
- Domestic policies emphasize the importance of strategic nuclear force and conventional military capability to counter perceived threats.
- Domestic and foreign policies to maintain a strategic sphere of influence, or buffer zone, between Russia and NATO countries.
- Foreign policy efforts are expanding Russia's influence beyond its near-abroad. Russia is actively involved in the Middle East and Africa, working to establish domination in the Arctic, and joining cooperative agreements in Asia. It also continues to develop its strategic relationship and cooperation with China.
- Russia retains permanent member status on United Nations Security Council, enabling it to effectively counter attempts by this organization or many other international organizations to act against Russian interests.

MILITARY

1-28. Russia's National Defense Strategy focuses on the following principles to counter possible United States' and their European Allies' aggressions to Russian Territories:

- A modern and effective military is essential to providing Russian security and to achieving world power status.
- Modern nuclear forces and means from strategic to tactical levels are essential elements of Russia's military power.
- Modernization efforts are a priority for all areas of the military, including nuclear, air, maritime, and land power.
- Capabilities development is focused on improving precision fires, anti-tank, and high mobility systems.
- Integration of military capabilities using automated command and control complexes to prevent aggressor's access to Russia's periphery are a priority for expansion.

ECONOMIC

1-29. Russia's economic policies focus on the following:

- Economic strength is necessary to not only fuel the other elements of national power but also to attain or retain status as a world power. Economic considerations influence or direct political actions.
- Economic policies target exploitation of domestic natural resources (for example, hydrocarbons, minerals, fisheries), including those found in the Arctic.
- Export and trade controls are a means to influence or coerce other European countries.
- Power generation, military materiel, and technical expertise are key economic commodities.

SOCIAL

1-30. Russian leaders rely heavily on ensuring its social construct aligns with their strategic goals:

- Support of the Russian population is essential to maintain the nation and to achieve great power status. Russian leaders view the threat of hybrid warfare used to create internal unrest in the form of a popular revolution as a significant threat.
- Russian culture creates a strong basis to oppose Western liberal policies and initiatives.
- The ethnic Russian diaspora is a legitimate resource used to support national objectives.
- The Russian Orthodox Church has a key role to play in establishing social and military conditions in Russia.

INFORMATION

1-31. Russia's operational environment relies heavily on controlling information:

- Russia views the information environment of utmost importance for both its domestic and foreign policy efforts.
- Russian overt and covert efforts to control the information environment and manipulate perceptions of reality will continue to target its domestic population as well as aggressors.
- Confrontations and conflicts may be won primarily—or even exclusively—by using IPb or warfare. Information actions ultimately focus on defeating a competitor's will to fight.

INFRASTRUCTURE

1-32. Russia continues to improve infrastructure with the following considerations in mind:

- Development efforts are focused on military equipment storage sites to facilitate brigade, division, and army deployment.
- Construction and maintenance of underground facilities to protect the nation's leaders and strategic forces around Moscow will continue.
- Russia's size causes it to emphasize maintenance and improvement of its interior lines of communication, primarily rail, to facilitate rapid movement of military forces.
- Efforts to develop new contracts to build nuclear power facilities outside of Russia further Russian influence and status.
- Development of the coastal city of Kaliningrad as well as the Kaliningrad Oblast is ongoing to mitigate the effects of changing sea levels.

PHYSICAL ENVIRONMENT

1-33. Russia's large land mass poses a variety of challenges within its operational environment:

- Russia must capitalize on the effects of climate change to exploit the Arctic region before its competitors do the same.
- Russia's vast border dictates that it requires military forces that can rapidly deploy in response to a wide variety of threats.

● Military complexes must be designed to operate in areas with numerous water obstacles and Arctic conditions.

TIME

1-34. Russia understands the importance of swift actions and strategic patience to achieve its strategic goals:

● The Kremlin recognizes the timing complications that the United States faces due to the deployment distances involved to bring land forces to bear in the event of a conflict.

● Russia looks to take advantage of NATO's decision-making process, which often requires consensus and can be time consuming.

● Russia's political leaders understand that IPb takes time to develop and becomes more effective by directing the same or related messages at the target population through various channels over an extended period.

● Russia has demonstrated the ability to employ unconventional means (proxy forces, IPb, or cyber-attacks) over an extended period to undermine U.S. interests and shape potential future battlefields in their favor.

This page intentionally left blank.

Chapter 2

Russian Military Overview

This chapter focuses on the historical background and basis of the Russian military. It also reviews the military doctrine and thought that directs the evolution of the military. It presents the factors that influence the latest organizational restructuring of Russia's security and military forces, as well as national-level integration of forces and means to accomplish strategic goals and objectives.

NATIONAL LEVEL SUPPORT TO MILITARY OPERATIONS

2-1.   The advent of what has been dubbed New Generation Warfare, or 6th Generation Warfare, has ushered in a host of new concepts resulting in an updated Russia military doctrine. Russia's doctrinal evolution greatly influences future conflicts down to the tactical level. To set favorable conditions in an operational environment Russia relies on the integration of national level capabilities to attain strategic advantage.

2-2.   The military philosopher Sun Tzu first highlighted the ability to destroy an aggressor's will to resist without battle as a sign of military prowess. Russia's evolving concept of warfare wholeheartedly embraces this idea. Russia's warfare concept demonstrates a growing capability in its approach to warfare, rather than focusing the traditional elements of warfare—materiel and organization—Russia now emphasizes psychological and IV. Russia's perception that there is little, or no separation of peace and conflict resulted in the evolution of Russia's understanding of warfare. Every action it takes across its diplomatic, information, military, and economic elements of power is specifically calculated to achieve effects in what it sees as psychological battlespace. This approach to warfare, developed from analysis of Western military actions, shows Russia's materiel approach to warfare will rely on the effects of precision targeting and massed fires as well as the type of IV embodied in previous descriptions of New Generation Warfare.

2-3.   Russia believes that to win any future conflict, it must dominate in IPb, harness the population to support its operations, and use integrated strikes to defeat any aggressor. These characteristics, taken together, form the current Russian concept of warfare as primarily focused on the political will of an aggressor. These concepts have been central to Russia's military reorganization and prioritization of future capabilities development, and they have been particularly impactful on the SV. Modernization efforts for the SV focus on creating a force that can capitalize on national assets, such as those that set the conditions in the social and information environments, and on increasing its competence with precision reconnaissance and targeting coupled with weapon systems with significant improvements.

2-4.   Military doctrine complements this modernization by accounting and planning for the contributions of national-level actions as part of a Russian integrated campaign. While national-level actions impact and are often conducted at a tactical level, they are rarely, if ever, controlled by tactical-level commanders. Should the United States find itself embroiled in conflict with Russia, it will be confronted in a tactical fight with efforts to dominate the information environment, proxies working among the population on behalf of Russia, and the presence of precision strike capabilities on the battlefield.

> ***Note.*** Russia's emphasis on precision fires capabilities, referred to as Russia's "Strike" capability, is discussed in chapter 5.

INFORMATION SUPERIORITY

2-5.   Russia recognizes that domination of the information environment prior to and during combat is critical to successful operations. Information warfare consists of information-technical or information-psychological actions. Information-technical actions employ physical means to manipulate or attack information reliability while information-psychological means concentrate on the individual or population perception of the information.

2-6.   Russia categorizes information actions into two groups: IPb and IV. These groups encompass hostile actions in which information is a tool, a target, or a domain. Primarily IPb involves covert measures employed by Russia during ongoing competition prior to and during large-scale war. Information warfare focuses on those aggressive actions in the information environment, including electromagnetic warfare, that support SV combat actions. Strategic and operational IV units integrate with tactical formations to perform actions that support tactical units and subunits.

2-7.   Efforts to dominate the information environment are not limited to periods of war; rather, Russia conducts IPb throughout competition, crisis, and conflict. During competition, Russia uses IPb to protect its forces and populace against adverse information, to degrade aggressor capabilities, and to set the conditions in the OE. The protection measures are continuous and transition into the initial period of conflict when military forces become employed. Active IV attacks may begin in the initial period of conflict and continue into large-scale war. National-level information campaigns continue in support of Russian strategic objectives while the SV employs integrated IV actions in support of all combat actions.

2-8.   Russia's IV means are combined systematically and continuously to target the aggressor's political will to wage war and its decision-making processes. Russia uses a host of methods to accomplish information dominance: propaganda, counterpropaganda, deception, deflection, provocations, reflexive control, disinformation, and psychological pressure. These multiple forms of information manipulation and attack present a believable compilation of information and corroborating evidence, as a deception, that guides decisions that seem to be reasoned and correct to an aggressor but support Russian goals. Russian reflexive control manipulates information and other forms of sensory presentation so that apparently true data obtained by the IV target is mutually supporting misinformation.

2-9.   Russia also uses electromagnetic warfare methods that allow an aggressor the freedom to continue its use of the electromagnetic spectrum (EMS), and that do not cause suspicions of intrusion; this is enabled by Russian deception or disruption practices. Russian protection and security measures ensure the actual situation, and its IV manipulation are not uncovered. At designated times, key information-gathering and -transmitting nodes will be disrupted or destroyed using jamming or spoofing and are designed to combine with other IV means to provide false electromagnetic signatures or incorrect targeting data.

2-10. Russia includes several elements under the IV umbrella: computer network operations, psychological operations, strategic communications, influence, intelligence, counterintelligence, disinformation, electromagnetic warfare, disruption of communications, jamming or spoofing navigation systems, destruction of aggressor computer and network capabilities, and various deception/denial (*maskirovka*). Russian maskirovka employs camouflage, deception, denial, subversion, sabotage, espionage, propaganda, and psychological operations, to degrade or deny an aggressor's ability to fully understand and adequately respond to the OE situation. All the different elements in the information environment are treated as a coordinated whole under the heading of IV.

2-11. Russia may employ IV methods or tools from both civilian and military sources and from assets of third-party actors. Tools for waging IV can include but are not limited to: Conventional physical and electromagnetic destruction means, malicious software, denial-of-service attacks, manipulation on the Internet, manipulation of the media, manipulation of public opinion, exploitation of communication networks and employment of various types of reconnaissance, espionage, and eavesdropping technologies.

2-12. The types of IV do not exist in isolation from one another and are not mutually exclusive. The overlapping of functions, means, and targets requires that they all be integrated into a single, integrated IV plan. However, effective execution of IV does not necessarily involve the use of all elements concurrently. In some cases, one element may be all that is required to successfully execute an IV action. Nevertheless, using one element or sub-element, such as camouflage, does not by itself necessarily constitute an application of IV.

RUSSIAN PROXY FORCES

2-13. Russia regularly uses, and will continue to use, proxy forces (private military companies, separatist forces in areas of frozen conflict, allies, and partners) to achieve success in conflicts and throughout the competition period. Russia's use of proxy forces provides it an umbrella of plausible deniability and enables it to achieve tactical, operational, and strategic goals that it otherwise might not. These forces, that may not be controlled by Russian tactical commanders, have significant influence on the tactical battlefield and provide Russia the added advantage of undermining Western tactical, operational, and strategic objectives. The United States is most likely to encounter three forms of Russian proxies: local militant (separatist) groups, private military companies, and criminal organizations.

Militant Groups

2-14. Russia typically uses local militant groups in its near-abroad to influence local conditions to shift a conflict to benefit Russian strategic interests. These groups have historically been composed of regular Russian soldiers, Russian mercenaries, criminals, local pro-separatist groups, Russian right-wing extremists, Russian nationalists and communists, soccer hooligans, motorcycle gangs, and deserters from the local (non-Russia) army and security services. These groups may conduct independent or coordinated actions separate from or in concert with Russian military or security forces. Under these conditions, these groups can capably pressure the local governments to aid Russian activities and provide political cover for Russia's attempt to control its near-abroad.

Private Military Companies

2-15. Russia has a history of employing private military companies (PMCs) or security forces that dates to the tsar's use of Cossacks in the 18th century for internal security and actions on Russia's periphery. Individuals employed by PMCs may be recognized as mercenaries by the international community. The traditional international definition of a mercenary is a person that fights for monetary gain rather than loyalty to a particular nation and that is indifferent to issues of legality. While Russian law prohibits the use of mercenaries, Russian PMCs' continued involvement in conflicts in Syria and some African nations indicate the use of PMCs is something Russia will continue.

2-16. There is a close connection between the Russian government and some PMCs. For example, one of the foremost PMCs trains its personnel at a Russian military-intelligence special operations force training center. Still others, while perhaps lacking in access to the facilities as described above, are closely aligned with the Kremlin's agenda and their command-and-control system mirrors that of the Russian ground forces (SV). In many of their overseas operations, PMCs have trained with and conducted actions that support the Russian Ministry of Defense as well as being equipped in a manner akin to the SV. PMCs have employed tanks, multiple rocket launchers, air defense systems, and artillery with success. As they do not officially represent Russia, the PMCs can adopt any organization, equipment, or uniform as they attempt to blend in with the local forces.

Criminal Organizations

2-17. Transnational criminal organizations play a large role in persistent conflict. Organized crime is deeply rooted in Russian society and is likely a major tool of Russian statecraft. Several countries on Russia's periphery and across the world accuse Russia of using criminal activity to undermine control of their countries. Russia has used, and will likely continue to use, organized criminal networks as a geopolitical weapon. It has used such networks to support separatist actions throughout Eastern Europe, including arming pro-Russian separatist groups. Criminal organizations have formed part of the pro-Russian separatist forces, in many cases making them indistinguishable from separatists.

2-18. Russian criminal organizations, assisted by Russian intelligence specialists, are known to work together with local political activists, fringe political parties, and powerful oligarchs. Their actions can support Russian political campaigns and objectives designed to undermine the power of local governments.

THE MILITARY'S ROLE

2-19. Russia's 2021 National Strategy sets the framework to achieve national interests by prioritizing its goals and objectives for security. The following national actions are emphasized: strengthening the country's defense, ensuring political and social stability, economic modernization, preserving and developing Russian culture, and strengthening Russia's status as a leading world power. Of these actions, the military is tasked with the first and last, respectively strengthening the country's defense and strengthening Russia's status as a leading world power.

2-20. Russia's expectations for the military's role in executing these actions is found in its military doctrine, the most recent of which was published in 2014. Notably, doctrine allows for expansive military involvement in prevention and deterrence activities as well as calls for protection of peoples and activities abroad. Below is a summary of the specified tasks from the latest revision to Russian doctrine:

- Protect national sovereignty.
- Ensure strategic (nuclear and non-nuclear) deterrence, including the prevention of military conflicts.
- Maintain combat-ready strategic nuclear forces, their support units, and facilities.
- Provide timely warning of an air or space domain attack as well as notification of military risks and military threats.
- Maintain combat readiness of the Armed Forces, and other troops and bodies.
- Defend air and space domain critical ground facilities as well as maintain readiness to counterattacks from the air and space domains.
- Deploy and maintain space vehicles to support the activities of the Armed Forces.
- Protect and defend important state and military facilities.
- Build new military infrastructure facilities—as well as modernize and develop existing ones, of the Armed Forces and other troops and bodies.
- Protect Russian citizens abroad from armed attack.
- Participate in peacekeeping operations to restore peace, eliminate threats, and suppress acts of aggression in accordance with international law.
- Combat piracy and ensure safety of navigation and security of economic activities on the high seas.
- Combat domestic terrorism and suppress international terrorist activities.
- Participate in domestic law enforcement activities and emergency management to ensure public security and restoration of post-emergency services.
- Protect national interests in the Arctic region.

2-21. The 2014 doctrine highlights areas of particular concern for Russia, identifying military risks and threats expected to be encountered by Russian forces. Among these is an expected build-up of power among NATO countries, destabilization in some states and regions, deployment of aggressor militaries in the vicinity of Russian interests, existence of strategic missile systems, and growth in separatist and extremist groups in some regions of the world. The use of information technologies and subversive techniques and organizations—to target Russian interests politically and militarily—is also listed.

DEVELOPMENT OF THE MODERN RUSSIAN MILITARY

2-22. The Russian military, while much smaller than its Soviet predecessor, has significantly expanded its capabilities in IV, prioritized acquisition, and development of technology to better enable its fires assets, and increased its efforts to professionalize its enlisted ranks. New formations like the (Батальонная Тактическая Группа - battalion tactical group or BTG) have also appeared; however, even during the Soviet period military actions involved the task organization of troops for battlefield missions. The Soviet view of the battlefield was linear with forces connected on both flanks. The new Russian assessment is that, because of the devastating effects of precision weapons, battlefields will be dispersed and nonlinear with brigades and divisions defending in separate actions or launching attacks on separate avenues. Russian tactics are a result of a combination of innovations and a continuation of past Soviet practices.

2-23. Russian analysis of both its own performance and the United States' performance in recent conflicts has led to a significant restructuring and reorganization of the Russian military to capably compete against potential aggressors. Years of budget constraints, personnel shortages, and training deficiencies were highlighted by Russian combat performance in 1994 to 1995 in Chechnya and 2008 in Georgia. These conflicts highlighted a requirement to reorganize and modernize Russian military forces to create the forces necessary to conduct 6th Generation Warfare and meet Russia's strategic and doctrinal mandates.

2-24. After a sub-par performance in Chechnya and Georgia, Russian leaders realized that much of the military's ground troops were understaffed, poorly trained, ill equipped, and inadequately led. With these factors as motivation, the Russian political and military leaders used the analysis of Western military forces to identify strengths and weaknesses of those forces and warfighting methods to develop new organizations and formations. The results of that analysis precipitated the reorganization of Russia's military as shown in figure 2-1.

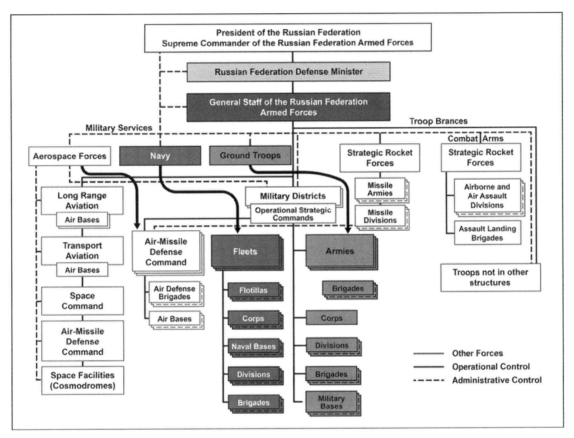

Figure 2-1. Russian Ministry of Defense forces

2-25. Russia labeled its reorganization concept the "New Look." The concept's primary object is to exploit the perceived weaknesses of Western forces and minimizing exposure of the ground forces to direct combat with those forces unless battlefield overmatch is achieved. Russian leaders stated that information dominance in all spheres, as a main tenet of the concept, was necessary to engage future aggressors. This motivated developments in new reconnaissance, electromagnetic warfare, and automated command-and-control complexes, among others.

2-26. The New Look concept incorporated several goals:
- Elimination of mass mobilization by creation of permanent readiness units.
- End all cadre units.
- Transition from an army-division-regiment structure to an army-brigade structure.
- Increased leader and soldier professionalism.

2-27. New Look evolution launched a massive re-armament program, including the establishment of "permanently ready forces" that caused significant force reorganization and revamping the personnel staffing practices of field units manned by professional voluntary contract soldiers (контрактник - kontraktnik). Inadequately manned Russian divisions and regiments were restructured into separate combined arms brigades. Before long, however, Russia re-established the divisional/regimental structure, in a limited manner, to improve its span of control in some military districts based on the most likely threat. It also opted to preserve many of its separate combined arms brigades. Both divisions and separate brigades are subordinate under a combined arms or tank army (TA).

2-28. Russian analysis of recent conflicts resulted in the requirement for ground troops capable of independent actions against modern aggressors. The desired end state is a combined-arms force capable of conducting short, high-intensity campaigns during the initial period of war to achieve Russia's objectives. To accomplish this the Russian leaders defined the components of the new force:

- Smaller combined-arms formations, based on brigades and BTGs, capable of launching and sustaining combat in a high-intensity environment.
- Use of all elements, including irregular forces, to create the conditions that allow the SV to advance into designated regions. This approach ostensibly portrays that the SV is there to support and protect endangered populations or regimes and establishes defensive positions to oppose any attempts to remove those forces. This presents the international community with a surprise attack.
- Reduced manpower requirements through development and increased use of robotic systems as combat enablers. Manning habitually plagues Russia's modernization plans through a shortfall in available manpower and reliance on conscripts.
- Layered offensive and defensive systems capable of denying penetration by Western forces and of transitioning to offense or defense as dictated by battlefield conditions.
- Reliable platforms constructed on standardized running gear to simplify logistics and maintenance.
- Reconnaissance and visibility of contested areas across all domains.
- Strike systems, both lethal and nonlethal, to allow strikes at the necessary times and locations to facilitate ground success. The strike concept maintains the basic principle from Soviet era/history that fires lead the ground maneuver fight to establish conditions for success. Strike includes direct, indirect, and nonlethal electromagnetic fires up to and including nuclear weapons.
- An evolved decision-making process for new organizations and systems that did not discard the "scientific approach" of the decision process. Use of correlation of forces, nomograms, and battle drills at all echelons remain key elements of the SV's approach to decision-making and combat.

2-29. Forces were reorganized to provide a spectrum of deployment capabilities. The initial ground troops at the brigade level should be able to form and deploy one or two combined arms BTGs with predominantly contract soldiers and the latest combat systems in less than 24 hours. These units are followed by brigades or regiments with a larger share of conscripts and older equipment, but still manned at a level capable of deploying in D+10 days, followed by troops from other military districts that mobilize using brigade and battalion equipment sets at designated mobilization sites, or storage and maintenance bases, for deployment within D+30 days. Army and division-level headquarters with their own combat forces command the deploying units, with the capability to allocate additional forces and means as needed based on the combat calculations.

2-30. In the last few years their continuing analysis of likely future conflicts has come to view the most likely to be large scale war against U.S. and NATO forces. This resulted in a shift away from separate maneuver brigades back to divisions with subordinate regiments. The organization of the divisions is dependent on the most likely threat to the military district where they are based. Division organization is not standard and may be tank heavy or motorized rifle heavy with four regiments or less.

MILITARY DOCTRINE AND THOUGHT

2-31. Russia's military is key to achieving the country's strategic objectives, as outlined in chapter 1. These objectives underpin Russia's view that it must develop forces and means capable of 6th Generation warfare to be a leading world power. This concept motivates the reorganization and modernization of the SV as well as leads it to develop new techniques and procedures to employ those forces. It also reinforces Russia's reliance on nuclear weapons, both strategic and tactical, to deter aggression while it modernizes and reorganizes its military. Much like U.S. strategic concepts, Russia wants to present an aggressor with an opponent that possesses significant capabilities to exert simultaneous pressure in all domains.

2-32. Russian strategies are intended to increase the costs of confrontation to make aggressor missions unsupportable from political, economic, and diplomatic perspectives. Russia's objective is to weaken an aggressor's national or collective will to maintain the conflict by inflicting highly visible and embarrassing casualties and related losses on aggressor forces. Modern nations have shown a sensitivity to domestic and world opinion in relation to protracted conflict and seemingly needless casualties. The Russians believe they have a comparative advantage against militarily superior forces because of what it perceives as its stronger collective national will to endure hardship or casualties.

2-33. Russia intends to win conflicts with minimal close combat and ensure any engagements that do occur are on terms favorable to its interests. It will attempt to set the information environment conditions so that deployment of aggressor forces is ultimately counter to the aggressor's interests. If the aggressor does deploy forces, Russian goals are centered on creating information environment constraints that prevent success of the aggressor's campaign. The balance of Russian methodologies focuses on four key areas:

- **Disrupt or prevent understanding of the information environment. Russian** IV activities manipulate the acquisition, transmission, and presentation of information to suit its preferred decision outcomes.
- **Enable targeted instability.** Russia fosters instability in key areas and among key groups so that regional security does not match aggressor operational requirements.
- **Disaggregate partnerships.** Russia undermines partnerships, reducing the ability of the aggressor to operate in its preferred combined, joint, and interagency manner.
- **Deny or complicate access.** Russia focuses pre-conflict activities to deny access to an aggressor force, using nonlethal means initially and transitioning to lethal means if necessary. It will undermine relationships; raise political stakes; manipulate public opinion; attack resolve; and constrain or deny basing rights, overflight corridors, logistics support, and concerted allied action. Establishment and employment of an integrated air and missile defense system serves as a key to degrade and disrupt an aggressor's capability to close with and engage Russian forces.

2-34. As it applies instruments of national power, Russia integrates those forces and means at selected times and locations to achieve desired effects as part of its overall campaign. The country uses offensive and defensive tactics and techniques, including crime and terrorism, to counter an aggressor. Russia can also employ these actions to manipulate population perceptions and dissuade support to an aggressor's military forces or other institutions. When necessary, Russia uses acts of physical and psychological violence to gain influence and develop willing or coerced cooperation in a target population. Concurrently, it uses indirect means to progressively degrade an aggressor's combat power and infrastructure, and to influence otherwise psychologically the political, social, economic, military, and information variables of the OE. As an example, Russia seeks to influence and control the flow of information by using its radio-electromagnetic combat capabilities to disrupt the official communications channels of a target country and to insert psychological warfare messages in social media targeting soldiers' families.

SCIENTIFIC SUBSTANTIATION

2-35. Russia uses scientific substantiation to understand the types of current and future conflicts, those most likely to occur, and the capabilities necessary to succeed in those conflicts. This understanding guides the development of its military forces. Although it creates the theory of why and how the military must evolve, the actual application depends on many other factors, including public support, economic viability, and technological advancements.

2-36. The Russian General Staff uses analysis by the military scientific community to define the conditions of modern conflicts as well as to develop and validate the forms and methods of employing its military forces. The analysis incorporates both the classical and asymmetrical means of military employment in support of strategic objectives, as well as operational and tactical actions.

In 2009, Russia established the Military Science Committee of the General Staff of the Russian Federation Armed Forces. The Military Science Committee is tasked with providing scientific evidence about construction, development, training, and the actual and predictable conditions of political-military, economic, and demographic situations. The Military Science Committee also promotes innovation in future warfare. The principal objectives of the committee are—

- Force development.
- Forecasting the development of construction, training, and use of the armed forces.
- Developing recommendations on the enhancement of force structure, forms and methods of conducting combat.
- Development of arms and military equipment.
- Study of related issues, such as nuclear and non-nuclear deterrence, countering unmanned aerial vehicles, and conducting IV actions as well as others.
- Improvement of the military science complex of the armed forces, including its composition, structure, and staff size based on actual needs to accomplish military actions.
- Development of modeling and experiments into process automation, including systems of information support.
- Direction of work on military history.

2-37. For the military and ultimately the ground forces, military science also plays a key role in development and validation of military theory and practice. These are a few of the key missions performed by The Military and Scientific Center of the Ground Forces:

- Scientific substantiation of the concepts, programs, and plans for the construction of the ground forces.
- Development of operational art and tactics.
- Improving combat and mobilization readiness.
- Improvement of weapons and military equipment.
- Study of problems associated with military education and training.

ARMED CONFLICT

2-38. The latest Russian military doctrine demonstrates a nuanced understanding of conflict. Russia views local wars and armed conflicts as the most likely and common types of direct clashes between it and any aggressors. Russia's current doctrine defines local war as a conflict with limited political and supporting military goals where military actions are limited to the border of the warring states and mainly affects only the interests of those states. This judgment is based on its analysis of current trends and the capabilities of its most likely aggressors. Russia believes that large-scale war will most likely be the result of the expansion and escalation of hostilities from the regional to the international level. Russia views the characteristics of these conflicts as follows—

- Integrated employment of military forces in conjunction with the other elements of national power.
- Weapons and military equipment based on advanced technologies that include high-precision, hypersonic weapons; electromagnetic warfare; use of new physical principles, automated information, and control complexes; unmanned aircraft and maritime vessels; and guided robotic weapons.
- Global simultaneous attacks in the land, air, maritime, space and cyberspace domains, and the information environment.
- Task-organized and rapidly deployed forces and means to inflict large-scale damage on aggressor facilities and forces.
- Reduction of the time needed to conduct military actions and strikes.
- Enhanced automated command and control (C2) of both units and weapons using a global networked computer complex.
- Permanent military operations zones in the territories of conflicting sides.
- Integration of irregular and private military companies in military actions.
- Use of indirect and asymmetric actions.

- Financing and directing opposition political or public groups outside the conflict area.

RUSSIAN CAMPAIGNS

2-39. Russia's recent campaigns highlight its strategy towards modern and future conflicts. Russian forces have intervened in local conflicts while continuing to wage IV against nations involved in the conflict, operating on its periphery, and against those it considers as aggressors. Russia's deployment of military forces for these operations provided officers with combat experience, tested new weapons platforms, and showed itself to be a successful military force internationally.

2-40. As observed in recent campaigns, Russia may employ irregular forces or special operations forces to exploit familiarity with the physical environment of a region and the ability to blend into a local populace. Its activities occur over extended periods of time, but may change in tempo, speed, and duration. While timing of Russian action may appear random, the actions and activities are deliberate decisions and part of a long-term campaign or stratagem. Even when circumstances are beyond its control, Russia has an ability to deftly seize on unexpected opportunities to achieve desired effects.

2-41. Russia can use international protocols and conventions, national laws, and moral codes that guide or regulate behavioral norms and social interactions to limit an aggressor's use of overmatch weapons systems or other capabilities. Military affiliates comply with these codes of conduct when advantageous for the IV campaign or for overt or clandestine actions. If Russia incorporates clandestine use of combat power, the country can then claim plausible deniability for actions considered illegal or immoral.

2-42. Although an individual, organization, or combination of forces often receives immediate notoriety for violent actions, Russia complements physical violence with methodical, long-term psychological warfare. The overarching agenda includes but is not limited to the following methods:
- Spotlight popular grievances for resolution.
- Establish influence, popular recognition, and support of a targeted segment of a population.
- Expand active or passive support in an area or region.
- Deter opposition to Russian goals and objectives within a specific population.
- Marginalize the governance or extra-regional influence of an aggressor.
- Develop general acceptance and legitimacy of Russian programs and actions.
- Achieve Russian political or national objectives without alienating critical segments of indigenous or extra-regional populations.
- Expand physical control and governance in an area or region.
- Attract an international or global audience, or external organizational sources of influence that support Russian aims.

2-43. Russia seeks to gain the approval and support of certain elements within a target population in order to obtain active or passive assistance. The methods must eventually communicate a compelling narrative of legitimacy that is accepted by the population. Legitimacy may require a gradual process of convincing the population that Russian military or security forces are an acceptable means to achieve desired social, economic, religious, or political effects. However, Russia can also attempt to confer authority on itself without regard to the population's goals. It may declare that its actions are justifiable under existing conditions and attempt to degrade the legitimacy of a targeted government.

2-44. Russian actions may encompass a complex array of irregular and regular organizations, units, or individuals with various coordinated or perceived disparate single agenda aims. A particular geographic, political, cyberspace, or ideological environment may lead to alliances or affiliations that are dynamic and constantly changing in purpose and actions.

2-45. Internal security forces or law enforcement organizations infiltrated by Russian security services can also be used to support military actions. The collaboration among organizations, units, and individuals of a population may be based on coercion, contractual agreement, or common goals and objectives—either temporary or long term. Russia may prefer indirect approaches such as subterfuge, deception, and nonlethal action to achieve strategic objectives. However, when necessary, the country is committed to violent action in order to compel an aggressor or opposing government to submit to its intentions.

2-46. Some irregular organizations, such as affiliated criminal gangs, exist for their own commercial profit and power. These elements intend to influence or coerce, with no interest in a populace's quality of life or civil security. Other forms of Russian subterfuge include use of rogue individuals or groups with single-issue agendas that are willing to use criminal activity or terrorism to achieve their objective. Russia seeks opportunities to co-opt or affiliate with these varied types of organizations for mutual temporary benefits.

Integration of All Domains

2-47. Russia does not use the term multidomain operations, but it does work to integrate all of its elements of national power across all domains with any battlefield actions.

2-48. Russia's emphasis on information and psychological warfare does not translate to de-emphasis of physical warfighting capabilities. The SV continues to maintain and improve its capabilities to conduct combat actions at the tactical level using long-established tactics and non-prescriptive techniques to conduct effective mission tasks and drills. The continuing evolution of these techniques and procedures achieves the desired immediate or near-term effects and supports the aims of higher headquarters to weaken or defeat an aggressor's resolve to prolong a conflict.

2-49. The Russian military uses the term strike to refer to the convergence of multiple effects, to include multiple domains, focused on an aggressor force. These strikes incorporate everything from pre-conflict IV to nuclear fires.

2-50. Strategically, Russia uses the threat of nuclear fires at all echelons and considers the threat of escalation as a valid means of de-escalating conflict to avoid large-scale combat. Such threatened strikes are designed not to necessarily defeat the United States on a battlefield, but to cause enough political pressure that the United States cannot sustain its political resolve to continue the conflict. However, Russia likely has a lower threshold for use of low-yield, nonstrategic nuclear weapons assessing them to be less escalatory.

2-51. At the tactical level, strike predominantly relies on fires from direct and indirect forces and means to achieve the desired outcomes in combined-arms battle. The ground-force use of strike seeks to integrate all effects, whether they are from IV, REB, aerospace support, or irregular warfare actions.

National Battle Management

2-52. Russia's national command and control authority begins with its President and flows down through the Minister of Defense and General Staff. The President is the Supreme Commander in Chief of the armed forces and is authorized to assume direct C2 over the military during times of crisis and martial law. Subordinate to the President, the Minister of Defense oversees and directs the operations of the General Staff. The General Staff is tasked with ensuring Russia's national security and developing operational plans for armed forces C2. The Joint Strategic Commands (known as OSK) are joint force elements that have operational control in peace and wartime of all general purpose forces—across military services—stationed within the geographic boundaries of a military district.

2-53. The National Defense Management Center (Центр управления национальной обороной - Tsentr upravleniya natsional'noy oboronoy – known as NTsUO), based in Moscow, is the single organization that orchestrates the integration of all national, regional, and territorial actions to defend Russia. It coordinates and manages the actions of ministries, departments, and civil authorities in support of security actions. As a unified interagency system, it serves to integrate all Russian organizations and forces involved in national security, including 159 federal and state agencies as well as 1,320 state corporations and military-industrial companies.

2-54. Using modern communications complexes, the NTsUO generates real-time situational updates disseminated to all levels: strategic, operational, and tactical. It manages all national-level security actions to include nuclear attack early warning, retaliation status, and air and missile defense, as well as directing combat actions in specific theaters. The NTsUO uses the latest automated C2 complex to enable automatic collection and analysis to generate situational estimates. The NTsUO complex can send orders, direct missions, manage strikes and fires, and synchronize logistics support of forces.

2-55. Russia places strike as the leading function in its joint and tactical actions, with all other forces and means enabling it to set the conditions for successful land operations. Strike involves engaging all lethal and nonlethal forces and means to attack an aggressor at a planned location and time on the battlefield. The NTsUO integrates reconnaissance and intelligence collection to create targeting information and, using its network-centric capability, conducts command and control (C2) of strike complexes to engage those targets. This complex allows passing automatic target engagements directly to the firing or launching platform without going through the intervening headquarters levels. In addition, the firing or launch complexes may be able to operate in an autonomous mode—without the need for operator initiation of the strike.

2-56. Russian equipment modernization programs incorporate the requirement to include automated command and control system communications and data systems to send and receive information. These Avtomatizirovannyye Sistemy Upravleniya - Автоматизированные Системы Управления – (ASUs) are intended to provide near-real-time information sharing between SV soldiers using Strelets reconnaissance, command and control, and communications system (known as KRUS) (комплекса разведки, управления и связи (known as КРУС)). The Strelets can interface with the Airborne troops (VDV) Andromeda-D, and Air-Space Force (VKS) Metronom strike-aviation, naval vessels, and high-precision missiles and massed artillery fire.

2-57. Three subordinate C2 centers of the NTsUO monitor and control Russia's nuclear forces, conduct battle management to identify developing threats, and focus on day-to-day actions from strategic to tactical levels. The NTsUO and its subordinate centers integrate all elements of Russian power through Army and Corps commands to allow the Russian military to transition away from large formations and massed fires to a more refined and precise force.

RUSSIAN MILITARY FORCES

2-58. Russia's military forces have several components organized to conduct or support actions on land. The focus on the military forces in this ATP is on military services that interact with or support the SV. Each service has a distinct mission focus and has forces assigned to Russia's five Joint Strategic Commands (OSKs), based on the geographic boundaries of military districts. OSK West, South, Center, East, and Northern Fleet are the joint commands that manage, control, and direct all forces in their areas of responsibility. The OSKs, as a joint-force element, incorporate all forces and means as opposed to just the land forces of the former military districts. Figure 2-2 on page 2-12 shows the geographical laydown of the respective military districts and associated OSKs.

- OSK West conducts joint efforts focused on the Baltic States. The Baltic Fleet falls under this OSK.
- OSK South cover actions in the eastern European region. This OSK has the most recent experience with the reorganization and joint-force ground actions in Ukraine and Crimea. The Caspian Sea Flotilla is subordinate to this OSK.
- OSK Center focuses on actions in Central Eurasia.
- OSK East focuses on the Pacific and Asian areas. The Pacific Fleet falls under OSK East.
- OSK Northern Fleet focuses joint efforts to improve the ability to project military campaigns into the Barents Sea and Arctic region.

Figure 2-2. Geographic regions of Russia's military districts

NUCLEAR FORCES

2-59. The Russians consider their tactical, operational, and strategic nuclear arsenal to be the ultimate safeguard against any attack on their homeland. The nuclear forces comprised the Naval Forces, Strategic Rocket Forces, and Long-Range Aviation.

2-60. Russia constantly trains for nuclear war, and nuclear, biological, and chemical defense units are well resourced and play a fundamental role within tactical maneuver units. The Russian military regularly employs simulated nuclear strikes in its war games and field exercises. While Russia is prepared to fight in a nuclear-threatened environment, it deems this scenario unwise because of the possibility of escalation.

2-61. Russia is a signatory to the Nuclear Non-Proliferation Treaty and Intermediate-Range Nuclear Forces Treaty and states that it adheres to a "no first use" policy about nuclear weapons. However, like all nuclear powers, Russia continues to modernize its nuclear capabilities. Russia retains approximately 2,000 nonstrategic nuclear weapons capable of delivery by naval vessels, aviation, surface-to-surface missiles, or artillery, in addition to the approximately 4,500 strategic weapons in its inventory.

SECURITY SERVICES

2-62. Russia possesses numerous militarized intelligence and security services. These forces may field units with similar equipment and training to that of the SV. All of these organizations concentrate their efforts on internal security, while the ground forces under the Ministry of Defense are primarily concerned with external threats but will assist with internal security when required. Russian leaders show an increasing concern over internal threats and have allocated resources to modernize the security services that may have previously gone to the Ministry of Defense. The following list shows the different ministries or agencies and their estimated size:

- Ministry of Internal Affairs: 904,800 personnel.
- Federal Security Services Border Guards: 170,000 personnel.
- Ministry of Justice: 32,000 personnel.
- Ministry of Emergency Situations: 289,000 personnel.

- Federal Protection Service: 20,000 personnel.
- National Guard: 340,000 personnel.

AEROSPACE FORCES

2-63. Russia reorganized its aerospace forces in 2015 to combine the Space operations, Air Force, Aerospace Defense, and Air Defense forces into one branch, the Air-Space Force (Vozduzhno-kosmicheskie sily - VKS). The VKS' main missions are air/space control to degrade aggressor capabilities and intelligence collection focused on aggressors. The current organizations used to support the SV are Air Force and Air Defense Armies, with one for each of the military districts.

2-64. Russia's military doctrine tasks the VKS with sole responsibility for air and space defense and long-range transport. The VKS tasks and complexes include—

- Air and space defense.
- Communication.
- Intelligence.
- Electromagnetic warfare.
- Unmanned aerial vehicles.
- Automatic engagement weapons.
- Military transport.
- Personal protective equipment.

2-65. VKS support to the SV includes three components: long-range aviation, frontline aviation, and integrated air defense forces. As part of the reorganization, the VKS also received the space and missile defense forces. Air or surface-to-surface fire support for tactical maneuver forces—primarily from frontline aviation and missile defense forces—is planned and delivered through the VKS.

NAVY

2-66. The Russian Navy focuses on protection of territorial waters but does have limited power projection capabilities. The Navy's power projection capability primarily rests with its fleet of ballistic missile submarines. The Navy includes two forces with land-based missions: Naval Infantry and Coastal Missile and Artillery Troops. Separately, the Coastal Forces of the Navy primarily focus on defense of Russia's coastline from aggressor surface fleets as well as from air and sea landing forces. It assists the SV with anti-landing defenses in the coastal area.

Naval Infantry

2-67. The Naval Infantry (Морская пехота – known as MP) is subordinate to the fleet commanders but does not have a set organization within each fleet. Missions include amphibious assault, coastal defense, counterterrorism, anti-piracy, as well as ship and naval base security. It is considered an elite force with counter-diversionary capabilities to defeat aggressor intelligence gathering units associated with water or seaborne actions. As an elite force it conducts training and actions with VDV units.

2-68. The Naval Infantry is smaller in number than other ground force units, with only 9,000 personnel. It is similar in organization to the motorized rifle units of the SV. The Naval Infantry consists of four independent brigades, a separate brigade, and three separate battalions.

Coastal Missile and Artillery Troops

2-69. The Coastal Missile and Artillery Troops (Береговые ракетно-артиллерийские войска – known as BRAV) have the mission of defending Russian ports, harbors' shore-based facilities, and the 38,000 km of shoreline. As the name implies, its forces are composed of long-range artillery and missile units with the capability to engage aggressor surface fleets attempting amphibious assaults or air landings on the coast.

2-70. Russia is modernizing the Coastal Missile and Artillery Troops units with long-range surface-to-surface and cruise missile complexes. Engagement ranges are between 300 and 600 km, with fire direction generated by internal sensors, organic radars, or by linked automated C2 complexes from airborne or ship sensors. Mobile complexes are rapidly deployable with approximately a 5-minute setup and a maximum operational duration of 120 hours, based on fuel availability.

RUSSIAN GROUND FORCES

2-71. Several forces conduct land-based actions in the Russian military. The Russian Ground Forces are composed of the Ground Troops, Airborne, and National Guard, as well as those associated with the Navy.

Ground Troops

2-72. The SV contains the mainland-based combat power of the Russian military with tank and motorized rifle brigades and divisions with subordinate regiments, both subordinate to combined arms armies. The SV manning goal is a total of 350,000 officers, noncommissioned officers (warrant officers), kontraktniki, and conscript soldiers. As part of the evolution of the SV, Russia's goal is to generate brigades and regiments with the capability to create two-to-three task-organized BTGs.

2-73. Included in the main headquarters of tank and motorized rifle units are missile, artillery, and air-defense units. Additional supporting units consist of reconnaissance; engineer; nuclear, biological, and chemical defense; materiel technical support; electromagnetic warfare; and signal.

Airborne Troops

2-74. The VDV is an independent service within the military and is employed as a rapid response or strategic reserve force. It consists of four maneuver divisions, four maneuver brigades, and a separate special purpose (spetsnaz - спецназ) reconnaissance brigade. Like Naval Infantry and Main Intelligence Directorate Spetsnaz units, VDV forces often remain under the direct control of their respective higher headquarters. The component headquarters may retain centralized control of these elements, which permits flexibility in the employment of relatively scarce assets in response to national-level requirements.

National Guard

2-75. The Russian National Guard (Национальная гвардия - Natsional'naya gvardiya - NG) is a national security service and not part of its deployable ground forces. Any operations or actions crossing into Russia proper will be opposed by these forces. The NG was recently organized from elements of the existing security services.

2-76. The NG's primary mission is to ensure internal security and territorial defense. Internal security includes stopping riots, fighting terrorism, and deterring crime. Territorial defense includes protection of important military, state, and communication sites, combating sabotage and reconnaissance, defeat of terrorists and aggressor troops, establishing and maintaining martial law.

2-77. Since the NG's role is more for security and law enforcement functions, it has that type of equipment in addition to many of the same systems as the ground forces. The NG has its own airfields, aircraft, helicopters, unmanned aerial vehicles, and armored personnel carriers. The intent is for it to be capable of conducting ground combat actions against terrorist organizations such as those affiliated with the Islamic State of Iraq and Syria in Russia's Muslim regions.

JOINT STRATEGIC COMMANDS

2-78. The OSK is the highest level of command in a particular geographical military district; it controls all general purpose forces stationed in or deployed to the district, both in peacetime and conflict. The organization of specific general purpose land forces for each OSK is unique and depends on the most likely aggressor threat and conditions in that area.

2-79. Each of the OSKs plans, trains, and directs the forces in its geographic district. In crisis periods, the OSK conducts training of active and reserve units, mobilizes, and deploys to threatened areas, and prepares to conduct defensive actions. In the event of war, the OSK coordinates joint actions to repulse aggressor attacks, conducts an integrated defense including protection of critical infrastructure, and launches counteroffensives to defeat the aggressor forces. To accomplish these missions, the OSK land forces are organized in combined arms armies or corps.

Northern Fleet

2-80. The land forces in the Northern Fleet OSK are primarily composed of a single Naval Infantry brigade and an army corps (AC) with two subordinate motorized rifle brigades. Training specifically prepares these land units to conduct tactical actions in the Arctic environment using equipment modified to operate effectively in the harsh cold. Northern Fleet forces are shown in figure 2-3.

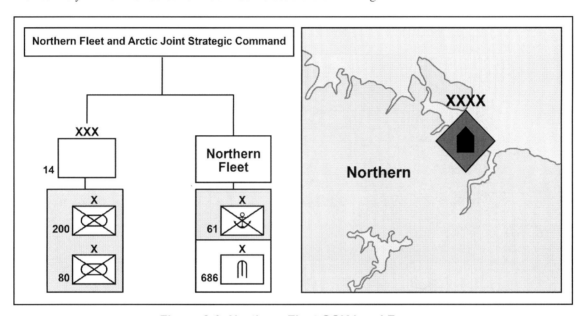

Figure 2-3. Northern Fleet OSK Land Forces

Western

2-81. The main part of the Western OSK borders Finland, Estonia, Latvia, Belarus, and Ukraine, from north to south. Kaliningrad, as a detached territory sandwiched between Lithuania and Poland, contains forces subordinate to the Western OSK. Land forces in the Western OSK, which face what Russia believes is the main threat from NATO, are organized into two combined arms armies (CAAs), one in the north and one in the south, one TA in the central part of the military district, and one AC in Kaliningrad with the Baltic Fleet. The forces in each of the CAAs and the TA are shown in figures 2-4 through 2-7 on pages 2-16 and 2-17, respectively.

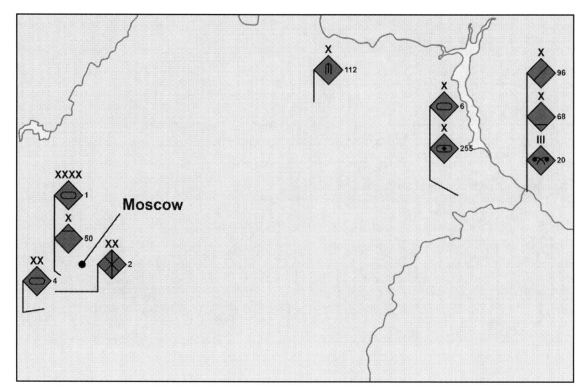

Figure 2-4. Guards Tank Army

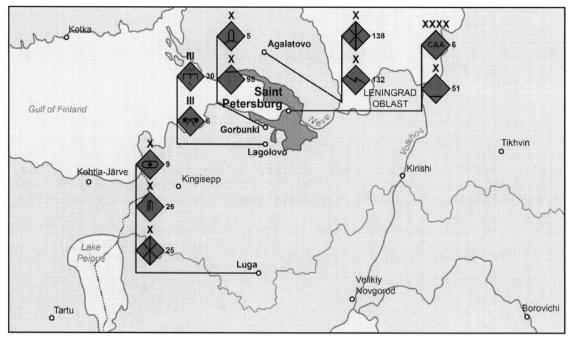

Figure 2-5. Combined Arms Army – North

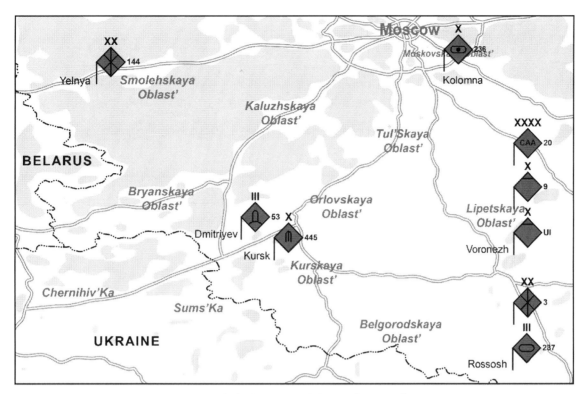

Figure 2-6. Combined Arms Army – South

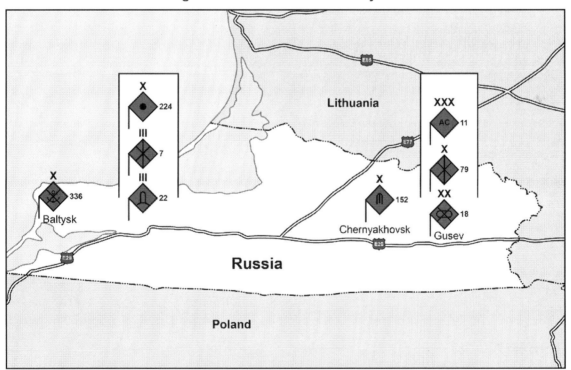

Figure 2-7. Army Corps – Baltic Fleet

Southern

2-82. The Southern OSK borders Azerbaijan, Georgia, and Ukraine, with three CAAs, an Army Corps in Crimea, and two Naval Infantry battalions in the Caspian Sea Flotilla. The forces in each of the CAAs and AC are shown in figures 2-8 through 2-12 on pages 2-18 through 2-21, respectively.

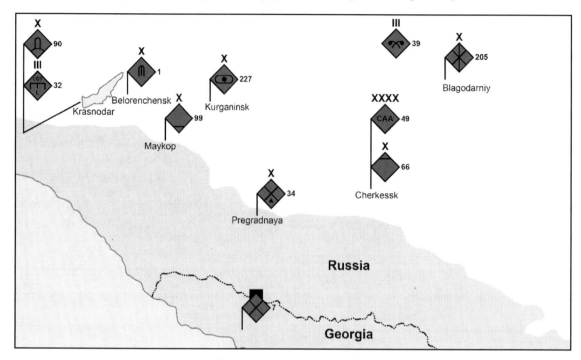

Figure 2-8. Northern OA

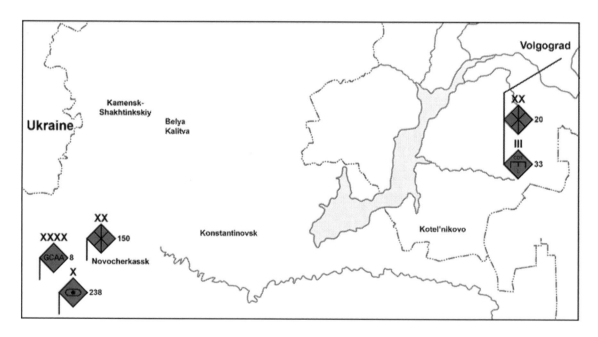

Figure 2-9. Central OA

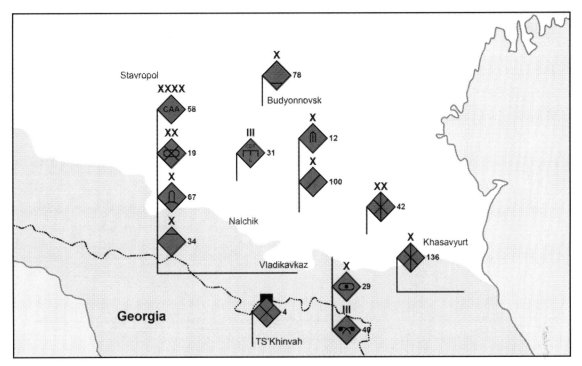

Figure 2-10. Southern OA

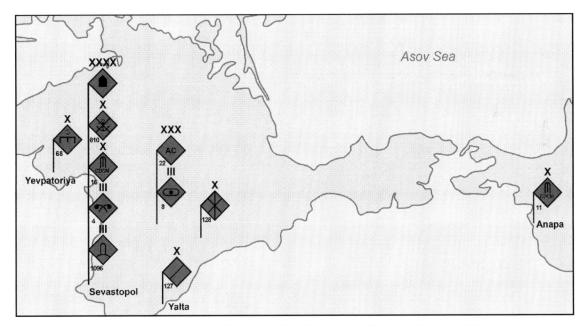

Figure 2-11. Army Corps of the Black Sea Fleet in Crimea OA

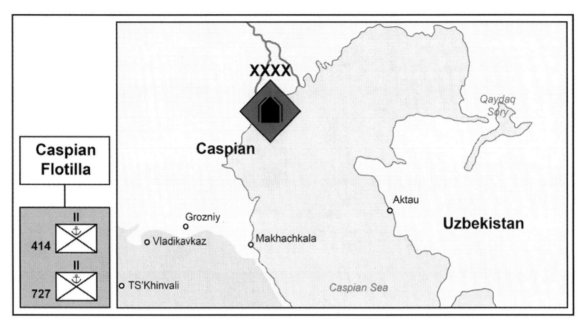

Figure 2-12. Naval Infantry battalions of the Caspian Sea Flotilla

Central

2-83. The Central OSK borders Kazakhstan, China, and Mongolia, and has two CAAs as shown in figure 2-13. This OSK's main mission is to defend the central Asian region, but it also is intended to reinforce other OSKs to the east or west.

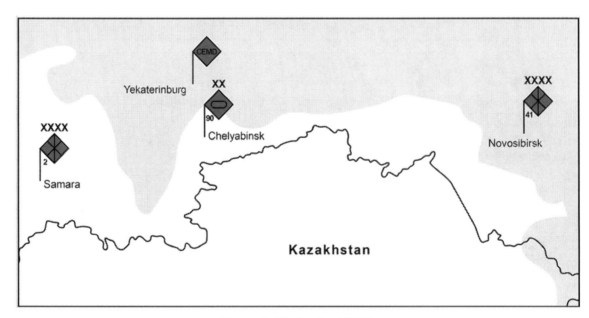

Figure 2-13. Central OSK

Eastern

2-84. The Eastern OSK—bordered by Mongolia, China, North Korea, and Japan—has four CAAs, an AC, and two Naval Infantry brigades subordinate to the Pacific Fleet. The current disposition of these units is shown in figure 2-14.

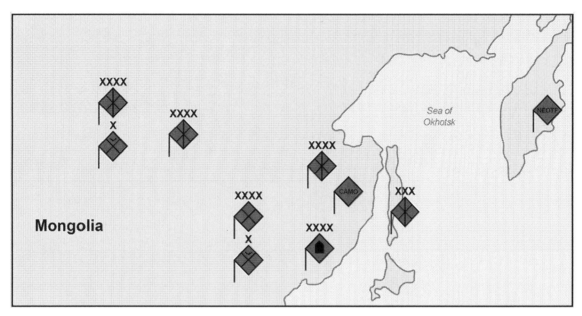

Figure 2-14. Eastern OSK CAAs and army corps

This page intentionally left blank.

Chapter 3

Ground Forces of the Russian Federation

Chapter 3 addresses the guiding principles used by the Russian Federation ground forces (сухопутные войска РФ - sukhoputnyye voyska RF - SV), in tasking and subunits with missions. It presents the SV decision-making process including the use of correlation of forces and means calculations, the use of normative factors, and battle drills. Finally, it discusses the Russian concept of battle management that includes controlling and directing tactical-level forces.

ORGANIZATIONAL CONSIDERATIONS

3-1.   Since the 1920s, Russian tactical-level units have fought as combined arms entities to exploit the effects of more precise targeting combined with integrated fires. A basic principle of Russian military actions is to use the effects of strike actions to create the conditions for military success. The SV combines both maneuver and artillery strikes to achieve success on the battlefield. Further discussion of Russia's "Strike" concept can be found in chapter 5.

3-2.   Russian divisions with subordinate regiments as well as brigades reporting directly to an army higher headquarters, are task-organized for combined arms missions. Combined arms units integrate available forces and means allocated by the senior commander. Both brigades and regiments will form task-organized tactical groups. Often these include BTGs to perform assigned missions. Russia will employ all available national elements of power prior to launching maneuver forces and after force-on-force operations begin, the country will continue to employ these integrated capabilities to support tactical maneuver. To execute tactics, the Russians apply analytic intelligence methods and scientifically substantiated decision making to—

- Understand the battlefield conditions that will impact operations.
- Determine the tactical functions required and calculate the required allocation of combat power needed to accomplish a mission in concert with time and location.
- Understand the psychological dimension and cognitive issues among competing friendly forces, aggressor forces, and other possible actors and the local population.

3-3.   This analysis results in a graphic depiction of how the SV is likely to conduct battlefield actions using capabilities, dispositions, and time to accomplish a particular type of mission. Russian capabilities and actors are planned, analyzed, and allocated based on required combat power functions as a synchronized and integrated force ordered to accomplish a mission task.

> *Note.* The SV considers a unit to be a division, regiment, or brigade capable of sustained action, while a subunit is a battalion tactical group, battalion, detachment, or subordinate that requires support.

3-4.   The SV conducts three general types of actions at the tactical level:
- Defensive actions.
- Offensive actions.
- Local war and armed conflict actions.

DEFENSIVE ACTIONS

3-5.   The SV's defensive actions are conceptually based on the intent to maneuver to points of advantage against an attacking aggressor force or to occupy designated positional defenses. At the tactical level of division, regiment, brigade, battalion tactical group, and battalion, defensive mission tasks are identified with the following descriptions:

- Defense in direct contact.
- Defense out of direct contact.
- Withdrawal.
- Relief operations.

Defensive actions by the SV will employ both maneuver and positional defenses. Since 2011, the SV's field regulations stated that maneuver defense has priority over positional defense, but they continue to train for both. Maneuver defense is considered a fundamental type of defense, and it is primarily used to disrupt an attacking aggressor force, inflict losses on the attacking units, and protect critical areas or objects.

3-6. Planned actions typically involve sufficient time, knowledge, and situational understanding of an OE to prepare forces for specific tasks. Nonetheless, battlefield conditions can change often and suddenly, precluding actions as originally planned. In instances such as being surprised or finding SV forces at a significant disadvantage, conditions can require a temporary situational defensive posture until the SV can regain the initiative.

Note. See chapter 6 for discussion and examples of defensive actions at the division, regimental, brigade, and subordinate unit levels.

OFFENSIVE ACTIONS

3-7. The SV employs four basic types of tactical offensive actions at division, regiment, brigade, battalion tactical group, and battalion echelons:

- Attack against a defending aggressor.
- Meeting battle.
- Pursuit.
- Withdrawal from encirclement.

3-8. SV units at the tactical level perform the below offensive methods using established battle drills. To perform a combat reconnaissance, the SV will normally task-organize the force to achieve the optimal mix of sensors and platforms to achieve sufficient detection and target acquisition of aggressor forces. At the tactical level the SV recognizes four basic methods employed in conducting offensive actions:

- Ambush.
- Assault.
- Raid.
- Combat reconnaissance.

Note. See chapter 7 for discussion and examples of offensive actions at the division, brigade, regimental levels, and subordinate units.

LOCAL WAR AND ARMED CONFLICT ACTIONS

3-9. Local war and armed conflict (LW/AC) tactics are a normal aspect of SV operations and often occur concurrently with other ongoing defensive or offensive actions. These types of actions leverage the variables of an OE, persistent conflict, and a targeted population to create conditions that enhance Russian physical, informational, and cognitive goals and objectives in support of the mission.

3-10. Offensive and defensive tasks in armed conflict and local war actions can be simultaneous and continuous at various levels of intensity. The SV sustains or modifies the frequency and levels of physical and cognitive violence and coercion to destabilize an OE. Actions are at times sudden and massive in effects but are more often a series of gradually escalating incidents that cause long-term debilitating effects to an aggressor and targeted population. Whether sudden and massive or gradual and insidious, armed conflict and local war actions seek to degrade the capabilities of an aggressor and manipulate OE conditions to Russian advantage.

3-11. At the tactical level, the SV adds three primary tasks to actions conducted during local wars and armed conflicts:

- Blokirovanie (blocking action).
- Reconnaissance-search action.
- Outpost or traffic control point duty.

Note. These tasks are discussed in chapter 6 because Russia anticipates that it will initially conduct defensive tactical operations and that local war and armed conflict (LW/AC) are the most likely form of modern conflicts.

BATTLE MANAGEMENT

3-12. The SV is adaptive, flexible, and agile, and can readily change force composition and focus to optimize organizational capabilities for use against known or perceived aggressor vulnerabilities. Once combat begins, the tempo and rapid changes—common on the modern battlefield—will greatly decrease a unit's or subunit's ability to generate and distribute new intelligence or prepare new plans and orders. As a result, the SV believes battle management at the tactical level should be decentralized but remain under centralized operational control.

3-13. Battle management for the SV is driven by commanders. The rapid implementation of a plan or development of a supporting action is often a key to success. SV tactical commanders have increased authority and a corresponding expectation of using initiative to quickly respond to sudden battlefield changes.

3-14. Russian officers are trained to apply their military standards to the current battlefield conditions to develop a plan. Templating Russian forces in absence of an aggressor force based on the doctrinal template distances and unit laydown locations is neither realistic nor practical.

SV PLANNING

3-15. The commander analyzes the mission assigned, the OE situation, and the forces and means available, then directs a course of action for the unit to follow. To accomplish the commander's plan, the SV relies on well-defined and practiced combat drills, as well as swift and efficient staff scientific calculations to increase the speed of decision making and resulting action. In the SV's approach, rapidity in planning and implementing tactical operations is considered more important than flexibility.

3-16. A key component of the SV decision-making method is the calculation of correlation of forces and means (COFM). The SV uses COFM as an indicator of the relative combat power comparison between its forces and those of an aggressor to determine the probable superiority of one force over the other. The SV commanders and staffs calculate COFM at the strategic, operational, and tactical levels throughout an entire area of operations, in not only the main sector, but in other sectors as well.

3-17. Scientific substantiation using mathematical verifications supports planning and identification of the actions and resources necessary to successfully accomplish the tasked mission. Proficiency in combat drills, COFM, and other mathematical confirmations allow the SV to greatly reduce operational and tactical planning times. It is not surprising that an SV motorized rifle brigade's operations section contains only five personnel—two officers, two sergeants, and one civilian technician.

3-18. The SV tactical decision-making process is a continuous cycle (see table 3-1 on page 3-4). It validates information and intelligence and engages SV leaders in critical thinking and effective decision making. This mission planning process includes consideration of all variables within an OE.

Table 3-1. Illustration of the SV commander decision-making process

Steps	Key Inputs	Key Outputs
1. Commander's plan	• Receive mission • Evaluate intelligence • Allocated attachments and supporting units and subunits	• Commander's concept • Commander's plan
2. Conduct commander's terrain reconnaissance (Razvedka) with key subordinates	• Coordinate directives • Configure task organization	• Staff issues warning orders
3. Staff verification	• Correlation of forces and means (COFM) analysis • Coordinate task organization • Allocation of: • Fires and maneuver • Combat support • Combat service support	• Unit and subunit mission assignments • Mathematical verification • Mission brief to commander • Coordination of route and area designations
4. Issue final plan	• Confirm COFM • Assess situational updates	• Final plan as map with concise narrative annex, signed by commander and chief of staff • Subordinate commanders acknowledge mission receipt • Incorporate tactical updates to adjust plan
5. Prepare for combat	• Reconnaissance (Razvedka) • Assess situational updates	• Incorporate contingencies to plan • Situational running estimates

3-19. SV tactical units focus on the purpose or function of their tactical mission and act toward achieving mission intent, even when the details of an original plan have changed through aggressor action or unforeseen events. Flexible and agile actions and reactions in tactical situations are the result of training, practical experience, and unit conditioning. Some basic functions are reflexive, as in combat drills, and require minimal deliberate decision making and orders. The capability for the commander to rapidly decide, knowing how their subordinate units will and can respond, gives them flexibility as the battle unfolds.

3-20. Tactical deployment of units and subunits into battle formation is governed by specific factors such as combat power, aggressor readiness, SV status, terrain, weather, time of day, and season. The SV commander will vary formations and position of units and subunits based on their understanding of the battlefield. Rigid combat drills executed by SV tactical units and subunits create a predictable outcome that creates operational flexibility for higher level commanders.

BATTLEFIELD ORGANIZATION

3-21. CAA or TA commander's order specifies the initial organization of forces within their level of command according to the specific missions assigned. At brigade, regimental, and higher echelons, subordinate forces are referred to as units. At battalion and subordinate echelons, they are called subunits. Battalions, companies, and below are subunits that are allocated based on the higher echelon commander's order.

3-22. Current SV tactical formations include divisions with subordinate regiments, brigades, BTGs, and company tactical groups (CTGs). Battalions include subordinate companies, platoons, and squads. The SV considers an army as an operational-level formation designed to carry out campaign actions.

3-23. Infantry units and subunits in the SV are mounted on armored personnel carriers or infantry fighting vehicles (IFVs) and are called motorized rifle units. These units and subunits are mounted on armored personnel carriers (APCs) such as infantry combat vehicles (Boevaya Mashina Pekhoty - BMP)], armored transport (Bronetransporter - BTR), or multi-purpose towing vehicle light armored (Mnogotselevoy Tyagach Legky Bronirovanny - MT-LB) BMPs, BTRs, or MT-LB tracked or wheeled vehicles. Motorized rifle battalions using BTRs and MT-LBs are slightly larger than those battalions with BMPs. This is because the BTR/MT-LB units have additional antitank weapons that are not necessary for BMP subunits due to the increased firepower of the BMP.

ELEMENTS OF THE COMBAT FORMATION

3-24. The SV division of forces based on functions executed to accomplish missions is translated as "echelonment." Russian units and subunits typically form two echelons in both the offense and defense. In the offense, a division or brigade first echelon conducts the initial attack; its function is to achieve the army's immediate objective. In the defense, the first echelon occupies the main forward position, and its function is to disrupt the aggressor's attack in front of or within this position and to reposition in a maneuver defense.

3-25. In both the offense and defense, the second echelon is tasked with a specific function, and this assignment distinguishes it from a reserve. In the offense, the second echelon is to exploit the success of the first echelon and achieve the primary objective of the parent organization. Other specific second-echelon functions may be to conduct pursuit, destroy bypassed aggressor elements, or defeat a counterattack. During defensive actions the second echelon counterattacks any aggressor penetration of the first echelon defensive belt, defeats those units and, if conditions are favorable, launches a pursuit to exploit success. The SV almost always plans for a counterattack against an attacking aggressor.

3-26. The SV units are assigned to function as elements of the combat formation. Most of these elements relate to both offensive and defensive battle. These elements may deploy into any of the march, pre-battle, or battle tactical formations, depending on the assignment and the combat situation. Units or subunits that are created to fill a mission specific requirement are—

- Reconnaissance (разведка - razvedka).
- Forward detachment (peredovoi otriad - передовой отряд).
- Raiding detachment (рейдовый отряд - reydovyy otryad).
- Flanking detachment (фланговый отряд - flangovyy otryad).
- Advance guard (авангард - avangard).
- Combat security outpost (боевой пост охраны - boyevoy post okhrany - CSOP).
- Assault Detachment (Штурмовой отряд).
- Combined arms reserve (общевойсковой резерв - obshchevoyskovoy rezerv).
- Antitank reserve (противотанковый резерв - protivotankovyy rezerv).
- Anti-air assault reserve (резерв противовоздушной обороны - rezerv protivovozdushnoy oborony).
- Special reserve (специальный резерв - spetsial'nyy rezerv).
- Flank and rear security (фланговая и тыловая охрана - flangovaya i tylovaya okhrana).

Forward Detachment

3-27. A forward detachment is typically a reinforced maneuver battalion and is practiced at independent action. In offensive operations, the brigade or regiment forward detachment moves ahead of the advance guard but behind the reconnaissance patrol (RP), with mission tasks of seizing key objectives or penetrating deep into aggressor territory. In a positional defense, the forward detachment occupies defensive positions in the brigade or regimental security zone. A forward detachment is also an essential component for pursuit operations and may also conduct raids.

Advance Guard

3-28. An advance guard formation is formed from first-echelon battalions of first-echelon brigades or regiments. Its purpose is to ensure the high-speed maneuver and unrestricted advance of the main body of the brigade. As a security unit, its mission is to protect the main body by fighting any aggressor units encountered to destroy or fix them and allow the main body to continue its advance unimpeded.

Raiding Detachment

3-29. A raiding detachment is typically a reinforced battalion designed to operate independently, and is used to destroy valuable military targets, dislodge aggressor command and control (C2), secure key terrain, and impede aggressor reserves. It can also be the follow-on mission of a battalion reserve that, once successful in destroying the aggressor, transitions to raiding in the depths of the aggressor defense.

Reconnaissance Detachment

3-30. A reconnaissance detachment is normally a mounted, reinforced company or battalion capable of performing observation, searches, raids, ambushes, and installing or removing observation equipment. This detachment is usually created by the parent brigade or regiment. If required, it can also engage the aggressor.

Flanking Detachment

3-31. A flanking detachment is normally a mounted, reinforced company or battalion capable of performing observation, searches, raids, ambushes, and installing or removing observation equipment. This detachment is usually created by the parent brigade or regiment. If required, it can also engage the aggressor.

Reconnaissance Patrol

3-32. Usually a platoon-sized unit reinforced with engineers and other specialists, the RP will conduct reconnaissance missions up to 10 km in front of the parent unit. There are four types of RPs: combat; officer reconnaissance; nuclear, biological, and chemical; and engineer.

Reconnaissance Group

3-33. A reconnaissance group typically consists of motorized rifle or Spetsnaz squads. This group's mission is to scout behind aggressor lines and identify nuclear delivery systems, aggressor forces, headquarters, airfields, and other high-priority targets.

Combined Arms Reserve

3-34. Combined arms reserves are formed by brigades, regiments, and battalions. A brigade or regiment will typically form a battalion as the reserve, while a battalion will designate a platoon.

Anti-Airborne/Air Assault Reserve

3-35. The anti-air assault reserve is used in defensive situations and is composed of combined arms subunits taken from the second echelon. The Russians will only create this formation if they are opposed by an aggressor with the capability to airland or airdrop forces into combat.

Armored Group

3-36. The armored group (Bronegruppa) forms after motorized rifle forces dismount from their armored vehicles to conduct an attack or defense. The armored fighting vehicles are then formed into an armored maneuver reserve or support subunit. On occasion, tanks augment the armored group. It is used by a battalion to strengthen the defense by increasing maneuverability and firepower to blunt any penetrations of the defense.

Special Reserve

3-37. Special reserves—such as chemical defense or engineer—may also be formed, depending on the tactical situation. They are not normally found at battalion level due to their limited organic assets.

Antitank Reserve

3-38. Antitank elements from brigade, regimental, or battalion level will form an antitank reserve. These reserves are often reinforced with engineer and artillery assets.

Flank and Rear Security Forces

3-39. During march movements, every battalion and regiment in both the first and second echelon performs flank security, while units of the second echelon also provide rear security. Forward detachments and the advance guard provide their own advance, flank, and rear security.

Air Assault Detachment

3-40. An air assault detachment consists of a reinforced rifle company that is trained to conduct air assault into aggressor rear areas. This detachment is often used for containment or counterattack tasks.

Combat Security Outpost

3-41. The first-echelon companies of defending first-echelon battalions will normally employ platoons or squads as CSOPs. A CSOP provides security to the main body in the defense and is typically within direct fire support range of the main body.

ORGANIZATION

3-42. The "New Look" restructuring changed the SV from the traditional Soviet four-tiered organization of military district, army, division, and regiment to the modernized, three-tiered force of military district, army, and brigade. The General Staff sees the brigade as the best organizational building block with the capabilities to fight local wars and armed conflicts and at least initially fight large-scale war. The continuing analysis of likely combat actions is now causing a return to division organizational structures. In the initial reorganization the Soviet-era divisions and regiments were downsized to brigades, with 3,000–4,500 personnel in motorized rifle brigades (мотострелковая бригада - motostrelkovaya brigada - MRB) and 3,000 in tank brigades (танковая бригада - tankovaya brigada -TB).

> *Note*. Throughout the ATP the term motorized rifle is used for simplicity to address both wheeled and tracked units and subunits rather than motorized/mechanized rifle.

3-43. The smaller brigade formation provides a level of strategic mobility that Russia was unable to achieve using the former Soviet divisional structure. The new motorized rifle and tank brigades are high-readiness units, manned mainly with contract soldiers, and are capable of rapid deployment via rail or air over strategic distances. These smaller units provide capabilities on order with a former Soviet division, can cover more tasks, and cover more of Russia's extensive borders.

3-44. Russia is reforming maneuver divisions in those military districts where the expected threat requires a broader span of control. Primarily the Western and Southern military districts are those receiving new divisions formed with a separate maneuver brigade as the core. After the creation of the new brigades, the General Staff retained some divisions with subordinate regiments in military districts where long-range deployment was not viewed as necessary. Divisions are primarily found in the Western, Southern, and Central Military Districts. Analysis of likely future combat actions caused the General Staff to reconstitute divisions using existing maneuver brigades as the core building block. These divisions are located at their peacetime bases near the border areas where Russia believes there is the likelihood of an aggressor attack.

3-45. Motorized rifle (мотострелковый дивизион - motostrelkovyy divizion - MRD) and tank divisions (танковая дивизия - tankovaya diviziya -TD) have a larger number of contract and conscript soldiers, with total personnel strength of approximately 8,500 and 6,500, respectively. Airborne divisions and Naval Infantry brigades, as elite units, are predominantly manned with contract soldiers and have approximately 5,500 and 2,500 personnel, respectively.

3-46. These changes were a significant departure from the supposed predictability of Soviet-era ground force organizational structures. The reorganization of the SV resulted in brigade and regimental level structures that are somewhat standard, but at higher level echelons the emphasis is on the perceived threat.

SYMBOLOGY

3-47. Unit symbols for all SV units in this ATP use the diamond-shaped frame as defined in DOD MIL-STD 2525D. All SV task-organized units use the "task force" amplifier placed over the "echelon" (unit size) modifier above the diamond-shape frame. Figure 3-1 shows ways in which SV units can be portrayed.

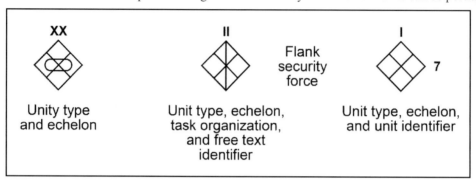

Figure 3-1. SV unit/organization symbols

3-48. The symbology used by Russia is significantly different and communicates a great deal of information to its users. Leaders in the SV use map symbology and a working map or card to capture decisions and transmit plans to subordinates. The signed commander's map is the equivalent of an order directing unit missions and tasks.

DIVISIONS AND BRIGADES

3-49. Unlike the United States and NATO, brigades in the SV are not subordinate to divisions, but rather are directly subordinate to a CAA or TA. Divisions throughout the SV are not standardized or fixed and have varying numbers and types of maneuver regiments.

3-50. There are two brigade types MRB and tank TB. The SV consolidated existing divisions and regiments into brigades under the "New Look" reforms. These brigades are structured to fight local wars but can also be successfully employed in large-scale wars.

3-51. Brigades and division-subordinate regiments are required to be capable of forming task-organized BTGs. The number of BTGs task organized by either a regiment or brigade depends on the level of modernization, but all must be capable of creating at least one BTG. A task-organized BTG performs independent combined-arms combat missions.

3-52. The largest tactical formation in the Russian Army is the division. The Russians believe the division structure is necessary to confront any aggression by the United States and NATO. Some of these divisions have the classic Soviet six-regiment structure, with a motorized rifle division containing three motorized rifle regiments, one tank regiment, one artillery regiment, and an air defense regiment. Tank divisions may contain three tank regiments and one motorized rifle regiment, plus artillery and air defense regiments. The regiments within the division will most likely resemble the Soviet-era regimental structure, with the addition of air defense and multiple rocket launcher (MRL) battalions. Current Russian divisions have about 8,500 personnel and are considerably smaller than Soviet-era divisions. Figure 3-2 and figure 3-3 show examples of a motorized rifle division and TD force structure.

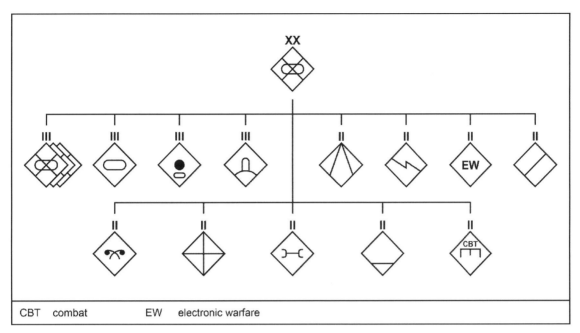

Figure 3-2. Motorized (Mech) rifle division

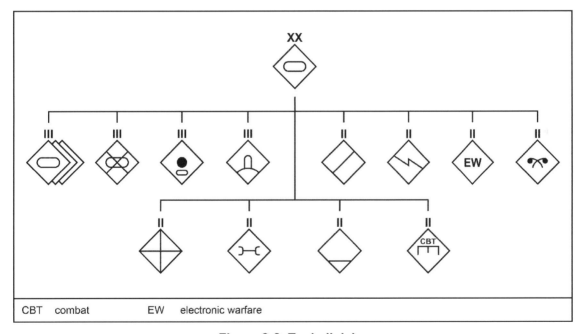

Figure 3-3. Tank division

REGIMENTAL FORCE STRUCTURE

3-53. Russia's regimental structure is still developing but is most likely similar to the combined arms brigades which contained four maneuver battalions. A motorized rifle regiment would contain three motorized rifle battalions and one tank battalion, while a tank regiment would contain three tank battalions and one motorized rifle battalion. Figure 3-4 on page 3-10 shows an example of a Russian regiment.

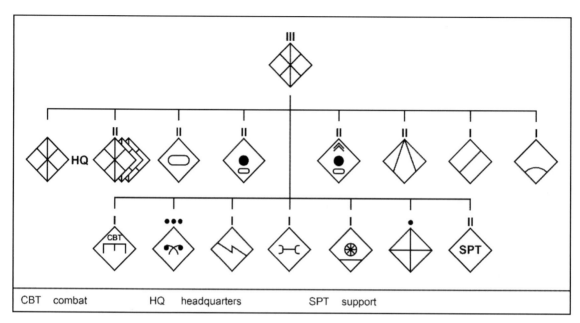

Figure 3-4. Motorized rifle regiment

SEPARATE COMBINED ARMS BRIGADE FORCE STRUCTURE

3-54. Separate combined arms brigades differ from divisions in that they have fewer personnel and less military equipment. They can execute missions with the very same high effectiveness as divisions, but in a smaller zone of responsibility. While these brigades can certainly operate independently, they will commonly conduct operations as part of a CAA or TA. Brigades will often have additional subunits attached to them from their parent army, such as artillery, engineer, antitank, and air defense.

3-55. The subunits of MRBs and tank brigades TBs are different in number and type. The MRB has three motorized rifle battalions, one tank battalion, one antitank battalion, one artillery battalion, and one MRL battalion. Figure 3-5 shows an example of a motorized rifle brigade.

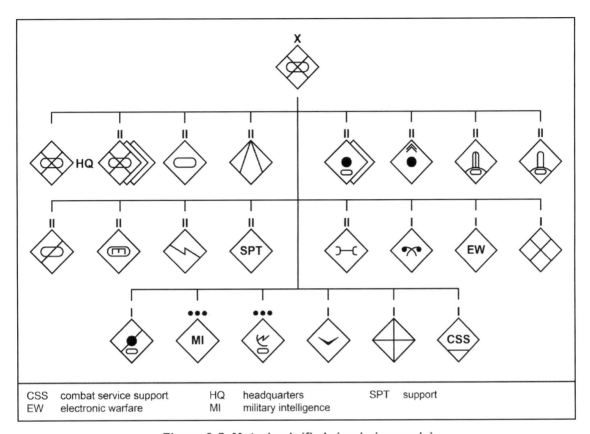

CSS combat service support   HQ headquarters   SPT support
EW   electronic warfare   MI military intelligence

Figure 3-5. Motorized rifle brigade (example)

3-56. The TB has three tank battalions and one motorized rifle battalion but, unlike the MRB, has no antitank subunit, artillery battalion, or MRL battalion.

BATTALION TACTICAL GROUP

3-57. A BTG is a task-organized or ad hoc motorized rifle or tank battalion created by either a brigade or regiment with additional forces and means for a specific mission. Russian BTGs are composed almost exclusively of contract soldiers. A BTG will be used to accomplish the most challenging and complex assignments allocated to its parent unit. The SV goal is ultimately to field the tactical groups with combat power equivalent to Soviet-era brigades and battalions while requiring a much lower level of manpower.

3-58. BTGs regularly train together with enablers and are semipermanent structures. Like the brigade or regiment that often receives additional assets from higher headquarters, the BTG receives additional tanks or motorized rifle units, artillery, engineers, antitank, air defense, electromagnetic warfare, and other assets. With these extensive attachments, the BTG executes independent combined arms combat missions.

3-59. A BTG contains significantly more combat power than a regular battalion; however, a standard Russian motorized rifle or tank battalion always receives additional assets when in combat. These additions do not intrinsically make the battalion a BTG. Figure 3-6 on page 3-12 shows an example of a BTG.

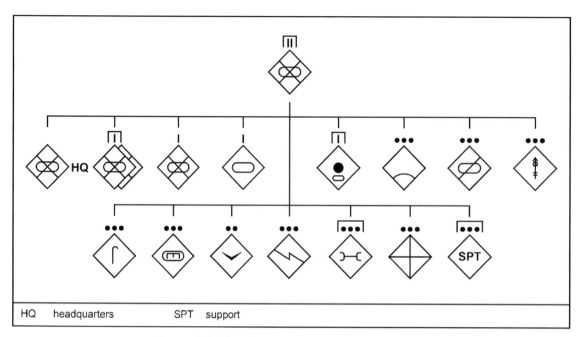

Figure 3-6. Battalion tactical group (example)

COMPANY TACTICAL GROUP

3-60. The CTG, like the BTG, is an ad hoc subunit, organized for a specific mission or task. The SV trains to establish habitual relationships between maneuver and supporting subunits to increase the combat power and overall tactical capabilities. The CTG may be task-organized with additional indirect fire subunits depending on the type and priority of its aggressor target. An example of a CTG with additional tank, reconnaissance, antitank, air defense, engineer, sniper, and electromagnetic warfare support subunits follows in Figure 3-7.

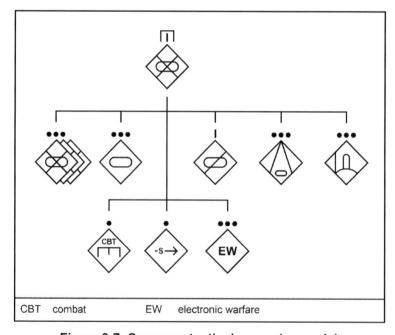

Figure 3-7. Company tactical group (example)

BATTALION

3-61. In the Russian system, battalions are subunits and are the primary forces of brigades and regiments. The motorized rifle battalion normally has three motorized rifle companies, a mortar battery, and one platoon each of reconnaissance, grenade launcher, antitank, signal, engineer, and combat support. A tank battalion normally has three tank companies. A battalion performing an independent mission receives additional assets from the brigade or regiment. Figures 3-8 and 3-9 provide examples of battalions.

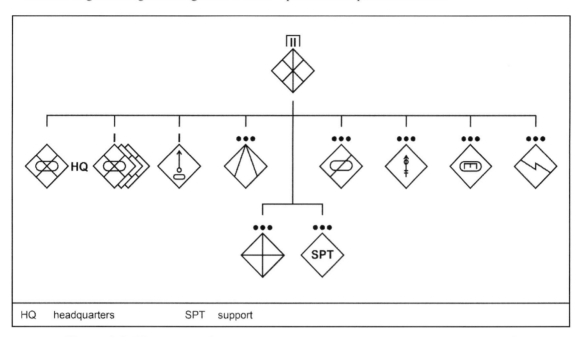

| HQ | headquarters | SPT | support |

Figure 3-8. Motorized rifle battalion and task-organized support (example)

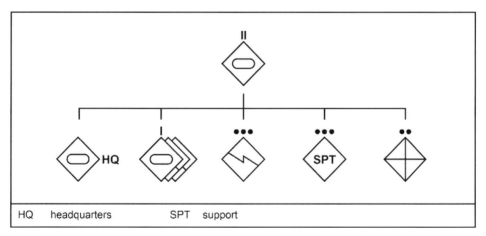

| HQ | headquarters | SPT | support |

Figure 3-9. Tank battalion (example)

COMPANY

3-62. Russian companies vary in size, but most have two to four platoons averaging 30–100 soldiers each. Most companies belong to a battalion; however, in some cases a company might report directly to brigade, regimental, or even higher echelon units. A Russian motorized rifle company has three platoons commanded by a captain. A motorized rifle company in a BTR battalion might have an additional antitank squad.

SPECIALIZED FORCES AND MEANS

3-63. The Reconnaissance - Fire Complex (разведывательно-огневые комплексы - razvedyvatel'no-ognevyye kompleksy - RFC) at the tactical level integrates the constituent and dedicated fire assets retained by its level of command. This can include aviation, artillery, and missile units. The RFC also links reconnaissance and intelligence assets allocated to it. (See chapter 5 for more detail on the RFC missions.) While not specifically stated or named, division and brigade level SV organizations can form at least one RFC structure—staff, command post, communications and intelligence architecture, and integrated/automated fire control system. Brigades and subunits may form a limited RFC using integrated fires of the brigade artillery group (BrAG). The RFC may integrate some or all the unit types depicted in figure 3-10.

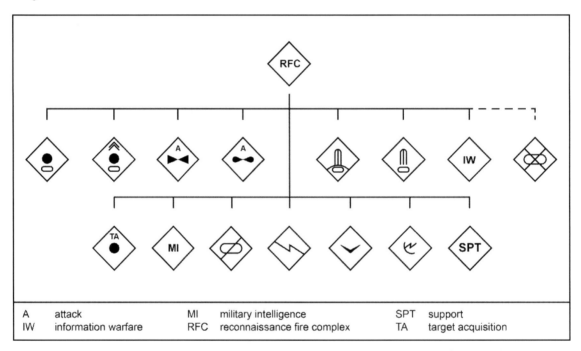

| A | attack | MI | military intelligence | SPT | support |
| IW | information warfare | RFC | reconnaissance fire complex | TA | target acquisition |

Figure 3-10. Functions or type units organized as elements of the RFC

COMMAND POST TYPES

3-64. Russian units may have several types of command posts, such as main, forward, air, and auxiliary to ensure redundancy and continuity of action. No single attack against one command post will disrupt an SV tactical action. Typical Russian command posts are shown in figure 3-11.

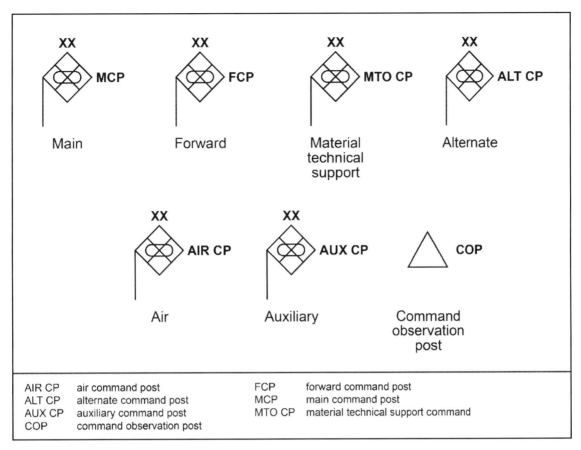

Figure 3-11. Command post symbols

Main Command Post

3-65. Each army, corps, division, brigade, and separate regiment has a main command post (MCP). This command post is the primary one and is augmented by forward and alternate command posts. The MCP will be protected by a platoon of ground based tactical air defense systems.

Forward Command Post

3-66. Commanders often establish forward command posts (FCPs) with small groups of staff members. Much smaller and more mobile than the MCP, the FCP provides the commander with information and communications that facilitate their decisions. It is deployed at a point from which the commander can more effectively and personally observe and influence the battle. The FCP is often used when control is difficult from the MCP, or when the MCP is moving or destroyed.

Command Observation Post

3-67. Command observation posts are typically an armored command vehicle. It is the only command post formed below brigade and regimental level. Artillery commanders will also have command observation post (COP) vehicles. Artillery battalion and battery commanders will normally collocate with the supported maneuver commander to relay calls for fire and quickly deal with targets of opportunity.

Materiel Technical Support Command Post

3-68. A materiel technical support (MTO) command post, also known as a rear area command post, will be established by MTO brigades, battalions, and companies. A MTO brigade will establish a command post behind an army MCP, and a MTO battalion will establish one to the rear of a division or brigade MCP. A MTO company will establish a command post behind a maneuver battalion's COP.

Airborne Command Post

3-69. When subordinates are spread over a wide area or when the MCP is moving, a commander may use an airborne command post to control fluid situations. This is common in army, corps, and division command, and can occur in separate brigades. These command posts are typically aboard helicopters.

Alternate Command Post

3-70. The alternate command post provides for the assumption of command should the MCP and its commander become incapacitated. This command post operates with a greatly reduced staff.

Auxiliary Command Post

3-71. The auxiliary command post is established by army and higher levels of command when the situation requires an additional command post. It is often used to control an operation on a secondary axis.

CONTROL MEASURES

3-72. The SV typically uses a minimum number of control measures to orient or regulate unit or subunit actions. They analyze an OE to facilitate rapid transition, when necessary, between defense and offense or between linear and nonlinear dispositions. SV analysis also adapts to the nature of conflict conditions and provides clear expectations of a mission—as well as limitations or constraints to mission expectations—in written, verbal, or graphical instructions.

3-73. When a division or brigade participates in the army's combat formation it is assigned a defensive zone. Units establish defensive belts within the assigned defensive zone. For independent action on a separate axis or during an armed conflict, the unit is assigned a zone of responsibility (zona otvetstvennosti - ZOR).

3-74. For a defense by motorized rifle or tank units, there are several control elements that interconnect and layer the formation to create an integrated defense:

- Combat formation—the task organized units and subunits included in the defense.
- Zones—Successive designated areas that define the responsibilities for reconnaissance, security, and defensive echelonment of forces for Army subordinate units.
- Strong points—Prepared fighting positions interconnected by trenches and fortified with engineer obstacles to form a 360-degree defensive position.
- Fires system—All organic and allocated fire complexes integrated to create fire ambushes and fire sacks, and to ensure coverage of the unit frontage.
- Engineered obstacles—Emplaced obstacles, including mines, wire, flame, electric fences, and other obstacles, designed to slow and canalize the attacking aggressor units.

Zone of Responsibility

3-75. The expected nonlinear nature of the modern battlefield will likely result in units being assigned a ZOR for independent actions. The ZOR is the combination of a unit area of operations (AO) and the area outside the AO that can be observed by the unit's reconnaissance and security technical sensors. The zone of responsibility can extend into the AOs of other units. The ZOR depends on the type of defense the unit was engaged in before launching a counterstrike. From a positional defense, the ZOR planning distances for a brigade include a front area of up to 10 km long with a depth of 15 km. The planning distances for an attack from a hasty defense plan for brigade's frontage to be up to 20 km with a depth of 30 km. These planning distances are based on SV COFM and nomogram calculations and are subject to modification based on battlefield conditions.

Covering Force Area (Security Zone)

3-76. The covering force area or security zone is part of the battle area of the unit or subunit assigned the mission of protecting the main defensive belts from surprise by aggressor units. A unit assigned the security zone mission, such as a forward detachment, is tasked with disrupting an attacking aggressor by delaying it or causing it to prematurely deploy its forces. The security zone is a geographical area and airspace in which the assigned unit fixes or disrupts an aggressor and sets conditions for successful combat actions throughout an AO. Units in this zone begin the attack on specified components of the aggressor's combat system to start the disaggregation and defeat of that system, primarily by precision or massed fires. Successful actions in the security zone will create a window of opportunity that is exploitable by battle zone units. SV states that a tactical security zone may be formed at a depth of up to 40 km in front of the forward edge of the defense. The purpose of such a deep security zone is to draw out the aggressor unit and accomplish the following actions, including:

- Defeat aggressor reconnaissance and counterreconnaissance forces.
- Maintain reconnaissance or surveillance of critical aggressor systems.
- Deny aggressor ability to acquire and engage battle zone units with long-range fires.
- Disrupt aggressor air defenses.
- Disrupt aggressor engineer capabilities.
- Disaggregate aggressor movement and maneuver.
- Interrupt effective aggressor logistics support to its combat force.
- Deceive the aggressor on disposition and actions of SV units, main effort, or main defenses.

3-77. The boundaries of the security zone consist of the battle line and the reconnaissance limit of the overall AO. In nonlinear offensive combat, the higher headquarters may move the battle line and reconnaissance limit forward as the unit continues to move and maneuver in successive offensive actions. A higher headquarters commander can adjust the security zone boundary as units adopt a temporary defensive posture while consolidating gains after a successful offensive action or in preparation for subsequent offensive actions. Similarly, a higher headquarters commander can adjust the security zone boundary based on emergent conditions during defensive actions.

3-78. Security zones between SV units may be contiguous or noncontiguous. They can also be layered, with the security zone of a subordinate command being integral to the security zone of the next higher command. Security zone units and subunits may be directed to conduct disruption actions within the security zone of a higher headquarters.

Battle Area

3-79. The battle area is the portion of an AO where the SV plans to fight. In a positional defense it will usually consist of a first and a second echelon. Echelons are lines of units arranged in mutually supporting positions in a defense or in sequential formations during an attack. The battle and support lines separate the battle zone from the security zone and the support zone (see paragraph 3-50), respectively. Lateral boundaries are part of the ZOR. Units in the battle zone exploit opportunities created by actions in the security zone. The primary action in the battle zone is to use all subunits of combat power to engage the aggressor in close combat and achieve tactical mission success.

3-80. In the battle area, forces are typically tasked to accomplish one or more of the following:

- Create a penetration in aggressor defenses through which exploitation units can pass.
- Deceive aggressor attention from a main offensive effort or supporting defensive effort.
- Prevent movement or maneuver of an aggressor force that might otherwise impact SV actions in an AO.
- Seize or defend key terrain.
- Inflict significant casualties on aggressor forces.
- Defeat aggressor command and control (C2), units, or logistics.
- Destroy aggressor high-value equipment or facilities.

A division or brigade does not always form a division- or brigade-level battle zone, as the battle zone may be the aggregate of the battle zones of its subordinate subunits. In nonlinear situations, there may be multiple, noncontiguous brigade or regimental battle zones. The brigade and regimental battle zones provide each of the subordinate unit commanders the terrain to conduct decisive tactical actions. Battalion and other subunits may have AOs that consist primarily of a battle zone with a small support zone contained within it.

Support Zone

3-81. The support zone defines the area occupied by units and subunits that support the mission. Security units operate in the support zone in a combat role to defeat aggressor forces that might otherwise impact effective AO logistics and administrative support. Camouflage, concealment, cover, and deception measures, as in other zones, improve defense against aggressor reconnaissance and precision attack. Logistics support and services integrate direct and general support to ensure maintenance of effective combat power for the performance of missions and supporting tasks.

3-82. A division's support zone can be dispersed within the support zones of subordinate regiments, or the division may have its own support zone that is separate from subordinate-unit AOs. As the battle moves during the course of the defense or an attack, the support zone repositions based on command direction to ensure timely and continuous support to the command. The support zone may be in a sanctuary that is noncontiguous with other zones of an AO.

Reconnaissance Zone

3-83. A reconnaissance zone is the combination of a unit AO and the area outside of an AO that can be observed by the unit's reconnaissance and security technical sensors. A reconnaissance detachment created by a brigade or division based on the tactical situation may have a zone that is up to 10 km wide for a battalion detachment or 5 km for a company.

Attack Zone

3-84. The commander assigns an offensive mission and associated attack zone to a subordinate unit to clearly delineate where units will conduct offensive maneuver. Attack zones are often used to control offensive action by a subordinate unit inside a larger defensive battle or operation.

Fire Ambush

3-85. A fire ambush is a designated terrain position that is favorable for engaging aggressor forces from hidden positions with sudden fires: direct and concentrated short-range fire effects augmented by mines. The SV commander designates a fire ambush to inflict maximum damage to and defeat of aggressor forces, using the concentrated forces and means available. Designated platoons, either motorized rifle or tank, execute the fire ambush and are task organized with sniper teams, flamethrowers, and engineer sappers.

Fire Sack

3-86. Fire sacks define where aggressor forces are targeted and destroyed. A fire sack may be within the security, battle, or support zone of an AO. It is a three-dimensional target area defined by depth, width, and height to facilitate the integration of coordinated joint weapons strikes. Fire sacks may use either single or multiple fire ambushes to destroy an aggressor force. As a joint coordination and control measure, fire sacks facilitate effective and timely use of air and indirect fires in support of the ground maneuver commander's mission. A fire sack may include no-fire areas, restricted operations areas, and airspace coordination areas. When used as a joint coordination and control measure, a fire sac enables Russian aerospace army air support assets to engage surface targets without further coordination or terminal attack control.

PART TWO

Tactical Actions

Part Two addresses several primary areas of tactical actions of the Ground Forces of the Russian Federation (Сухопутные войска Российской Федерации – sukhoputnyye voyska RF - SV). Chapter 4 discusses reconnaissance and security actions, Chapter 5, strike actions, Chapter 6, defensive actions, and Chapter 7, offensive actions.

Chapter 4

Reconnaissance and Security

Reconnaissance and security are essential components to any SV mission, whether conducted during armed conflict and local wars or full-scale defense or offense. This chapter covers the concepts, methods, formations, and mission tasks the SV uses when conducting reconnaissance and security actions. This chapter also includes pertinent information related to security and protection provided by the Integrated Air Defense System (IADS), as well as electromagnetic warfare reconnaissance and security actions.

INTRODUCTION TO RUSSIAN RECONNAISSANCE AND SECURITY

4-1.   Russian reconnaissance and security are ongoing actions regardless of the type of competition, crisis, or conflict. The SV uses all forces and means available to conduct reconnaissance to gain information on the battlefield as well as security actions to deny an aggressor information and understanding of the SV's forces. The Russian military recognizes the critical need to obtain battlefield information through reconnaissance and security to maintain freedom of action for its forces. Reconnaissance and security are essential to creating and sustaining situational awareness and understanding of an OE including friendly and aggressor forces, potential adversaries, and civilian populations.

4-2.   Information and its resulting intelligence are essential to support successful execution of a commander's plan. Likewise, preserving freedom of movement and combat power of the SVs' forces and actions is also critical to that success. Gaining and maintaining information allows the SV commander to develop and execute battlefield plans rapidly. Fielding of automated command and control complexes such as the Strelets allows rapid transmission of reconnaissance and security information to provide intelligence that supports actions taken at all echelons.

Note. Russia uses the descriptive term "complex" сложный - slozhnyy) to refer to equipment with supporting infrastructure while "system" система - sistema) refers to a group of complexes or system of systems. A complex indicates the relation linking networks and C2 elements rather than systems. Throughout the ATP the term complex or complexes are used in place of the typical system or systems used by the United States and NATO.

4-3.   Security protects and enhances the flexibility and adaptability of SV leaders to take risk to create or seize opportunities in a deliberate, integrated, and synchronized manner. Reconnaissance and security provide the means to achieve specified tasks in support of a higher commander's mission. Security actions provide early and accurate warning of adversary or aggressor actions and intent and provide SV commanders with time and maneuver space to preempt or react to conditions for effective use of SV combat power.

4-4.   Reconnaissance and security tasks combine the capabilities of SV units and formations to provide the best possible collection and tactical effects to achieve the commanders' intent. Capabilities are a combination of cyber, space, ground, and manned and unmanned aerial resources and sensors. Technical sensor complexes at various SV echelons support reconnaissance or surveillance, information collection, intelligence production, target acquisition and targeting. Resource capabilities can overlap in coverage to provide redundancy and mitigate possible shortcomings of a particular reconnaissance or security complex forces and means. Resource capabilities often integrated for reconnaissance and security operations, include but are not limited to—

- Cyber and electromagnetic spectrum.
- Artillery range finding and signals target acquisition.
- Manned and unmanned aerial and ground complexes.
- Space complex collection downlinks with interface into tactical command and control complexes.
- Integrated air defense early warning and target acquisition.
- Engineer mobility and counter mobility.
- Nuclear, biological, and chemical (NBC).
- Reconnaissance scouts including special purpose forces.

4-5.   Mission tasks occur for the SV within a designated area of responsibility (AOR) and can include a zone of reconnaissance responsibility (ZORR). Russian national-level assets perform special reconnaissance missions that overlay all echelons to provide support in areas contiguous or noncontiguous to SV operations.

RECONNAISSANCE FUNDAMENTALS

4-6.   Commanders direct the appropriate combinations of dismounted, mounted, manned and unmanned aerial, ground, and other technical sensor complexes to accomplish a mission. Reconnaissance and security methods apply the SV fundamentals and principles for efficient and effective configuration and employment of resources over the duration of a reconnaissance or security mission. This section will cover the following fundamentals of Russian reconnaissance: razvedka, principles, objectives, missions, actions, and formations.

"RAZVEDKA": THE FOUNDATION OF RUSSIAN RECONNAISSANCE

4-7.   Russian SV situational awareness and understanding are products of razvedka—the Russian term that encompasses reconnaissance, intelligence, surveillance, and target acquisition. The SV continues to refine its integrated complex to collect information, create and update timely intelligence, and direct units and complexes to monitor, target, and strike an aggressor at an advantageous time and location. All levels of command in the SV are responsible for conducting razvedka, in all situations and circumstances. Razvedka can be strategic, operational, or tactical; however, all three levels are closely interconnected. An attack with fires will often require near real-time or immediate execution to achieve effective results and razvedka forces and means provide the necessary precision target acquisition to support those strikes. The razvedka complex also provides subsequent data and analysis to estimate and confirm the expected damage assessment on targets. Describing the elements of razvedka unites the individual functional capabilities to create an integrated set of complexes paraphrased as follows:

- Reconnaissance is an action to obtain information about the activities and resources of an aggressor or adversary, and to secure data concerning the meteorological, hydrographic, or geographic characteristics of a particular OE.
- Surveillance is conducted in aerospace, cyberspace, surface or subsurface areas, places, on individuals or groups, or things, by visual, aural, electromagnetic, photographic, or other means.
- Target acquisition is the detection, identification, and location of a target in sufficient detail to permit the effective employment of selected complexes, weapons, or both. An adjunct to

acquisition is the battle damage assessment that follows a mission to estimate the effectiveness of physical or other nonkinetic effects on a target.

- Intelligence is a requirement-directed end-product that results from the collection, processing, integration, evaluation, analysis, and interpretation of available information on an aggressor or adversary and the characteristics of a particular OE.

4-8. The reconnaissance and surveillance of an area or point of interest is an integrated group of activities that prioritize and optimize available sensors to locate, study, and exploit a potential or assigned target to create an intelligence product. These capabilities combine to indicate when and how to attack an acquired target most effectively. The decision to attack is often a time-sensitive action but can also be a decision conducted upon confirmation of specific conditions.

4-9. The SV recognizes that defeating the ability of aggressor maneuver, its reconnaissance, and its fires complexes can be problematic to pinpoint or monitor in time and location. Notwithstanding the tactical challenges, razvedka combines SV capabilities and actions to apply relevant intelligence in compressed decision cycles to achieve selective situational understanding of an aggressor, potential adversary, or an OE. However, the SV also considers a more inclusive use of multiple razvedka capabilities. In addition to providing a high degree of reliability to committing fires on high-payoff targets, razvedka complements IV effects that cause predictable impacts on the cognitive agility of an aggressor. Deceiving or decreasing the skills, moral resolve, and ability of an aggressor to act effectively is a fundamental aspect of the SV seizing the initiative, creating tactical opportunities, and applying combat power in an integrated and synchronized manner.

RECONNAISSANCE PRINCIPLES

4-10. The SV applies the following principles to all reconnaissance actions to ensure that the information gathered supports the intelligence requirements for battlefield situational awareness.

Continuity

4-11. Reconnaissance provides constant coverage to collect battlefield information specified by the senior commander. Continuous reconnaissance by multiple complexes improves the corroboration or confirmation of accurate and reliable information and resulting intelligence. Continuity provides multiple indicators of suspected aggressor actions and allows the SV commander the time necessary to defeat those actions. The SV achieves their reconnaissance objective with overlapping, successive, and alternating resources.

4-12. SV commanders commit resources to ensure constant reconnaissance. If coverage gaps emerge during preparation or execution of a mission, the commander informs higher headquarters, acknowledges the gap and risk, and coordinates for capabilities to remedy the potential collection vulnerability. Reconnaissance plans and actions are a continuum focused by the SV commander on critical information requirements and priority tactical issues.

Aggressiveness

4-13. Aggressiveness is a vigorous behavior to identify and collect required information to support production of timely required intelligence. Reconnaissance units willingly fight for information when other forms of collection are inadequate to accomplish a reconnaissance objective. Reconnaissance forces or elements may be required or directed to transition from reconnaissance to direct action tasks to achieve a reconnaissance objective.

Timeliness

4-14. Timely information reporting is critical to situational awareness and understanding in rapidly changing OEs. The ability to acquire, report, target, and deliver capabilities in near real-time is essential to command and control and effective use of the SV integrated fires complex. Timely reporting enables SV commanders and subordinate leaders to exploit temporary tactical opportunities and aggressor vulnerabilities.

4-15. Timeliness also considers factors of speed, pace, and tempo required to efficiently and effectively collect and report information, decide on action, and act. Tempo, pace, and speed relate to the period allowed to conduct a reconnaissance mission, the intent for covert and overt reconnaissance activities, and the level of detail anticipated from a focused collection effort.

4-16. The SV facilitates the acquisition and distribution of reconnaissance combat information using digital, automated, and unified command and control networks. The purpose of these complexes is to gain and maintain an advantage in battlefield awareness that spans the range from the individual soldier up to national command echelons. This capability allows the SV commander to gain an understanding of the battlefield situation and act on that understanding in a rapid manner. Automated C2 complexes facilitate the commander's ability to allocate fires very rapidly and accurately.

Accuracy

4-17. The SV uses all available reconnaissance means to verify the accuracy of reported information. A commander bases decisions on accurate reconnaissance information and professional experience in deciding and acting. The accuracy of reconnaissance information is critical to the targeting and destruction of high-value targets such as aggressor weapons of mass destruction, precision weapons, attack aviation, logistics centers, C2, and communications. The SV achieves accuracy through the creation of overlapping coverage and the use of improved automated command and control technologies. The NTsUO and the Joint Strategic Commands (OSK) integrate reconnaissance and intelligence for strategic and operational actions.

Reliability

4-18. For the operational and tactical level, the army serves as the focal point to integrate the various reconnaissance and intelligence collection capabilities. Reconnaissance must reliably clarify the aggressor situation despite aggressor counterreconnaissance actions including camouflage, cover, concealment, and deception. Commanders select and allocate reconnaissance forces and means according to unit capabilities matched with missions and targets. Subsequent analysis compares, validates, and integrates reconnaissance reports from multiple sources. The study and integration of reconnaissance information collected by multiple sources assists in identifying and assessing false targets and other false indicators of aggressor actions or intentions. (See table 4-1 on page 4-5 for concise descriptions of reconnaissance missions.)

RECONNAISSANCE OBJECTIVES

4-19. The reconnaissance objective focuses a reconnaissance task as a clearly stated requirement for specified information. The focus is often a terrain feature, geographic area, aggressor force, adversary capability or limitation, and information on a different variable of the battlefield.

4-20. The objective may also require a professional assessment based on human observation and data collection such as engineer determination of the capacity of a bridge to support tank traffic. Priorities of effort and available resources determine the specific objectives assigned that will inform, confirm, or deny plans for current and projected operations. In achieving the reconnaissance objective, the SV commander estimates the risk expected in developing the tactical situation while retaining freedom of movement and maneuver. This assessment of risk and decision making in reconnaissance operations includes higher headquarters guidance on engagement, disengagement, displacement, tactical task handover, and bypass criteria for a particular mission.

4-21. Reconnaissance units are assigned mission tasks to collect battlefield information that supports the following objectives:
- Ascertaining the aggressor's order of battle, current preparations for battle, and warning signs of surprise attack.
- Determining the aggressor's composition, position, echelons, status and capabilities of forces, and system of command and control.
- Ascertaining which targets to engage and their locations.
- Locating important aggressor theater-level weapons and equipment, detecting aggressor engineer field fortifications and integrated obstacle complex.

- Ascertaining the problems of crossing terrain, the status of communications, the nature of water obstacles, the boundaries, and the size of areas of destruction, fires and floods, NBC contaminated areas, and the possible axes of surmounting or bypassing them.
- Identifying new aggressor weapons and methods of warfare, as well as the conduct and measures required for all around security of the operation or combat.
- Ascertaining the morale of aggressor forces and the local population, and the economic status of the area of operations.

RECONNAISSANCE MISSIONS

4-22. For tactical offensive and defensive actions, SV reconnaissance missions are usually grouped in the categories of combat reconnaissance, signals intelligence, radar, electro-optical, artillery, engineer, medical, route, and NBC. The typical reconnaissance missions are route, area, and zone. During local war and armed conflict operations, SV units and subunits perform a variation on area reconnaissance labeled as a reconnaissance search activity. Another category is special reconnaissance typically conducted by special operation forces or other designated forces operating in the depth of an aggressor AOR or at selected sites. Special reconnaissance supports operational and strategic operations. See table 4-1 for descriptions of reconnaissance missions.

Table 4-1. Reconnaissance mission descriptions

Mission	Description – Using forces and means to gain detailed information.
Route	On a specified route, trafficability, lateral routes, adjacent or controlling terrain, aggressor forces and relevant populations on or along the route that an aggressor could use to impact movement and maneuver.
Area	Within a specified area identified by commander-specified boundaries that includes aggressor forces, terrain, and relevant populations that impact mission accomplishments. SV units conduct reconnaissance-search to identify aggressor forces and key terrain features.
Zone	Within a zone identified by a boundary that includes all routes, obstacles, terrain, aggressor forces, and relevant population considerations that have the potential to impact mission success.
SV	Russian ground forces

Route Reconnaissance

4-23. Route reconnaissance is a mission to obtain detailed information for a specified route and all terrain from which the aggressor could influence movement or maneuver on or adjacent to that route. The route may be a manmade transportation feature, cross-country mobility corridor, and several routes in an axis of advance. A route reconnaissance can be a discrete mission task or a specified task within a zone or area reconnaissance. Route reconnaissance is not a route classification mission that requires technical measurements and analysis typically performed by mission-tailored engineer reconnaissance teams. However, basic route classification information can be collected by units other than engineer teams. (See figures 4-7 and 4-8 for a platoon echelon route reconnaissance mission.)

Area Reconnaissance

4-24. Area reconnaissance is a mission to obtain detailed information about the terrain, adversary or aggressor activity, and civilian activities, infrastructure, and other OE features within a designated geographic area. The area may be identified as a single geographic point, or a specified area defined by a boundary. A difference between an area reconnaissance and a zone reconnaissance is an area reconnaissance focuses typically on a geographic area smaller than a zone. (See figures 4-12 and 4-13 on pages 4-21 and 4-22 for an example of a reconnaissance platoon of a motorized infantry reconnaissance battalion, reinforced with engineer reconnaissance squads that are conducting an area reconnaissance oriented on possible river crossing sites.)

4-25. When conducting operations under conditions of armed conflict and local wars, the SV performs a variation of the area reconnaissance, a reconnaissance-search. The purpose of this reconnaissance action is to secure a defined area within the ZORR and then conduct a search of that area to gain information on an aggressor force to enable detention or destruction. This type of reconnaissance supports development and execution of a Blokirovanie (blocking action). Blokirovanie is the isolation of a specified area to locate and target an aggressor force to prevent breakout and either capture or destruction.

Zone Reconnaissance

4-26. Zone reconnaissance is a mission to obtain detailed information on all routes, obstacles, terrain, and aggressor forces in a zone defined by boundaries. Operations validate the commander's concept by confirming or denying items of interest such as natural and manmade obstacles, trafficability of routes, viability and utility of key terrain, and areas with possible or known NBC contamination or other limitations that can affect a mission. Zone reconnaissance is a deliberate and time-intensive operation that takes more time to conduct than other forms of reconnaissance to refine detail and understanding of an OE, adversary and aggressor composition, disposition, and readiness, and civil considerations of a relevant population.

4-27. Special reconnaissance includes reconnaissance and surveillance conducted as a special action in hostile, denied, or politically sensitive environments to collect or verify information of strategic or operational significance. This type of reconnaissance usually employs military capabilities not resident in regular SV forces.

4-28. The most widely known special reconnaissance activity is the General Staff Main Intelligence Directorate (GRU) Spetsnaz (*спецназ*). Spetsnaz are not equivalent to U.S. special forces and are primarily focused on intelligence collection. Spetsnaz as a term includes any specialized unit with a narrow area of specialization like signal intelligence, engineering, is experimental, or performs highly important tasks.

4-29. As part of the changing force structure, the SV formed the Special Operations Forces Command (командование силами специальных операций - KSSO) to provide capabilities more in line with the Western special forces units. These forces are in addition to and not part of the GRU Spetsnaz and conduct strategic and operational level deep reconnaissance and combat actions. Irregular forces affiliated with SV regular or KSSO can employ a wide range of reconnaissance skills from simple human observation and collection to use of sophisticated sensor complexes. Surveillance by irregular forces can occur over extended periods of time and be the complement to KSSO or regular forces at selected points in time, as regular and irregular forces operate within a relevant population of an AOR or ZORR.

Unmanned Aircraft System Reconnaissance

4-30. The SV continues using all the reconnaissance techniques available but has significantly expanded its capability to use unmanned aircraft systems (UAS) reconnaissance as a means of gathering battlefield information. Maneuver brigades and divisions employ their organic UAS to support the senior commander's plan principally focused on supporting target acquisition for indirect fire strikes. The typical flight profiles for the different UAS search patterns follow in figures 4-1 through 4-6, on pages 4-7 through 4-12.

4-31. A UAS flight pattern set to search a designated zone attempts to identify group and single targets in tactical and near operational depths of an aggressor's combat formation. It serves as a relatively simple method to plan and covers a large area. The main disadvantage is that it exposes the UAS to detection and engagement by aggressor air defenses and can consume a large amount of time depending on the search zone.

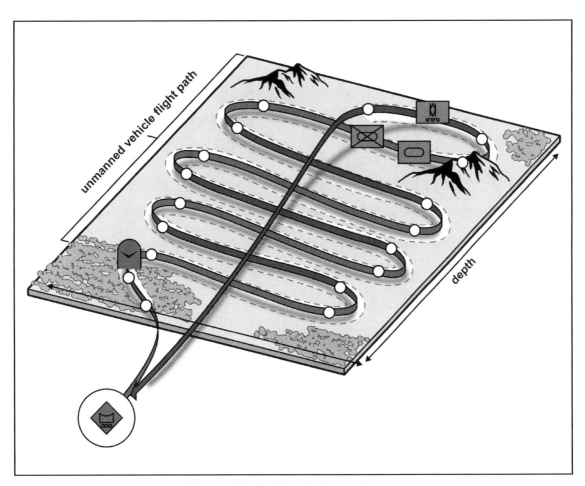

Figure 4-1. Designated search zone

4-32. Using a specified line to fly over a suspected aggressor formation can be highly effective if the selection of the line is refined by other reconnaissance methods during planning. Using REB or counter-battery radars can narrow the search footprint to refine the planned flight path. This pattern is more covert and stealthier, allowing the UAS to make a single transit of the suspected line of the targeted aggressor unit. This method reduces the exposure of the UAS to air defense fires. Disadvantages include increased difficulty in transmitting information collected in real-time with any delay causing targeting information to be degraded over time.

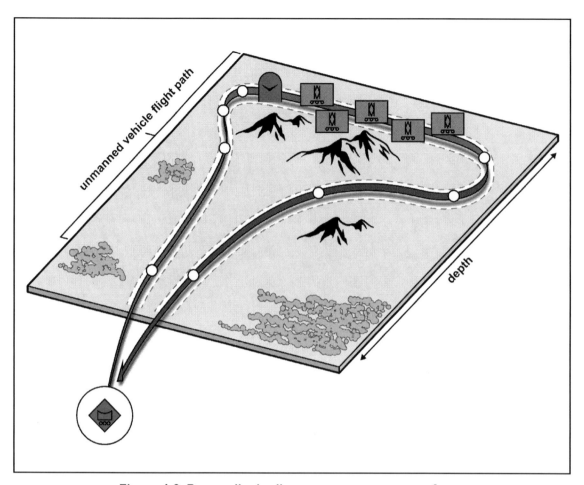

Figure 4-2. Perpendicular line across an aggressor force

4-33. The search of an angular sector orients the UAS on an angular search zone. The planning and selection of the search zone can be based on a likely march route of an aggressor force that is limited by terrain or other mobility factors. This method is particularly effective when there is no continuous line of contact between SV units and a targeted aggressor.

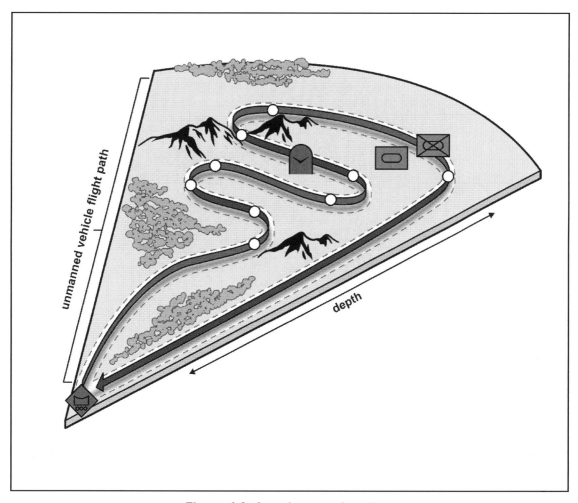

Figure 4-3. Angular search pattern

4-34. Continuous patrol of a designated area is best accomplished by a long-duration UAS with side-looking radar or electro-optical sensors. These characteristics allow the UAS to observe a search zone without entering the air defense zone of the aggressor unit. It is not a particularly stealthy flight pattern with repetitive tracks in a relatively restricted airspace. Predictable patterns and sensor emanations increase the platform's vulnerability to aviation or anti-radiation missiles.

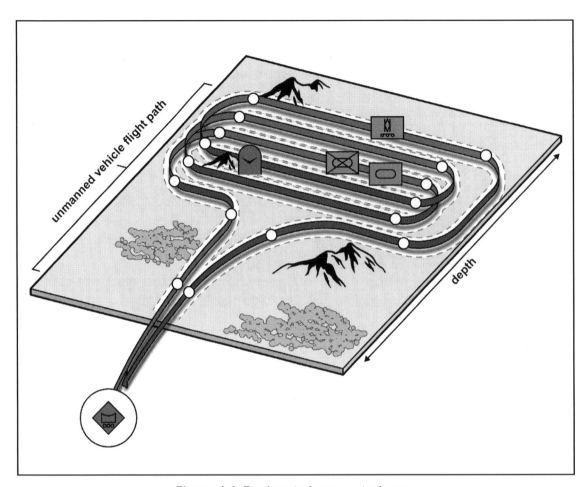

Figure 4-4. Designated area patrol zone

4-35. Reconnaissance of a specific point is used when the coordinates of a target are known to confirm current status. Coverage of choke points such as bridges or other defiles or confirmation of signals intelligence (SIGINT) locations for C2 complexes are examples of designated points. This method provides the greatest stealth and least exposure to aggressor air defenses. Its main disadvantage is that it provides a very limited amount of information.

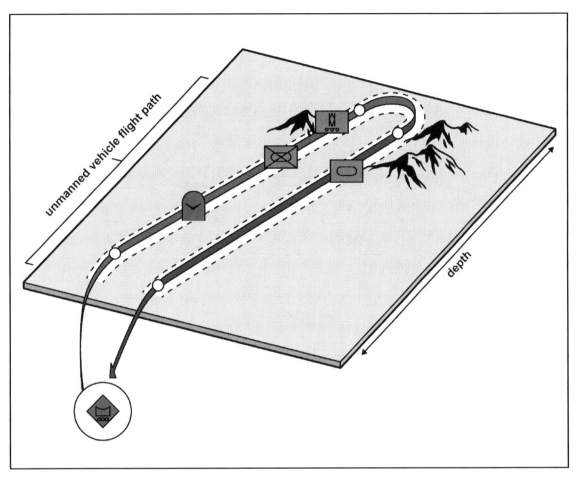

Figure 4-5. Search of a designated point

4-36. A flight path to search a given route may be used when there is information about the location of an aggressor unit or group of targets whose movement routes are constrained by terrain. It uses a low altitude high-speed flight profile to search designated waypoints on the route.

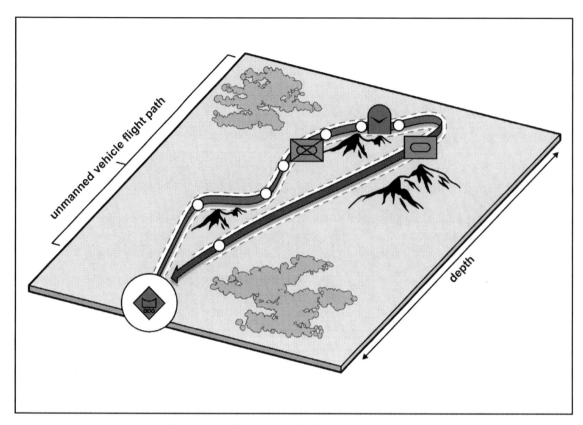

Figure 4-6. Designated flight route search

RECONNAISSANCE ACTIONS

4-37. SV units and subunits perform reconnaissance missions by conducting observation, infiltration, searches, raids, ambushes, and reconnaissance by battle actions.

Observation

4-38. Tactical-level commanders rely on direct observation by reconnaissance that is mounted, dismounted, aerial, radio-electromagnetic warfare (радиоэлектронная война - radioelektronnaya voyna - REB), and personal observation of the battlefield to create an understanding of the situation. Increasingly the SV collects and integrates battlefield information using automated collection complexes such as battlefield surveillance radars, unmanned aerial vehicles (UAVs), and unmanned ground vehicles to create situational awareness. The information gathered by reconnaissance forces is integrated using newly fielded automated command and control complexes.

4-39. Dismounted reconnaissance can provide detailed information collection about the aggressor, terrain, civil considerations, and infrastructure with human observation and technical complexes. Dismounted actions are typically the most time-consuming method performed by ground units. National-level forces, main forces of the SV, and irregular elements all conduct ground reconnaissance to provide OE information to the Russian command and control complex.

4-40. Mounted reconnaissance employs complexes with greater collection range and stand-off capabilities and enhances collection abilities based on the speed and range of mounted complexes. The testing and eventual fielding of remotely directed complexes, such as the unmanned URAN-9 (a tracked unmanned combat ground vehicle designated to provide fire support for special forces), allows operators to maneuver the platform and its sensors to an advantageous observation position for collection of battlefield information without exposing soldiers to direct or indirect fires.

4-41. Manned and unmanned reconnaissance integrate with and complement mounted and dismounted ground capabilities to collect information with increased speed, range, and coverage area by sensor complexes. To support tactical actions, automated command and control complexes integrate information collected from all UAV assets. Strategic and operational level reconnaissance is performed by fixed-wing and rotary-wing platforms. Electromagnetic warfare complexes complement Razvedka with the abilities to monitor, intercept, track, and collect electromagnetic information in the EMS. The complexes and platforms of sensors for electromagnetic radiation are classified by wavelength into radio wave, microwave, terahertz (or sub-millimeter) radiation, infrared, the visible region perceived as light, ultraviolet, X-rays and gamma rays. Electromagnetic warfare complexes integrated with dismounted and mounted, aerial, cyber, and space sensors provide flexibility for the mix and redundancy of technical assets and methods in order to focus special or unique capabilities on a comprehensive reconnaissance task.

Infiltration

4-42. Infiltration of aggressor defensive positions is conducted in conjunction with an attack to cover the penetration of the defensive line. The infiltrating RP rapidly moves into the depths of the aggressor defensive position to make observations that pinpoint high-value targets such as C2 complexes, artillery, strongpoints, and reserve units.

Search

4-43. Searches focus on an area instead of a targeted aggressor unit. It still uses covered approaches to the search area and once in the area combs through it to locate the target unit or facility. The reconnaissance unit conducting the search launches an attack to capture prisoners, weapons and equipment, and any documents or items of intelligence value. Reconnaissance searches are used extensively during local wars and armed conflicts and support both defensive and offensive actions.

Raid

4-44. Raiding detachments conduct missions to reveal the aggressor's disposition including strongpoints and obstacles. It identifies concealed avenues of approach to selected aggressor defensive positions and conducts attacks to seize prisoners, weapons, equipment, and documents of intelligence value.

Ambush

4-45. SV reconnaissance units and subunits conduct ambushes, much like raids, to capture prisoners, weapons and equipment samples, documents, and to destroy the aggressor unit. An ambush is conducted for reconnaissance during both defensive and offensive actions. It typically is set on the most likely avenue of aggressor movement that affords the best level of concealment from detection. SVs use ambushes in any terrain, weather, or level of visibility.

Reconnaissance by Battle

4-46. Reconnaissance by battle is typically an attack including direct or indirect fires, targeted on a suspected aggressor position to cause that target to disclose its presence by movement or return fire. This type of engagement can be direct, indirect, a combination of direct and indirect fires as well as IV engagements. When available, indirect fires support an SV reconnaissance force such as sniper teams that remain undetected as it observes possible aggressor reactions. A reconnaissance by fire does not ensure that an aggressor will disclose itself and is typically used only when other reconnaissance means are not available, and timeliness of intelligence collection requires this action. The SV also launches IV reconnaissance by fire engagements using psychological methods to convince the aggressor unit commanders that displacement is critical for continued survival. As the IV engagements are slow to develop, they are often combined with planned direct or indirect fires to enhance the impact on the aggressor force. Figures 4-7 through 4-10 on pages 4-14 through 4-17 depict types of reconnaissance actions.

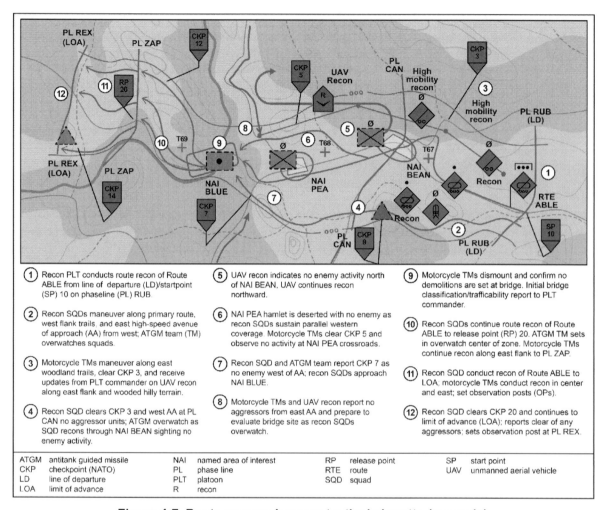

Figure 4-7. Route reconnaissance tactical vignette (example)

1. Recon PLT conducts route recon of Route ABLE from line of departure (LD)/startpoint (SP) 10 on phaseline (PL) RUB.

2. Recon SQDs maneuver along primary route, west flank trails, and east high-speed avenue of approach (AA) from west; ATGM team (TM) overwatches squads.

3. Motorcycle TMs maneuver along east woodland trails, clear CKP 3, and receive updates from PLT commander on UAV recon along east flank and wooded hilly terrain.

4. Recon SQD clears CKP 3 and west AA at PL CAN no aggressor units; ATGM overwatch as SQD recons through NAI BEAN sighting no enemy activity.

5. UAV recon indicates no enemy activity north of NAI BEAN, UAV continues recon northward.

6. NAI PEA hamlet is deserted with no enemy as recon SQDs sustain parallel western coverage. Motorcycle TMs clear CKP 5 and observe no activity at NAI PEA crossroads.

7. Recon SQD and ATGM team report CKP 7 as no enemy west of AA; recon SQDs approach NAI BLUE.

8. Motorcycle TMs and UAV recon report no aggressors from east AA and prepare to evaluate bridge site as recon SQDs overwatch.

9. Motorcycle TMs dismount and confirm no demolitions are set at bridge. Initial bridge classification/trafficability report to PLT commander.

10. Recon SQDs continue route recon of Route ABLE to release point (RP) 20. ATGM TM sets in overwatch center of zone. Motorcycle TMs continue recon along east flank to PL ZAP.

11. Recon SQD conduct recon of Route ABLE to LOA; motorcycle TMs conduct recon in center and east; set observation posts (OPs).

12. Recon SQD clears CKP 20 and continues to limit of advance (LOA); reports clear of any aggressors; sets observation post at PL REX.

ATGM	antitank guided missile	NAI	named area of interest	RP	release point	SP	start point
CKP	checkpoint (NATO)	PL	phase line	RTE	route	UAV	unmanned aerial vehicle
LD	line of departure	PLT	platoon	SQD	squad		
LOA	limit of advance	R	recon				

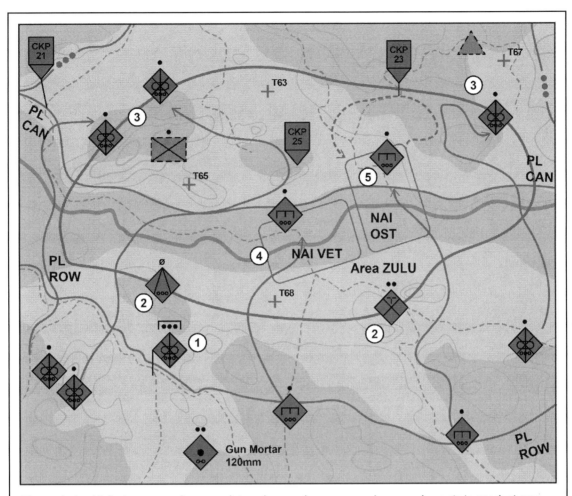

The motorized infantry reconnaissance platoon has engineer reconnaissance elements to conduct area and obstacle reconnaissance in an assigned area. The primary obstacle area is a river that crosses a proposed axis of advance for future offensive operations. Actions to obtain detailed information on the terrain and enemy activity in the area are as follows:

1. PLT occupies OPs south of river line for Area ZULU reconnaissance.
2. Antitank team, sniper section, and mortar section report readiness.
3. Security squads maneuver across river and conduct reconnaissance of probable enemy OPs.
4. Engineer squad performs area, river, and obstacle reconnaissance.
5. Engineer squads perform reconnaissance of near/far banks and staging areas.

CKP	checkpoint (NATO)	NAI	named area of interest	PL	phase line
mm	millimeter	OP	observation point	PLT	platoon

Figure 4-8. Area reconnaissance and tactical vignette (example)

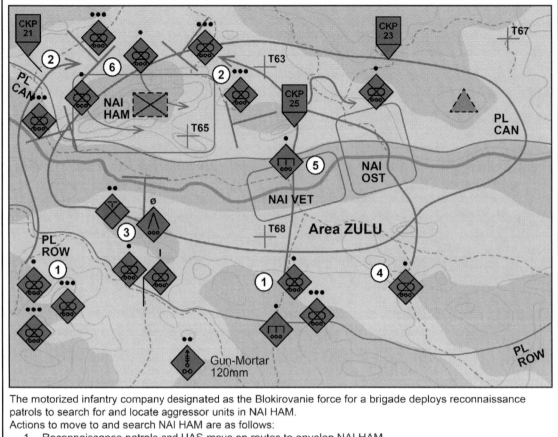

The motorized infantry company designated as the Blokirovanie force for a brigade deploys reconnaissance patrols to search for and locate aggressor units in NAI HAM.

Actions to move to and search NAI HAM are as follows:

1. Reconnaissance patrols and UAS move on routes to envelop NAI HAM.
2. PLTs follow and move to occupy blocking positions on all sides of NAI HAM.
3. Supporting mortar, antitank, and sniper subunits position to observe NAI HAM and report readiness.
4. Security element screens eastern flank.
5. Engineer reconnaissance moves to identify crossing sites in NAI VET and NAI OST
6. Reconnaissance patrols search NAI HAM for aggressor units.

| CKP | checkpoint (NATO) | NAI | named area of interest | UAS | unmanned aerial system |
| mm | millimeter | PL | phase line | | |

Figure 4-9. Reconnaissance-search vignette (example) for a Blokirovanie action

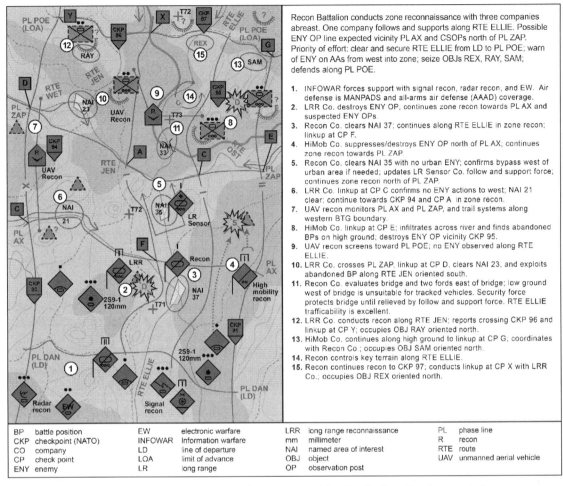

Recon Battalion conducts zone reconnaissance with three companies abreast. One company follows and supports along RTE ELLIE. Possible ENY OP line expected vicinity PL AX and CSOPs north of PL ZAP. Priority of effort: clear and secure RTE ELLIE from LD to PL POE; warn of ENY on AAs from west into zone; seize OBJs REX, RAY, SAM; defends along PL POE.

1. INFOWAR forces support with signal recon, radar recon, and EW. Air defense is MANPADS and all-arms air defense (AAAD) coverage.
2. LRR Co. destroys ENY OP, continues zone recon towards PL AX and suspected ENY OPs.
3. Recon Co. clears NAI 37; continues along RTE ELLIE in zone recon; linkup at CP F.
4. HiMob Co. suppresses/destroys ENY OP north of PL AX; continues zone recon towards PL ZAP.
5. Recon Co. clears NAI 35 with no urban ENY; confirms bypass west of urban area if needed; updates LR Sensor Co. follow and support force; continues zone recon north of PL ZAP.
6. LRR Co. linkup at CP C confirms no ENY actions to west; NAI 21 clear; continue towards CKP 94 and CP A in zone recon.
7. UAV recon monitors PL AX and PL ZAP, and trail systems along western BTG boundary.
8. HiMob Co. linkup at CP E; infiltrates across river and finds abandoned BPs on high ground; destroys ENY OP vicinity CKP 95.
9. UAV recon screens toward PL POE; no ENY observed along RTE ELLIE.
10. LRR Co. crosses PL ZAP, linkup at CP D, clears NAI 23, and exploits abandoned BP along RTE JEN oriented south.
11. Recon Co. evaluates bridge and two fords east of bridge; low ground west of bridge is unsuitable for tracked vehicles. Security force protects bridge until relieved by follow and support force. RTE ELLIE trafficability is excellent.
12. LRR Co. conducts recon along RTE JEN; reports crossing CKP 96 and linkup at CP Y; occupies OBJ RAY oriented north.
13. HiMob Co. continues along high ground to linkup at CP G, coordinates with Recon Co; occupies OBJ SAM oriented north.
14. Recon controls key terrain along RTE ELLIE.
15. Recon continues recon to CKP 97; conducts linkup at CP X with LRR Co.; occupies OBJ REX oriented north.

BP	battle position	EW	electronic warfare	LRR	long range reconnaissance	PL	phase line
CKP	checkpoint (NATO)	INFOWAR	Information warfare	mm	millimeter	R	recon
CO	company	LD	line of departure	NAI	named area of interest	RTE	route
CP	check point	LOA	limit of advance	OBJ	object	UAV	unmanned aerial vehicle
ENY	enemy	LR	long range	OP	observation post		

Figure 4-10. Zone reconnaissance and tactical vignette (example)

RECONNAISSANCE FORMATIONS

4-47. Reconnaissance units are branches of the SV that conduct reconnaissance actions to support the commander's plan. Maneuver brigades, divisions, and subordinate regiments each have a designated reconnaissance unit while subunits use task-organized subunits to provide the essential reconnaissance function. Reconnaissance is an implied task that requires all echelons to report information in order to sustain and improve situational awareness and understanding for current and future missions.

4-48. Conducting reconnaissance before, during, and after a particular action provides information for the SV to confirm, deny, and modify ongoing or future missions. Typically, Russian military reconnaissance units and formations can include the following: combined arms, special operations forces, electromagnetic warfare, UAV, or unmanned ground vehicle (UGV) complexes, electromagnetic warfare, aerospace, space operations or dedicated SV reconnaissance subunits. Intelligence, motorized rifle, tank, airborne, and air assault all have the capability to perform tactical reconnaissance. In the SV, tactical reconnaissance is split into several categories which include combat reconnaissance, signals intelligence, radar, electro-optical, artillery, engineer, medical, route, and nuclear, biological, and chemical detection.

4-49. Reconnaissance exists as a function at every echelon of the SV beginning with an individual observer and extending to all SV activities, task organizations, and unit echelons. Some reconnaissance formations are designated reconnaissance units with specific reconnaissance capabilities. Functional maneuver units, such as infantry or tank units, receive additional capabilities for specified reconnaissance mission tasks. In either case, reconnaissance formations are typically task-organized combat and combat support units and subunits that conduct reconnaissance operations.

4-50. The commander's mission analysis and guidance on reconnaissance methods identifies the capabilities allocated to a designated unit headquarters. Units may receive a mission for independent reconnaissance actions or be directed to conduct synchronized reconnaissance actions as a task-organized force or element with specialized capabilities not organic to the unit. Reconnaissance tasks may require augmentation with additional combat or specialized support such as infantry, armor, aviation, artillery, engineer, chemical, unmanned complexes, or other combat support and combat service support expertise.

4-51. Before the "New Look" reorganization units below brigade and division echelons did not have dedicated maneuver reconnaissance subunits. With the reorganization of the SV some battalions now have specialized subunits, typically a platoon, dedicated to reconnaissance support. Battalions that do not have a specialized reconnaissance subunit train select maneuver companies and platoons to conduct reconnaissance as a secondary task. For maneuver reconnaissance, the SV does have a distinct method for task-organizing subunits to perform reconnaissance missions. The following shows various echelons and their task organized reconnaissance units.

Brigades and Divisions

4-52. Task-organized reconnaissance units of brigades and divisions include the following:
- Reconnaissance forces.
- Battalion—Each "New Look" maneuver brigade has either an organic reconnaissance battalion or as a possible interim measure, a company as the reorganization continues.
- Company—A task-organized reconnaissance company performs observation, searches, raids, ambushes, emplacement, and recovery of observation complexes, and engages aggressor units as necessary. A reconnaissance company can serve as the basis for the formation of a reconnaissance detachment.
- UAV company.
- Radar platoon.
- NBC company.
- Engineer reconnaissance platoon.
- Detachment.
- Patrol.
- Group.
- Search units.
- Ambush units.
- Reconnaissance by battle.
- Observation post.
- Sniper teams.

Regiments (In a Division)

4-53. Task-organized reconnaissance units of regiments (in a division) include the following:
- Reconnaissance company.
- Reconnaissance detachments.
- Reconnaissance patrols.
- Commander's reconnaissance.
- Search units.
- Ambush units.
- Observation post.

Battalions

4-54. Task-organized reconnaissance units of battalions include the following:

- CRPs
- Ambush units.
- Patrol squads
- Observation post.

Companies or batteries

4-55. Task organized reconnaissance units of companies or batteries include the following:

- Patrol squads.
- Observation squads.
- CRPs.
- Fire control platoon.

Platoons

4-56. Task organized reconnaissance units of platoons include the following:

- Patrol squads.
- Observation squads.

Observer Team/Observation Post

4-57. Reconnaissance observation is an expectation of every member of a unit, subunit, or activity. At a small subunit activity such as squad or platoon, a recurring task is reconnaissance in conjunction with security measures. Although one individual can act as an observer, the typical configuration is to use at least two soldiers as a team to observe and report with specified responsibilities, as well as sustain team security. The size, number, and location of observation posts (OPs) depend on the mission, duration of tasks, and available capabilities in the SV force.

4-58. An OP is a position within which a team of varied size and capabilities conducts surveillance of activities in each zone or location. An OP receives communications assets and sensors based on mission requirements to ensure the ability to locate, track, and report on its reconnaissance targets and assigned areas of interest. An OP can be stationary or be expected to periodically shift location to accomplish its purpose and intent.

4-59. Sensors include unmanned platforms that allow electromagnetic detection and physical observation to target aggressor units. Electromagnetic warfare platforms support reconnaissance missions by performing initial identification and location of targets. Ground and aviation units use the electromagnetic warfare information to conduct either additional reconnaissance or engaging the aggressor with indirect fires. The sensor to shooter window after detection is estimated at 12–15 minutes for ground targets and 4–6 minutes for counter-battery fire. Direct electromagnetic attacks to degrade or damage aggressor communication or networks are also possible using UAV platforms with jamming or interception capabilities. These platforms are increasingly semi-autonomous to reduce counter-UAV effects caused by interrupting the command link.

Reconnaissance Group

4-60. Reconnaissance groups are elements that operate with small tactical units, typically at squad or platoon level. The group's mission is to locate aggressor nuclear delivery systems, forces, C2, signal sites, airfields, and other high priority targets. See figure 4-12 on page 4-21 for a variant of a reconnaissance platoon of a reconnaissance brigade (separate), augmented with a signal intelligence team. Missions are often conducted with a very small number of task-organized individuals that can also temporarily combine functional capabilities such as infantry, engineer, and artillery, to conduct a mission as a large-scale grouping of combat power and subsequently dispersing back into smaller teams or detachments.

4-61. GRU Spetsnaz can organize reconnaissance teams from within their organization in their AOR. Typical tasks for a team can be to identify and collect information on targets such as precision munitions and weapon sites, weapons of mass destruction, C2 facilities, force reserves, airfields, or other assigned priority targets or objectives. A reconnaissance team may infiltrate dismounted or mounted or be inserted and recovered by air or similar methods. Reconnaissance tasks for this type of team do not typically include direct combat action to collect reconnaissance. These teams may conduct actions in tactical-level zones of responsibility, but they do not typically work with or for SV tactical level units. The intelligence they collect is integrated into the overall battlefield situational view shared with tactical-level units. See figure 4-11.

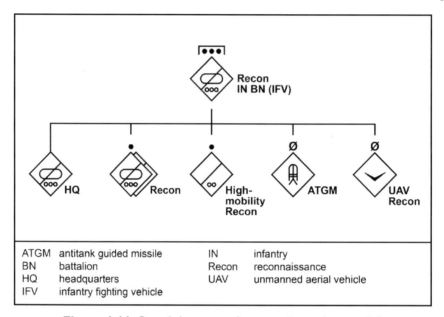

Figure 4-11. Special reconnaissance team (example)

Reconnaissance Patrol

4-62. A RP is generally a platoon-size tactical reconnaissance element with the mission of acquiring information about the aggressor and the terrain. Reconnaissance patrols aim to avoid direct fire action with an aggressor; however, a reconnaissance patrol is capable of self-defense and engagement with limited combat power. While an RP may vary in size depending on the commander's requirements, forces available, and tactical situation, mission focus determines the functional capabilities and task organization of a patrol. Typical mission options are as follows—

- Signals reconnaissance assets include radio intercept and direction-finding complexes. Technical equipment exploits signals from cellular, digital, satellite, and computer network complexes.
- Engineer capabilities usually consist of engineer specialists at squad or platoon echelon. Engineer reconnaissance focuses primarily on aspects of terrain in support of the mission, and generally analyzes for mobility and counter mobility tasks.
- Chemical defense assets can establish chemical and radiological observation posts to complement mobile NBC reconnaissance to confirm or deny NBC contamination. Chemical defense reconnaissance identifies and marks areas of NBC contamination, determines the extent and nature of any contamination, locates potential bypass routes around contaminated areas, and conducts doctrinal NBC monitoring to report and warn of terrain and downwind NBC hazards.

4-63. Patrols or detachments can be task-organized with artillery-specific capabilities such as battlefield surveillance radar, target acquisition radar, and counter-battery radar. The sound-ranging and flash-ranging complexes typically remain in the support area. Direct and indirect fires can be used for reconnaissance by fire with considerations for unmasking of SV locations. Reconnaissance by fire employs fires on suspected aggressor positions or selected locations to prompt a reaction by the aggressor or individuals in a target area.

(See figure 4-12 on page 4-21 for an example of an RP [reconnaissance platoon] from a mechanized infantry battalion.)

4-64. The SV distinguishes among various types of patrols under the general descriptive term, RP. Patrols are tasked with specialized functional capabilities when required such as signals sensors, engineer mobility and counter mobility assessments, or reconnaissance for the presence of NBC contaminants.

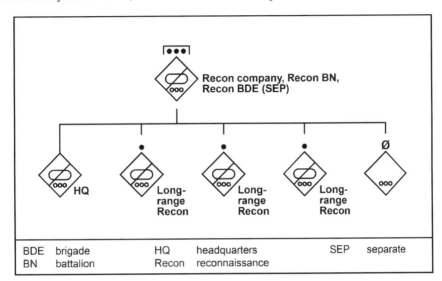

Figure 4-12. Reconnaissance patrol, reconnaissance platoon (example)

Commander's or Officer's Reconnaissance Patrol

4-65. Tactical commanders conduct personal reconnaissance as part of a mission planning and execution process. Commanders go to a site in the vicinity of planned actions to conduct a visual study of the aggressor forces, terrain, and other battlefield conditions. Subordinate commanders and leaders and special staff members or subject matter experts accompany the commander in support of the reconnaissance task and purpose. During RPs commanders issue guidance to enhance mission accomplishment.

4-66. Reconnaissance patrols are limited in task, scope, and duration. A commander or staff can order an officer RP to update information on tactical conditions by on-site observation and sensor collection. An officer RP is typically small and can comprise one to three officers and two to five other members for operating communications equipment, providing specialized expertise, and ensuring local security to the patrol.

Combat Reconnaissance Patrol

4-67. Combat reconnaissance patrols (CRPs) are platoon-sized elements typically task-organized from within a maneuver unit with an expectation that direct action combat may occur to achieve its reconnaissance objective. Nevertheless, the CRP typically avoids direct fire action with an aggressor if possible. Patrols operate normally within areas that can be supported by indirect fires of the parent force headquarters. Specialized capabilities, such as engineer or NBC reconnaissance, can be allotted to patrol when required to support mission tasks. Forces or elements employ one or more CRPs based on the tactical situation. A CRP mission can include a reconnoiter task, or a security task. The security task anticipates direct action combat and indirect fire support when an aggressor is in the patrol mission area. (See figure 4-13 on page 4-22 for an example.)

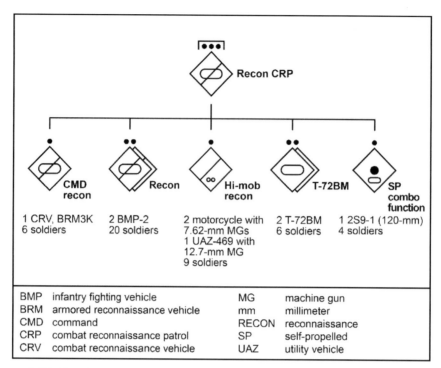

Figure 4-13. Combat reconnaissance patrol, task-organized platoon (example)

Reconnaissance Platoon

4-68. The SV motorized or tank company can task-organize a reconnaissance platoon. Tracked vehicles, all-terrain wheeled vehicles, and motorcycles of the platoon provide mobility for multiple types of terrain in support of its battalion headquarters. Additional capabilities are task-organized to the platoon based on mission requirements.

Reconnaissance Detachment

4-69. The largest subunit maneuver forces use at the tactical echelon is the reconnaissance detachment (разведывательный отряд - razvedyvatel'nyy otryad - PO). A combat arms company or battalion is the basis for a detachment task organization. The primary mission is reconnaissance; however, a reconnaissance detachment is task-organized with the capabilities to fight for information to accomplish its mission. The range of a PO fluctuates by mission. Typically, a company-sized detachment will have a reconnaissance depth of 50 km while a battalion-sized detachment can have a depth of 80 km.

Reconnaissance Battalion

4-70. The SV motorized or TD is organized with a separate reconnaissance battalion with significant capabilities. Brigades will also contain a reconnaissance battalion in their force structure. This is a recent change which came about after SV brigade commanders criticized the lack of intelligence, surveillance, and reconnaissance capabilities in the reconnaissance company. Modernization initiatives have expanded from a company to a battalion-size unit for organic reconnaissance capabilities in the division and brigades.

4-71. The reconnaissance battalion of an SV mechanized division, with modernized IFVs, has the subunit functions presented in figure 4-14. Other maneuver battalions have similar reconnaissance assets. Additional capabilities, as in the example, are often task-organized to the battalion based on mission requirements.

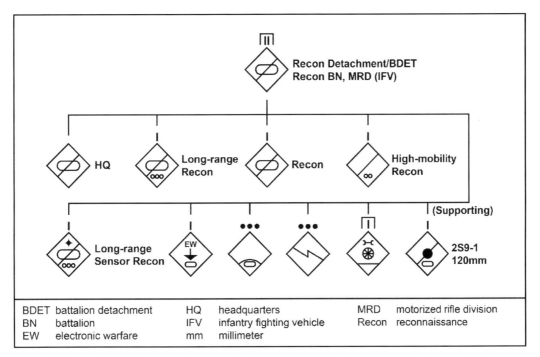

Figure 4-14. Reconnaissance battalion, mechanized division (example)

Reconnaissance Brigade

4-72. The reconnaissance brigade (разведывательная бригада - razvedyvatel'naya brigada – known as Pb) is a separate brigade at the operational echelon and has capabilities that can be selectively task-organized to support tactical actions. The SV currently has a limited number of reconnaissance brigade forces operating in or beyond a tactical force's AOR which can include long-range reconnaissance, long-range sensor reconnaissance, intelligence, and electromagnetic warfare, and mounted and dismounted reconnaissance. When directed the Pb can augment capabilities with selective mechanized, armor, antitank, artillery, air defense, sniper, and engineer support. Aviation and air assault forces, and extensive UAVs of a reconnaissance brigade can also be allocated to support tactical actions.

Special Brigades

4-73. Each military district has a Spetsnaz brigade that functions as district-subordinate scouts. To conduct signal intelligence collection each military district has a SIGINT or OSNAZ brigade.

SECURITY FUNDAMENTALS

4-74. Security missions protect supported forces with designated levels of early warning and combat power. The security function includes maneuver subunits as well as other forces and means allocated to degrade an aggressor's ability to gain full OE situational awareness. In addition to maneuver subunit security missions, air defense and REB act as integrated complexes to deny an aggressor's ability to observe and target main body maneuver units. Security and reconnaissance operations complement each other in developing and sustaining situational awareness and understanding of an OE and conditions that impact mission success.

4-75. Security applies the SV principles in chapter 3 and the reconnaissance fundamentals presented there. The fundamentals of reconnaissance and security operations complement each other with a different focus for security tasks. This section covers the following fundamentals of Russian security: objective, missions, actions, and formations.

SECURITY OBJECTIVE

4-76. Protection of the supported force is the security objective. All actions focus on accurate and timely warning of OE conditions that can hinder the mission of the supported force and security actions that protect the supported force from an aggressor. A security force understands and acts in conjunction with the supported unit's scheme of maneuver and mission. These factors cause the security force to typically operate between the protected force and suspected or known aggressor forces. Security forces conduct stationary or mobile actions dependent on the mission of the supported force to be protected. The level of combat power task-organized in a security force is based on the level of required security and the degree of risk the tasking headquarters commander is willing to direct in assigning a mission.

Timely Warning

4-77. Provides effective alerts of known, probable, or possible conditions that can adversely impact on a mission. Timely reporting of information and intelligence on adversaries, aggressors, and other OE conditions enables informed decisions and actions to protect supported forces. Security forces detect, observe, and monitor OE conditions and acts to protect supported forces.

Maintain Aggressor Contact

4-78. Real-time and accurate information requires reconnaissance and security forces to gain and maintain contact with the aggressor. Reconnaissance fundamentals are integral to all security operations. Developing tactical situations involve continuous activities that provide options in reaction time and available maneuver space decisions, and how to shape or place an aggressor at a position of disadvantage in relation to the protected force. The duration required for a security mission task depends on the protected force's situation and mission guidance that can be terrain, time, or force oriented. The security force receives mission guidance that includes security force engagement criteria, disengagement criteria, and displacement criteria. Engagement and disengagement criteria identify conditions of when or how the security force can attack aggressor forces and conditions that restrict engagement of the aggressor to preserve camouflage, cover, concealment, and deception of the protected force. Displacement criteria state conditions, typically based on time and the tactical situation, that allow or deny movement and maneuver to subsequent locations or fighting positions.

SECURITY MISSIONS

4-79. Security forces are assigned an AOR in support of a force to be protected. with an adequate area and distance to provide early warning of an approaching aggressor and prevent aggressor ground and air forces from observing or engaging the protected force with direct fires. Protecting a force from aggressor indirect, aviation, and missile fires is problematic due to the various types of long-range weapon complexes that are available to an aggressor. Reconnaissance and security actions synchronize capabilities to provide an integrated fires command ability of razvedka and effective target engagement throughout an AOR and ZORR. The intent of security missions is to provide effective early warning and protection actions that support SV unit freedom of action and maneuver in the conduct of a mission.

4-80. Security operations focus on the tactical missions of screen, guard, and cover. Defeat of aggressor reconnaissance efforts is a mission conducted to support security actions. (See table 4-2.)

Table 4-2. Security mission descriptions

Mission	Description
Screen	Provides early warning to the main body of an aggressor's forces in a specified zone. Maintains contact with the aggressor force to support the commander's plan that states engagement, disengagement, displacement, and other screen criteria.
Guard	Protects the main body, destroys, or repels aggressor reconnaissance, destroys or fixes advance units, causes aggressor forces to deploy, prevent observation of SV forces, disrupt or prevent indirect and direct fires, and provide time for the SV main body to execute defensive or offensive actions.
Cover	Protects the SV main body, inclusive of screen and guard security and zone reconnaissance subunits. Ensures the main body remains beyond effective detection or engagement ranges from both direct and indirect fires while also providing time for the main body to execute defensive and offensive actions.
Reconnaissance defeat	Destroys, defeats, or repels all aggressor reconnaissance within the specified zone to defeat aggressor situational understanding of SV force disposition, formations, actions, and intent.

Note 1. Defeating aggressor reconnaissance efforts is an implied action for all security missions.
Note 2. A covering force is typically a BTG, brigade, or larger echelon mission due to the higher echelon SV units it protects, such as, a division, corps, or combined arms army; and is a self-contained unit that performs as an independent or semi-independent force.

BTG	battalion tactical group	SV	Russian ground forces

4-81. Additional security missions that occur in an operation can include—

- Area security actions to protect friendly installations, routes, units, and facilities within an AOR. Mission task identify specific requirements within a designated objective area and specified points in the area.
- Local security is a responsibility of all units and activities as a force protection measure. Situational awareness and early warning to a protected force provides time for proactive or reactive actions in support of a protected force operation. Mission tasks identify specific requirements within a local security mission.
- Subsets of area security and local security are route security and convoy security.

4-82. Security screens provide early warnings to the main body of the force. Screen mission tasks combine defensive and offensive actions to disrupt and possibly delay aggressor forces, and defeat or destroy aggressor reconnaissance from collecting information and intelligence on the main body. The screen orients on aggressor avenues of approach into its assigned area as an economy of force action that supports security to a main body, facility, or area.

4-83. OPs and mounted, dismounted, and aerial patrols in a zone ensure observation and surveillance of an assigned area to gain and maintain aggressor contact—without becoming decisively engaged. Indirect fires of the screening force are typically provided from the main body as a complement to direct fires of a screening force. The intent is to prevent the screening force from being decisively engaged by an aggressor as the screening force displaces and reduces its direct fire capabilities.

4-84. Reconnaissance patrols are typically assigned to the flanks or rear of a main body and can also be forward of a main body force. However, a screen does not occur forward of a moving main body. In the case of a maneuvering force, forward security to the main body occurs as a zone reconnaissance mission, reconnaissance in force, and guard mission. Reconnaissance missions can be assigned when tactical operations have extended flanks, coverage gaps occur between major subordinate maneuver units of a force, and when required to provide early warning in areas not considered critical enough to require security tasks of greater combat power such as a guard mission.

4-85. The depth of a screen zone is typically terrain dependent to prevent aggressor direct observation of the main body. Depth provides the main body with more time to react to approaching aggressor maneuver units and allows for reconnaissance and security handover. A screening force employs depth by positioning OPs and other sensor collection assets between a designated forward-oriented limit of advance (LOA) and the rear boundary of the security force. The number of OPs or patrols required considers zone depth, width, duration of mission, and orientation of the screen in task-organizing a screening force. Available time and allowable distance from the main body are significant additional factors in planning and conducting a screen, reconnaissance handover, and battle handover of a screening force to another force.

4-86. A screen displaces to subsequent positions based on event or time criteria stated in a mission order. A rearward passage of lines continues defensive actions and maintains aggressor contact while conducting the passage and handover. These passage actions may or may not be conducted under aggressor pressure. The force accepting handover typically accepts control of the AOR forward of a handover line after two-thirds of the screening force's combat elements clear designated passage points. Execution of a screen requires forces dependent on the level of protection directed by the main body commander. Execution considerations for a screen include—

- Conducting surveillance of all avenues of approach that can affect the main body's mission.
- Detecting and reporting all aggressor forces approaching the screen zone.
- Disrupting, defeating, and destroying all aggressor reconnaissance elements.
- Delaying aggressor maneuver of ground forces in the screen zone.
- Disrupting aggressor movement and maneuver of aerial forces in the screen zone.
- Identifying probable aggressor main effort.
- Providing the protected force early warning of aggressor activities, locations, and movement or maneuver.

4-87. A screen is designated either a stationary screen or a moving screen. A screening force is typically assigned a zone with a wide frontage and has subordinate forces normally deployed abreast with zones in depth. A screening force conducts a moving flank or rear screen like a stationary screen but employs movement and maneuver dependent on the tactical situation of the main body. (See figure 4-15 for a defensive screen vignette with delay actions conducted by a mechanized (armored/wheeled) infantry company detachment.

Stationary Screen

4-88. Stationary screen missions require terrain-oriented and time duration guidance. Air and ground force integration enables security area coverage and acceptable risk determined by the force commander for the screen mission. A phase line located along identifiable terrain graphically identifies the forward LOA of the screen. Phase lines also identify lateral and rear boundaries of the screen. The screening force is responsible for the area between the screened force and the screen rear boundary. The rear boundary can be a reconnaissance handover or battle handover line. Other phase lines control forward, lateral, and rearward movement and maneuver of the screening force in its mission. The screening force uses checkpoints, contact points, other control measures as required, and named areas of interest to identify specific areas of interest and to coordinate razvedka and movements or maneuver. Engagement, disengagement, and displacement criteria prompt actions of the screening force.

4-89. The screen orients to a forward LOA and is considered a restrictive control measure that requires coordination when forces move beyond it into a ZORR. Key considerations include the maximum range of supporting indirect fires available to the screening force in determining fields of fire, requirements to observe specific named areas of interest or target areas of interest, and control measures for area target acquisition, fire support, and airspace and air defense support. Occupying a screen zone considers time available and the SV situation, and typically uses infiltration or tactical road march. When conditions allow, a zone reconnaissance is the norm to collect information and intelligence as a screening force occupies terrain and identifies any aggressor forces already in the screen zone.

4-90. The screen integrates multiple sensors from the force main body or higher headquarters to collect and monitor conditions. Ground maneuver forces may also be task-organized with attack/reconnaissance aviation, UAV or ground-based sensors, and signal intelligence complexes in depth. Reconnaissance management of cueing, mixing, and redundancy provide effective coverage and internal security of assets. Aerial reconnaissance, when integrated into the ground screen, can act as a supporting or independent screen for early warning of approaching aggressors or aggressors in selected areas of the security zone. Fires planning includes integration of direct and indirect fires, attack aviation, and other direct air support. Kill zones are the focus for fires along likely aggressor avenues of approach. Engineers provide mobility, countermobility, and survivability capabilities for specific tasks such as improvement of roads and trails for lateral movement, emplacement of obstacles, and observation post survivability. Situational obstacles disrupt or delay an aggressor in conjunction with fires. Obstacles are planned and prepared and are armed or executed based on emplacement criteria and emergent tactical conditions. Mine dispensing complexes can rapidly and precisely emplace a minefield with predetermined self-destruct times. A screen force tailors logistics support in depth throughout its assigned security zone.

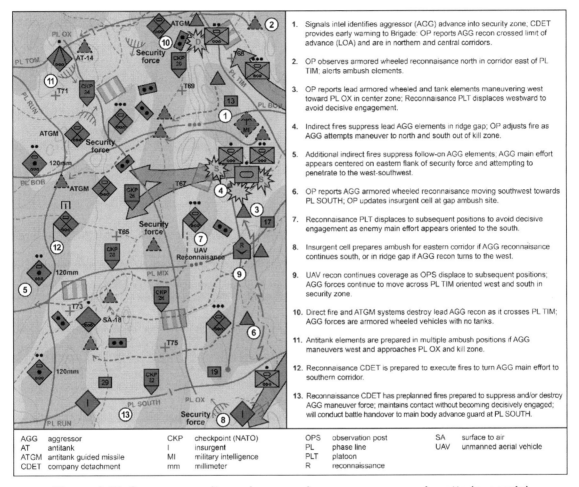

1. Signals intel identifies aggressor (AGG) advance into security zone; CDET provides early warning to Brigade: OP reports AGG recon crossed limit of advance (LOA) and are in northern and central corridors.

2. OP observes armored wheeled reconnaissance north in corridor east of PL TIM; alerts ambush elements.

3. OP reports lead armored wheeled and tank elements maneuvering west toward PL OX in center zone; Reconnaissance PLT displaces westward to avoid decisive engagement.

4. Indirect fires suppress lead AGG elements in ridge gap; OP adjusts fire as AGG attempts maneuver to north and south out of kill zone.

5. Additional indirect fires suppress follow-on AGG elements; AGG main effort appears centered on eastern flank of security force and attempting to penetrate to the west-southwest.

6. OP reports AGG armored wheeled reconnaissance moving southwest towards PL SOUTH; OP updates insurgent cell at gap ambush site.

7. Reconnaissance PLT displaces to subsequent positions to avoid decisive engagement as enemy main effort appears oriented to the south.

8. Insurgent cell prepares ambush for eastern corridor if AGG reconnaissance continues south, or in ridge gap if AGG recon turns to the west.

9. UAV recon continues coverage as OPS displace to subsequent positions; AGG forces continue to move across PL TIM oriented west and south in security zone.

10. Direct fire and ATGM systems destroy lead AGG recon as it crosses PL TIM; AGG forces are armored wheeled vehicles with no tanks.

11. Antitank elements are prepared in multiple ambush positions if AGG maneuvers west and approaches PL OX and kill zone.

12. Reconnaissance CDET is prepared to execute fires to turn AGG main effort to southern corridor.

13. Reconnaissance CDET has preplanned fires prepared to suppress and/or destroy AGG maneuver force; maintains contact without becoming decisively engaged; will conduct battle handover to main body advance guard at PL SOUTH.

AGG	aggressor	CKP	checkpoint (NATO)	OPS	observation post
AT	antitank	I	insurgent	PL	phase line
ATGM	antitank guided missile	MI	military intelligence	PLT	platoon
CDET	company detachment	mm	millimeter	R	reconnaissance

SA	surface to air
UAV	unmanned aerial vehicle

Figure 4-15. Screen security and reconnaissance company vignette (example)

Moving Screen

4-91. Maneuver and movement of a moving screen orients on the main body and specified mission tasks assigned for early warning of aggressor actions. Coverage for a moving flank screen begins at the front of the main body lead combat element and ends at the rear of the protected force. Front and rear security forces are responsible for their own early warning protection. A line of departure phase line integral to the main body mission initiates the screen mission and becomes the initial rear boundary of the moving screen.

4-92. As the main body maneuvers or moves, its screening force occupies a series of successive screens with options of four basic methods of movement. Movement options are as follows:
- Alternate bounds by individual OPs.
- Alternate bounds by subordinate security forces or elements.
- Successive bounds.
- Continuous march.

4-93. The screening force adjusts to time and distance factors required by the main body commander. Coordination is continuous with other security forces that may be protecting the main body beyond the screening force such as a guard force or covering force.

GUARD

4-94. Guard is a security mission task to protect the main body by fighting the aggressor to create reaction time and maneuver space for the main body. The guard force also observes and reports information on its AOR and ZORR and prevents aggressor ground observation of and direct fire on the main body. A force conducting a guard mission cannot operate independently because the guard force relies on additional fires and other functional support from the main body. A guard force expects contact with an aggressor and provides protection to the main body that a screen force cannot provide. Figure 4-16 shows an example of flank security.

4-95. A guard force conducts multiple mission tasks, when stationary or moving, to include reconnaissance. Reconnaissance defeat actions by a guard force seek to destroy aggressor reconnaissance within its security zone. A guard force is prepared to accept decisive engagement with an aggressor, and can attack, defend, and delay to enable reaction time and maneuver space to the protected main body. Three types of guard missions are as follows:

- Advance guard.
- Flank security element.
- Rear security element.

4-96. A guard force operates within the range of designated indirect fire weapons of the main body and accomplishes all the tasks of a screen but operates over a narrower zone frontage to permit the concentration of combat power. Battalion detachment or larger echelon groups are the norm for guard missions based on the combat power required to counter an anticipated aggressor. The guard force differs from a screen in that the guard force contains sufficient combat power to defeat, cause to withdraw, or fix lead aggressor forces before they can engage the protected main body. Aerial assets typically support a guard force by screening between gaps and in front of force arrays or battle positions that the guard force establishes in its security zone. Aviation tasks can include—

- Reconnoitering the area between the guard force and the main body.
- Maintaining contact between the security force and the main body.
- Providing early warning and a degree of security to the guard force.

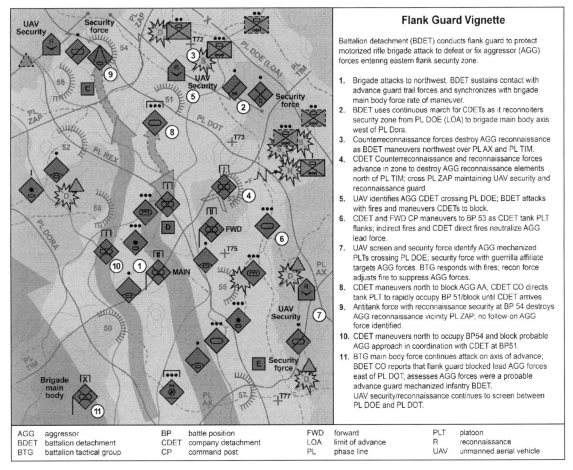

Figure 4-16. Flank security and battalion detachment vignette (example)

4-97. Timely development of the tactical situation by a guard force along the axis of advance of the main body enables situational awareness and understanding of an OE. Maintaining tactical initiative in contact with the aggressor enables main body options to continue its primary mission, conduct an appropriate defensive task such as defend, or an act with an offensive task such as counterattack.

4-98. A guard force executes its mission with several tactical expectations. The intent of guard force actions includes but is not limited to—

- Maintaining surveillance of avenues of approach into and in the guard security zone.
- Detecting and report all aggressor forces approaching the security zone.
- Destroying or disrupt aggressor reconnaissance elements.
- Defeating the aggressor advance guard.
- Denying the aggressor the ability to place effective direct fires on the protected force.
- Delaying the aggressor approach and cause the aggressor main body to deploy.
- Defending security zone.

4-99. Guard forces deny aggressor ground maneuver forces the ability to penetrate through the guard security zone. Indirect fire considerations for a guard force are like a screen; however, a guard force typically has more indirect fire support combat power allocated for its guard mission task. The guard force customarily operates within supporting range of the main body's indirect fires and can call for fires from these assets if the situation warrants. Engineers support a guard force with mobility, countermobility, and survivability tasks.

4-100.   Other combat support and combat service support are task-organized in depth throughout its security zone. Immediate logistics support forces move with the flank security force, while additional logistics support move with the main body axis or as directed by the guard force commander.

4-101.   In a noncontiguous AOR, advance, rear, or flank security forces can be based on cardinal direction or general orientation to an aggressor. Mission tasks of defend, delay, and disrupt are typical for a rear guard, and may include a task to fix the aggressor until other forces such as a quick reaction force arrive to an engagement.

Advance Guard

4-102.   An advance guard for a moving force is offensive in actions to locate and defeat aggressor forces along the axis of advance of the main body it protects. Every first echelon division, and brigade forms an advanced guard. Advance guards enable uninterrupted movement of the protected main body. Terrain appreciation of an AOR and expected tempo of movement or maneuver of the main body are key considerations of how far the guard force operates from the main body.

4-103.   Task organization internal to the advance guard provides capabilities in forward elements to immediately engage and defeat or fix any aggressor that might impede the momentum of the main body. Based on timely CRP intelligence, these forward elements mass task-organized direct and indirect fires, and engineer mobility or countermobility support to set conditions for the remainder of the advance guard to maneuver and defeat or destroy the aggressor. The main body should not have to deploy from its march or attack formations; however, if the advance guard cannot defeat the aggressor forces, it fixes them to enable the main body to bypass or deploy forces against the aggressor.

4-104.   An advance guard for a stationary force is primarily defensive in nature and deploys forward of a main body to protect it from engagement with the aggressor. Once the guard force obtains and maintains contact, it defends, delays, and disrupts in support of the main body. Typical mission tasks include deceiving the aggressor to the location of the actual main defenses of the battle zone, force the aggressor to deploy its main body, and target critical aggressor assets such as command and control, artillery groupings, and mobile logistic sites such refuel on the move points or ammunition transfer points. Offensive actions such as ambushes, raids, or limited counterattacks can support advance guard security in an AOR.

Flank Security Guard

4-105.   A flank security force protects a flank of a defending main body. For a defending SV unit, it performs a zone or area reconnaissance when establishing its initial security positions. Upon reaching the initial battle positions and observation posts, flank security establishes a defensive array oriented on kill zones in probable or possible aggressor avenues of approach. Once the flank security contacts an aggressor force, it defends or delays to protect the main body in compliance with the main body commander's criteria for guard force engagement, disengagement, and displacement.

4-106.   A moving flank security force mission task presents additional considerations and requirements. Moving flank security has many of the same considerations as a moving flank screen; however, a moving flank security can occupy a series of battle positions to protect a main body axis of advance. The main body commander assigns a security objective to orient the flank security force in its security zone. Tasks for the moving flank security include but are not limited to—
*   Maintaining continuous surveillance of aggressor avenues of approach along the main body axis of advance.
*   Establishing and occupying a series of battle positions to guard the main body.
*   Reconnoitering the zone between the main body and flank security force battle positions and LOA.
*   Maintaining contact with the lead to rear elements of the main body and other security forces protecting the main body.
*   Destroying or disrupt aggressor reconnaissance forces in the guard security zone.
*   Protect the main body.

4-107.   A moving flank security force conducts its maneuver in successive bounds, alternate bounds, or continuous marches. Occupation of battle positions is situationally dependent on the aggressor threat to the main body. In a sequential maneuver of a flank security, the flank security force crosses the line of departure separately and sequential to the main body movement. A sequential method is typical when a main body has already penetrated a line of contact, or the main body being protected is not in contact with an aggressor. In a simultaneous method, a flank security force crosses the line of departure within the main body and then deploys from that same main body axis into its flank security zone. A simultaneous action is appropriate when the main body conducts its own penetration of aggressor defenses along a line of contact. The flank security force follows the lead combat elements of the protected main body through the departure point(s) and deploys into its guard force array in the security zone. The lead element of a moving flank security force conducts a zone or area reconnaissance with three key mission tasks:

- Maintain contact with the main body.
- Reconnoiter the zone between the main body and moving flank security force route or routes of advance.
- Reconnoiter the moving flank security force routes in the flank security zone.

4-108.   The moving flank security force maneuvers along the routes of advance to occupy battle positions and observation posts parallel to the main body axis of advance. Commanders establish phase lines that run parallel and perpendicular to the direction of the movement of the main body. If the aggressor attacks into the protected flank, the guard force uses parallel phase lines to the main body to control a delay or defense. Phase lines perpendicular to the main body are used to control movement forward adjacent to the main body axis of advance. The guard force regulates movement along its routes of advance by the pace of the protected main body. The following are three methods of movement: successive bounds, alternate bounds, or continuous movement.

4-109.   If the protected force stops, the guarding force occupies blocking positions oriented to likely aggressor axes of advance toward the SV main body. As the speed, pace, or tempo of the main body changes, the guard force adjusts its movement and maneuver to provide protection to the main body. If the guard force anticipates being overextended in its ability to protect, the guard force commander informs the main body commander and recommends one of the following courses of action:

- Reinforce the flank security.
- Reduce the area of responsibility.
- Screen a designated area of the flank security zone and guard the remaining area of the flank security zone.

Rear Guard

4-110.   A rear guard protects the rear of the main body. The rear guard is created by second-echelon battalions or regiments. Rear guards are appropriate when conducting offensive tasks, when the protected main body breaks contact with flanking forces, or during a retrograde operation. The rear guard deploys and defends to protect the moving and stationary main body. The tasks described for a stationary flank security apply to a rear-guard mission. The rear guard for a moving force displaces on the order of the senior commander.

4-111.   The commander establishes a rear guard during a main body withdrawal, retirement, or delaying action in one of two typical ways:

- The guard force relieves main body units in place and occupies battle positions, as the main body moves or maneuvers in a direction away from an aggressor.
- The guard force establishes battle positions in depth to the rear of a main body and conducts multiple passages of the main body moving or maneuvering forces through the guard force defensive array.

4-112.   If a rear guard cannot defeat an approaching aggressor or aggressor operating in the support zone, the rear guard fixes the aggressor force until the main body can support additional security actions.

COVER

4-113.   Cover is a security mission task to protect the main body by fighting the aggressor to create reaction time and maneuver space for the main body. The typical mission intent is to defeat or destroy aggressor forces within its cover force capabilities. A covering force is tactically self-contained and task-organized for extended operations, and capable of operating independently from the main body it protects. A covering force operates typically at a significant distance from the main body to—

- Develop the tactical situation with early warning to provide the main body commander with the optimum situational awareness and understanding for main body mission decisions.
- Prevent aggressor observation of the main body.
- Prevent aggressor direct and indirect fires on the protected main body.
- Protect the main body from effective aggressor direct and indirect fires.

4-114. The covering force collects and reports information on its AOR and ZORR in support of the protected main body commander's priorities and may include complex capabilities to disrupt and prevent selective aggressor long-range indirect fires from affecting the main body it protects.

4-115. A covering force conducts actions to destroy aggressor reconnaissance within its security zone. As a covering force develops the tactical situation at an extended distance from the protected main body, mission tasks can vary among reconnaissance, screen, guard, disrupt, attack, defend, and delay to protect the main body. Missions anticipate decisive engagement with an aggressor if required to achieve protection of the main body and does not allow aggressor forces to bypass the cover force array. A covering force expects to confront aggressor combat power normally greater than that expected of a guard or screen mission force. Actions can include disrupt, fix, and block in conjunction with other tactical tasks to provide time and space for the main body to be successful in its mission.

4-116. Integration of aerial assets is critical to the task organization for a cover mission. Aviation assets assist in security tasks between a covering force and main body, maintain contact with the protected main body when extended distances involve the security zone and battle zone, and screen to the front of the covering force.

4-117. A covering force may be offensive or defensive in nature. All covering force actions employ an offensive orientation as opportunities evolve or are created in a tactical situation. The covering force executes its mission and intent as an aggressor force-oriented reconnaissance throughout its assigned AOR and conducts security tasks typically in the context of guard and screen tasks.

Offensive Cover

4-118. Offensive cover retains or seizes the initiative to provide the main body commander with time and the ability to maneuver. An offensive covering force can operate to the front or flanks of the main body. Offensive covering forces conduct the following key tasks:

- Reconnoiter along the main body axis of advance.
- Identify aggressor dispositions, capabilities, and probable axes of approach.
- Maintain continuous surveillance of aggressor avenues of approach.
- Destroy aggressor reconnaissance and security forces in the AOR.
- Deny the aggressor information about the size, strength, composition, and objective of the main body.
- Disrupt, fix, block, and defeat aggressor forces in the cover security zone.
- Exploit tactical opportunities in support of main body fires and maneuver.
- Protect the main body from effective observation, surveillance, and direct and indirect fires.

4-119. Advance cover and flank cover are two forms of offensive cover. An advance covering force is to locate and penetrate the aggressor force security zone and forward defenses. When the aggressor is a moving or maneuvering force, an advance cover destroys aggressor reconnaissance, and defeats advance guard units and first-echelon units of the aggressor main body. A flank cover is conducted like a flank security mission.

4-120. Differences of a cover force from a guard force are the larger tactical scope of the cover mission, the significant task organization of forces for tactical operations, and the greater distance from the main body as a semi-independent or independent security mission. A covering force typically clears the area between its route of advance and the main body; however, the main body commander can assign missions to other security forces which designates the zone responsibilities to protect the main body.

Defensive Cover

4-121. A defensive cover forces the aggressor to reveal their main effort, disrupts aggressor offensive actions, and creates conditions for successful SV main body tactical actions. A defensive covering force operates to the front, flanks, or rear of a main body deploying into an AOR or already deployed to defend. Planning and execution considerations are applicable to all three types of defensive cover. Defensive covers—

- Maintain continuous surveillance of aggressor avenues of approach.
- Destroy aggressor reconnaissance and security forces in the security zone of the AOR.
- Deceive aggressor situational understanding of main body dispositions and capabilities of the defensive array.
- Determine the size, strength, composition, and direction of the aggressor's main effort.
- Maintain contact with aggressor forces and cause commitment of aggressor second echelon forces.
- Exploit tactical opportunities in support of main body fires and maneuver.
- Protect the main body from effective observation, surveillance, and direct and indirect fires.

4-122. A rear covering force protects a main body moving away from the aggressor. A rear covering force can be directed to conduct a relief in place of a main body as integral to a deception plan with covering forces deployed abreast and in depth. Another tactical option is a covering force deploying behind the main body, supporting battle handover and passage of lines with the main body in contact with the aggressor, and conducting a defense or delay. A covering force displaces typically to subsequent phase lines in depth in accordance with the defensive mission. The covering force maintains contact with the aggressor until relieved of that task by the main body commander.

RECONNAISSANCE DEFEAT

4-123. Reconnaissance defeat is a task that encompasses reconnaissance and security measures taken by a SV commander to counter aggressor reconnaissance and surveillance efforts. It is the sum of all actions taken at each echelon of headquarters to protect SV forces, mission plans and intentions, unit dispositions, and ongoing actions. The purpose is to destroy, defeat, or repel all aggressor reconnaissance elements throughout an assigned AOR and ZORR. This is a task that can be performed during both defensive and offensive actions.

AREA SECURITY

4-124. Area security is a security task conducted to protect friendly forces, installations, routes, and actions within a specified area. Area security is essential to all operations. The security intention is to preserve the main body commander's freedom of maneuver in tactical missions, preserve the ability to move reserves and position fire support assets, and provide effective logistics and other sustainment actions. Area security degrades the aggressor's ability to affect friendly actions in a specific area by denying the aggressor's use of an area for its own purposes. The SV commander may task subordinate units to conduct the following actions in support of area security operations:

- Area, route, or zone reconnaissance.
- Screen or guard security actions.
- Offensive and defensive tasks.
- Route and convoy security.
- Protection of high-value assets.

4-125. Security actions at and among designated area security perimeters or areas, complemented with other reconnaissance and security tasks, are based on risk assessment of aggressor force capabilities and intentions and available forces to employ in missions assigned by the main body commander. Area security can be assigned to a force or element when tactical conditions warrant within contiguous and noncontiguous perimeters and boundaries in an AOR. The commander positions reaction forces and reserve forces in the AOR for rapid response to probable aggressor actions. Other missions or tasks in support of area security may include but are not limited to the following:

- Conduct route or convoy security of designated lines of communications.

- Monitor and control movement with checkpoint or combat outpost operations in the AOR and on critical lines of communications.
- Employ patrols to provide reconnaissance, intelligence, and security between secured perimeters.
- Maintain an observable presence to the relevant population of an AOR.

ROUTE SECURITY

4-126.   Route security missions prevent aggressor forces from affecting freedom of maneuver along a protected route. A route security force operates on and to the flanks of a designated route. Route security operations are typically defensive in nature and are terrain-oriented to the protected route. A route security force enables force traffic flow along a route with actions that include the following tasks:

- Conduct mounted, dismounted, and aerial reconnaissance and security tasks for designated routes and key locations along routes.
- Occupy key terrain along or near designated routes to prevent aggressor observation and direct fire weapons use that could disrupt route operations.
- Conduct engineer reconnaissance and maintenance to ensure satisfactory trafficability for force operations.
- Cordon sections of the route with periodic searches for suspected aggressor materiel, actions, and intentions.
- Conduct offensive actions to ambush, disrupt, defeat, and destroy aggressor forces intent on affecting route security and freedom of force movement.

4-127.   Convoy security is a subset of area security and route security. Convoy security missions are offensive in nature and orient on the protected force. This type of security mission can be conducted in conjunction with route security operations. A convoy security force operates to the front, flanks, and rear of a convoy moving along a designated route and is typically integrated into the body of the convoy. A security force conducts tasks that include but are not limited to—

- Reconnoiter a route the convoy is to travel.
- Provide early warning of aggressor presence along a designated route.
- Clear a designated route of obstacles.
- Prevent an aggressor force from influencing convoy actions along a designated route.

4-128.   Local security includes all actions to prevent or interdict aggressor efforts. Local security is continuous in all missions, and essential to maintaining mission task initiative. Active patrolling and continuous reconnaissance are measures that support local security. Passive measures include camouflage, cover, concealment, and deception; noise and light discipline; standardized movement control; and concise standardized communications.

SECURITY FORMATIONS

4-129.   Before entering battle, either offensive or defensive, SV maneuver brigades and regiments and their subsidiary units will organize into a combat formation. A unit not in a combat formation is typically arranged to perform various reconnaissance and security missions.

COMBAT RECONNAISSANCE PATROL

4-130.   A CRP mission conducts security and reconnaissance functions for the force or element it supports. CRP security actions anticipate direct combat when an aggressor is in the security zone. As in reconnaissance missions, a CRP is a typically platoon-size element that is task-organized from within a maneuver unit with an expectation that direct action combat will occur. The CRP can be directed to avoid direct fire action with an aggressor or can be directed to initiate combat actions with an aggressor for situational understanding of the aggressor and to deceive an aggressor. Normally within the indirect fire support range of the supported force, a CRP can also have indirect fires task-organized within its maneuver and support elements.

4-131. When required to support a particular mission task, specialized capabilities such as engineer and NBC reconnaissance capabilities are allocated to the patrol. Forces employ one or more CRPs based on the tactical situation.

COMBAT SECURITY OUTPOST/OBSERVATION POST TEAM

4-132. A CSOP conducts defensive actions. A grouping of CSOPs, typically reinforced maneuver platoons, provides early warning along aggressor probable main and secondary axes of advance in an AOR. Combat action can include—

- Identify approach and entry of the aggressor.
- Disrupt the momentum of aggressor movement and maneuver.
- Defeat aggressor reconnaissance.
- Deceive the aggressor to the actual location of the main body.
- Act as a stay-behind capability to maintain situational understanding of follow-on aggressor forces.
- Continue reporting if flanked or bypassed by aggressor units.
- Assist in movement and maneuver transition of the main body between defensive and offensive missions.

4-133. Engineer countermobility support and other functional support of direct and indirect fires concentrate fires into kill zones and typically present substantial defenses in depth. Once kill zones are identified, normal configurations include primary and alternate fighting positions of the battle position, and development of a comprehensive defensive all-round perimeter. Engineers progressively emplace and maintain viability of obstacles of wire entanglements, tripwire, mines and demolitions, and other techniques to channel or contain an aggressor. Subsequent and supplemental fighting positions usually include the withdrawn CSOP. Weapons are dug in. Interconnecting trench lines and overhead protection are constructed as part of cover, concealment, camouflage, and other deception and protection measures. Underground shelters within the CSOP protect storage of munitions, materiel, and living quarters separate from the fighting positions. Observation teams provide visual and sensor awareness on activities in assigned areas of interest and kill zones, and support adjustment of direct and indirect fires on the aggressor.

4-134. The defensive actions of CSOPs in the forward security area forward of the main battle area mask the exact location of the main defense. The main body higher headquarters can direct selected CSOPs to remain in the security zone.

4-135. The CSOP can support transition to main body offensive actions from the defense. Situational awareness of the aggressor and terrain provides the main body with real-time observation and sensor data to support decision making and timing of actions.

SCREEN FORCE

4-136. A screen unit or subunit provides early warning to the main body of the force that the screen is subordinate to in a tactical action. When task-organized in support of and from a brigade or higher headquarters, screening unit is the appropriate title. When task-organized in support of and from a battalion or lower-level headquarters, screening subunit is the appropriate title. The screen orients on aggressor avenues of approach into its assigned area as an economy of force action.

4-137. In addition to fundamental aspects of ensuring a degree of local security in all unit echelons and preventing surprise by an aggressor, defensive and offensive screening actions support the defeat of aggressor reconnaissance efforts. The screen's purpose is to defeat or destroy aggressor reconnaissance to prevent collection of information and intelligence on the main body. A screening force maintains contact with the aggressor without becoming decisively engaged and conducts a battle handover at a time and place designated in the commander's plan to the main body.

GUARD FORCE

4-138.   A guard force employs a task-organized formation, typically structured around a maneuver battalion that is part of a brigade tactical group. The guard force protects the main body with a security/disruption zone to the main body's front, either flank, and rear. Conditions and risk assessment by the brigade commander may indicate that a task-organized company detachment is sufficient to provide the required guard protection.

4-139.   Guard actions provide early warning of aggressor activity in the assigned security zone, and they conduct counter-reconnaissance to destroy any aggressor reconnaissance elements that evade other security actions in the security zone. An intent of protection prevents aggressor situational understanding of main body actions and critical locations. A guard force is prepared to decisively engage aggressor forces. If the guard force cannot defeat an approaching aggressor, the guard force fixes the aggressor force to provide the main body commander with time to decide on supporting offensive or defensive actions.

COVER FORCE

4-140.   A cover force is typically a brigade or larger force that protects a higher headquarters main body such as a division, corps, or combined arms army. Tactical conditions could exist for a battalion to be assigned a cover mission for a brigade or division with an exceptional mission task and supporting task organization.

4-141.   A covering force is employed in either offensive or defensive operations and reflects the mission of the main body it protects. A covering force accomplishes all the tasks of screening and guard forces but has significant additional capabilities in force capability and use.

FORWARD DETACHMENT

4-142.   A forward detachment (разведывательная бригада - Peredovoy otryad - PRO) is typically a task-organized battalion or regiment, capable of semi-independent or independent action. The higher headquarters assigning the mission and task organization synchronizes its other reconnaissance and security forces in the AOR to inform the PRO mission on directional orientation and maneuver in relation to the aggressor and an assigned PRO objective.

4-143.   In offensive operations, the PRO maneuvers to its objective on an axis other than the main body axis of advance. The brigade commander assigns PRO missions to enable the rapid maneuver of the main body by seizing key terrain or water crossings. It maintains position behind the brigade's RPs and well ahead of the advance guard. Maintaining situational understanding from higher headquarters reconnaissance forces to its front, the PRO avoids contact with aggressor forces until it nears its objective. When directed, forces within a PRO can conduct raids and other offensive actions that support the rapid maneuver to and seizure or occupation of the PRO objective. An example is linkup of PRO and air assault forces on key terrain deep in an AOR and behind aggressor forces that enables continued momentum of the higher headquarters main body in its attack.

4-144.   A PRO can also perform a flanking mission. However, this should not be confused with a SV flanking detachment. Given appropriate terrain and an aggressor situation that allows a rapid envelopment, the objective is to attack a flank or rear of an aggressor array that is in contact with the main body. Whether attacking an aggressor flank, or rear, or seizing an objective in the depth of the battle zone, or security zone, the enveloping detachment is often under the C2 of a headquarters senior to the main body attacking the aggressor frontage.

4-145.   In defensive operations, a PRO can be assigned defend, delay, and disrupt tasks in the security zone usually along secondary aggressor axes of advance. It establishes a series of successive defensive positions in the brigade's security zone along main avenues of approach into the main defensive zone. Tactical actions slow or halt aggressor advances in a security zone and deceive the aggressor to the location of the actual main defenses of the battle zone. Forces within a PRO can be directed to conduct ambushes or limited counterattacks in support of the security zone defenses.

SNOW DOME

4-146. The SV uses a series of interconnected capabilities radiating outward from a critical asset, rather than a single impenetrable layer to secure critical maneuver assets from attack. The Snow Dome is a set of mutually supporting capabilities that create a combined arms effect with the purpose of deterring and disrupting aggressor attacks. The Snow Dome denies aggressor access from the air, ground, space, and cyberspace to target SV units and subunits. While some components of the Snow Dome have range capabilities that span the entire battlespace, others have shorter ranges that require maneuver with the covered units and subunits. Capabilities that contribute to the Snow Dome include, but are not limited to—

- Medium- and long-range air defense systems.
- Mobile short-range air defense systems.
- Man-portable air defense (MANPADS) systems.
- Manned and unmanned aircraft.
- Tube and rocket artillery.
- Direct fire/maneuver systems.
- Ballistic and cruise missiles.
- Information warfare, with particular emphasis on cyber and electromagnetic warfare.

Note. The label "Snow Dome" is not a Russian term but is used in this ATP to label all of the complexes and system of systems that serve to protect SV combat power. There is no specific Russian term that encompasses all of the integrated protection or defensive systems. Snow Dome is used to differentiate it from the U.S. and Western anti-access and area denial concepts. Figure 4-17 illustrates the Snow Dome concept.

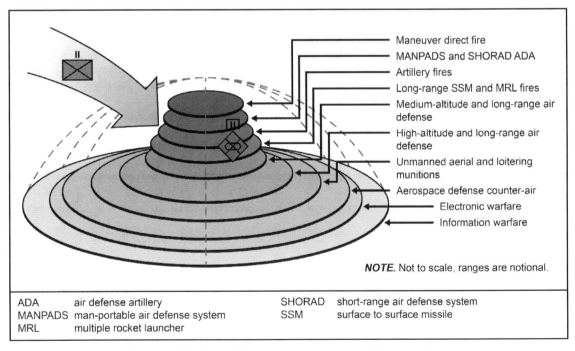

ADA	air defense artillery	SHORAD	short-range air defense system
MANPADS	man-portable air defense system	SSM	surface to surface missile
MRL	multiple rocket launcher		

Figure 4-17. Snow Dome integrates multiple complexes

4-147. Each one of these capabilities reinforces or supports others, mitigating weaknesses or gaps through all domains. Air defenses create localized air superiority from the ground, dissuading or neutralizing air and missile attacks on Russian forces. Artillery is used against aggressor artillery and maneuver forces, defending fragile and highly visible air defense assets from aggressor suppression efforts. Maneuver forces defend air defense and artillery forces from ground attack. Ballistic and cruise missiles attack the highest-value targets at extended ranges on land and at sea. Electromagnetic warfare protects key systems such as radars and communications from electromagnetic attack, while simultaneously disrupting aggressor electromagnetic emitters. Other IV elements reinforce the psychological deterrent effect of all forces and seek to disrupt aggressor systems with cyber and information attack.

4-148.   The result is a three-dimensional geographic area wherein there are no significant weaknesses for an aggressor to exploit. The objective of the Snow Dome is not to completely prevent aggressor attack but rather to make attack so costly that a deterrent effect is achieved. If deterrence fails, the Snow Dome attrits and suppresses the aggressor so effectively that it is unable to close with and destroy the SV in close combat.

4-149.   In support of tactical level actions, the Snow Dome complexes disrupt the buildup of aggressor combat power. Snow Dome components attrite the aggressor maneuver units to deny the use of key terrain, particularly valuable airspace. Key contributors at this echelon include—
*   MANPADS: SA-24/25.
*   Short-range air defense systems: SA-13, SA-19.
*   Tube and rocket artillery: 2S19 self-propelled gun, BM-21/27 MRLs.
*   Direct fire/maneuver systems.
*   Electromagnetic warfare.

4-150.   The brigade's portion of the Snow Dome extends across its AO and integrates with higher echelon components. The brigade commander relies on MANPADS and short-range air defense to deter or defeat low-altitude fixed- and rotary-wing air attack; perhaps more importantly, these systems must defeat aggressor surveillance from small, unmanned aircraft. Artillery complexes provide counterfire and fire support. Counterfire falls largely to rocket systems, while fire support falls to tube systems. Maneuver forces defend both air defense and artillery systems from ground attack, while electromagnetic warfare enables Russian electromagnetic emitters and disrupts aggressor sensors. The primary intent of the Snow Dome at the tactical level is to disrupt the aggressors' lower echelons (battalion and below) as they attempt to close with and destroy the brigade.

4-151.   The following sections address the integrated air defense and electromagnetic warfare components as part of the security function of the SV. Artillery and ground maneuver are addressed in subsequent chapters.

INTEGRATED AIR DEFENSE SYSTEM

4-152.   Integrated air defense complex (IADS) is a key feature in the Russian military and is also a key component of Snow Dome. It is designed to provide overlapping coverage to keep the aggressor's airpower at a distance and protect Russian combat power. Recognizing that the United States and NATO rely on airpower to deliver close and deep precision strikes that enable successful ground maneuver, IADS at the tactical level is intended to deprive the aggressor of regular close air support during the ground battle.

AIR DEFENSE

4-153.   The SV expects significant aggressor threats from attack aviation and missile forces. To counter those threats their force development programs created an IADS to provide security and protection. Generally, the strategic level air defense units and subunits are subordinate to the Aerospace branch while operational and tactical level air defense is subordinate to the SV. There are some air defense units that bridge between the strategic and operational-tactical levels.

4-154.   Tactical, operational, and strategic IADS units and subunits form a layered network of complexes. A complex includes the acquisition and tracking radar with the firing unit, either guns or missiles. For tactical-level units and subunits, most of the air defense complexes are single, self-contained, subunits on a wheeled or tracked chassis. Tactical-level air defense, using both guns and missiles, create protection bubbles for the SV maneuver, artillery, and support units. Each complex is linked through automated C2 networks to create a zone defending against aggressor ground and air complexes as shown in Figure 4-18 on page 4-40. It should also be noted that information collected by UAVs and UGVs is automatically distributed to all linked complexes via the automated command systems. The resulting intelligence improves air defense engagements by directing and refining the acquisition of airborne targets.

4-155.   The SV ground air defense units and subunits integrate with fixed-wing fighter aircraft that target and engage aggressor air platforms at long-range with air-to-air missiles. Russian Aerospace Defense Forces include not only fixed-wing fighter aircraft but also high-altitude, long-range air defense missile subunits such as the S-300 series (NATO SA-10 Grumble, SA12A Gladiator, SA-12B Giant, SA-20 Gargoyle or SA-20B Favourite) and S-400 (NATO SA-21 Growler) at the military district level.

4-156.   Prior to large-scale combat operations, the SV units of the strategic-operational echelons are anti-aircraft missile brigades from the military district level. The Air Defense Brigades of the Combined Arms Armies field BUK-M1 (NATO SA-11 Gadfly), BUK-M2 (NATO SA-17 Grizzly). The Army echelon allocates subunits from the air defense brigades to subordinate divisions to create the IADS coverage during ground combat operations.

4-157.   The IADS supporting actions create a multi-layered defense that provides security for SV not only against aggressor airborne information collection efforts but also against air strikes and cruise missile attacks. SV air defense units include both gun and missile complexes that allow engagement of aggressor airborne platforms starting at ground level up to 12,000 m altitude. The Russian military consider their air defense zones as extremely low - ground level (up to 200 m), low (200 to 1000 m), average (1000 to 4000 m), and large (4000 to 12000 m). Aerospace defense units, such as the S-400, provide the upper levels of the air defense envelope with the reported ability to engage targets from 100 to 27,000 m altitude.

4-158.   At the operational and tactical echelons, the IADS secures SV units by providing both point and area air defense detection and fires. Complexes are man-portable, wheeled, or tracked depending on the force and area covered (See Appendix D for specifications). In addition, the individual complexes are self-contained with the capabilities of detecting, tracking, targeting, and engaging targets autonomously and, in some cases, automatically.

4-159.   The IADS complexes form a dense network of coverage starting at ground level with shoulder-fired launchers, low-altitude close-range gun and missile launchers, medium-altitude missiles, and finally high-altitude missiles. Integrated with this network of IADS the SV uses electromagnetic warfare complexes to jam search and targeting radars that degrade the capability of targeting and strike by aircraft or surface-to-surface missile complexes.

4-160.   Using a standard mobile control complex for all air defense complexes, the SV automates command, control, and direction of air defense units and subunits of regiments, brigades, battalions, and batteries. It automatically shares acquisition information from the radar detecting the target to the short-range missile and missile-gun complexes as well as higher command posts and their subordinate subunits.

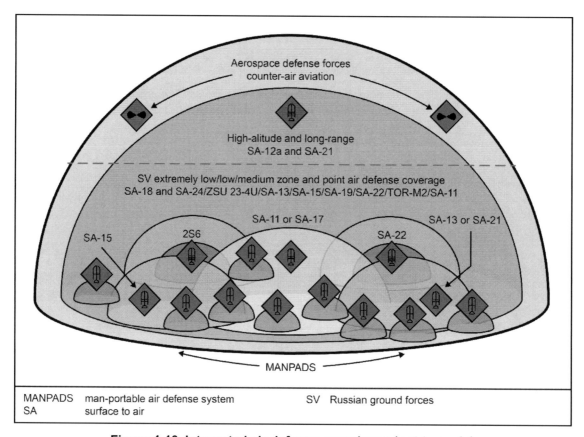

Figure 4-18. Integrated air defense complexes (not to scale)

4-161. Motorized (Mech) and tank brigades have organic air defense units and subunits that provide tactical level IADS. Each brigade has one anti-aircraft missile-artillery battalion and one anti-aircraft missile battalion. The commander allocates air defense subunits to each maneuver battalion and the BrAG based on forces and means calculations from their plan.

4-162. Maneuver divisions have a subordinate air defense regiment composed of two battalions of SA-15 Gauntlet complexes. These units provide area coverage that maneuvers with the division for both defense and offensive actions. The SA-10 air defense complexes (from Army or higher levels) can identify and engage fixed and rotary-wing aircraft, drones, cruise missiles and high-precision loitering munitions.

4-163. The anti-aircraft missile-artillery battalion is organized with three battery subunits as well as a support platoon as figure 4-19 shows:
- Missile (SA-13 or SA-24)—Six air defense complexes.
- Missile-artillery (SA-19)—Six air defense complexes.
- Missile MANPADS (SA-18/24/25)—Twenty-seven man-portable launchers.

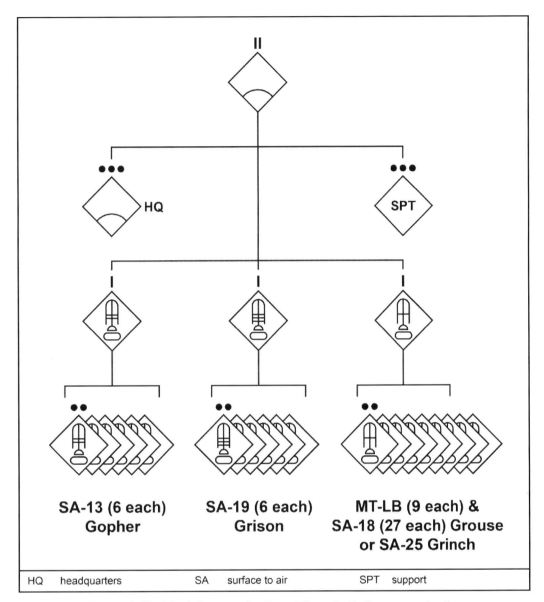

Figure 4-19. Air defense missile-artillery battalion organization

4-164.   The anti-aircraft missile battalion also is organized with three battery subunits but also has an additional radar, support, and maintenance platoons per figure 4-20 on page 4-42:

- Radar platoon.
- Missile (SA-15)—Four complexes per battery.

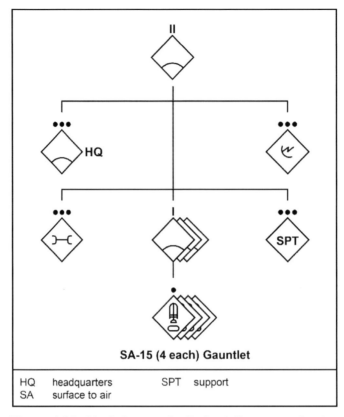

Figure 4-20. Air defense missile battalion organization

4-165. Short-range MANPADS, such as the SA-18, integrate with the IADS using the common mobile control network shared across missile and missile-artillery subunits. The SV MANPADS achieve rapid maneuver using tracked or wheeled platforms to embed with designated maneuver subunits.

4-166. As all air defense complexes at the tactical echelon are on highly mobile platforms, they can provide coverage of moving motorized (mech), tank, or artillery subunits as they perform their assigned mission. Air defense subunit actions support the maneuver or artillery units by combating aggressor aviation reconnaissance collection, detection aggressor aviation and warning of all SV units, engaging and destroying aviation attacks, and engaging cruise missile strikes.

4-167. Maneuver brigades benefit from additional area protection from complexes operating at the strategic-operational level. The air defense brigades may also allocate short-to-medium range SA-11 Gadfly complexes that provide 30 km coverage up to 14 km in altitude. The SV is replacing the SA-11 with the SA-17 Grizzly that carries a larger missile load and an increased envelope of 70 km coverage up to an altitude ceiling of 35 km.

ELECTROMAGNETIC WARFARE RECONNAISSANCE AND SECURITY ACTIONS

4-168. Russia's analysis of the Georgian War and other modern conflicts identified the importance of precision strike capabilities to offensive operations and the critical nature of managing battlefield information. That analysis led to the conclusion that the effects of precision strikes are equal to or potentially more effective than nuclear weapons in certain situations. This realization prompted an expanded emphasis on the modernization of the SV including a significant increase in radio-electromagnetic battle (радиоэлектронная борьба - radioelektronnaya bor'ba - REB) capabilities.

4-169.   This emphasis is reinforced by the close integration of REB capabilities with air defense and artillery to create significant early detection capabilities of aggressor actions. The importance of REB is revealed by the fact that the SV integrates REB support to accomplish aggressor C2 disruption, intelligence collection, and security of its own C2 complexes. For Russia and the SV, REB is generally the equivalent of the Western term electromagnetic warfare but the capabilities are much more pervasive in the SV. REB functional developments focus on not only on reconnaissance capabilities to detect aggressor C2 and communications and on enhancing security of SV C2 complexes but also on defeating or degrading potential aggressor strike capabilities.

4-170.   At the tactical SV level, smaller portable electromagnetic reconnaissance and jamming complexes with direction-finding capabilities are found in both dedicated REB units as well as maneuver reconnaissance units and subunits. The multifunctional capabilities of many REB complexes are common. An example is the Infauna complex that is primarily used to jam improvised explosive devices (IEDs) but is also a multifunctional reconnaissance and jamming complex used to both identify aggressor attacks and provide security warnings to SV units and subunits. The Infauna's capabilities are reported to not only jam radio-controlled IEDs but also jam controlling radio communications and optical missile tracking. These capabilities protect soldiers, military equipment, and objects from guided weapons equipped with video or laser homing.

4-171.   Within the SV, the REB leads in the integration and automation of command-and-control complexes. Automated complexes using modern and redundant communication networks share battlefield information on a real-time basis. The automated cycle consists of the REB complex performing radio survey/detection, jamming, signal analysis, and providing real-time battlefield information of the EMS.

4-172.   This allows the OSK to monitor and control REB units and subunits through the RB-108S General Staff level complex. This complex allows the SV to integrate all REB domains, which include ground, air, and space. It also enables special targeting against terrorists' communication networks. Security actions of organic electromagnetic complexes in SV units and subunits are performed by separate units focused on controlling emanations and compatibility of electromagnetic complexes.

4-173.   The C2 complex permits REB units and subunits to not only feed and share current EMS information with other REB units but also enables integration with non-REB units and subunits. This capability allows REB units to pass tracking and targeting information to the air defense or artillery, again in real time.

RADIO-ELECTROMAGNETIC BATTLE ACTIONS

4-174.   The SV categorizes REB actions into four areas: electromagnetic attack, electromagnetic protection, comprehensive technical control, and radio-electromagnetic information support measures. See figure 4-21 on page 4-44, for the actions under the three categories supporting reconnaissance and security of SV units and subunits. The fourth category of electromagnetic attack focuses on degrading or defeating aggressor strike capabilities. The REB information in this chapter addresses the three categories shown, while electromagnetic attack is addressed in the fires section of chapter 5.

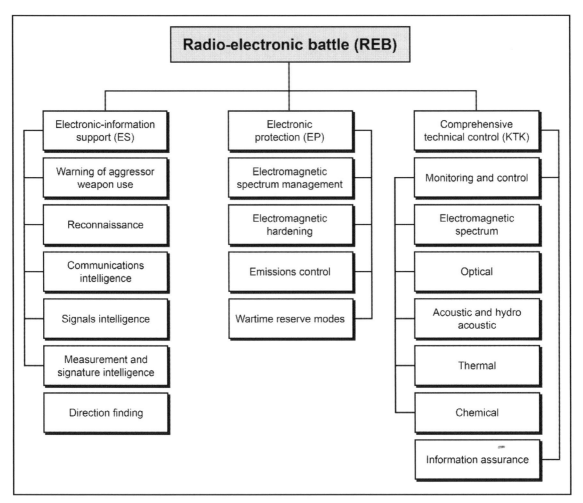

Figure 4-21. Radio-electromagnetic battle reconnaissance and security actions

4-175.   Radio-electromagnetic information support measures enable the other REB categories. Information support provides the capability to suppress radio communications or deploy countermeasures against an incoming missile by detecting the radio signal or the missile itself. These support measures consist of the radio-electromagnetic reconnaissance means to collect, analyze, and disseminate battlefield data to support electromagnetic attack direct strikes. These complexes are integrated into armored, wheeled, aerial, and man-portable variants at the tactical, operational, and strategic levels.

4-176.   Electromagnetic protection actions for the SV serve to ensure that equipment complexes remain fully capable in an electromagnetically threatened environment. Electromagnetic protection actions prevent equipment degradation or disruption due to targeting by electromagnetic, optical, or infrared sensors, jamming of radio or data transmissions, directed energy attacks, and in some cases countermeasures against direct fire. Electromagnetic protection actions fall into the categories of electromagnetic hardening and electromagnetic compatibility.

4-177.   Electromagnetic hardening integrates protection capabilities in new and existing equipment complexes. Hardening primarily takes place during the engineering development of new equipment complexes. The expanding integration of automated C2 capabilities makes electromagnetic hardening essential to counter any aggressor attempts to degrade or disrupt them. Hardening of electromagnetics closely follows the development of aggressor electromagnetic attack capabilities.

4-178.   An example of the electromagnetic hardening aspect of maneuver complexes can be found in the development of the Armata T-14 tank. The Armata includes an active protection complex that has a phased-array radar linked to launchers for specially designed fragmentation munitions mounted on the turret. The Afghanit active protection complex detects incoming fire, calculates an intercept point, and launches a fragmentation munition to destroy the round. Testing of the Afghanit complex indicates it is capable of not only defeating attacks by antitank guided missiles but also armor-piercing fin-stabilized discarding sabot (known as APFSDS-T) rounds. This and other electromagnetic protection complexes are integrated into ongoing equipment development for unmanned ground and aerial vehicles.

4-179. Electromagnetic compatibility actions focus on ensuring that each SV equipment complex is compatible with all other SV complexes. Electromagnetic compatibility also takes place during combat actions to deconflict the use of the EMS and ensure that SV non-REB complexes such as radars and radio communications continue to operate effectively.

4-180. The REB comprehensive technical control (kompleksny tekhnicheskii kontrol) (KTK) actions secure and protect SV units and subunits against aggressor technical reconnaissance. The KTK actions focus primarily on self-monitoring of the EMS to identify unintentional emissions by SV communications or C2 networks. It monitors not just the EMS, but also several other sources capable of disclosing information about the whereabouts of SV forces and means. Examples include optical, acoustic, hydroacoustic, thermal, and chemical signatures of SV battlefield actions.

RADIO-ELECTROMAGNETIC BATTLE ORGANIZATION

4-181. The reorganization of the SV resulted in significant increases in its REB capabilities. The new formations included REB brigades for each of the military districts. These REB brigades, with four battalion subunits, maintain the most modern and powerful electromagnetic warfare complexes that provide integrated area coverage as well as support for maneuver actions. Brigades conduct collection and analysis of the EMS in each district during peacetime and are available for immediate support of the corresponding OSK during conflicts.

4-182. Each of the battalion subunits of a REB brigade focuses on a specific type of electromagnetic warfare defined by its targets. Those target categories against aggressor forces are as follows:
- REB–N for those targeting ground-based complexes.
- REB–S targeting aerial platforms.
- REB–K targeting space complexes.
- REB–Atd for specialized targets such as terrorists and UASs.

4-183. REB units support the SV with both offensive and defensive electromagnetic warfare capabilities. They provide not only jamming of aggressor communication networks but also direction finding, ranging, and monitoring of radio communications. Based on the OSK or Army commander's plan, REB brigade units and subunits are allocated to support operational and tactical actions in addition to the organic REB subunits within each maneuver brigade.

4-184. The REB brigades provide many complexes that complement those at the tactical level. The effects generated by brigade-level complexes are characterized by extended ranges and jamming power. The automated and integrated characteristics of REB complexes allow reconnaissance collected by the REB brigade to pass in real-time to maneuver units and subunits.

4-185. REB UAS complexes also provide reconnaissance as well as electromagnetic attack capabilities. UASs are predominantly found in the SV and Navy as opposed to the Aerospace branch. As a result, the SV directly controls REB UAS as organic units and subunits. A platoon in the REB brigade operates the Leer-3 complex that consists of three Orlan-10 UAVs and a truck-based command and control post. Its reconnaissance capabilities allow detection of cellular base stations for Global System for Mobile Communications (GSM) networks and possibly 3G and 4G within 6 km of the UAV. The Orlan-10 can operate at up to 300 km from its ground control station.

4-186. The brigades also provide KTK complexes to increase the security of SV networks. The Dziudoist, Plavsk, and Svet complexes perform automated signal analysis of SV emissions. These truck mounted complexes allow identification and mitigation of emissions to lessen the possibility of aggressor technical reconnaissance detecting and targeting SV units and subunits.

4-187. In addition to the REB brigades, a separate REB company was added to each maneuver brigade. The company is tailored to provide tactical-level support that provides overall EMS situational awareness, targets and degrades aggressor C2, provides protection from precision-guided munitions and IEDs. This subunit can provide area coverage for REB reconnaissance functions of up to 50 km for brigade operations and point defense against precision-guided munitions and IEDs of up to 400 m. The structure and functions of the company are shown in figure 4-22.

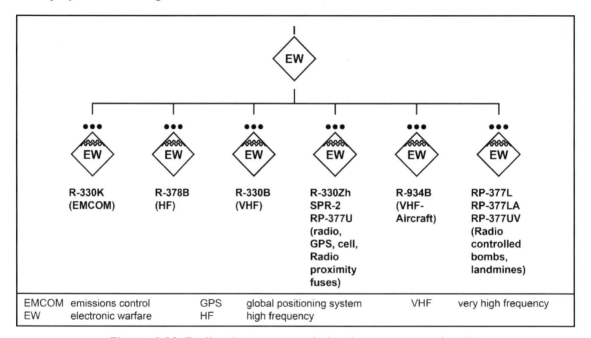

Figure 4-22. Radio-electromagnetic battle company subunits

4-188. The reconnaissance and security functions provided by the REB company are made possible by the various complexes found in its subunits. Those complexes provide not only targeting information but also warning of aggressor attacks and disruption of weapons relying on the EMS for targeting and tracking. Descriptions of the REB complexes found in the company appear in Table 4-3.

Table 4-3. REB complex descriptions

REB Complex	Purpose
RP-330KPK	VHF Automated Command Post
RP-330K	Automated Control Station
R-378B	HF Automated Jamming Station
R-330B	VHF Frequency Jammer linked to the *Borisoglebsk*-2 HF Automated Jamming Complex
R-330Zh	Automated Jammer against INMARSAT and IRIDIUM satellite communication complexes, GSM, and GPS
R-SPR-2	VHF/UHF Radio Jammer cover and thereby protect troops in an area of up to 50 hectares for up to 6 hours
RP-377U	Portable Jammer (against IEDs)
R-934	Automated VHF-UHF aerial radio communication jamming complex provides automated detection, direction finding and signals intelligence of aerial radio sources. It also detects and jams VHF radiotelephone and mobile radio complexes
RP-377L	IED Jammer
RP-377LA	Portable Automated Jammer
RP-377UV	Portable Automated Jammer

GPS	Global Positioning System	INMARSAT	satellite phone company
GSM	global system for mobile communications	IRIDIUM	satellite phone company
HF	high frequency	UHF	ultra-high frequency
IED	improvised explosive device	VHF	very high frequency

4-189.   The Borisoglebsk-2 is the latest iteration Russian REB complex that replaces the Soviet-era R-330 Mandat. It is a mobile complex that consists of nine MT-LB armored tracked vehicles to provide tactical signal intelligence and communication jamming. It disrupts mobile satellite communications and satellite-based navigation signals, jams HF/UHF (both terrestrial and aircraft) radio channels as well as the global positioning system (GPS). It is the main tactical level REB complex in the maneuver brigades.

4-190.   The R-330Zh REB complex used at the tactical level reportedly integrates with signal intercept to identify and target communications. The TORN complex composed of three truck mounted signal intercept has a reported range of 2,000 km. The three vehicles allow the REB unit to conduct direction finding, ranging, and location reconnaissance of satellite and cellular communications as well as GPS guidance signals.

4-191.   The SV will continue to develop and rely on REB capabilities to support strategic, operational, and tactical actions. The emphasis on integrating new REB capabilities will continue and grow, possibly to the level of the REB becoming a separate branch within the Russian military.

This page intentionally left blank.

Chapter 5

Strike

This chapter describes Russian ground forces (Сухопутные войска Российской Федерации – Sukhoputnyye voyska Rossiyskoy Federatsii - SV) doctrinal capabilities and employment of strikes from Missile and Artillery Troops (RViA), radio-electromagnetic battle (REB), nuclear, biological, and chemical (RHBZ), and supporting Russian Aerospace Forces (VKS).

INTRODUCTION TO RUSSIAN STRIKE

5-1.   The Russian military integrates effects from all available forces and means against an aggressor force as a strike that incorporates everything from pre-conflict IV to nuclear fires. Where the Soviet-era ground forces relied on massed artillery to create the desired battlefield effects, the current and future SV will integrate the capabilities of more precise reconnaissance, improved fire range and rates, and automated C2 complexes and still use massed fires to achieve the desired level of damage on aggressor targets. Russian drones routinely train with maneuver and artillery units and subunits to provide real-time target acquisition. These new capabilities continue the Russian principle that fires create the conditions that allow successful battlefield maneuver.

5-2.   The SV's use of strike seeks to integrate all effects whether they be from IV, RViA, REB, RCBZ, VKS, or irregular warfare actions. Integration of these different capabilities at strategic and operational levels are Russia's primary focus with tactical-level fires considered a secondary or culminating action to defeat or destroy an aggressor. At the tactical level, strike predominantly relies on fires from direct and indirect units and subunits to achieve the desired outcomes in combined-arms battle. The main focus of this chapter is the direct and indirect fires that the SV uses to achieve mission success and the other strike elements to support tactical ground actions.

5-3.   The reorganized SV continues to evolve the capabilities of ground maneuver forces while integrating network-centric warfare capabilities in a shift towards information dominance on the battlefield. Improved information flow in the SV allows a greater reliance on use of more precise targeting of fires to accomplish required battlefield effects. The SV considers the effects of precise targeting and fires to equal the impact of tactical nuclear weapons. This evolution does not change the SV use of fires as the leading force and means to accomplish actions during local wars and armed conflicts, defense, and offense. As the basis for the evolving integrated fires concept, the Russian military culture continues to view artillery fires as the true "God of War" as attributed to Joseph Stalin during World War II.

5-4.   Russia's vast, modernized nuclear arsenal and a stated willingness to use that arsenal to engage aggressors from the strategic to tactical levels serves as its basis for military deterrence. This component serves as the predominant source of national power that Russia employs to maintain its position on the world stage as well as defend the nation. Russia's latest military doctrine states strategic and nonstrategic nuclear weapons prevent the outbreak of strategic nuclear conflict. As one of Russia's main security tasks it emphasizes the maintenance of its nuclear force as a deterrent to global and regional conflicts. To that end the SV incorporates nonstrategic nuclear fires in all major exercises and continues to maintain tactical level proficiency to integrate those fires.

5-5.   Russia employs fires from nonstrategic nuclear forces (нестратегические ядерные силы - nyestrategicheskiy yaderniy sili - NSYaSh) and conventional high-precision weapons (Высокоточное оружие - vysokotochnoye oruzhiye - vysokotochnoye oruzhiye - VTO) complexes to conduct strategic operations for the destruction of critically important targets (стратегические операции по уничтожению критически важных целей - strategicheskiye operatsii po unichtozheniyu kriticheski vazhnykh ob"yektov -

SODCIT). Russia states that the effects of VTO fires can be equal to those of NSYaSh in some circumstances meaning NSYaSh may supplement VTO capacity shortfalls in a firing complex or be planned for specific target effects. The SODCIT concept involves the application of progressive fire engagements used with the intent of de-escalation of local or regional conflicts. The strikes demonstrate to an aggressor Russia's resolve and its strike capabilities to deter escalation to large scale ground combat. Fire demonstrations increase over time with an intended effect of, first, deterring aggression towards Russia, then escalating to strikes that serve the dual purpose of deterrence and degradation of aggressor capabilities. At the tactical level, SODCIT focuses on three target categories:

- Category 1
  - Conventional VTO strike forces.
  - Artillery.
  - Military command posts.
- Category 2
  - Air defense units.
  - Armor concentrations.
  - Communication nodes.
- Category 3
  - Logistics infrastructure.
  - Transportation infrastructure.
  - Ammunition, equipment, and material stockpiles.
  - Petroleum, oil, and lubricant depots or transmission lines.

5-6. The SV integrates NSYaSh and higher yield nuclear fires into training and actions at all levels. The destructive power or yield of nuclear munitions are generally distinguished by the carriers at the strategic, operational, and tactical levels. The destructive power or yield of nuclear munitions of—

5-7. Strategic carriers include—
- Intercontinental mobile-based missiles.
- Nuclear submarines with ballistic or cruise missiles.
- Strategic bombers and missile carriers.

5-8. Operational-tactical carriers include—
- ballistic and cruise missiles operational-tactical range.
- medium bombers and missile carriers.
- anti-ship missiles of submarines and surface ships of operational-tactical range.

5-9. Tactical carriers include—
- Artillery.
- Tactical missiles.
- Frontline aviation (fighter-bombers).
- Torpedoes, depth charges, anti-submarine missiles.
- Anti-aircraft missiles.

5-10. The SV categorizes nuclear fires by the power of the explosion; nuclear weapons of all types are conventionally divided into five calibers:
- Very small (less than 1 kt).
- Small (1–10 kt).
- Medium (10–100 kt).
- Large (100–1000 kt).
- Extra-large (more than 1 MT).

5-11. Many fires systems are expected to be dual-capable of deploying chemical and conventional fires. The most likely uses are for covert or clandestine employment.

5-12. Russian understanding of nonlinear warfare also guides the evolution of the SV force and their doctrine. The Russians view the characteristics of this type of warfare as follows—

- Long-range destruction by aerospace, naval, and indirect fire ground forces of aggressor targets prior to contact.
- Rapid planning and execution of combined arms actions by highly maneuverable forces and means.
- Destruction of aggressor targets primarily by artillery and other strike assets.
- VTO fire capabilities allow target destruction without contact.
- Automated target acquisition and transmission to the strike delivery systems.

5-13. As indicated by the majority of the nonlinear warfare characteristics being associated with strikes and their employment, one gains an appreciation of the priority placed on the function. Russia's nonlinear battle concept anticipates the SV maneuver forces continuing to seize and hold terrain but only after strike complexes destroy aggressor units. The SV integrates all strike assets to focus on an aggressor force and remove its ability to affect the battle outcome. Strikes include artillery, rocket, and missile medium-to-long range massed indirect fires, engineer mines, nuclear, chemical, special operations forces, IV and REB attacks, as well as irregular forces that influence or affect the tactical battle.

Note. Russia uses the terms "complex or complexes" rather than the Western terms "system or systems." Complexes refer to not only individual weapons platforms but also to the integrated and supporting forces and means that create the battlefield capability for maneuver, artillery, air defense, REB, and others. As an example, an artillery unit or subunit may have several guns or launchers all with organic automated C2 that receive targeting information from ground radars of artillery reconnaissance units.

5-14. Priority of fire sets the battlefield conditions that correspond to maneuver unit actions. The SV's view is that by using long-range VTO fires to seize the initiative and employing all other fire elements in an integrated manner allows their forces to attain fire superiority. Improved reconnaissance and target acquisition capabilities using UASs, unmanned ground systems, REB, and all other IV complexes serve to create a responsive strike complex to interdict or destroy an aggressor.

Note. The abbreviation for unmanned aerial system (UAS) is used by U.S. forces in reference to the aircraft, its ground control station and communication link. The abbreviation for UAV is used in reference to the aerial vehicle itself. Russian terminology refers to UAV airframe as a drone and that an unmanned aerial complex includes the airframe, ground control station, launch and recovery subunits. A UAS includes all previous components as well as supply and support, training, and communications networks to transfer data.

5-15. The strike systems of the Russian military and the SV particularly rely on integration and layering of capabilities beginning at the strategic level down to tactical platoons. Organic system capabilities coupled with allocated weapons from higher level units and integrated with those of neighboring units serves to create a system of fire to defeat an aggressor attacking the front, flanks, or rear of the formation.

5-16. The SV's fielding of improved sensors in unmanned robotic complexes continues to increase the speed and precision of strikes. The use of UAS to provide more precise target identification greatly assists the SV in responding with more accurate indirect and direct fires. Development programs seek to expand this capability to unmanned ground systems as well as using artificial intelligence to prioritize and direct strikes. Automated and autonomous complexes are currently used by the SV in tank, air defense, and REB units and subunits to reduce manpower, improve soldier survivability, and to rapidly engage aggressor targets.

5-17. Information dominance on the battlefield in terms of the application of fires translates to improving the link between the acquisition sensor and a fire delivery complex. The desired end state is a complex that reduces the "sensor-to-shooter" delay to the lowest level possible. This evolution reinforces the application of fires based on the commander's plan that specifies targets, volume, and location necessary to accomplish specified missions.

DOCTRINAL APPLICATION (CONCEPT OF FIRES)

5-18. Russian military doctrine views indirect fires as a critical function for all combat operations. Destruction or suppression of aggressor forces using effective fire units and complexes are necessary to set the conditions for successful ground operations. Initially, the SV senior commander and their staff plan the application of fires from various levels using scientific substantiation that includes determining the correlation of forces and means and applying established normative quantities. Normative application defines space and timing of unit and subunit maneuvers, expenditure of forces and means, and the resulting required supply quantities.

5-19. For fires, these calculations stipulate the volume and timing of fires necessary to accomplish a specified mission. As the SV executes the commander's plan during armed conflicts/local wars, defense, and offense the fire units conduct precise targeting for selective and massed fires as well as responding to targets of opportunity identified by reconnaissance or maneuver of SV units. For tactical-level formations this process determines the use of organic fire systems within a brigade or regiment and any allocation of strike effects from units or subunits of higher level RViA formations and supporting actions from the VKS or REB units.

5-20. At the tactical level, doctrinal application of fires continues allocation of the type and volume of fire necessary to achieve the desired effect on the aggressor target. The SV employs several types of fires to accomplish actions during armed conflicts and local wars, defense, and offense. Their VTO capabilities continue to grow while they retain the ability to launch massed artillery fire strikes to support the commander's plan. The commander assigns artillery missions determined by the desired percentage reduction of effectiveness of a target. The mission type and size of the target area are variables used by nomograms to determine the volume of fire required from firing units to achieve the specified percent of damage. The following are examples of artillery missions with desired percentages of reduction—

- Annihilation (уничтожéние)—Reduction in effectiveness of 70–90%. Loss of complete combat effectiveness.
- Destruction (разрушение)—Reduction in effectiveness of 50–60%. Unfit for combat operations.
- Neutralization/suppression (нейтрализация)—Effectiveness reduction of 30%. Severe damage but still capable of combat operation.
- Harassment (изнурение)—Intended impact is psychological rather than a percentage of destruction. A limited number of firing units and rounds fired on a specified schedule, to disrupt aggressor forces in static positions.

5-21. The SV principles of artillery warfare are—

- Constant combat readiness of artillery forces and means.
- Matching objectives to unit capabilities.
- Close coordination between maneuver forces and fires units.
- Continuous fire support for motorized units.
- Rapid and extensive maneuver by artillery units, subunits, and fires.
- Solid and continuous control of fires.
- Suddenness of action.
- Use deception and cunning.
- Rapid restoration of combat capability of artillery units.
- Comprehensive unit protection.

PLANNING

5-22. The SV's planning of fires on an integrated battlefield focuses on achieving a required amount of damage of targets. As such, the commander plans to apply fires by massing effects rather than by massing units and subunits. In the past, the Soviet Army used physical formations of artillery units and subunits in large, massed artillery groups based on calculations of type targets and desired effects. The SV approach for calculating the forces necessary for indirect fire effects remains essentially the same but, depending on aggressor capabilities, they continue reducing the use of physical groupings of fire systems. For the present the divisional, regimental and brigade artillery groups continue to exist to create the desired battlefield conditions.

5-23. Aggressors with existing and growing VTO fire capabilities cause the SV to use dispersed positions and frequent movement to alternate positions as countermeasures. During tactical actions conducted for an armed conflict or local war, where the aggressor forces do not have VTO artillery or aviation capabilities, the SV may use some physical groups to deliver the required effects on a target. Given a relatively secure environment during armed conflicts and local wars they may deploy and fire individual systems depending on the type effects required by the commander's plan.

5-24. Commanders and supporting staff plan the type and amount of indirect fire required to accomplish commander-directed tactical actions. The SV continues modernization of the methods used to perform the necessary planning calculations, but the basic process used under the Soviet system remains valid. Using correlation of forces and means calculations and nomograms, the staff calculates the necessary mix of ground maneuver units, indirect fires, and corresponding logistics to accomplish the mission specified by the commander against a specified aggressor unit. This process essentially uses the big data sets accumulated since its World War II experience to establish standardized allocations to achieve likely battlefield success. That technical analysis results in an SV assessment that in modern battles the source of damage from fires is 12–15% for maneuver forces, 20% for fixed and rotary aviation, and 65–70% for RViA.

5-25. Initial calculations and resulting allocation of fires determines the task organization of the units and subunits necessary to achieve the required mission. As reconnaissance refines target information, the commander may adjust their fire allocation. For artillery forces and means, the result of this planning is the formation of artillery groups allocated for specific missions and phases of an operation.

5-26. Plans flow from higher, Army level, to lower, division and brigade levels based on immediate and subsequent missions for each unit. Correspondingly, the allocation or task organization of strike elements; RViA, REB, VKS, and organic systems provide a cumulative effect to achieve the directed missions. Artillery units and subunits allocated for tactical actions form into control groups designated as army artillery groups (армейска артиллерия группы - armeyskaya artilleriyskaya gruppa - AAG), division artillery group (дивизион артиллерийской группы - divizionnaya artilleriyskaya gruppa - DAG), regimental artillery groups (полковая артиллерия грцппа - polkovaya artilleriyskaya gruppa - RAGs), and brigade artillery groups (бригадная артиллерийская группа - artilleriyskaya gruppa brigady - BrAGs). The organization and control of the various artillery groups are discussed in the following sections.

5-27. Commanders and staff officers prepare their plans primarily on a "commander's map" that provides a detailed graphic of the scheme of maneuver. Each officer puts on the map only the data pertinent to their area of responsibility. The map is primarily for use by the individual officer, but it complies with standard graphics procedures so that the information is understandable by higher and adjacent commanders as well as subordinates. Positions and actions of maneuver units and subunits are shown in red. Aggressor units, known positions, firing points, defensive barriers, and other available data are shown in blue. SV supporting forces, artillery, air defense, engineers, chemical, REB, etc. are marked in black. See figures 5-1 and 5-2 for examples on page 5-6.

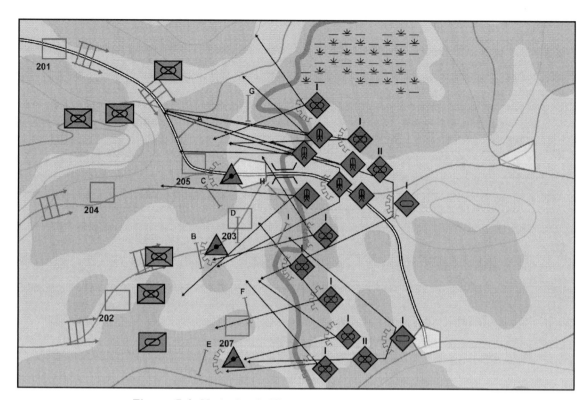

Figure 5-1. Motorized rifle commander's map for fires

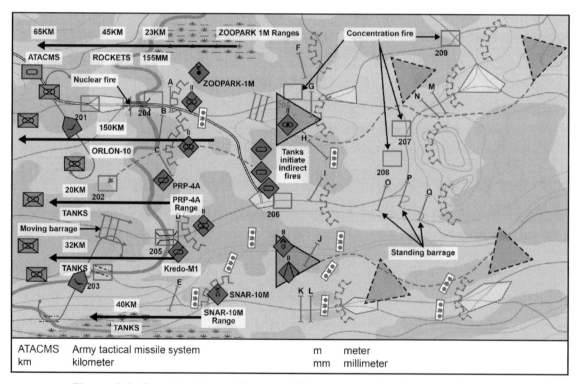

Figure 5-2. Combinations of types of fires supporting the security zone

COMMAND AND CONTROL

5-28. Allocated RViA units and subunits that deliver the required fires remain under the senior commander of their respective chain of command. Fires units and subunits attached to a BTG or regiment support those maneuver forces and respond to that commander in support of their plan and actions. For fires that carry out the senior commander's plan, the units and subunits remain under the control of the senior artillery commander. A supporting artillery battalion conducting action as part of a brigade, regiment, division, or army form artillery groups to conduct fires at the direction of the senior combined arms commander and supports several maneuver battalions with planned fires.

5-29. The senior artillery commander directs the fires of subordinate artillery units and subunits and collocates their command post with the senior maneuver commander. As required by the battlefield situation the senior artillery commander may be deployed forward to conduct target acquisition and fire direction. Reliable integrated C2 networks allow greater separation of command posts than the physical proximity used in the past. Real time data transmission networks, protected by extensive electromagnetic warfare complexes, facilitate rapid C2 of all SV forces and means.

5-30. Russian doctrine about the modern battlefield treats SV forces as a system of systems or complexes with fires in the lead. The concept seeks to link all supporting reconnaissance assets with automated command and control (C2), and VTO indirect fires to enable ground maneuver actions. Russia's most recent military doctrine specifies that development of the capacity and means of information exchange are critical tasks in development of its armed forces. Combining improvements in reconnaissance, automated command and control complexes, and improving long-range VTO fire systems serves to support the Russian concept of "noncontact" warfare. The concept views modern wars as simultaneous and integrated actions that rely on precise reconnaissance for target acquisition linked to automated C2 directed strikes to engage and destroy the aggressor before direct contact of forces.

5-31. The capability to effectively control and direct both targeting sensors and VTO fires at the tactical level are made possible through a network of COP vehicles. The vehicles equipped with communications, navigation, and sighting systems provide the artillery commander with fire control of allocated artillery units and subunits.

5-32. Fire direction centers pass all detected high-value targets directly to firing units without headquarters analysis and direction. The SV employs specific task organized groups at the operational level and below in organizations labelled a reconnaissance strike complex (разведывательно-ударный комплекс - razvedyvatel'no-udarnyy kompleks - RSC). The RSC is part of a network-centric complex that integrates operators, reconnaissance assets, command and control, and selective semi-automated or automated decision-making capabilities. It connects a full range of fires systems that include mortars, cannon and gun artillery, MRL, surface-to-surface ballistic and cruise missiles, attack aviation, strike UAVs, and naval gunfire. Currently the RSC controls exist as temporary or provisional measures used to strike high-value targets while AAGs, DAGs, RAGs and BrAGs are groupings that support maneuver formations at the specified levels.

5-33. The fire control complex prioritizes strikes on high-value aggressor targets that are detected and monitored by reconnaissance elements for attack throughout an AOR, including but are not limited to:
- Weapons of mass destruction launch and support including equipment with precision strike capabilities.
- Condensed groupings of tactical maneuver formations.
- Command and control nodes.
- Artillery and rocket unit concentrations.
- Logistics sites with critical bulk commodities such as ammunition and fuel.
- Air defense weapon/target acquisition nodes.
- Systems specialized for space vehicle downlink of navigational or other C2 data.
- Sensor systems with specialized optical, electro-optical, radar, thermal-imaging, acoustic, and other collection and targeting devices.

RECONNAISSANCE AND TARGET ACQUISITION

5-34. The planned fires of the artillery groupings enable maneuver by SV brigades, regiments, and battalion tactical groups (BTGs) to strike the aggressor force at the time and place specified in the commander's decision. These strikes engage aggressor forces or positions at the critical time with the volume and type fires necessary to annihilate, destroy, or suppress those forces.

5-35. In a defense there are artillery reconnaissance vehicles positioned behind the first echelon companies or the second echelon company strongpoints. These reconnaissance vehicles provide direct observation of the front and flanks of a defending unit. This capability allows the collection, analysis, and assessment of all detected battlefield actions and the resulting rapid adaptation to changing conditions. These vehicles provide additional target acquisition capabilities and feed information to a fire direction center that provides fire solutions to the firing subunits.

5-36. During offensive actions artillery reconnaissance vehicles maneuver with the forward reconnaissance detachments to provide fire direction to supporting artillery groups as much as 20 KM forward of the marching main body. Artillery reconnaissance vehicles such as the PRP-4A Argus at the brigade and regimental level provide radar detection of moving tank type targets at up to 12 KM. The Argus also uses electro-optical sensors to identify tank targets at up to 8 KM during the day and 3 KM during nighttime. Information gathered by UAVs is passed to artillery reconnaissance by ground control of the UAS unit or subunit and the maneuver command post.

5-37. In the brigade and division there are both man portable and vehicle mounted radars that add to the target acquisition capabilities. These reconnaissance platforms are linked by automated mobile field C2 systems such as the Strelets or Bylina to direct the actions of SV units. A conceptual graphic of the command network for an SV self-propelled howitzer battalion follows in figure 5-3.

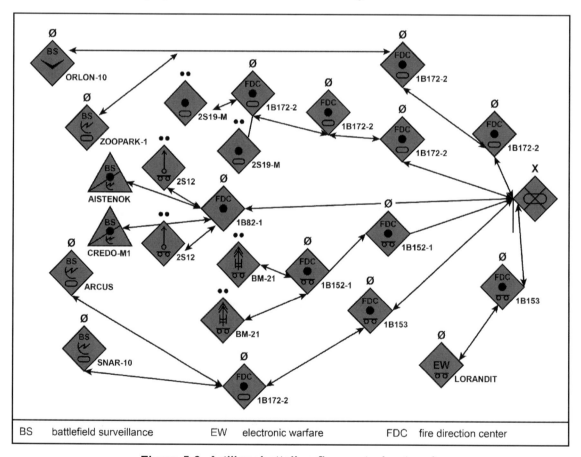

Figure 5-3. Artillery battalion fire control network

5-38. The development and integration of UAS into the SV ground forces greatly reduces the amount of time needed to strike a target. In addition, the precision target acquisition allows a reduction in the specified number of rounds to achieve the desired level of damage to a target. Integration with the networked and automated C2 systems allows direct transmission of UAV target detections to firing subunits for engagement. The UAS capabilities also allows rapid battle damage assessments of fires to determine if the specified level of damage was achieved and whether reengagement is necessary. Automated transmission of target information from the UAS to the designated firing unit allows almost instantaneous engagement when all factors conform to the commander's plan.

5-39. Targeting using the UAS complex involves one of four methods. These four methods are outlined in figures 5-4 through 5-7, on pages 5-9 through 5-15:

- Reference point — The location of a target is determined by its relation to a known point such as a road intersection. Observation from the UAV camera provides the relationship between the target and the known point. This method requires detailed maps and position data and is most suitable for massed weapons fire on an area target.

Figure 5-4. Known reference point

- Overflight — The ground station maneuvers the UAV to fly directly over the target to capture its position. This method exposes the UAV to ground fire from the target and is most likely used against an aggressor with limited or no air defense. Limited visibility targeting with UAVs equipped with thermal imaging sensors will most likely use this method due to the limited accuracy of the sensor.

Figure 5-5. Target overflight

● Range finding — If the UAV is equipped with an on-board gyro stabilized electro-optical camera and a laser rangefinder the ground station calculates the known location of the UAV as well as the direction and distance to the target. This method requires a complex UAV and exposes it to aggressor fire or electromagnetic countermeasures. It does provide targeting information for more precise fires against high-value targets.

Figure 5-6. Range finding from known point

- Multiple azimuths — The UAV is flown along multiple azimuths from the target to capture several reference points to use in calculating the target's exact location. This method also requires a complex UAV but allows precision engagement of multiple targets while remaining passive. It is the most likely method to be used on a modern battlefield against an aggressor with the capability to counter UAV observation and targeting.

Figure 5-7. Multiple azimuth correlation

5-40. In addition to UAS complexes, the RSC and RFC integrates all assets retained by its level of operation including army aviation, artillery, and missile units. Based on mission requirements, a brigade, division, or higher headquarters commander may include maneuver forces as an element of the RSC or RFC. The communication links between the reconnaissance complexes, fire direction, C2, and the firing systems follows in figure 5-8.

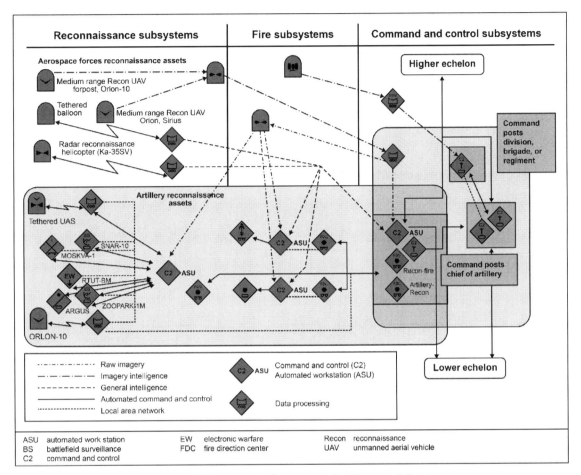

Figure 5-8. Fire control communication architecture

5-41. The RSC integrates sensors including UAS, REB, special operations forces, counter-battery radars, and cyber units to pinpoint high-value targets. These systems are directly linked to the allocated fire units to create an extremely efficient and short sensor-to-shooter complex for operational-strategic targets. Previous estimates of Soviet sensor-to-shooter times between target detection and resulting fire were as low as 3-7 minutes. Based on the modernization of the SV with integrated, automated C2 that period is reduced by as much as half and in some cases reaches the threshold of real-time indirect fires.

5-42. The RFC as a fires executing formation uses the operational-tactical reconnaissance targeting information to designate targets for indirect fires systems. The recon sensors including UAS, REB, and direct observers enables the SV to conduct precision-point or area targeting with near real-time fire missions on high-value targets and high-payoff targets from dispersed firing positions. Automated fire control complexes onboard indirect fire platforms allow batteries allocated to an RFC to disperse by 200 m or more.

5-43. The use of VTO fires is the desired SV norm for attacking targets in dynamic tactical situations; however, massed artillery fires often have effects beyond destruction of a particular target. Aggressor units experiencing or witnessing massed fires often suffer profound paralysis or psychological trauma. Selected targets are typically engaged with fires of short duration that are task-organized for maximum destruction or other effects. For either point target or area fire missions, the coordinated firing units quickly disperse from firing points to alternate sites within a firing position area to avoid effective counterfire by an aggressor.

5-44. Fire control functions under the umbrella of other complexes such as the integrated air defense system (IADS) provide the protection necessary to enable effective fires according to the commander's plan. The SV uses selective centralized and decentralized options to allow semi-autonomous and autonomous fires based on engagement criteria. When near real-time or immediate fires are not required the SV uses a standardized approval process by authorized leaders to direct fires. In the expected high-intensity combat with peer or near peer aggressor forces the trend is towards automated targeting and fires as the norm.

5-45. Division and higher headquarters conduct pre-established fire control with functional staff, command posts, communications and intelligence architecture, and automated fire control system. Divisions, which can have rotary-wing attack assets allocated can also request fixed-wing sorties for direct air support from higher headquarters. At brigade and regimental level, attack helicopters supporting a mission would typically remain under control of the brigade or regimental commander.

5-46. Support of fixed-wing or rotary-wing assets for a battalion or BTG mission would come from a higher-level headquarters. A battalion or BTG does not have constituent rotary-wing assets and normally does not have a dedicated forward air controller. If aviation support is provided for a mission to a battalion or BTG the brigade or division would provide a forward air controller for air support coordination.

5-47. Conditions could exist that require fire support relationships among service, joint, and combined forces. An example of possible task organization would be a brigade directed to command a division level advance guard, an exploitation force, or any other functional force whose actions must be closely coordinated with the delivery of fires.

INDIRECT FIRE SYSTEMS

5-48. The SV conducts maneuver by fire by shifting indirect fire from a designated target, barrage line, standing barrier, massed or other fire method from one target or axis of advance to another. This is accomplished with limited repositioning of units and subunits to guard against counter-battery fires to create a means of rapid response to engagement requirements. Firing units do reposition after engaging a target as each defensive position or offensive firing line involves creating 2–3 alternate positions. As one battery completes its fire another continues the mission while the first battery relocates to one of its alternates.

5-49. The capability to accomplish immediate fire defeat of an aggressor by a brigade or regiment in its zone of responsibility continues increasing as VTO complexes evolve. VTO fires are possible out to 20KM for heavy mortars and 70KM for tube artillery when linked to reconnaissance complexes such as UAVs or REB targeting. The SV continues modernization of both its indirect fire guns and MRL complexes to support VTO fires. These include the Coalition-SV reportedly capable of multiple round simultaneous impact missions from a single firing platform. Brigade and regimental commanders still have the capability to use massed fires against area targets with the same increased artillery and MRL ranges.

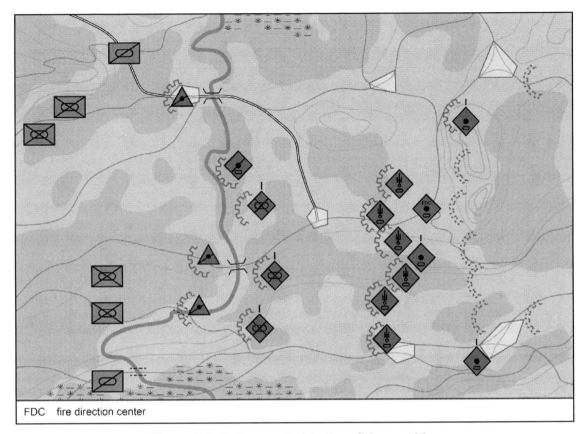

FDC   fire direction center

Figure 5-9. Self-propelled battery firing position

5-50. Indirect fire units composed of mortars are organic to motorized rifle battalions and additional artillery from the motorized rifle brigade may be attached based on mission tasks. Allocation of additional fires based on mission planning may include additional artillery, MRLs, and missiles. These units may employ a range of munitions; HE, precision-guided, chemical, and nuclear.

METHODS OF FIRE

5-51. The SV employs fires to accomplish the required level of damage or destruction specified by the commander's plan using the following fire types. The basis for the fire type or types selected by the commander are the artillery norms. Nowhere are norms more important than in their artillery application where artillery effectiveness is the prime means of reducing aggressor battlefield effectiveness.

5-52. Planned fire classifications and the combinations used to form various patterns that support combat action are found in Figure 5-10 through 5-12, on pages 5-17 through 5-21, following the descriptions:

- Armed Conflicts and Local Wars:
    - **Fire Blocks.** A line of fire designed to prevent an aggressor or irregular unit from leaving an area.
    - **Fire Sweeps.** A moving barrage used to drive aggressor or irregular forces in a desired direction.
    - **Defensive Box.** Fires on all sides of a defensive position protecting important facilities or units in an area of concentration.
    - **Fire Corridor.** Fires on both sides of a planned axis of advance for a unit and subunits during exit from an area.
    - **Fire Edge.** Carried out using barrage and concentrated fires on likely areas of action by militants and on the terrain in the rear and on the flanks of SV units and subunits.

- **Fire Vise.** Combination of moving barrage lines on the perimeter of the target that progressively advance towards the center of a target area where single or multiple fire concentrations complete the destruction of the aggressor force.
- **Layer cake.** Combination of different heights of artillery bursts including air, surface, and ricocheted rounds that skip the blast and fragments along the ground surface.
- **Fire sack.** Fire targeted at a central aim point with the points of impact from different subunits covering the breadth and depth of a 400-800 M area.
- Defense
    - **Individual targets.** (наблюдаемая одиночная цель - nablyudayemaya odinochnaya tsel') Fire on an individual observed target of opportunity as the aggressor unit advances towards the defense.
    - **Concentration.** Typically preplanned fires against an expected area of aggressor unit advance by several batteries or battalions.
    - **Barrier Standing barrage fire (неподвижнын загради-тельный огонь).** A single wall of fire planned against aggressor avenues of approach to stop an attack, destroy the attacking force and its antitank systems.
    - **Deep standing barrage.** Multiple lines of simultaneous and continuous fire on an expected aggressor attack axis.
    - **Double moving barrage.** Successive lines of fire from two battalions firing on an assigned line until the aggressor unit passes and then rolling back or leapfrogging back to the next line in the series. In a four-line series one battalion will fire on line 1 and then 3 while the second battalion will fire on lines 2 and then 4 if the aggressor continues the attack.
    - **Defensive rolling barrage.** A solid curtain of fire from supporting artillery on lines that are successively closer to the main defense as the aggressor attacks. Each firing gun is assigned a section of the line and shifts the targeted line closer to the defense as the attack progresses. Fire lines are 100 to 300m apart depending on the battlefield conditions.
    - Fire ambush - Surprise high density direct fire from all weapons including artillery and mortars.
- Offense
    - **Fire against an individual target (огонь по отдельной цели).** Fire by a single system or platoon against a single aggressor target. Individual target fires include direct fire and support maneuver units during battle in cities.
    - **Fire concentration (сосредоточение огня).** Simultaneous fires by a several batteries or battalions against a single target in the aggressor's defense.
    - **Successive concentrations of fire.** On the axis and flanks of the SV unit advance toward aggressor positions. Concentration's target known or suspected high-value targets such as C2 and antitank units into the depth of the aggressor formation.
    - **Massed Fire.** A simultaneous strike against an area target with planned battery or battalion concentrations. While VTO fire supported with UAV target identification is a growing capability, the use of massed preplanned fire remains an effective fire method used to destroy or degrade aggressor high-value targets when only general targeting information is available.
    - **Offensive rolling barrage.** A continuous set of preplanned fire lines that lead the SV attack on the axis of advance. Used against a prepared defense the rolling barrage is a solid curtain of artillery fire that proceeds the attacking SV subunits on successive lines 100-300m apart depending on the speed of advance.
    - **Deep standing barrage fire.** Executed by either single or multiple battalions to fire successive lines simultaneously and continuously.
    - **Moving barrage.** Fires targeted on the aggressor axis of advance with successive lines of concentration. The initial line is 2-4km from the forward edge of the SV units, the succeeding line is at 700-1000m, and the final line is 400-600m from the SV forward edge. The battalions' artillery systems are positioned so that they can perform direct fire engagements on aggressor forces penetrating the final standing fire line.

- **Double moving barrage.** Fires by multiple battalions for alternating barrage lines in depth. The first battalion fires barrage line one. The second battalion fires barrage line two closer to the SV maneuver units. After a specified fire volume, the first battalion lifts fire on line one and fires barrage line three a step closer to the SV line, and the second battalion shifts its barrage line to line four. Both battalions' position to allow direct fire on the advancing aggressor force if they can close with the SV maneuver units.
- **Ricochet fire.** Low angle fires between 2 to 25 degrees with a delayed fuze setting to time the burst height at 3–4 M.

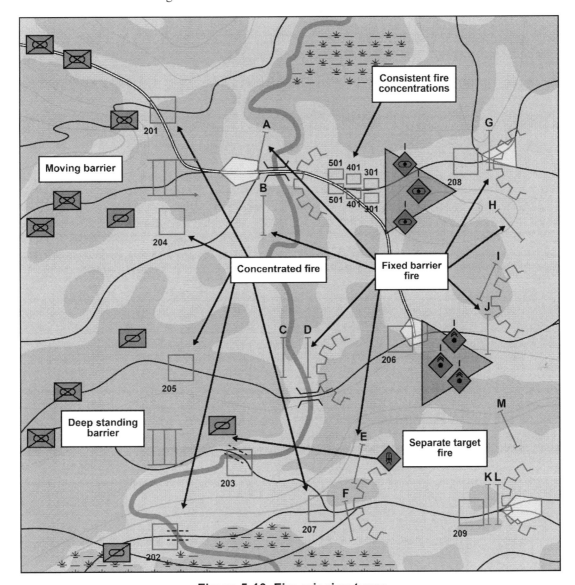

Figure 5-10. Fire mission types

5-53. The SV employs multiple fire mission types to create patterns of fire that support the specified mission:
- Fire block.
- Fire search.
- Fire edge.
- Fire vise.
- Layer cake.
- Fire sack.

- Fire combing.
- Fire cover.

ARTILLERY FIRE BY TYPE AND USE

5-54. This chart shows the types of fire most likely to be used during various tactical actions. A certain type of fire is not restricted during any tactical action as use depends on the commander's plan and battlefield conditions.

TARGETS OR FIRE TYPE	OFFENSE			COMMITMENT OF THE SECOND ECHELON	REPEL COUNTERATTACK	PURSUIT	MEETING ENGAGEMENT	DEFENSE						
	BREAKTHROUGH FIRES							COUNTER-PREPARATORY	INTERDICT AGGRESSOR ADVANCE	REPEL AGGRESSOR ATTACK	SUPPORT SECURITY FORCE	SUPPORT DEFENSIVE POSITIONS IN DEPTH	SUPPORT SECOND ECHELON BATTALION	ROVING GUN
	PREPARATORY	ASSAULT	ACCOMPANYING											
INDIVIDUAL	X		X	X	X	X		X	X	X	X	X	X	X
SEPARATE	X						X							
GROUP	X						X							
MASSED	X													
ASSAULT	X													
CONCENTRATED		X	X	X	X	X	X	X	X	X	X	X	X	
DIRECT			X				X					X		
SUCCESSIVE		X	X											
CURTAIN		X												
FIXED BARRIER			X	X	X	X	X			X	X			
MOVING BARRIER		X	X		X					X				
HARASSING	X													X
OBSERVATIONAL	X													
SCREENING SMOKE	X									X	X			
COUNTER-BATTERY												X		
REGISTRATION	X		X											
DUMMY TRANSFER	X													X
PAUSES	X													
DEMOLITION		X						X						

TYPES OF FIRE AND USE

Figure 5-11. Fires to facilitate tactical actions

ORGANIZATION

5-55. During the conduct of local wars and armed conflicts, defense, and offense the SV organizes strikes to facilitate tactical mission accomplishment. Tactical level units such as divisions and brigades organize organic fire assets as well as those allocated from other units of the army group. Using the growing automated C2 complex to organize and direct fires, the SV still allocates units and subunits to mission groups but has the capability to direct fires from any firing unit or subunit against a priority aggressor target.

5-56. The SV task organizes RViA units into groups to achieve C2 of units and subunits allocated for mission accomplishment. The integration of improved communication and automated C2 systems allows these groupings to focus the fire effects without occupying a specified unit area on the battlefield. As indicated below, former-Soviet offensive operations against a prepared aggressor defense provide an initial planning factor for the artillery groups. Modernized planning and grouping of forces accounts for the increased precision and speed of employment to arrive at the number of indirect fire systems required to accomplish the level of damage or destruction specified in the commander's plan. Examples of the possible task organization of RViA units to form the following formations at the tactical level.

- DAG - 4-6 battalions.
  - Division subordinate Regimental Artillery Group (RAG) - 3-4 battalions.
- Brigade Artillery Group (BrAG) - 3-4 battalions.
- Separate roaming guns or battery - Small artillery sections used to decoy aggressor artillery into a counter-battery battle. Tank fire may also be used to draw an aggressor into a counter-battery battle.

5-57. The indirect fire units and subunits of the SV include two major subcategories:
- Field artillery: field guns, gun-howitzers, howitzers, mortars, and MRLs.
- Antitank artillery: AT guns, recoilless guns, and antitank guided missile launchers. Antitank units and subunits are not part of the artillery groups.

5-58. Artillery formations locate as far forward as security allows which is usually behind the first echelon or main defensive line in the defense or behind the lead battalion in an offense march formation. This applies to the anti-tank subunits as well as the artillery. Example artillery laydowns are depicted in figures 5-13 and 5-14 on pages 5-22 and 5-23. Note that the locations in the figures are doctrinal and do not depict how the units and subunits will locate in an actual battle during large scale war.

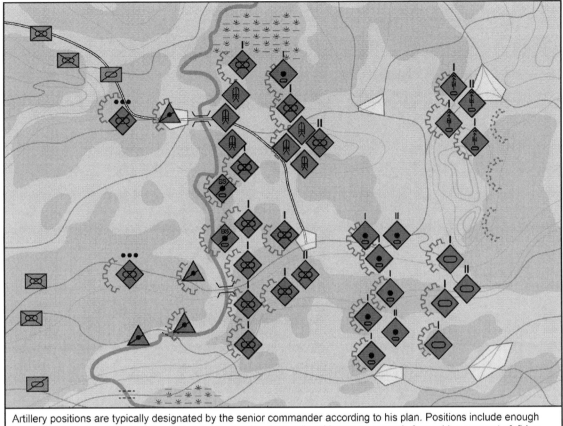

Artillery positions are typically designated by the senior commander according to his plan. Positions include enough area to allow gun and battery dispersion (up to 4km2) . Generally, with access to roads for rapid movement of firing units, supplies, and materials.

BS   battlefield surveillance

Figure 5-12. Artillery units and subunits in a positional defense

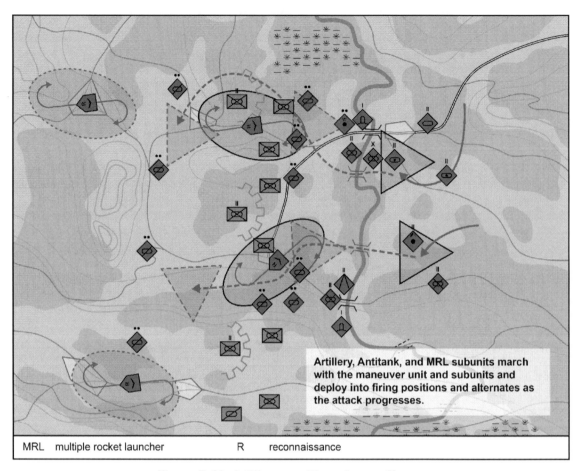

Figure 5-13. Artillery positions in an offense

5-59. Artillery conducts fires from positions that are "open" or "closed" based on the commander's plan. An "open" position is a firing point that is not hidden from ground surveillance and a "closed" position is a firing point that is hidden or not observed from ground level while firing. Battery firing positions include gun emplacements, ammunition bunkers or holding areas, command vehicle placement to direct fires, personnel shelters and defensive positions, reloading site for rocket artillery, and meteorological support.

Note: Open firing positions are hasty and don't offer the firing unit protection from observation once it begins an engagement. Closed firing positions are more deliberate with protection from observation; allow large adjustments for fire missions, and the capability to conduct direct fire against aggressor units and subunits.

5-60. When planning and emplacing fire positions the SV senior commander designates two or three positions for each battery. These firing positions allow for displacement after firing to avoid hits from aggressor counter-battery fires. The positions have a minimum of 300m separation between them. These positions receive priority for emplacement to establish readiness to strike any aggressor force.

5-61. The commander also designates duty guns that cover the most likely sector of an aggressor attack. The tasks of the duty gun are to observe the designated sector, identify and destroy newly identified aggressor fire weapons that impede the advance, and if necessary, replace disabled guns. In addition, as part of the deception plan, the SV prepares decoy fire direction posts as well as firing positions. Roving gun positions are another technique used as part of the deception. A gun will fire 1–2 rounds and then move to be replaced by a dummy gun in the position.

5-62. Commanders prefer maneuver of fire over actual maneuver of units or subunits. As a battle unfolds the artillery groupings formed according to the senior commander's plan change to reflect the fluid nature of the battle and to employ the strengths of the artillery units and subunits to engage aggressor targets. Artillery groups established for the defense normally remain intact until the counterattack or launch of the offense.

5-63. In a march formation, when a meeting battle is not anticipated, the artillery battalions or groups are integrated into the column based on the commander's plan. In some instances when the aggressor threat is low or multiple routes are necessary to accomplish a rapid advance the artillery may march in a separate column. When contact with the aggressor is expected and the march column will deploy into pre-battle formation, the artillery will be positioned between the advance guard at the head of the main body. Anti-tank subunits will be at the head of the artillery march formation to support long-range engagements of aggressor tank and mechanized targets.

5-64. Groups formed for the offense are often dissolved or reorganized when the supported maneuver units enter the exploitation or pursuit phase. The centralization of logistics support makes substantial regroupings relatively quick and easy.

5-65. Higher headquarters forms or dissolves DAGs and BrAGs in accordance with plans and the tempo of operations. The DAGs or BrAGs are considered artillery groups if they retain one or more organic artillery battalions. When higher headquarters dissolves these groups, army groups and army assets may revert to centralized control. Thus, they can provide long-range reinforcement for divisional or brigade artillery. The SV's ability to organize and reorganize artillery forces and means facilitates the execution of RSCs and RFCs.

5-66. At the tactical level, the SV focuses on the indirect fire units and subunits that set the conditions to allow maneuver forces to complete the destruction or defeat of aggressor forces. Motorized rifle brigades organically possess two self-propelled artillery battalions and one MRL battalion. The SV also considers anti-tank units and subunits as part of its artillery so as an example, a battalion equipped with the AT-14 Kornet is included with the motorized rifle artillery.

5-67. The SP artillery battalions typically field 18x 2S19 or 18x 2S3 152mm howitzers and the MRL battalion 18x BM-21 launchers. The SV is in the process of improving its range to cover dispersed units and for effective counter-battery fire by fielding the 2S35 SP 152mm howitzer. Reports are that the 2S35 has an extended maximum range of 70 km or more using rocket-assisted projectiles. It also reportedly has a range of 40 km with standard rounds. The size of artillery battalions and number of artillery pieces continue to fluctuate as the SV experiments with different unit configurations to accomplish long-range VTO fires. Some self-propelled artillery battalions may include as many as 24 systems while mortar batteries may have 6, 8, or 9 systems.

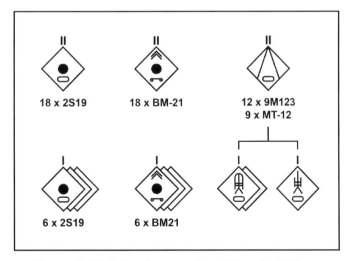

Figure 5-14. Brigade organic artillery battalions

5-68. Division artillery regiments consist of 3-4 battalions. See figure 5-15.

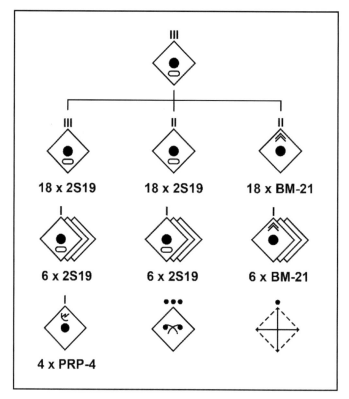

Figure 5-15. Division self-propelled artillery regiment

5-69. Army artillery groups task organize to support tactical units with long range fires. See figure 5-16, and figures 5-17 and 5-18 on page 5-25.

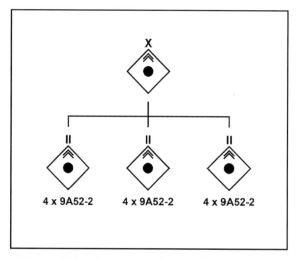

Figure 5-16. Army reactive artillery brigade

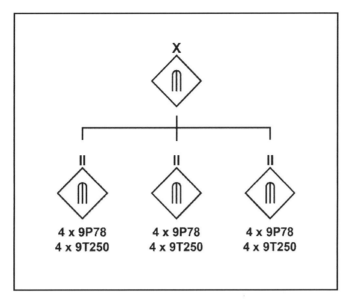

Figure 5-17. Army surface-to-surface missile brigade

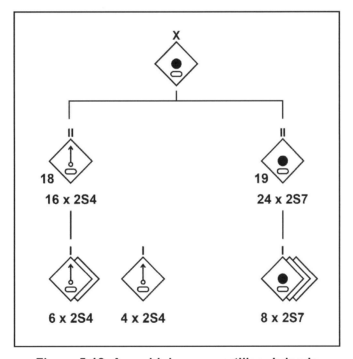

Figure 5-18. Army high power artillery brigade

5-70. AAG also task organize and may conduct fires to facilitate tactical support missions using long-range multiple rocket launcher (MRL) systems. Indications are that the SV also employs high-power indirect fire systems such as the 203mm 2S7 Pion with a 37.5 km range or the 240mm 2S4 Tyulpan with a 9.6 km range for high-value targets and to support urban combat. The Army commander retains the 9K720 Iskander (SS-26 Stone) as a reserve for priority strikes.

ANTITANK FIRES

5-71. Antitank units and subunits are a significant force within the motorized brigade or regimental structure. Antitank fires in the SV brigade consist of those from tanks, IFVs, mines, grenade launchers and antitank guided missiles (ATGMs). Density of ATGMs on a brigade frontage of 10km will include 4–5 in a tank brigade from allocated forces and 9–10 in a motorized brigade. Battalions based on BTRs and MT-LBs typically include an antitank platoon. Motorized rifle brigades have an organic antitank battalion, and that battalion commander normally commands any antitank reserve formed to support the commander's plan.

5-72. Tanks and antitank units and subunits are typically located behind the first echelon or second echelon motorized rifle battalions. These units and subunits orient on the most likely axis of aggressor tank advance and set fire sacks to destroy any penetration of the defense. In the offense the same generally holds true with the motorized rifle battalions attacking the aggressor defensive lines where the antitank subunits concentrate on engaging aggressor tanks, fighting vehicles, and armored personnel carriers. Training after-action assessments calculate that during an attack 70% of the antitank units and subunits engage tanks and 30% other armored carriers. If required, antitank fires may be used to destroy or breach aggressor bunkers or fortifications.

COMMAND AND CONTROL

5-73. The senior SV commander conducts forces and means calculations using established norms as is performed during all other planning and combat management. Once the antitank platoon commander receives their mission tasks to support the commander's plan, they develop the commander's map card to include the following information:

- Information about the aggressor and the most tank-threatened direction.
- Primary and alternate command post locations.
- Battery (platoon) positions, boundaries, primary and secondary fire lanes.
- Engagement lines.
- Route and order of march.
- If dismounting from carriers their support location.
- Signals and communication.

5-74. During offensive actions the commander determines the location of the AT units and subunits in the march column based on the final position when the column deploys to combat order. Based on reconnaissance information the commander determines the timing of deployment from march column, unit and subunit boundaries, initial positions, resulting zones of fire, and alternate positions.

5-75. AT fires integrate with other firing complexes and interlock with other AT units and subunits. AT units deploy command (командно-наблюдательный пункт - KNP) and observation posts (наблюдательный пункт - NP) on the possible breakthrough routes of aggressor tanks and mechanized infantry forces of in positions offering the best long-range observation. The observation posts conduct reconnaissance of aggressor activity directly in front or flanks of the combined-arms units and within visual range of firing complexes as shown in Figure 5-19 on page 5-27. Communications with the COP and firing complexes is maintained using automated command and control networks, radio, wire, flares, flags, or lights.

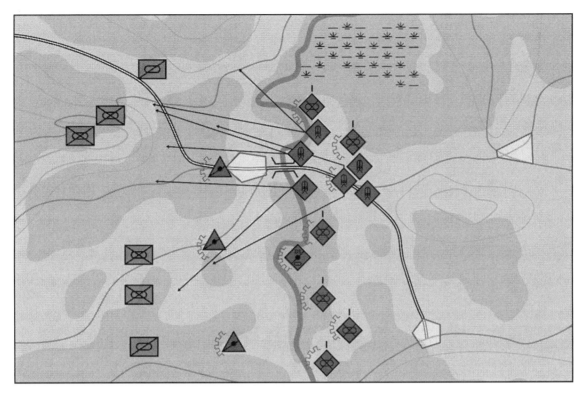

Figure 5-19. AT scheme of fire

METHODS

5-76. Based on the higher commander's plan, the brigade commander allocates forces and means to strike the aggressor in an integrated and synchronized manner. All decisions are prepared and maintained graphically using the commander's map. During defensive actions, the AT units and subunits operate using a fire ambush technique that uses terrain and emplaced obstacles to channel aggressor forces into a fire sack. The commander positions a battery or platoons in advantageous firing sites on the routes of the greatest tank and mechanized threats. Minefields, barriers, and flamethrower units aid in establishing fire sacks supporting the fire ambush. The commander locates AT complexes in carefully camouflaged positions on—

- The reverse slope of hills or highpoints.
- Terrain controlling routes through defiles.
- The periphery of urban areas hidden in structures.
- The edge of forests at a minimum distance of 30–50m from roads or gaps.
- Positions that avoid power lines, gas, and oil pipelines.

5-77. Antitank guided missile (ATGM) batteries conduct the following battle tasks:

- During armed conflicts and local war actions:
  - Cover the deployment of units and subunits into battle.
  - Engage counterattacks of aggressor tanks and armored vehicles.
  - Cover the deployment of the combined-arms reserve.
  - Cover open flanks.
  - Participate in the consolidation of captured lines.
- During the defense:
  - Engage and destroy aggressor tanks and other armored vehicles that penetrate the defense.
  - Cover gaps created by massive fire strikes.
  - Cover gaps between defending units and subunits as well as open flanks.

- Cover the advance of the second echelon units to the firing line and support the counterattack.
- Engage and destroy aggressor airborne or air assault units as well as illegal armed formations.
- Cover the withdrawal and regrouping of combined-arms units.
- During the offense:
    - Cover the deployment of units and subunits from march formation.
    - Cover the regrouping of units and subunits.
    - Engage counterattacks by aggressor tanks and armored vehicles.
    - Cover the deployment of the combined-arms reserve from the second echelon.
    - Cover the consolidation of captured lines.
    - Cover open flanks.
    - Engage and defeat or destroy aggressor air assaults or airborne landings.
    - Engage as tasked to destroy aggressor weapons, specifically focusing on antitank and armored equipment, at the forward edge of attacking units and subunits.

ORGANIZATION

5-78. Motorized rifle brigades have four battalions of artillery with one of those being the AT battalion. The AT battalion has three subunit batteries: one battery of six each MT-12 AT guns and two batteries of ATGMs. The ATGM batteries are composed of either six each AT-15 Springer (9M123 Chrysanthemum—Хризантем) or AT-14 Spriggan (9M133 Kornet—Корнет) man-portable launchers on a BMP-3 variant. The AT-15 has both radar and laser guidance capable of guiding two missiles at once. The AT-14 has laser targeting guidance and is also capable of launching and guiding two missiles simultaneously.

5-79. Munitions for the ATGM complexes include standard and dual-tandem high explosive antitank types used to target tanks and armored carriers as well as thermobaric used against fortifications, buildings, or entrenchments. The battery of antitank guns is equipped with the MT-12, 100mm smoothbore typically towed by an MT-LB tractor and operated by a crew of six. The MT-12 has a basic load of ten armor piercing fin stabilized discarding sabot, four high explosive-fragmentation, and six high explosive antitank rounds of ammunition.

5-80. The AT battalion of the motorized rifle brigade can serve in several roles in addition to its main function to provide fires that engage and destroy aggressor tanks and armored equipment. It may be allocated to support the battalions forming BTGs. It may also serve as a subunit of an antitank reserve or be designated as the anti-tank reserve.

5-81. The battalion commander receives taskings from the senior artillery commander and remains in command of the battalion whether assigned or attached to a motorized unit. The battalion commander reports to the maneuver battalion commander to receive fire tasks and priorities, order of march instruction, and communication procedures. The maneuver commander conducts close and constant interaction with the AT unit to integrate its fire capabilities with those of supporting aviation, artillery, and direct fire from maneuver subunits.

RADIO ELECTROMAGNETIC BATTLE

5-82. The use of electromagnetic warfare has historically been a key support capability of Russian forces. Since its first use to support Russia's defense of Port Arthur during the Russo-Japanese War in 1904 until the present day, electromagnetic warfare has been an essential combat multiplier of Russia's combat power. With its historical basis in Russian military actions, electromagnetic warfare continues to be the leading element of IV along with cyber and psychological warfare actions. Electromagnetic warfare capabilities continue to be an element of Russia's development and expansion of integrated and automated C2 complexes. The advent of network-centric warfare has only served to increase Russia's expansion and emphasis on its integration as a strike action.

5-83. As part of the strike package, the SV employs REB complexes in the same manner as indirect, rotary or fixed-wing aviation fires to counter aggressor capabilities. Recognizing that information management is a key element of successful battlefield operations, the SV uses REB to degrade, disrupt, and destroy the information network of an aggressor to accomplish disorganization (дезорганизация - C2D). Disorganization or C2D targets aggressor electromagnetic assets to disable, maintain technical control over electromagnetic countermeasures, counters reconnaissance technical assets, degrades precision weapons and electromagnetic systems, and disrupts command, control, and coordination of forces. By using C2D the SV actively protects networks and complexes to maintain stability and control of friendly forces.

5-84. REB identifies and monitors the emanations of electromagnetic objects and collects, analyzes, and defines priority targets. The SV uses REB actions through electromagnetic suppression of aggressor control complexes, weapons, reconnaissance, and electromagnetic warfare complexes. The SV uses units and subunits specifically organized for electromagnetic emissions monitoring and control (kompleksny tekhnicheskii kontrol (KTK) of its own command and control, equipment, and reconnaissance (razvedka) complexes.

5-85. As part of the battle plan, the commander directs REB actions at a specific time and place to strike the aggressor force in conjunction with the other integrated fires systems. REB subunits are closely integrated with other battlefield systems, reconnaissance, artillery, air defense, and aerospace. The REB officer at brigade level assesses the EMS situation and develops the REB plan to support the commander's plan. A C2D element is included in SV plans down to the brigade level.

5-86. The SV employs REB platforms that include satellites, fixed-wing, rotary-wing, UAVs, and ground platforms. The capabilities of these systems include direction finding and ranging, GPS and C2 system jamming, emanation deception, and defeat of electromagnetic proximity fuzes.

5-87. As discussed in chapter 4, the SV categorizes REB into four areas: electromagnetic attack, electromagnetic protection, countermeasures against technical reconnaissance, and radio-electronic information support measures. Figure 5-20 on page 5-30 shows the actions specifically focused on electromagnetic attack. REB information in this chapter addresses electromagnetic fires, with electromagnetic protection, comprehensive technical control and radio-electronic information support addressed in Chapter 4 as part of reconnaissance and security.

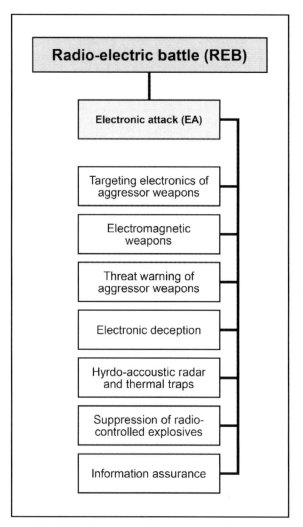

Figure 5-20. Electromagnetic attack action categories

5-88. Electromagnetic attack targets aggressor C2 networks and suppresses or neutralizes weapons systems. REB capabilities provide a rapid and effective means of targeting and disrupting aggressor electromagnetic systems. Electromagnetic attack uses means categorized as functional attack, electromagnetic countermeasures, anti-radiation missiles, and electromagnetic deception. A REB functional attack targets aggressor C2 and weapons systems to degrade capabilities or to damage components. Employing directed energy weapons such as lasers or radio-frequency weapons such as ultrahigh frequency microwave emitters, the REB subunits strike optical, infra-red guidance, network transmitters, and receivers to directly damage or degrade their operation.

5-89. The SV uses a series of REB platforms to cover the entire spectrum of aggressor electromagnetic communications and reconnaissance sensors. Each platform serves one primary function with secondary capabilities that overlap with other REB platforms. To conduct REB, the Russian military categorizes electromagnetic capabilities into those targeting ground, aviation, space, and terrorist operations. For tactical support this chapter concentrates on REB targeting of ground and aerial complexes:

- REB-N targeting ground combat systems.
- REB-S targeting aerial systems.
- REB-K targeting space systems.
- REB-Atd targeting terrorist electromagnetic capabilities.

COMMAND AND CONTROL

5-90. The capabilities of tactical level electromagnetic warfare complexes are integrated using a dedicated mobile command post such as the R-330K or R-330KPK. Continuing development of automated C2 is a priority for SV electromagnetic warfare complexes. The central C2 complex at the electromagnetic warfare brigade level for modernized units is the RB-109A Bylina. The complex integrates the capabilities of subordinate platforms to enhance electromagnetic warfare information sharing and provides significantly improved situational awareness of the electromagnetic zone of operations. This enhanced capability will allow the SV to generate an improved electromagnetic maskirovka that creates a false electromagnetic picture and provides an aggressor with false targets.

5-91. Russian analysis of recent conflicts leads it to the understanding that current and future wars are dependent on information and information operations. This understanding translates to a continuing emphasis on new equipment, integration of capabilities, and development of new forms of REB. The diversity and complexity of Russian REB is reflected by a constantly growing list of complexes that conduct ever more wide-ranging electromagnetic warfare. Unlike the ROK [reconnaissance-strike] and RUK [fires] complexes linked for indirect fires the REB conducts its own reconnaissance, analysis, targeting, and fire to perform electromagnetic attacks.

5-92. Like indirect fire the REB forms networks to conduct electromagnetic attacks at strategic-operational and operational-tactical levels. At the strategic-operational level the radio-electromagnetic strike complex (known as REUK) integrates and coordinates REB actions. At the operational-tactical level the radio-electromagnetic fires complex (known as REOK) engages aggressor information networks.

RADIO-ELECTROMAGNET BATTLE METHODS

5-93. Electromagnetic attack encompasses the measures and operations of REB units and subunits to degrade and disrupt aggressor C2 and reconnaissance capabilities. REB targets command-and-control systems, arms and military equipment by means of fire (self-guided weapons), functional (electromagnetic weaponry), and informational (active and passive electromagnetic jamming) destruction, as well as altering the conditions for the broadcast (reflection) of electromagnetic waves (electromagnetic maskirovka [camouflage, concealment and deception]).

5-94. Just like other SV combat complexes the REB units and subunits provide successive layers of coverage to target the aggressor and protect friendly forces. To disrupt or destroy communication capability of the aggressor units and subunits at the point of contact with SV forces, REB deploys its complexes within 1–3 km of the line of contact. These units and subunits conduct interception and direction finding of C2, communications, and radars. At the next level, approximately 15–30 km from the line of contact, REB units deploy complexes that target ground-based emitters using high frequency (HF), very high frequency (VHF), and ultrahigh frequency (UHF) GSM cell towers, and 3G and 4G networks. REB unites can also target satellite transmissions. These complexes not only jam communications but also conduct intrusion into aggressor communications by introducing psychological warfare messages into aggressor networks.

5-95. In the SV brigades an organic REB company provides tactical-level electromagnetic warfare strike in support of the maneuver units and subunits. Several different electromagnetic warfare complexes provide a range of capabilities in support of brigade tactical actions. The various electromagnetic warfare functions are described below with the complexes used to support tactical actions.

Jamming

5-96. SV REB subunits at the tactical level contain capabilities for jamming of both REB-N and REB-K electromagnetic systems. The REB company organic to each motorized rifle and tank brigade employs jamming of GPS, radio networks, satellite links, and radars, to strike at aggressor command, control, communication, intelligence, surveillance, and reconnaissance systems. Tactical level jammers are listed in table 5-1 on page 5-32.

Table 5-1. Tactical-level REB complexes

REB Complex	Purpose
R-378B	HF Automated Jamming Station
R-330B	VHF Frequency Jammer linked to the Borisoglebsk-2 HF Automated Jamming System
R-330Zh	Automated Jammer against INMARSAT and IRIDIUM satellite communication systems, GSM, and GPS
R-SPR-2	VHF/UHF Radio Jammer cover and thereby protect troops in an area of up to 50 hectares for up to 6 hours
RP-377U	Portable Jammer (against IEDs)
R-934	Automated VHF-UHF aerial radio communication jamming complex provides automated detection, direction finding and signals intelligence of aerial radio sources. It also detects and jams VHF radiotelephone and mobile radio systems
RP-377L	IED Jammer
RP-377LA	Portable Automated Jammer
RP-377UV	Portable Automated Jammer

GSM	Global System for Mobile Communications	INMARSAT	International Maritime Satellite
GPS	Global Positioning System	IRIDIUM	satellite phone company
HF	high frequency	VHF	very high frequency
IED	Improvised explosive device	UHF	ultrahigh frequency

5-97. The SV can take advantage of the time prior to an aggressor attack to emplace expendable jammers (EXJAMs). These jammers can disrupt aggressor communications nets. When used in conjunction with terrain (such as at natural choke points, mountain passes, or valleys), they can achieve significant results despite their short range and low power. The SV can also use them to support a deception plan, without risking expensive vehicle-based systems. While limited in number, artillery delivered expendable jammers may be employed. These jammers are especially useful in those areas where support is not available from more powerful vehicle-mounted jammers.

Intercept

5-98. Signals reconnaissance or interception is action taken to detect, identify, locate, and track high-value targets using the EMS. It includes both intercept and direction finding, which may enable a near-real-time attack on the target. SV commanders determine the priorities for signals reconnaissance by determining which high-value targets must be found to have the best chance for success of their plan. If the collected intelligence value is of higher significance than the destruction of the target, the commander determines the best tactical action to accomplish their objective. He may decide either to destroy the target, to jam it, or to continue to exploit the collected information from the intercept. The REB units pass radio and radar intercepts to artillery units as targeting intelligence.

5-99. Other intercept actions involve detecting and retransmitting a modified signal to confuse or misdirect systems using that signal for navigation or targeting. The SV can employ low-cost GPS jammers to disrupt aggressor precision munitions targeting, sensor-to-shooter links, and navigation.

Interdiction

5-100. Proximity fuses used on some artillery projectiles rely on return of a radio signal reflected from the target to detonate the round within lethal range of the target. Proximity fuze jammers cause the round to explode at a safe distance. The SV can deploy such jammers to protect high-value assets that are within indirect fire range from aggressor artillery. This jamming complex is mounted on a tracked vehicle with a crew of two and integrates into the defense or march formation of a brigade or regiment. The crew emplaces the complex in 10 minutes and covers an area of .5 square kilometer.

Deception

5-101. The SV integrates deception actions into all plans including IV actions to conduct active deception. The SV employs all forms of deception, ranging from physical decoys and electromagnetic devices to tactical activities and behaviors. The key to all types of deception activities is that they must be both realistic and fit the deception story.

5-102. Due to the sophistication and variety of sensors available to the aggressor, successfully deceiving an aggressor requires a multispectral effort. To accomplish effective deception the SV creates false or misleading thermal, visual, acoustic, and electromagnetic signatures. Nonlethal means used by the SV may include the deployment of corner reflectors, protective countermeasures, and deception jammers.

5-103. Deception actions also involve manipulation of aggressor perceptions of the battlefield. The SV uses penetration of aggressor electromagnetic networks to insert false data or psychological messages to mislead or deceive aggressor decisionmakers. Psychological messages may also target tactical-level leaders and soldiers to create uncertainty, mistrust, and fear.

ORGANIZATION

5-104. The reorganization of the SV resulted in significant increases for electromagnetic warfare capabilities. The new formations included a REB brigade of four battalions for each of the military districts organized as shown in figure 5-21. These REB brigades maintain the most modern and powerful electromagnetic warfare complexes that provide integrated area coverage as well as support for maneuver actions. They support each district with REB capabilities from the strategic to tactical levels. REB units support the SV with both offensive and defensive electromagnetic warfare capabilities. They provide not only jamming of aggressor communication networks but also direction finding, ranging, and monitoring of radio communications. Based on the front or army commander's plan REB brigades are allocated as units or subunits to support maneuver brigades in addition to the organic REB company within each maneuver brigade.

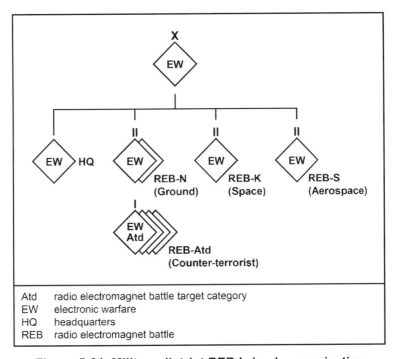

Figure 5-21. Military district REB brigade organization

5-105. In addition to the REB brigades, a separate REB battalion is included in the organization of each of the 12 CAAs and a separate REB company was added to each maneuver brigade. The separate REB battalions support operational-tactical level actions for the CAAs.

5-106.   Maneuver brigades and regiments also use REB command and integration complexes such as the Baikal-1ME to maintain situational awareness of the electromagnetic operational environment. In addition to the separate REB battalions, each motorized rifle and tank brigade has an organic REB company. This subunit provides area coverage of up to 50 km for brigade actions. The structure and functions of the company are shown in figure 5-22.

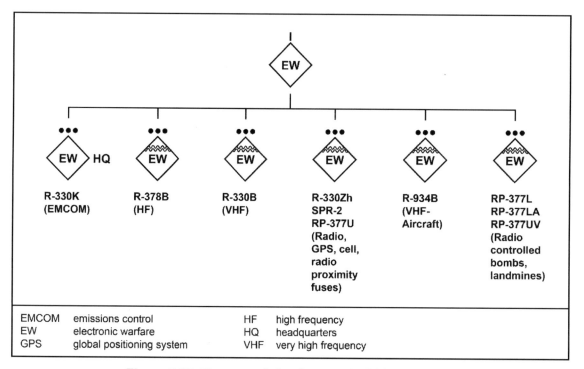

Figure 5-22. Maneuver brigade organic REB company

5-107.   The REB company subunits integrate into the maneuver formation of the brigade as shown in an example for an offensive action in figure 5-23.

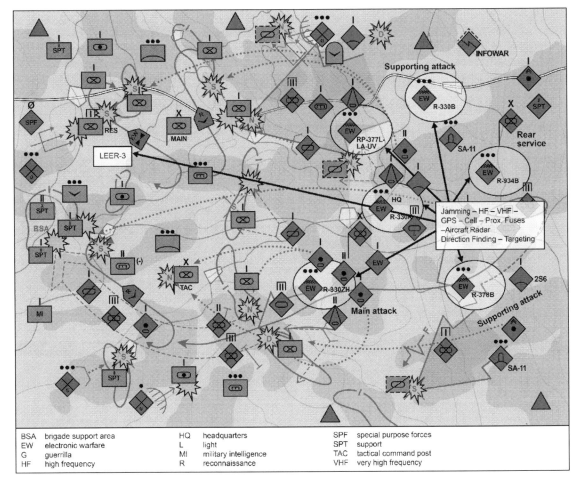

Figure 5-23. REB platforms in MRB/TB maneuver formation

BSA	brigade support area	HQ	headquarters	SPF	special purpose forces
EW	electronic warfare	L	light	SPT	support
G	guerrilla	MI	military intelligence	TAC	tactical command post
HF	high frequency	R	reconnaissance	VHF	very high frequency

AEROSPACE SUPPORT

5-108.   Russia reorganized its aerospace forces in 2015 to combine the Space, Air Force, Aerospace Defense and Air Defense forces into one branch, Aerospace Force (Vozduzhno-kosmicheskiesily - VKS). The VKS main missions are air-space control to degrade aggressor capabilities and intelligence collection focused on threats. The current organization used to support the SV are Air Force and Air Defense Armies with one for each of the military districts.

5-109.   The VKS is composed of three components that support the SV with reconnaissance, air defense, and strikes:

- Military air forces (Voyenno-Vozdushnye Sily - Военно-Воздушные Силы - VVS)
  - Frontal aviation (Фронтовая Авиация - Frontovaya Aviatsiya -FA)
  - Army aviation (Aviatsiya Sukhoputnykh Voysk - Авиация Сухопутных Войск - ASV)
  - Transportation aviation forces (Voyenno-Transportnaya Aviatsiya - Военно-Транспортная Авиация - VTA)
- Air and missile defense forces (Voiska Protivivozdushnoi Oborony - Войска Противывоздушной Оборону – known as VPVO)
- Space Forces (Космические войска - Kosmicheskiye voyska - KV)

5-110.   The VVS coordinates closely with the air defense forces to defeat aggressor air attacks on the SV. Both provide early warning to SV of any aggressor air attacks entering a particular zone of operations.

COMMAND AND CONTROL

5-111.   The aviation regiment commander manages the unit and subunits with the support of their deputies for flight, training, engineering and aviation services, and chiefs of services. Under the direction of the commander, the headquarters performs actions to maintain combat readiness of all aerospace complexes, constantly evaluate the aggressor, track the status of support subunits, communications, and center for flight operation.

5-112.   Air missions supporting SV actions remain under the command of the aviation regiment but rely on integrated planning and close coordination to effectively support the SV during local wars and armed conflicts, defensive, and offensive actions. Frontline aviation fighter-bombers, army aviation helicopters, and UAVs coordinate actions using common radio complexes using shared frequencies.

5-113.   Planning for supporting ASV strikes is integrated by the Joint Strategic Commands (OSK) that subsequently passes instruction down through the army to division or brigade command level. These preplanned strikes occur at a designated time and place to support the senior commander's plan. Targets that develop during a defensive or offensive action are directed by SV or ASV ground forward air controllers (FACs). Designated aircraft from airborne alert areas attack first and as necessary alert aircraft on 5 - 15-minute standby provide on-call strikes.

5-114.   Maneuver brigades and battalions receive FAC support to direct strikes by both fixed and rotary-wing aircraft. Using integrated automatic command and control communication complexes the ground FAC has good situational awareness, clearly understands the maneuver commanders support requirements, and applies aviation strikes to the best advantage possible. The FAC corrects the targeting trajectory of the attack aircraft until the flight leader detects the designated aggressor target.

METHODS OF FIRE

5-115.   The battle order of VKS aerospace units is determined by the tasked mission and the OE conditions. The mission tasks for ASV units are shown in figure 5-24.

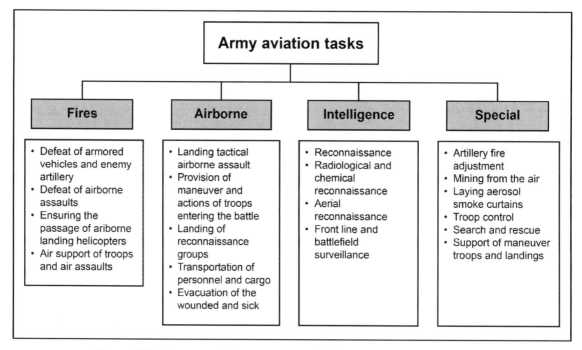

Figure 5-24. Army aviation support of SV maneuver force actions

5-116.   The unit forms into the following groups:
- Main. Performs the primary task of a mission whether it is to strike the main aggressor targets, engage and destroy opposing air forces, landing air assault units, or delivering materiel.

- Support. Performs tasks to support the successful completion of the main groups mission. There are several categories within the support group:
  - Reconnaissance. Collects battlefield information to clarify the situation by identifying aggressor target locations, direction, and speed of movement, identifying mission reference points, and location of aggressor air defense. The Russian military and the SV are rapidly developing and deploying UASs to increase the reconnaissance capabilities provided by these complexes.
  - Search and designation. Performs target illumination during limited visibility conditions.
  - Guidance. Determines the optimal flight path to and from targets or landing zones including the flight conditions along the routes.
  - Electromagnetic warfare. Suppresses active and passive aggressor systems that may detect the main group using either electromagnetic attack or direct surface-to-surface or air-to-air missiles.
  - Anti-aircraft missile strike.
  - Covering.
  - Landing support.
  - Search and rescue.
  - Reserve.

5-117. The basic Russian helicopter formation consists of a pair of aircraft with one aircraft acting as flight lead. The type of spacing used by the flight lead will likely dictate the horizontal and vertical spacing between each aircraft in the flight. Additions to the flight will often consist of another pair of aircraft; however, singles can be added as well. By making additions in pairs, VKS groups can divide the flight into smaller formations while still providing mutual support between aircraft within each pair.

5-118. Options for rotary-wing flight formations may include any combination of the following considerations: control of the formation, formation profile, maneuverability, spacing (between aircraft and above the ground), weapon employment, ground threats, air threats, mission, other factors of combat. These factors determine different spacing options (closed/concentrated, open/dispersed, scattered) and formation options (column/trail, wedge, abreast, echelon, etc.). These options allow the flight lead to maneuver their flight in a manner best suited to the threat and mission.

5-119. Closed/concentrated: Aircraft spacing is close for greater control of the flight and presents a smaller target profile. Concentrated spacing limits overall maneuverability and the flight's ability to quickly react to threats. This type of spacing is more suitable for admin flights consisting of small number of aircraft.

5-120. Open/dispersed: This type of spacing spreads out the flight, providing greater horizontal distance between aircraft. Flights using dispersed spacing, can move more freely and provide greater focus on elements external to the flight. The flight lead maintains visual contact for added control, while aircraft are allowed to maneuver more independently to accommodate for terrain, and threats. This type of spacing is more useful for tactical flights.

5-121. Scattered: This spacing allows for flight separation beyond visual range and can accommodate multiple missions. Increased dispersion between aircraft or formations of aircraft help to mitigate threats; however, control/coordination and mutual support between aircraft or formations is limited.

5-122. The nature of formation flight also depends on the flight mode, which is defined by relative altitude and is a function of the threat environment. Flight safety considerations alone would generally lead to higher flight altitudes, but against an enemy that can defend their airspace rotary-wing aircraft are pushed to toward lower altitudes to mitigate against air defense threats. The low altitude modes of flight can be broken up into three groups: high, low, and extremely low and can be equated to the U.S. terms: low level, contour, and map-of-the-earth (MOE). The general distinctions between these flight modes are that low level flight maintains a constant altitude that provides clearance of terrain and obstacles, contour flight follows the general contour of the terrain, and NOE is flown in very close proximity to the ground. See figure 5-25 on page 5-38.

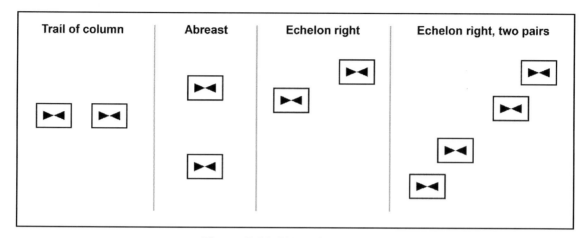

Figure 5-25. Flight formations

5-123. The formations chosen for the flight are selected based on their suitability for each task or phase of the mission. Among these considerations are how best to maneuver the flight to the objective area based on the threat and terrain, and once in the objective area, determine what attack profile to use based on the target and type of weapon systems possessed by the flight. The formations shown in figure 5-25 are examples of formations that can be employed by the flight lead to accomplish a particular task. Trail/column formations can be used to provide sustained fire on a target as preceding aircraft pull off or are used by fights moving through constrictive terrain. Conversely, aircraft in a flight can be brought abreast to maximize fires while simultaneously engaging a target. Other formations might be used tactically to provide mutual support both for the flight as a whole and within each pair, like what is depicted in the echelon right with 2 pairs.

5-124. Formations strike aggressor targets using one of five flight types shown in figure 5-26.

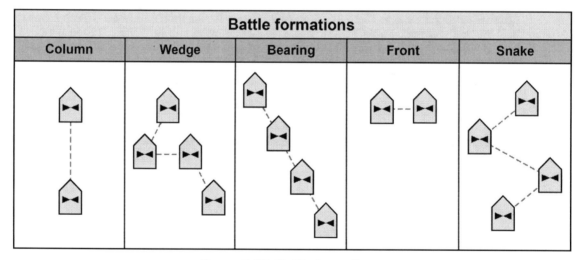

Figure 5-26. Battle formations

5-125. Both fixed and rotary wing aircraft have the capability to use air-to-ground guided missiles, unguided rockets, air-to-air missiles, free fall bombs, and cannon fire. Fixed wing front-line bombers also can employ homing missiles, adjustable bombs, cluster bombs, incendiary tanks, chemical munitions, and nuclear bombs. Typical safe distances from SV ground forces are 1,000 m for free-flight rockets, 500 m for helicopter cannon, and 300 m for helicopter machine guns.

5-126. To help de-conflict artillery and VKS fires, the aircraft normally engage from the flanks of the supported ground formation or in gaps between forces as shown in figure 5-27. The SV may create designated flight corridors through ground formations by directing ground air defense complexes to place their weapons on hold or weapons tight. Fixed and rotary wing strikes can occur simultaneously by designating separate engagement boxes that segment the aggressor target unit.

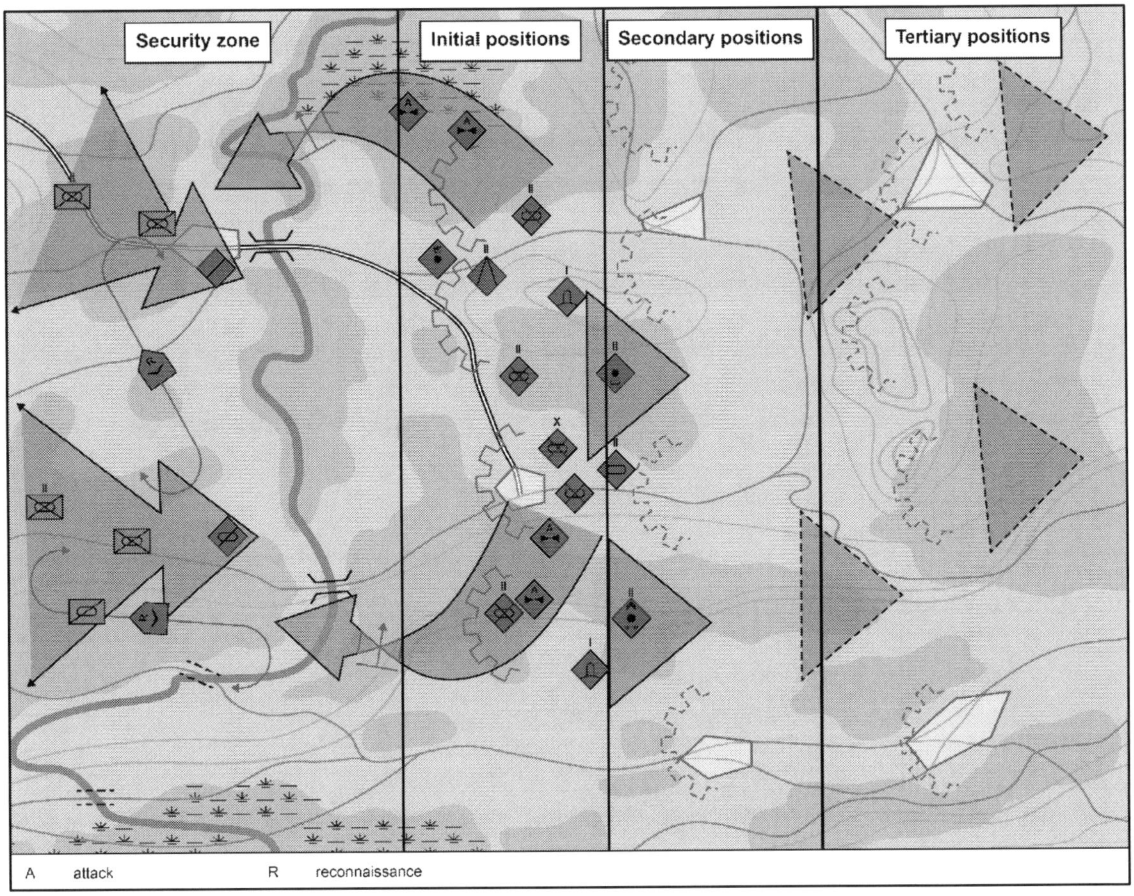

Figure 5-27. Aviation ground attack

Fixed Wing

5-127.   Frontline aviation provides fixed wing support to SV maneuver forces. During combat actions fighters will disrupt aggressor command and control, engage, and destroy their aircraft or nuclear delivery complexes, and support SV ground maneuver. Attack aviation strikes are planned at the Army level and conducted to support high-speed attacks, air assaults, and against aggressor forces beyond the range of artillery.

5-128.   On-call strikes against aggressor units discovered during an attack or defense are initiated by the embedded FAC. If there are aircraft flying in loitering areas, they may be called on to engage the general area of the target. It is more likely these attacks will be conducted by squadrons from designated airfields, either established or tactical, by immediate readiness flights capable of launching in 5 to 15 minutes. In many cases, fixed-wing aviation will not be available so the mission will be performed by on-call ASV units.

Rotary Wing

5-129.   Army aviation are the aerospace forces and means employed by commanders of military districts, combined-arms armies, and divisions (corps) to support SV ground actions. The ASV rotary-wing units and subunits conduct combat actions in coordination with SV ground maneuver units; motorized rifle, tank, airborne as well as VVS. In support of the SV the ASV is assigned fire, combat, and engineering service and logistics tasks. The main firing tasks include attacking aggressor units, airborne incursions, raiding forces, advance reconnaissance forces, bypassed detachments, landing of friendly air assault units and subunits, as well as logistics support. Combat tasks involve fires against aggressor helicopters and close support fixed-wing aviation, nuclear delivery complexes, tanks and armored vehicles, command and control complexes, communications, and supporting infrastructure.

5-130.   Army aviation units and subunits support SV ground actions by conducting; fires, airborne support, reconnaissance, and special support actions. The primary targets of ASV units against aggressor forces are tanks, IFVs, armored personnel carriers, self-propelled guns, artillery, strong points, air assaults, and low-altitude fixed-wing and helicopters that are airborne and on the ground.

5-131.   To destroy aggressor air assault incursions or attacking helicopters the ASV will overfly the SV positions or formations. This complicates the control of ground air defense complexes to avoid fratricide. The supporting fires are categorized as follows:

- Containing. Primarily targeting aggressor forces on the main avenue of attack.
- Maneuver. Fires in support of ground forces in succeeding lines of attack or defense.
- Raid. Deep fires to support ground forces that penetrate the aggressor defense and advance into the depths of the defense.
- Flank. Fires to provide security of the main body and suppression of aggressor attempts to flank the SV.

5-132.   The main methods of rotary-wing fire missions are—

- Simultaneous attack.
- Successive strikes.
- Attacks by pairs.
- On call from a loitering area.
- Independent search and destruction.

Unmanned

5-133.   While the majority of UAS are found in the SV not the VKS, there are development efforts underway to expand UAV capabilities into all Russian military forces. As with ground fire complexes, UAVs in the SV are using established platforms to perform several different functions, reconnaissance, targeting, REB, and direct strikes. The UASs used to support tactical level actions are typically robust and easily transported. They launch either by catapult or by hand and are recovered by parachute or balloon. The VKS UAS on the other hand require an airfield for launch and recovery.

5-134.   Tactical support UAS tie into the ASU of the maneuver and artillery units and subunits. Using this link, they can provide real-time battlefield information to ASU equipped combat vehicles. They are capable of not only communications retransmission over encrypted links but also of forming a common network between multiple platforms.

5-135.   The Russian military continues to study and develop the capability of direct ground attack UAS. These complexes are anticipated to be a stealthy design with the capability to conduct strikes using preprogrammed or ground station-controlled attacks against fixed or stationary targets. Initially these complexes will likely attack high-value targets such as C2, communications, precision weapons, and nuclear capable complexes.

ORGANIZATION

5-136.   Aerospace forces in the VKS are organized into aviation regiments as the primary administrative and tactical structure. These regiments have several subordinate aviation squadrons and an engineering services squadron. The units of the squadrons, 2–3 in number, are detachments with 3–4 aircraft in each. Regiments are located on permanent airfields when there is no conflict, but during hostilities they may operate from temporary airfields using prepared dirt runways and temporary structures. The aircraft of the VKS are designed to conduct actions using the austere support infrastructure found in temporary fields. Temporary fields are selected based on expected requirements for combat support, aircraft range, concealment, day and night operations, and expected axis of attack by the aggressor.

5-137. Aviation support for the SV comes from fixed bases that consolidate all fixed and rotary wing squadrons. A VVS base typically has 2–3 squadrons with 2–3 subordinate units per squadron. The aviation units have 3–4 aircraft with a subordinate detachment of 1–2 aircraft as the smallest formation depending on tasked missions. During heightened readiness in the initial period of conflict the bases continue operations but deploy aviation units to forward temporary airfields near the supported SV units.

5-138. Front-line bombers are the main strike unit that supports the SV's ground maneuver actions. It delivers attacks against aggressor units, facilities, and infrastructure at a depth of 250-400 km from the front-line of the action. The front-line bombers priority targets are as follows:

- Weapons of mass destruction and support vehicles (this includes precision strike artillery)
- Aggressor reserves
- Command and control complexes and facilities
- Air-land aggressor units
- Maneuver control and coordination points

5-139. During competition prior to large-scale combat operations, the army aviation units are part of the military district permanent airbase. They consist of the command and control, combat squadrons, and technical (TEC) squadron.

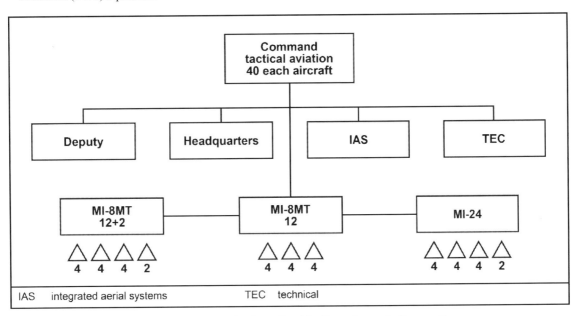

Figure 5-28. Typical tactical helicopter aviation unit

MISSILES AND ROCKETS

5-140. Surface-to-surface missiles and heavy rocket launch complexes are typically held at the Army level as a commander's special reserve and not allocated to subordinate forces. Russian military forces continue developing and demonstrating the ability to launch cruise and ballistic missiles to support ground actions. These complexes are typically very precise in their strike and are employed against high-value targets.

Note: This section largely describes defensive capabilities. Refer to Sections 5-1 through 5-9 for offensive nuclear, chemical, and biological capabilities.

NUCLEAR, CHEMICAL, AND BIOLOGICAL

5-141. Nuclear, chemical, and biological troops (Радиационные, Химические, Биологические войска - Radiatsionnyye, Khimicheskiye, Biologicheskiye voyska - RHBZ) are not solely defensive in nature, but also have very effective means to contribute to SV fires These units and subunits provide both the defensive nuclear, chemical, and biological capabilities as well as the offensive delivery of flame and smoke fires. The RHBZ units also possess the units and equipment complexes to deliver indirect fires with thermobaric munitions using TOS batteries and generate particulate smoke against designated targets. These units are distinct from the forces tasked with employing nonstrategic nuclear and chemical fires.

5-142.   Motorized rifle subunits have organic capability to add flame and smoke fires to direct combat engagements using generators built into tanks and armored personnel carriers as well as hand-held or direct-fire missiles. Each motorized rifle battalion has a platoon in the organic RHBZ company. The platoon delivers missile launched thermobaric, flame, and smoke fires to support the maneuver force. Integration and application of those fires is discussed in chapters 6 and 7.

COMMAND AND CONTROL

5-143.   Once allocated to the maneuver brigade, the TOS-1A battery provides direct support to senior commander. Reconnaissance information flows from the Orlon-10 UAV to the firing subunit over the Strelets automated C2 network. The TOS-1 Buratino Russian 220mm Heavy Flamethrower System is the original variant of the TOS family; it is equipped with a 30-tube rocket launcher and based on a T-72 main battle tank. It is designed to provide massed indirect and direct fire support. The TOS-1A Solntsepek Russian 220mm Heavy Flamethrower System is an improved version of the TOS-1. Its launch vehicle is designated BM-1 and is designed to perform the same missions as the original vehicle. However, it has an increased range because of longer rockets. The latest variant of the TOS complex is the TOS-2 based on a wheeled chassis with fully automated C2 and fire direction.

METHODS OF FIRE

5-144.   The main launch platform for thermobaric fires is the TOS-1 and TOS-1A configured as a multiple rocket launch (MRL) complex. This MRL complex is primarily used against area targets such as dug-in light infantry and vehicles. It is also used to destroy bunkers and against targets in urban buildings.

5-145.   Employment of the TOS-1/1A is as an allocated fire subunit to a tank brigade or TD conducting a penetration of defending aggressor. The firing batteries of the TOS-1/1A battalion move to the forward edge of the SV forces to launch a barrage against the planned point of attack. The 24-missile barrage uses thermobaric munitions to kill all aggressor personnel in a target area of 4 square km with flame and overpressure. The TOS 1/1A may be employed at breach sites. The tank units and subunits exploit the breach of the aggressor defense to penetrate and seize objectives or complete the destruction of the aggressor units.

ORGANIZATION

5-146.   The MRL fire complex typically consists of a battalion of eighteen launchers with three companies of six launchers. MRLs are organic to the RHBZ brigade in each military district. They are also found in the RHBZ regiments of the combined arms army. Each launcher is accompanied by two reloading vehicles that have the capability to reload the launcher in 24 minutes or less. A single TOS-1A firing complex consists of the combat launch vehicle, two transport-loading vehicles, and up to 72 unguided missiles.

LOGISTICS

5-147.   The required levels of materiel and technical support for tactical-level fires is defined during the commander's planning process. By allocating the type and source of fires for the operation, the commander defines the resulting requirements for supplies and maintenance necessary to accomplish the fire missions. Using nomograms that define the quantities or tonnage of ammunition, transport, and other services based on the type of fires selected dictates the logistics support required for initial and subsequent missions.

5-148.   These known quantities simplify the process for planning and supporting SV actions. Supply and resupply are push logistics based on the expenditure norms. Units receive initial ammunition allocations based on the planned volume and type of fire against a given target. Transport of resupply moves to the receiving unit based on the planned sequence of fires or as required to support the senior commander's plan. MTO units create ammunition caches at designated open or closed firing positions based on the commander's plan. This allows firing units to move to a firing point and have designated ammunition quantities on site and ready for use.

This page intentionally left blank.

Chapter 6

Defense

Over the course of the last two decades, the Ground Forces of the Russian Federation (Сухопутные войска Российской Федерации – sukhoputnyye voyska RF - SV) have emphasized defensive tactics. And, while SV units train in both positional and maneuver defense, recent SV doctrinal papers have emphasized the value of the maneuver defense over the positional defense. In all cases however, the SV considers the tactical counterattack as the ultimate method for destroying an aggressor on the battlefield. This chapter explains the theory and rational behind the SV's defensive objectives, as well as, how the SV design, arrange, and execute tactical defensive actions. Additionally, the tactical defensive requirements and characteristics for units are described in detail.

PURPOSE OF THE DEFENSE

6-1.   The SV is not the ground force of World War II or the Cold War, which involved massive armies and millions of soldiers in a linear, cohesive, side-by-side defense. Indeed, contemporary Russian military writers suggest that the future conventional battlefield under nuclear-threatened conditions and precision weapons will be fragmented. The SV will fight with open flanks protected by fires, counterattacks, strong points, difficult terrain, and obstacles. Battles in the security zone combined with maneuver defense will be common leading to a positional defense where the greatly weakened and disorganized aggressor will crash into a toughened and prepared defense.

GOALS OF THE DEFENSE

6-2.   The goals of the defense for the SV are—
- Repel attacks by superior aggressor forces.
- Produce maximum losses.
- Hold important areas, objects, and key terrain.
- Generate advantageous conditions for the conduct of an offensive.

REQUIREMENTS FOR THE DEFENSE

6-3.   According to SV tactical regulations, the defense must be both stable and active. Numerous Russian military academics deem stability and activeness as primary prerequisites for an effective defense. The defense must be able to defeat large aggressor attacks and protect key areas. The defense must also be able to annihilate any aggressor breakthrough of defensive positions. Notably, SV forces can assume the defense in or out of contact with the aggressor. SV defensive doctrine states that to achieve these requirements, the defense must include—
- Echeloned positions capable of defending against weapons of mass destruction, precision-guided munitions, and electromagnetic warfare.
- Antitank resources.
- Air defense resources.
- Anti-air assault capabilities.

ACHIEVING STABILITY IN THE DEFENSE

6-4. To achieve stability in the defense, SV ground units must be able to survive impacts of nuclear weapons and maintain a low exposure to aggressor precision weapons. To accomplish this, units must be dispersed, covered, concealed, and use resources to mask their positions from radar and thermal imaging devices. To maintain stability, SV ground units must also have the means to protect against precision munitions using electromagnetic warfare. Stability measures also include—

- Antitank capability to deter attacks by tanks and armored vehicles.
- Ability to defend against tactical and operational air strikes.
- Ability to resist airborne and air assault attacks and aggressor reconnaissance efforts as well as the capability to deter attempted sabotage.

ELEMENTS OF AN ACTIVE DEFENSE

6-5. An active defense must be capable of placing the aggressor under planned and integrated fires, and, as a rule, create adverse conditions for the aggressor to manage the battle. Active defensive measures also include extensive maneuver of systems and forces in the conduct of fires and assaults. A key attribute of the active defense is the ability to conduct decisive counterattacks. The active defense is achieved by thorough organization and adroit implementation of the means of nuclear and conventional fires to annihilate the aggressor. The active defense also includes—

- Judicious maneuver of forces and systems, which includes the use of planned, integrated fires and obstacles against a threatened axis of advance.
- Countering aggressor C2 systems, weapons, fixed wing, rotary wing, and UAVs.

ECHELONMENT OF FORCES

6-6. Russian tactical combat formations, units, and subunits are normally deployed in two echelons in both the offense and the defense. The first echelon in either offense or defense is a combined arms force often comprising as much as one-half to two-thirds of the brigade's or division's available combat power. In the positional defense, the first echelon occupies the main forward position and is responsible for stopping the aggressor's attack in front of or within this position. In a maneuver defense, the first echelon seeks to force the aggressor to deploy, disrupt the attack, and expose key elements and systems to counterattack.

6-7. The second echelon is assigned an explicit mission that distinguishes it from a reserve. The second echelon is also a combined arms force often representing one-third to one-half of available combat power. In a maneuver defense, the second echelon shields the repositioning of combat forces and reserve to provide a basis from which strikes and counterattacks are launched. In a positional defense, the second echelon's mission is to—

- Retain the depths of the defensive positions.
- Prohibit the aggressor from penetrating into the depths of the defense.
- Replace units and subunits from the first echelon who have lost combat effectiveness.

TYPES OF DEFENSE

6-8. The SV uses several different tactics during defensive operations, with their use informed by the principles discussed earlier in this chapter.

POSITIONAL DEFENSE

6-9. The positional defense is designed to exact the utmost losses on the aggressor by tenaciously holding prepared defensive positions. The positional defense is used to defend critical terrain and significant objectives considered too important to lose to the aggressor. An SV positional defense will be significantly echeloned by a system of defensive positions, lines, and areas and a prepared system of planned and integrated fires designed to defeat the aggressor. SV units may also adopt a brief positional defense, typically a nonfortified firing line. This temporary defense could be employed during a meeting battle or while moving within a defensive combat formation. Typically, the temporary positional defense is used to fend off aggressor counterattacks, hold key terrain, or to protect exposed flanks before shifting to offensive operations. SV manuals stipulate that a brigade's main defensive zone in a positional defense will be up to 15 km wide and up to 20 km deep. As always, though, the width and depth will be situationally dependent.

MANEUVER DEFENSE

6-10. When circumstances arise in which the aggressor has substantial advantage over SV forces, and when it is possible to trade maneuver space for time, the SV will use a maneuver defense. Maneuver defense is designed to win time, allow for the reorganizing of forces, and at the intended time, strike a critical blow on the attacking aggressor. In short, the maneuver defense is achieved by echeloned, sequential defensive actions planned, and culminating in a decisive blow against the aggressor forces. A brigade's main defensive front in a maneuver defense can be up to 20 km wide and up to 30 km in depth. However, the width and depth of the main defense will be situationally dependent.

DEFENSIVE BELT AND ZONE OF RESPONSIBILITY

6-11. If the brigade or division is part of an army or corps, it comprises a defensive belt (polosa oborony - *полоса обороны*). If, however, the brigade/division is working separately on a distinct axis of approach or in a separate armed conflict, the brigade/division establishes a zone of responsibility (zona otvetstvennosti - *зона ответственности*). The radius of reconnaissance systems, combined with flank and rear boundary lines dividing the brigade/division from other friendly units determines how a defensive belt or zone of responsibility are distributed. The design of the belt or zone is predicated on the tactical support of all combat subunits within the brigade/division, as well as the ability of the brigade/division to provide increasing resistance to advancing aggressor elements. The layout is also based on sufficient area for freedom of maneuver and dispersal of subunits. The following are characteristics of a motorized rifle or tank brigade/division in the defense:
* Brigade/division combat formation.
* A system of defensive positions, areas, and borders. (Integrated defensive positions).
* A system of fire destruction on the aggressor. (Fire sacks for destruction of the aggressor).
* Integrated air defense. (Tactical-Operational-Strategic).
* Integrated antitank defense.
* System of engineering obstacles. (Integrated obstacles).
* A system for combating airborne assault forces. (Integrated air assault/air drop defense).
* Management system. (Integrated command and control).

PREPARATION OF THE DEFENSE

6-12. Formulation of the defense starts when the SV senior commander issues their orders. These orders will include—
* Organization for combat.
* Decision making.
* Giving orders to subordinate units.
* Reconnaissance.
* Establishment of cooperation and establishment of an integrated system of fires as well as wide-ranging logistic and C2 support.
* Development of diagrams for the battalion's area of defense, to include company strong points.
* Planning to conduct combat missions.
* Creation of combat orders and system of fires.
* Engineering collaboration for the establishment of strong points.
* Organization and direction of morale and psychological effort.
* Functional work by the commander, deputies, and staff with subordinate subunits and other planning activities.

THE MOTORIZED RIFLE AND TANK DIVISION IN THE DEFENSE

6-13. Not long after the implementation of the "New Look" reforms, the SV began re-establishing division-sized formations. Senior SV officers have concluded that the division delivers increased firepower and can conduct combat missions on a broader front. In general, senior SV officers believe that antiterrorist operations are currently less important than possible peer-to-peer confrontations. While the brigade is well suited to conduct smaller scale type operations, senior leaders deem the division a superior formation for conducting large-scale war.

6-14. The division allows the synchronizing of combat power through the activities of multiple regiments and their supporting elements. Recent SV educational material related to the defense uses the brigade and regimental structure interchangeably in its discussion. This chapter will also use the brigade and regiment interchangeably in examining the battalion in the defense.

BRIGADE IN THE DEFENSE

6-15. A brigade can defend in either the first or second echelon of an army, division, or corps. The brigade can also function as a reserve or defend a separate axis. A first echelon brigade defends on the first defensive axis, occupying two or three defensive positions. A brigade defending in the first echelon of an army or corps on the aggressor main axis of attack may be reinforced with two or more artillery battalions, and often such support as antitank subunits and rocket-propelled flamethrowers. If the brigade is a component of an army or corps, it typically becomes part of a defensive belt. If, however, the brigade is operating independently on a distinct avenue of approach or in an isolated armed conflict it establishes a zone of responsibility. Both the defensive belt and zone of responsibility are allocated based on the range of reconnaissance systems and the flanks and rear of the boundary line that divides the brigade from adjacent units. The assigned size of the zone and area of defense must take into account the counteraction against the attacking aggressor and tactical assistance between the combat elements of the brigade. Assigned size must also permit sufficient area for the freedom of maneuver and dispersal of subunits.

6-16. The brigade commander has the option for form a wider or deeper defense if necessary. For example, a brigade might place three maneuver battalions in its first echelon if operating on an extended frontage or if the commander perceives a limited threat of aggressor attack. Conversely, it may defend on a narrower frontage (and greater depth) because it is part of a larger defensive formation, or the commander expects a more powerful aggressor attack. Similarly, the brigade commander may decide to form or retain a smaller or larger combined arms reserve.

6-17. The construction of the defense for a brigade comprises—
- The brigade combat formation.
- A system of defensive positions, areas, and borders (lines).
- "Kill zones" for annihilation of the aggressor.
- Integrated air defense.
- Integrated antitank defense.
- Integrated obstacles.
- A system for combating airborne/air assault forces.
- Integrated combat control information system. Automated complexes that support rapid battlefield decision-making and battle management. (See Appendix J).

ELEMENTS OF THE COMBAT FORMATION

6-18. Subject to the situation, the brigade combat formation in the defense can be formed in one or two echelons. At least a company will be allocated to the combined arms reserve from one of the echelons. A brigade combat formation in the defense includes—
- The first echelon (often two or three battalions).
- The second echelon (or combined arms reserve) one or two battalions, often including a tank battalion.
- A brigade artillery group (BrAG).

- Air defense subunits.
- An antitank reserve.
- An obstacle construction detachment.
- Anti-airborne/air assault reserve.

6-19. The brigade combat formation can also include a forward detachment, tactical air assault units, and electromagnetic warfare subunits, subject to the situation.

6-20. Battalions of the first echelon of the brigade in the defense are intended to—
- Defeat the aggressor during its deployment and transition to the attack.
- Fend off the aggressor's offensive and retain the defensive area.
- Deny aggressor breakthrough into the depths of the defense.
- Destroy aggressor subunits pockets at established kill zones and lines.

6-21. The second echelon (or reserve) is intended to—
- Prohibit the aggressor from breaking into the depths of the defense.
- Prevent the aggressor from seizing strongpoints throughout the depth of the defense.
- Defeat aggressor pockets with subunits at planned positions and lines and conduct counterattacks to restore the situation along the front line/forward edge of the defense.

6-22. The combined arms reserve of the brigade is intended to—
- Deal with suddenly arising tasks (unexpected problems).
- Reconstitute units in the first echelon in the event of their loss of combat effectiveness.

6-23. Artillery-A motorized rifle or tank brigade in the defense will be supported by a Brigade Artillery Group (BrAG). The BrAG is designed to defeat the aggressor in the approach march, on the line of deployment, in the staging area, or should the aggressor penetrate the first defensive positions, to defeat them from interim firing positions. Artillery subunits will disperse to ensure greater survivability, as automated C2 complexes allow dispersed artillery units to converge and mass fires on designated targets. The BrAG can be allocated additional artillery units to accomplish the assigned mission task against attacking aggressor forces. The SV organizes indirect fire units into groupings to support missions at specific levels of the senior commander's plan. These groups are organized principally on the level receiving fires: strategic-operational- Army Artillery Group (AAG) and operational-tactical- DAG or BrAG.

6-24. If a brigade is operating as part of an Army, it may receive artillery support from the AAG.

6-25. Air defense. A defending brigade will be supported by its organic anti-aircraft and missile systems. The air defenses are intended to protect the brigade from air strikes and cruise missiles. The air defense missile battalion will provide zone-specific coverage to protect the brigade's subunits and command post from air strikes. The first echelon forces will be protected by a battery of Tunguska rocket artillery 2S6 Anti-Aircraft Systems. The BrAG is shielded by two platoons of the Strela-10 missile battery. Two Igla MANPADS equipped platoons protect the first echelon, while the third platoon defends the brigade command post.

6-26. Antitank reserves. The antitank reserve of the brigade is intended to destroy tanks and other armored vehicles which breakthrough into the depths of the defense. It is also designed to protect dangerous areas on the flanks. The antitank reserve comes primarily from the brigade's organic antitank artillery battalion.

6-27. Mobile obstacle detachment. The mobile obstacle detachment is designed to quickly lay antitank minefields on aggressor avenues of approach or to protect a flank during defensive and offensive operations. The mobile obstacle detachment operates in conjunction with the antitank reserve and is formed from the brigade's organic engineer-sapper company, integrating its mobile mine-layers.

6-28. Anti-air assault reserve. Usually formed by a motorized rifle company taken from the second echelon, the anti-assault reserve is designed to destroy aggressor airborne, air assault landings in areas deemed susceptible to sabotage or reconnaissance activities.

6-29. Forward detachment in the security zone. An advanced detachment/subunit created from the second echelon, designed to force the aggressor to deploy or attack prematurely in a disadvantageous direction..

6-30. Air assault detachment. The air assault detachment is part of a reinforced motorized rifle company created to conduct air assaults into the rear area of an aggressor breakthrough. This detachment will also assist other subunits from the second echelon during their counterattacks.

6-31. Electromagnetic warfare subunits. Subunits designed to electromagnetically suppress aggressor electromagnetic means and protect brigade units from being hit by electromagnetic proximity fuses and other signal detonated munitions.

6-32. Bronegruppa (Armored Group). When motorized rifle forces have dismounted from their BMPs BTRs or MT-LBs, the APCs/IFVs may remain with their dismounted personnel to provide fire support, or they may be may remain with their dismounted personnel to provide fire support, or they may be detached to form an armored maneuver reserve with substantial direct-fire capability. This armored reserve is customarily formed from platoon through brigade and is commonly found in second echelon subunits. It is often commanded by the deputy commander.

THE SYSTEM OF DEFENSIVE POSITIONS, AREAS, AND LINES

6-33. The system of defensive positions, areas and lines for a brigade includes—
* Forward security zone.
* Forward security outpost position.
* Two to three defensive positions.
* Alternative positions.
* Separate areas and defense nodes.
* Areas for the firing of the BrAG and other areas for artillery subunits and initial positions for anti-aircraft assets.
* Areas for the concentration of the second echelon (reserves).
* Firing lines for tanks and BMPs (infantry fighting vehicles).
* Deployment lines for counterattacks.
* Antitank reserve deployment lines.
* Mobile obstacle detachment deployment lines.
* Anti-assault reserve assembly area.
* Locations for the construction of fire sacs.
* Landing zones and ambush sites for combat helicopters.
* Locations for troop control points.
* False and reserve defensive areas (strong points, positions).

6-34. When the defending force is not in direct contact with the aggressor, a security zone can be formed forward of the defense out to the range of supporting fires. There can be multiple positions established within the security zone. These positions are typically spaced as to not be able to be decisively engaged by the same aggressor force, typically 6–8 km from each other. Individual company and platoon strong points will also be created to hold critical areas. These strong points will be strengthened with engineering obstacles.

6-35. When no forward security zone is established a motorized rifle or tank brigade can form a forward position 6 to 8 km from the forward edge of the defense. This position is designed to mislead the aggressor as to the actual location of the forward edge of the defense, repel hasty offensive actions on first echelon subunits, and to cause the aggressor to precipitately deploy its main combat elements. Reinforced companies will be obtained from first echelon motorized rifle battalions to shield the forward positions by establishing company and platoon strong points.

6-36. A combat security zone will usually be formed, up to two km from the forward edge of the defense. It is typically formed to defend approaches not covered by forward positions, and where there is no contact with the aggressor. The combat security zone is designed to prevent surprise attack and to thwart aggressor ground reconnaissance of the first echelon battalions. If there is no direct aggressor contact, the mission of the combat security zone may be performed by subunits from the first positions of the first trench. (See paragraphs 6-67 through 6-78 for information on battalion in the defense). The combat security zone is created by reinforced motorized rifle platoons allocated by the brigade's assigned battalions.

6-37. The main defensive position consists of combined company strong points integrated in the battalion defense area. The depth of the battalion defensive position can be up to three km and will be established within a trench system when time allows.

6-38. The first trench is in the first defensive position on the forward edge of the defense. The brigade commander will determine the outline of this position, while the battalion commander will determine the exact location. The first trench will be defended by platoons from the first echelon. Mines are typically placed in front of the first trench.

6-39. The second trench is normally established 400–600 m behind the first trench. Subunits located in the first trench will be covered by fire from the second trench. Subunits in the second trench will also cover the approaches to the forward edge of the defense and any obstacles laid out in its front.

6-40. The third trench is typically built 600–1000 m behind the second trench and placed to allow its subunits to provide direct fire on the zone between the second and third trench, on separate sections and in front of the forward edge of the defense. The third trench may also be used as a start point for maneuver against vulnerable areas in the event of an aggressor counterattack.

6-41. The fourth trench is established 600–1000 m behind the third trench. Subunits in the third trench will be covered by fires from the fourth trench. The fourth trench will also cover the approaches to the forward edge of the defense and any obstacles laid out in its front.

6-42. The first position in the brigade defensive belt is of the utmost importance. This belt is occupied/defended by the brigade's first echelon battalions. The second brigade defensive belt is defended by the brigade's second echelon battalions. These defensive positions of the brigade are made up of battalion areas of defense. These battalion areas incorporate company strong points linked from the front to the depth by interlocking fires, obstacles, trenches, and connecting corridors arranged to permit a three-hundred-and-sixty-degree defense.

6-43. Separate areas (nodes) of defense are created to protect various areas. These areas include road junctions, built-up areas, crossings, and other important objectives from aggressor air assault/airborne forces.

6-44. Firing positions for the BrAG are often selected based on axes which might be susceptible to aggressor tanks. Direct lay fire against armor remains an important SV artillery mission. If the BrAG is part of an army's first-echelon brigade, firing positions are located between the first and second defensive belt. While not under threat of significant counterfire, these will typically be just beyond direct fire range from the forward edge of the defense. Reserve and temporary firing positions are also prepared for the BrAG, as are routes to these locations.

6-45. A defending brigade will also be supported by its organic anti-aircraft systems. These systems are deployed to provide coverage to front line units. The mutual distances between the anti-aircraft batteries are designed to provide interlocking coverage.

6-46. The reserve concentration (assembly) area is placed in pre-battle order and prepares a second (sometimes third) brigade defensive belt. The firing lines of tanks and motorized rifle units of the second echelon (combined arms reserve) are directed to areas where precision weapons or massed tank assaults are anticipated.

6-47. A tank company or motorized rifle companies with BMPs is deployed on firing areas at the front, with 1.5 km intervals between companies, with the total length of the firing line extending up to five km. The firing line may overlap with the commitment line used in the conduct of counterattacks.

6-48. To carry out counterattacks in the defensive zone, battalions of the second echelon will plan one or two areas for a counterattack on the likely axes of the aggressor's attack. A primary and alternate line for the deployment of the counterattack will be designated, these will often be separated by 2–3 km.

6-49. In areas where the aggressor is likely to use precision weapons and substantial tank attacks, the SV will assign lines of deployment to the antitank reserve. While in the defense, the antitank reserve is in an assembly area. This assembly area will be located on an armor avenue of approach between the second and third positions or within the second position.

6-50. Three to five deployment lines or more may be assigned to the antitank reserve between the first and second positions. The antitank guided missile (ATGM) battery is deployed up to 2 km from the front, with the antitank battalion up to 5 km from the front. The mobile obstacle detachment is assigned to guard the lines of deployment for the antitank reserve. The POZ will be in reserve, near and sometimes in, the antitank reserve assembly area.

6-51. Ambush by fire locations are prepared on the aggressor's flanks and throughout the depth of the defense to limit the aggressor's ability to maneuver. SV doctrine states that the best locations for ambushes are reverse slopes of hills, the outskirts of towns, the edges of forest, and road intersections.

6-52. The anti-assault reserve assembly area should be in an area that will ensure rapid access to the most likely targets of an aggressor air assault/airborne landing. The brigade's anti-assault reserve is located within the boundaries of the second (or third) position. Primary and reserve control points are chosen throughout the depth of the defense typically in areas difficult for tanks to access, away from the direction of the main aggressor attack.

6-53. The brigade's command post is deployed at a distance from the forward edge of the defense that prevents engagement from aggressor direct fire weapons. From this point the commander should seek to view the most likely aggressor avenues of approach. The brigade's material technical support is deployed beyond aggressor medium range systems from the forward edge of the defense. It is located with the brigade trains (maintenance and logistics elements). A COP will be set up for the motorized rifle battalion located behind the first-echelon motorized rifle companies or in the vicinity of the battalion's second-echelon company, which is approximately two km from the forward edge of the defense. False strong points and firing positions will be created throughout the defense, between defending units, on the flanks, and other unoccupied places.

Fires

6-54. Fires include—
- Aviation strikes.
- Direct and indirect fire from the BrAG. (See Chapter 5.)
- Fires from the maneuver battalions.

Air Defense

6-55. The air defense system is formed throughout the entire depth of the brigade defense and includes—
- An integrated system of radar reconnaissance and early warning.
- An integrated system of anti-aircraft missile and anti-aircraft artillery cover.
- An integrated command and control system for air defense.

6-56. A system of command and control connects command post, communications systems and computers with air defense units and subunits to assist the control of units and subunits and to direct their fires.

Integrated Antitank Defense

6-57. The integrated antitank defense of the brigade includes—
- Artillery fire on aggressor tanks and other armored targets from hidden sites.
- Integrated antitank fires (planned direct fires of antitank weapons, tanks, and BMPs by subunits covering armored avenues of approach.

6-58. The antitank reserve and mobile obstacle detachment (POZ) should plan for the maximum destruction of aggressor tanks and other armored targets. Both the antitank reserve and the POZ will prepare an assembly area, mine lines and prepare lines of deployment during combat. This will start at the security zone and forward positions and is designed to defeat an aggressor massed tank assault and to destroy it as it attempts to wedge its way into the defense.

Integrated Engineer Obstacles

6-59. The SV defense also includes a system of engineering obstacles that impedes aggressor movement. These can include mines, electrified fences, and other barrier materials. Russia places a doctrinal priority on the establishment of engineering obstacles. As time permits, they will simultaneously establish obstacles in the depth of the defense: strong points along less likely avenues of approach; artillery firing positions; reconnaissance zones; command and control positions; combat service support positions, and rear area positions. Obstacles will be arranged throughout the entire depth of the brigade defense in combination with direct and indirect fires and natural obstacles.

Integrated Air Assault Defense

6-60. The air assault defense force will interdict and destroy aggressor forces before and after landing. It will also counter airborne and air assault sabotage and reconnaissance groups. The integrated air assault defense includes—

- Anti-air assault reserve.
- Subunits of the second echelon (reserve).
- Air strikes and air defense weapons fire.
- Integrated direct and indirect fires, as well as anti-landing obstacles in potential landing areas (zones).

Fire Engagement of the Aggressor by the Defense

6-61. Fire destruction of the aggressor is the coordinated fires targeted on the aggressor by designated forces and means of destruction applying conventional and incendiary ammunition to achieve the battle objectives. The aim of fire destruction is to reduce the combat potential or combat capabilities of aggressor units and subunits to a level that ensures that SV subunits can achieve their assigned mission while still maintaining their combat effectiveness. Fire destruction is organized by the senior commander in accordance with the actions of subunits that will carry it out during the period of fire destruction, which can include—

- Fire preparation to repel the aggressor offensive.
- Fire support the defending force.

6-62. Fire preparation for the repulsing of an aggressor's attack is carried out with the aim of disrupting the advance, deployment, and transition to attack to defeat the aggressor's first echelon units and subunits. This effort will continue until the aggressor goes on the attack. Fire preparation to support the defending forces is carried out with the aim of inflicting maximum damage on the aggressor and prohibiting his breakthrough into the depths of the defense.

6-63. When conducting the counterattack, fire destruction of the aggressor is carried out in the periods of fire preparation for the counterattack and fire support of the counterattacking force. To increase the effectiveness of the aggressor's destruction by fire, brigades, battalions, and companies create a system of fire which senior commanders use as the basis for their unit's system of fire destruction of the aggressor. This includes the fires of artillery, tanks, BMPs, BTRs, antitank missiles, grenade launchers, and small arms. It also includes the use of flame and incendiary weapons [thermobaric]. This system of fire for the brigade, battalion, and companies will also include aviation strikes within the range of allotted aviation resources.

6-64. The brigade, battalion, and company integrated fires are organized in strict accordance with the senior commander's plan of integrated fire destruction. This plan will be used in conjunction with radio-electromagnetic destruction and integrated obstacles. The mission is to destroy aggressor artillery subunits, command and control elements, troop control and forces and weapons of the mechanized infantry, tank subunits and other targets of the aggressor's first echelon.

6-65. When performing the tasks of fire destruction SV artillery uses the following types of fire:

- Fire on an individual target, fired from a battery, platoon or single gun, fired independently from an indirect fire position or using direct fire.
- Concentrated fire, fired simultaneously by several artillery batteries on one target.
- Standing barrage, a fire curtain on a predetermined target.

- Defensive rolling barrage fire. Sequentially transferred to designated lines as the aggressor moves.
- Successive fire concentration.
- Offensive rolling barrage fire.
- Massed fire.

6-66. Each SV brigade is assigned at least a UAV company and stand-alone reconnaissance fire missions can be conducted by the brigade as well as the battalion. With systems linked to the Strelets command, control, communications, and reconnaissance computer, detection-to-engagement time can be less than four minutes. While the best way to act on targets is with precision-guided munitions, the brigade will often respond with rapid massed fires of conventional rounds which in many cases can inflict similar damage. The UAV company is also useful in identifying targets, adjusting artillery fire, and performing post-strike damage assessments. See figure 6-1.

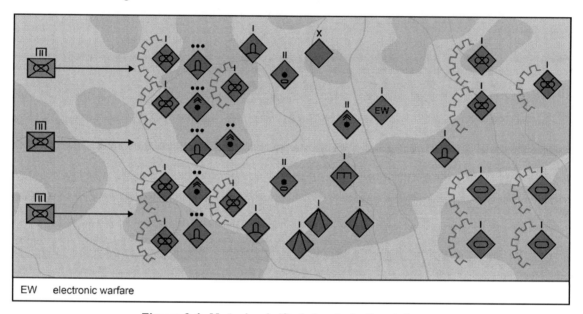

EW   electronic warfare

Figure 6-1. Motorized rifle brigade in the defense

Battalion in the Defense

6-67. A motorized rifle or tank battalion can operate in either the first or second echelons of a brigade or regiment. A motorized rifle or tank battalion can also operate in the security zone, forward position, or as part of the combined arms reserve. The first defensive position will be prepared and filled by a battalion of the first echelon. A second defensive position will be prepared and occupied by a battalion of the second echelon. The mortar battery and ASG-17 grenade launcher platoon are customarily directly subordinate to the battalion commander and remain as whole units to support defending subunits. The battalion defense will include a combat formation, system of strong points and firing positions, an integrated fire plan, as well as an engineer obstacle system. SV doctrine maintains that a battalion's area of responsibility (AOR) in the defense is typically up to 10 km wide and up to 10 km in depth, and the defensive area assigned to a battalion is typically up to 5 km along the front and up to 3 km in depth. As always however, these figures are situationally dependent and must factor in the terrain.

6-68. The elements of the battalion combat formation include—

- First echelon motorized rifle companies with reinforcements.
- A second echelon motorized rifle company or reserve platoon.
- Weapons systems controlled by the battalion commander (artillery battalion, mortar battery, antitank platoon, AGS-17 platoon, and air defense platoon).
- Bronegruppa (Armored Group).
- Ambush team.

6-69. As a rule, the motorized rifle or tank (maneuver) battalion in the defense will contain two echelons however, it can consist of only one echelon and a combined arms reserve of at least one maneuver platoon. The first echelon of the combat formation typically contains two or three maneuver companies. The second echelon will normally consist of a maneuver company or combined arms reserve of a least one maneuver platoon. Artillery subunits can include the mortar battery, though an artillery battalion can be attached to a maneuver battalion. The AGS-17 grenade launcher platoon, the antitank platoon, and the attached flamethrower company are directly subordinate to the battalion commander. A bronegruppa and ambush team may be added to this formation depending on the situation. The bronegruppa will typically position itself in an assembly area and will be given designated blocking positions and firing lines within the battalion defense.

6-70. A first echelon battalion is intended to—
- Defeat the aggressor during its deployment and transition to the attack.
- Repel the offensive.
- Prohibit a breakthrough of the forward defense.
- Hold strong points.
- Prevent an aggressor breakthrough into the depths of the battalion's defensive area.

6-71. The second echelon battalion is intended to—
- Prohibit the aggressor from breaking through the first position.
- Destroy or counterattack any aggressor breakthrough across the forward edge of the defense.

6-72. A motorized rifle company of the second echelon will also prepare strong points as fast as possible at the third and fourth trench.

6-73. The combined arms reserve of a motorized rifle battalion occupies a staging area behind the subunits of the first echelon, prepares a strong point, and prepares to carry out sudden developing missions.

6-74. The artillery subunits of the motorized rifle battalion remain intact and are used to support the companies of the first echelon. A battery from an artillery battalion may be attached to a motorized rifle company.

6-75. The grenade launcher (AGS-17) subunit, flamethrower subunit and other fire weapons remain subordinate to the battalion commander and occupy positions in the company strong points and remain intact to concentrate on the main aggressor effort. They also cover the flanks and support counterattacks.

6-76. The antitank reserve consists of the antitank platoon. It is intended to destroy tanks and other armored vehicles that have broken through into the depths of the defense. It also covers tank avenues of approach and the flanks.

6-77. The bronegruppa is created for the purpose of closing gaps that form due to aggressor fire strikes. It consists of tanks, BMPs, and BTRs from the first and second echelon units and will defend against main avenues of approach. It is commanded by the commander of a platoon of a first-echelon company.

6-78. A fire ambush team is deployed to inflict maximum damage on the aggressor with sudden direct fire and the use of minefields. It may consist of a motorized rifle platoon or squad reinforced by flamethrowers and sapper units. The firing positions for the fire ambush are put in fortified positions on tank avenues of approach, on flanks, and on the peripheries of populated areas.

System of Strong Points and Firing Positions

6-79. The system of strong points and firing positions of the battalion include—
- Strong points of companies, interconnected along the front and depth with an integrated system of fires and obstacles.
- Primary, alternate, and temporary positions for artillery, tanks, IFVs, and other organic and attached weapons.
- The positions of a CSOP.

6-80. The battalion's defensive area consists of three or four trenches composed of company strong points, firing positions for artillery subunits, firing positions for other weapons which remain under the command of the battalion commander, the assembly area, and the firing line for the bronegruppa. Gaps between company strong points are normally up to 1000 m, while the gaps between platoons are up to 300 m.

6-81. When trenches can be employed, the first trench is on the forward edge of the defense. The second trench is set up at 400 – 600 m from the first trench. The third trench is 600 –1000 m from the second trench, and the fourth trench is 400 – 600 m from the third trench. See figure 6-2.

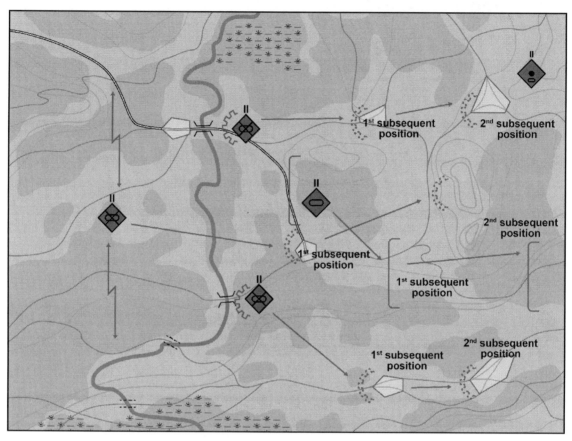

Figure 6-2. Motorized rifle regiment conducting a maneuver defense

Integrated Fire Plan

6-82. The system of fire (battalion's fire system) is an essential part of the senior commander's fire engagement system. The system of fire must be prudently integrated with the obstacle system. It includes—
- Zones of focused fire and lines of antiaircraft gun fire on the approaches to the defense, in front of the forward edge of the defense, on the flanks, and throughout the depth of the defense.
- Prepared maneuver fire.
- Antitank zones of fire and continuous multi-layer fire by all types of weapons before the forward edge of the battle area, in the gaps, on the flanks, and throughout the depth of the defense to destroy the first group of tanks and other armored vehicles of the aggressor.

6-83. The system of fire is shaped by considering—
- The firing capabilities of all the weapons systems involved.
- Their close integration.
- The effect when combined with the obstacle system and terrain conditions.

6-84. The readiness of the system of fire is determined by—
- Manning of the firing positions.
- Prepared range cards and firing data.
- Current supply of missiles and ammunition.

6-85. The battalion command-observation post is usually positioned in a dug-in location within the area of the first echelon companies or in the vicinity of the second echelon company or combined arms reserve strong point at a position where it can observe key target reference points.

Engineering Obstacle System

6-86. Obstacles will be emplaced in front of a CSOP, on the forward edge of the battle area, in gaps between subunits, and on the flanks of the battalion (company) throughout the entire depth of the battalion defensive area in accordance with the planned system of fires and terrain conditions, and after considering the maneuver of subunits and adjoining units. The system of engineer obstacles includes—
- Minefields.
- Mine clusters.
- Choke point obstacles.
- Locally fabricated obstacles.
- Different types of antitank and antipersonnel obstacles.

Means of Reinforcement

6-87. The following are frequent attachments for a motorized rifle battalion:
- Tank company.
- Artillery battery/battalion.
- Anti-aircraft battery.
- Engineer platoon.
- NBC reconnaissance subunit.

Sequence of Work on Receipt of Mission

6-88. When a battalion is not in direct contact with the aggressor, the battalion commander—
- Decides on the plan of defense.
- Conducts reconnaissance, during which the commander improves their decision.
- Gives their combat order.
- Organizes cooperation and integrated system of fires, support, and C2.
- Takes the battalion (company) onto a specified area of defense (strong point) and organizes its engineer support.

6-89. While moving from the offense to the defense, while in direct contact with the aggressor, the battalion commander—
- Organizes the seizure and fortification of designated (beneficial) lines.
- While fortifying the lines, decides on the plan of defense.
- Gives combat orders to their subordinate units.
- Organizes cooperation and an integrated system of fires, NBC defense, and countermeasures against aggressor precision weapons.
- Gives orders on basic issues of comprehensive combat support.
- Organizes engineering support in the area of defense (strong point).
- Conducts reconnaissance, and refines the subunit's order, the order of cooperation and other matters.

Considerations of the Battalion Commander

6-90. Battalion commanders take many factors into consideration when setting up the defense. The below items describe considerations by various elements.

6-91. For Companies of the First Echelon, commanders consider: reinforcements; strong points and direction on which to concentrate the main effort; tasks to repulse the offensive and destroy an aggressor which has penetrated into one's defenses; the number of trenches and their trace; field of fire, additional sectors of fire and zones of concentrated fire; what forces and means are needed to secure the flanks, joints and gaps, and who is responsible for them; who provides support.

6-92. For Companies of the Second Echelon, commanders consider: same duties as the companies (platoons) of the first echelon, plus, second echelon companies, their lines of deployment for counterattacks; for tank companies and motorized rifle companies with BMPs, their firing lines.

6-93. For Reserve, commanders consider: assembly area (strong point); on-order missions to prepare for; additionally for tank companies and motorized rifle companies with BMPs, their firing lines.

6-94. For Bronegruppa, commanders consider: group composition; assembly area and time to occupy it; firing lines; on-order missions to prepare for.

6-95. For Ambush Team, commanders consider: composition; place; mission for engaging an advancing aggressor; sequence of withdrawal.

6-96. For Attached Artillery and Mortar Battery Support, commanders consider: sequence of supporting fire for the security zone; fire missions during aggressor movement to the forward edge of the defense; deployment and transition to the attack; fire against aggressor wedged into the defense; support for the counterattack of the second echelon; main, alternate and temporary firing positions.

6-97. For Grenade Launcher (AGS-17), commanders consider: missions supporting companies of the first echelon and repelling aggressor infantry assaults; main and reserve positions; belts of fire; additional sectors of fire; zones of concentrated fire; lines of barrier fire.

6-98. For Antitank Subunits, commanders consider: their place in the defense; the direction of the aggressor's advance; lines of deployment; the sequence for occupying positions and on-order missions to prepare for; the signal for opening and ceasing fire; actions after mission is complete.

6-99. For Antiaircraft Units, commanders consider: launch or firing positions; sectors of reconnaissance to detect aggressor aircraft; time and degrees of readiness; sequence of the conduct of fire.

6-100. For Security Subunits in the Security Zone, commanders consider: position; mission; weapons designated for support; sequence of calls for fire; sequence of withdrawal.

6-101. For Concluding the Order, commanders consider: the time to be ready to fulfill the order, the time to occupy the defense, the time for readiness of the scheme of integrated fire and the time for engineering work to be completed, the order and sequence for camouflage and field fortifications of the area of the defense (strong point).

Chapter 7

Offense

This chapter serves to describe Russian ground forces (Сухопутные войска Российской Федерации – sukhoputnyye voyska RF - SV) tactical actions for offensive missions and indicates methods used to plan, prepare, and execute those actions to achieve the mission specified by the commander. Actions remain flexible to react to contingencies during conduct of an offensive mission. Subordinate commands can execute missions without direct control by a higher headquarters by understanding the objectives required by the higher unit commander's intent.

OVERVIEW OF OFFENSIVE ACTIONS

7-1.   Although Russia announced a new military doctrine in 2014 that emphasizes defensive preparations and actions, the military and the SV still consider the offensive as the decisive battlefield action and the ultimate means of defeating an aggressor. The Russian General Staff makes it clear that victory in a ground war can only be achieved through offensive actions.

7-2.   Russia's understanding of new generation warfare includes the concept of nonlinear, no-contact war where it is necessary to use all forces and effects to set the conditions for successful direct offensive engagement. This condition setting includes using proxy forces, rapid automation-supported decision making, precision targeting and fires for near real-time strikes, using simultaneous attacks throughout the depths of an aggressor's formation, and battle management complexes that integrate all forces and effects. Use of these capabilities effectively results in a disorganized and disrupted aggressor force incapable of defending or counterattacking against an SV offensive action.

7-3.   Integration of forces and effects at the strategic and operational levels create tactical opportunities for offensive action. Offensive actions continue to adhere to the historic principles of speed, mass, maneuver, and firepower. Integration is the key to delivering an offensive strike adhering to these principles. Tactical application has expanded to include not only ground maneuver units but also all forces and effects in all domains: land, maritime, air, information, and space domains. The aim of offensive action at the tactical level is to accomplish tactical missions in support of larger operations. A tactical command ensures that its subunits thoroughly understand both the overall goals of an operation and the specific purpose of a particular mission.

7-4.   The Russians identify the following specific characteristics of offensive action on a modern battlefield:
* Conduct aggressive reconnaissance to facilitate firm and continuous battle management.
* Reconnaissance-strike and fire complexes used to conduct swift and continuous attacks on an aggressor force.
* Breach aggressor defenses at weak points, gaps, flanks, and rear and bypass success.
* Conduct rapid maneuver of forces and fires in a decisive direction.
* Assign priority of fires to destruction of aggressor nuclear and precision-strike systems.
* Strike aggressor forces simultaneously throughout the depth of their tactical formation.
* Maintain momentum under all conditions.
* Use creative approaches to missions to deprive the aggressor the ability to predict likely courses.
* Employ REB and other IV actions.

7-5.   At the tactical level the SV anticipates that operational actions will set the conditions for offensive success. To achieve tactical mission success in modern warfare conditions, the SV continues modification of its offensive tactics, techniques, and procedures. These modifications continue to evolve based on Russian analysis of modern conflicts and technological advances. The following modifications will be evident on the tactical-level battlefield:

- Information warfare actions will influence local, regional, and world opinion in favor of the SV and seek to disrupt, degrade, and destroy aggressor command, control, and communication capabilities. The purpose of IV is to make it difficult, if not impossible, for the aggressor to effectively command and direct its units in response to the SV offensive action.
- Tactical SV units conduct maneuver using real-time reconnaissance information, automated C2, precision navigation and timing, electromagnetic suppression, and space-based support.
- Long-range indirect and direct fires are the determining factor in facilitating tactical maneuver. Using precise reconnaissance combined with long-range indirect fires reconnaissance-strike and reconnaissance-fire complexes gain the fire initiative and retain fire superiority. A growing technical capability is the introduction of top attack unmanned aerial munitions that loiter over the target area. The SV also currently maintains a direct fire range advantage with its antitank guided missiles and will initiate tactical offensive actions to take advantage of that capability.
- Integrated anti-aircraft gun and missile defense complexes are a key to protecting the maneuver force as it conducts an offensive. Russia's analysis of potential western adversaries reveals a heavy reliance on airpower. The SV seeks to defeat and disrupt air reconnaissance and precision strikes by using automated C2 to integrate air defenses and REB complexes. These layered and integrated complexes create the conditions to increase maneuver freedom for SV units and subunits conducting offensive actions.
- SV maneuver forces must avoid stereotypical deployments of units and subunits as well as using increased dispersion between vehicles in offensive formations and between platoons, companies, and battalions. Dispersion does not lead to dilution of mass which is accomplished by using automated C2 complexes to ensure simultaneous attacks against specified gaps or weakened areas. These complexes facilitate increased nonlinear maneuver of units and subunits including direct and indirect fires.
- Greater initiative by battalion- and brigade-level commanders to exploit battlefield success using combined arms actions. Battalion tactical groups (BTGs) task-organized for specific mission tasks exploit weakness in the aggressor defenses to accomplish rapid penetration or destruction of a specified aggressor unit or position.
- Modern combat actions depend on rapid maneuver with no solid front, open flanks, separate avenues of attack and gaps between maneuvering units. While large-scale wars may involve a protracted period of crisis and conflict, lengthy battles are a thing of the past replaced by rapid maneuver of fires and units. Units and subunits perform maneuver to rapidly shift from defense to offense or vice versa as required by the battlefield situation. Units conducting offensive actions use maneuver to launch swift strikes on an objective and then rapidly disperse as it conducts maneuver to the next objective or designated attack direction.
- Diversionary supporting attacks in the support areas of an aggressor force are also an element of offensive actions. Insertion of airborne or air landed units, attacks by deep reconnaissance, sabotage, raids, assassinations, sniper fire, and other special actions serve to tie down aggressor combat forces to degrade or divert combat capability.

PRINCIPLES OF COMBINED ARMS

7-6.   The SV combined arms units and subunits follow the principles of modern combined arms combat described in their doctrine. They are the fundamental building blocks that serve as the basis for the commander's initiative and creativity and facilitate making the correct decision that accomplishes designated objective. The principles the SV follows are:

- Constant high combat readiness for the main combat subunits; BTGs.
- High activity.
- Determination and continuity of combat actions.
- Suddenness of action.
- Maintaining continuous engagement in combat.

- Resolutely concentrating all efforts on the main objective at the right time.
- Maneuvering forces, means, and fires.
- Counting on moral and psychological factors to accomplish mission tasks.
- Comprehensive integration of all combat actions.
- Maintaining or rapidly restoring combat capability.
- Solid and continuous battle management.
- Intransigence in achieving the designated objectives.
- Full implementation of tasks assigned.

7-7. As SV commanders and soldiers execute an offensive their actions are informed by these principles. They set the perspective and approach the SV takes towards accomplishing assigned offensive missions. To succeed in modern conflicts not only must units and complexes be synchronized and integrated, but the commanders and soldiers must also have high moral, psychological conditioning, and highly developed combat skills.

7-8. The SV fully recognizes that strict adherence to guidelines and templates are a suboptimal approach to offensive actions. Adherence to the formal approach to combat management using templates, dogmatism, and stereotypical approaches can quickly lead to failure or achieving success only with high losses. Modern writings and discussion of SV tactical actions encourages initiative and developing creative solutions that do not allow an aggressor to use its best potential combat capabilities. Commanders are encouraged to find and use the best means to accomplish a mission objective with the least losses, in a shorter amount of time than defined by nomograms or combat manuals.

7-9. Combat manuals and doctrinal templates are the tools used by the SV to train and prepare junior officers as they enter the force. Junior officers use these basic tools coupled with repeated training of battle tasks to develop the skills and knowledge necessary to adapt combat actions to modern combat conditions.

7-10. It is not uncommon for officers to remain in leadership positions for extended periods of time. Through unit training, professional military education, and field exercises, the SV develops an officer's skills to read the battlefield situation and develop tactical plans that effectively use SV unit and subunit capabilities to accomplish offensive actions.

PLANNING OFFENSIVE MANEUVER

7-11. The SV tactical forces concentrate offensive actions on aggressor units. To accomplish the destruction of a designated aggressor force, the SV—

- Conducts reconnaissance to find a vulnerable point.
- Fixes aggressor forces with indirect fire or maneuver force.
- Uses fires to weaken the point of attack, and then penetrates to destroy aggressor reconnaissance, C2, and sustaining units.

While mission objectives for SV units and subunits are oriented on the aggressor units, depending on the battlefield situation, mission objectives may also include terrain-based objectives.

7-12. For large-scale warfare, the SV plans integrated attacks and anticipates that the battlefield situation will constantly change as the conflict unfolds. Training of battle drills and use of standard formations provide the means for the SV to respond to situational changes without extensive replanning or adjustments.

7-13. The SV uses the principle of interaction to achieve success in modern combined arms battle. Interaction is accomplished during planning by coordination and integration of the actions of all units and subunits of all combat and special forces. In addition to units and subunits, interaction planning includes weapons capabilities in terms of missions, timing, and methods of accomplishing assigned objectives. It requires constant situational awareness, correct understanding of the mission, synchronized battlefield information, initiative by the commander, and the necessary resources to support the mission objectives.

7-14. The SV accomplishes rapid decision making, planning, and battle management using network-centric automated command complexes (ASU). The Russian military and SV continue development and fielding of ASU complexes as discussed in chapter 2. These complexes integrate reconnaissance information gathered from the national to tactical levels. They also collect and analyze the status of units, material, and supplies using machine learning and aspects of artificial intelligence to enhance the speed and quality of the commander's decision process. With the aid of the ASU the commander and staff are capable of developing plans and decisions two to three times faster.

PLANNING ELEMENTS

7-15. Key elements of planning offensive missions are—
- Commander's decision for the scheme of maneuver and mission tasks.
- Disruption or destruction of the reconnaissance of the aggressor.
- Organizing combat support forces and means according to the commander's plan.
- Battle command and management organization and coordination.
- Defeating aggressor fire complexes especially aviation and artillery.
- Preparation and organization of subunits in the assembly area.
- Organizing and performing training as time permits.
- Initiating offensive actions.

7-16. In planning the offensive, the SV commander develops offensive actions to take advantage of a weakened aggressor and to use surprise to overwhelm a target when there is sufficient time and situational understanding to prepare forces for specific tasks. Key considerations in offensive planning include but are not limited to—
- Implement a plan for reconnaissance, intelligence, surveillance, and target acquisition (Razvedka).
- Determine the when, where, and how of aggressor plans, actions, and intentions.
- Identify aggressor vulnerabilities and how to exploit those weaknesses.
- Locate critical nodes of the aggressor's combat systems and when to most effectively interdict them.
- Enact functions that reinforce opportunities for offensive actions in the area of responsibility.
- Determine the offensive method that will deny the aggressor its tactical objectives.
- Task-organize forces to attack and exploit the effects of planned and opportunity fires.
- Create or take advantage of a tactical window of opportunity.
- Use successful defensive actions as the basis for attacks, penetration of the aggressor defense, and pursuit of its withdrawing units.

ORGANIZING FOR THE OFFENSE

7-17. The organization of modern SV units and subunits for offensive actions recognizes the integrated nature of modern combat. As SV commanders plan the action they incorporate forces and means to use all available elements from land, air, maritime, space operations, and cyberspace. The objective of organization for offensive action is to capitalize on the strengths and capabilities of all units in an integrated and synchronized manner.

7-18. As mentioned previously, the SV performs two types of offensive actions against a defending aggressor force: attack from the depths out of direct contact and attack from positions in direct contact. In the preparation phase, the SV organizes units and subunits in the AO and ZOR to optimize successful offensive actions and create or seize opportunities for actions. Offensive preparations integrate all forces and means to disrupt, disorganize, and degrade the aggressor's combat systems, deny integrated performance, and create vulnerabilities that SV forces can exploit.

7-19. The organization for the meeting battle anticipates that there is little time to adjust or react to an encounter with a maneuvering aggressor force. The offensive organization plans for sufficient combat power as a forward detachment to either destroy any aggressor units encountered or to block its advance and allow the main body to continue to maneuver.

OFFENSIVE ORGANIZATION – DIVISIONS, REGIMENTS, AND BRIGADES

7-20. The SVs combined arms maneuver units are currently mostly comprised of modernizing brigades. Recent announcements have indicated that division units with subordinate regiments are being reintroduced into the SV to meet the requirements of large-scale warfare. Divisions and brigades are task-organized based on the most likely aggressor threat in an assigned AO. Brigades and divisions conduct offensive actions under the direction of the army commander.

7-21. SV division, regimental, or brigade commanders specify the initial required mission objectives of the units and subunits within their commands. Commanders plans task-organize resources to achieve integration of all forces and means at their disposal to accomplish the offensive mission. At the tactical level of unit or task-organized units, multiple mission tasks can be assigned to a division, regiment, or brigade based on the resources available, including those allocated from higher levels. The commander will adjust force allocations during an offensive mission to address emergent tactical conditions and reinforce successes.

7-22. The SV senior commander at the brigade, division, and army levels plan the offensive in two echelons as shown in figure 7-1 on page 7-6. In the offense, the first echelon is a combined arms force composed of one-half to two-thirds of the available combat power sufficient to find, fix, and destroy the first echelon aggressor units. The first echelon conducts the main attack to achieve the immediate mission objective set by the next higher level typically oriented on an aggressor unit.

7-23. The second echelon correspondingly has one-half to one-third of the available combat power with a specific mission objective as opposed to a reserve's mission. The reserve executes emerging missions directed by the commander as the battle develops. The second echelon may reorient from the original attack plan to take advantage of the first echelon's success in creating gaps or breaches in the aggressor defenses. The second echelon mission objective is usually oriented on penetrating an aggressor unit to strike into the depth and destroy C2, support, or reserves. Its mission remains the same even when taking the initiative to exploit success.

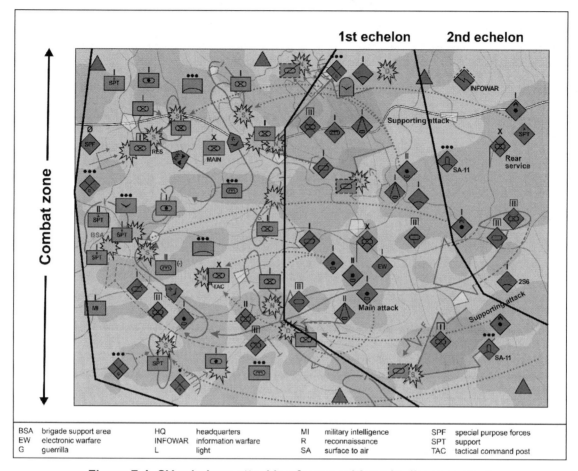

Figure 7-1. SV echelons attacking from positions in direct contact

7-24. First echelon units attacking in the main direction receive a significant artillery allocation to accomplish mission objectives. As an example, a brigade on the main attack axis may receive reinforcement of 2 to 4 additional artillery battalions from the AAG.

7-25. Precision missile, long-range multiple rocket launchers (MRL), and aerospace strikes controlled by the Army commander hit key aggressor targets such as bridges, airfields, and aggressor reserves. These strikes support not only army objectives but also tactical-level offensive actions by integration within the Army commander's plan.

ORGANIZATION OF SUBUNITS – DETACHMENTS, BATTALION TACTICAL GROUPS, BATTALIONS, AND SUBORDINATE UNITS

7-26. Detachments, BTGs, battalions, and companies are assigned mission tasks based on the objective it is to achieve. The SV can task-organize battalions and companies as detachments to accomplish a single tactical task. A detachment is assigned multiple mission tasks only in exceptional situations.

> *Note.* A commander allocates resources to create a mission-specific combined arms force for the tasks required to support their scheme of attack. For example, a detachment assigned to conduct a raid is called a raiding detachment.

7-27. As mentioned previously, the SV performs two types of offensive actions against a defending aggressor force: attack from the depths out of direct contact and attack from positions in direct contact. In the preparation phase, the SV organizes units and subunits in the area of operations and ZOR to optimize successful offensive actions and create or seize opportunities for actions. Offensive preparations integrate all forces and means to disrupt, disorganize, and degrade the aggressor's combat systems, deny integrated performance, and create vulnerabilities that the SV can exploit.

EMPLOYMENT PLANNING FOR SUBUNITS – PLATOONS, COMPANIES, AND BATTALIONS

7-28. Attacking from positions in contact with an aggressor defense provides subunits with better knowledge of the aggressor defensive organization and composition. Using this information subunit commanders designate landmarks to guide the attack and direct fires of organic and allocated weapons. Because of the threat of high-precision weapons fire the subunits may dismount further from the aggressor or use the terrain to mask and protect subunits as they move into the attack.

7-29. Engineer support for maneuver conducts breaches to overcome manmade or natural obstacles to ensure rapid passage. The NBC subunits identify contaminated areas to avoid, generate smoke or aerosol screens to obscure the attack, and as required use flame weapons to overcome defender strongpoints.

7-30. Subunits attacking from the march use dispersion and terrain masking to approach the defender positions as stealthily and rapidly as possible. The dismount line for mounted infantry is the last covered and concealed position closest to the aggressors as possible. Establishing the dismount line takes into consideration where the motorized rifle and tanks can place effective fire on the aggressor while safely advancing with supporting indirect fires. Once dismounted the carriers may accompany soldiers on the ground or may be used to form an armored group (бронегруппа - bronegruppa).

Employment Planning for Battalions, Brigades, Regiments, and Divisions

7-31. As the main units and formations in an attack against a defending aggressor, the brigade, regiment, or division plans and conducts battle management to ensure the integrated effects of its various subunits. In the senior commander's plan, the main attack is weighted with subunit allocations to provide the necessary combat power to successfully accomplish assigned mission objectives. These allocations not only involve combined-arms maneuver subunits but also security, maneuver support, indirect fire, air defense, REB, and MTO.

7-32. The SV position sufficient MTO logistics support in anticipation of offensive mission tasks and aggressor actions. Preparations consider mobile logistics support, caches, and other sustainment requirements as lines of communications extend with the directions of offensive actions.

7-33. Engineer and NBC reconnaissance conduct battlefield surveillance to identify obstacles to maneuver and create passages through them based on the commander's scheme of maneuver. Subunits in the movement support formation facilitate rapid maneuver by the main body to allow unrestricted maneuver. This can include breaching minefields, obstacles, clearing contaminated areas, and opening routes through urban areas.

7-34. The SV prepare for a primary concept of mission execution plan and the possibility of other contingencies including flexible responses with priorities of effort and support. The commander establishes the priority for critical action rehearsals. The force rehearses those actions in as realistic a manner as possible in the time allocated for preparation.

7-35. The SV establish priorities of effort and support. Typical actions rehearsed in preparation for an offensive mission include but are not limited to the—
- Razvedka updates.
- Counterreconnaissance.
- Integrated fires from reconnaissance strike and fires complexes.
- Massed fires on designated target lines and areas for the attack.
- Battle handover from security and disruption forces to main body attack forces.
- Main attack by the first echelon and support or exploitation by the second echelon.
- Mission, counterattack, and exploitation options.

EXECUTING THE OFFENSIVE

7-36. Successful execution of an offensive mission is often followed by continued offensive action to exploit tactical opportunities. In some situations, the offense may temporarily transition to the defense to consolidate gains, defeat aggressor counterattacks, or avoid culmination. The intent is to rapidly reconstitute forces and continue offensive actions.

EXPLOIT STRIKES AND FIRES

7-37. As described in Chapter 5, the SV plans and executes combat actions based on its integrated plan for reconnaissance strike complex (RSC) or reconnaissance fires complex (RFC) as well as those fires setting the conditions for successful maneuver of its combined arms units. The RSC/RFC uses real-time precision targeting supplied by reconnaissance assets to strike high priority targets of opportunity. The planned fires from indirect, direct, REB, and aerospace forces and means are maneuvered according to the senior commander's plan to allow ground maneuver forces to achieve mission objectives.

MAINTAIN CONTACT

7-38. Offensive actions maintain contact with aggressor forces for relevant situational awareness and situational understanding of an AO and probable or known aggressor actions. Effective reconnaissance and security guides prudent use of SV combat power to achieve the offensive mission. Reconnaissance and counterreconnaissance actions include rapid reorganization or reconstitution of assets to ensure no gaps in situational awareness and understanding of the aggressor and an AO and ZOR.

7-39. The SV ensure that its forces maintain contact with key elements of aggressor forces throughout the mission. Actions include rapid reconstitution of reconnaissance capabilities for a continuum of timely and accurate information and intelligence.

EXECUTE MISSION TASKS AND DRILLS

7-40. The SV conducts mission tasks and battle drills with aggressive and flexible actions that have been practiced to standards. As situational conditions evolve during a mission, clear and concise modifications to methodical and practiced combined arms actions allow the SV to rapidly adapt to new tactical conditions.

SEIZE TACTICAL OPPORTUNITIES

7-41. The SV emphasizes decentralized execution of a mission task and use of tactical initiative. Subordinate units are expected to take advantage of emergent opportunities and adapt tactical actions in concert with the purpose of a mission order and its intent. Indeed, Russian commanders are instilled with a full measure of combat initiative, rendering their tactical maneuvering flexible, and not readily templated or targeted.

DOMINATE THE TEMPO OF ACTIONS

7-42. The SV maintain the initiative with a focus on achieving the mission objective. The SV promote an adaptive, flexible, and agile approach to sequential, parallel, and successive actions with situational understanding of emergent aggressor conditions and an OE. Actions are continuous as the SV adjusts the speed, pace, or tempo of actions to create tactical opportunities with prudent risk assessment and an overarching requirement to accomplish the mission.

TACTICAL OFFENSIVE ACTIONS – BATTALIONS, DETACHMENTS, AND SUBORDINATE SUBUNITS

7-43. Russian commanders of detachments, battalion tactical groups (BTGs), battalions, and subordinate entities are tasked to conduct offensive actions with a mission purpose and intent. Subunits at this tactical level typically execute only one tactical mission at a time. Conducting simultaneous multiple missions by a detachment or subordinate type element would be rare. If simultaneous multiple missions were required as part of a larger mission set, more than one detachment or tactical subunit would be tasked and organized for actions within the larger mission.

ORGANIZATIONS OF OFFENSIVE SUBUNITS

7-44. Detachments, BTGs, battalions, and subordinate levels are labeled subunits while regiments are units and divisions and brigades are formations. An action subunit typically is an assault, ambush, or raid subunit. However, in a reconnaissance by battle the action subunit typically changes during the mission due to the multiple actions to find and fix selected aggressor elements and set conditions for a mission leader to order a decisive action such as an attack, assault, ambush, or raid.

ASSAULT

7-45. An assault is an attack that destroys a specified aggressor unit or strongpoint through firepower and the physical occupation and destruction of the unit or position by a designated assault group. It is typically used against established aggressor defensive positions and in cities. The assault group may be tasked to continue the attack in the direction of the offensive after completing its immediate objective. An assault is a basic form of SV tactical offensive combat. See an example in figure 7-2 on page 7-10.

ASSAULT ACTIONS

7-46. An assault is typically an integrated combined arms action. Russian assaults are characterized with actions to—
- Conduct tactical security.
- Isolate the objective.
- Fix designated aggressor elements.
- Suppress the objective with fires.
- Maneuver to seize the objective or destroy aggressor unit/position.

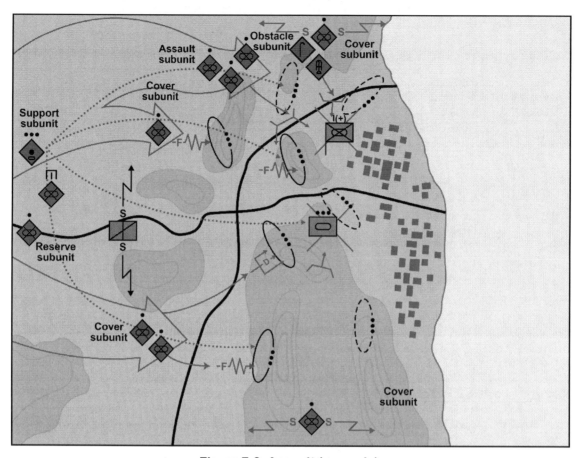

Figure 7-2. Assault (example)

Organization for an Assault

7-47. The battle formation in an offensive action may include a designated battalion as an assault detachment that forms motorized rifle companies as assault groups. Maneuver companies may also form assault groups built using a platoon as the core element. The assault groups are typically allocated reinforcements and additional capabilities based on the assigned mission tasks.

7-48. The detachment conducting an assault is assigned an AO and objective. A key coordination point with respect to an AO is whether a higher headquarters is controlling the airspace associated with the assault.

7-49. An assault group is organized into subunits designated to perform specific mission functions for attack, cover and reinforcement, fire support, obstacle, and, depending on the situation, a reserve. The attack group receives support from the other elements that allow it to close with and destroy an aggressor unit or position.

Assault Subunit

7-50. The assault combined arms subunit is the action subunit. Actions center on maneuver, supported by enabling fires, from an assault position to and beyond the objective. Typical tactical tasks expected of the assault subunit are—

- Clear.
- Destroy.
- Occupy.
- Secure.
- Seize.

7-51. The assault subunit is the main attacking element of the assault. It maneuvers to and seizes the specified aggressor position, and defeats or destroys any aggressor forces at the objective. Speed of execution is critical to an assault. The assault subunit will use surprise and situational factors of limited visibility, terrain, and camouflage, concealment, cover, and deception.

7-52. The basis for the assault group is a motorized rifle subunit that is allocated additional forces and means to include—

- Tanks.
- Self-propelled artillery.
- Mortars.
- ATGMs.
- Grenade launchers.
- Flamethrowers.
- Engineer sappers to breach barriers with explosive and demining charges.
- Additional ammunition, hand and antitank grenades.
- Aerosol generators.

7-53. The assault subunit may be composed of one or two motorized rifle subunits reinforced with tanks and flamethrowers. If possible, it moves in advance of the attack under conditions of limited visibility to occupy positions near the objective. If that is not possible then it approaches the objective under the cover of fire preparation for the offensive. The attack group launches the assault against the objective at the same time as the general attack by the first echelon units.

Fire Subunit

7-54. The fire support group that includes attached artillery and mortars uses its fires to perform several functions. Allocated fire support units and subunits—

- Suppress aggressor personnel and weapons, especially antitank.
- Breach obstacles on the approaches to the objective.
- Destroy buildings or other structures.
- Fire barrages that protect the flanks.
- Defeat any counterattacking units.

Security Subunit

7-55. Security subunits provide several functions including covering the flanks and rear of the assault group. It also secures the objective to prevent any aggressor counterattack units from breaking through to retake the position. The security group also locates and secures any underground approaches to the position. Typically, the security group is a motorized rifle subunit reinforced with antitank weapons, grenade launchers, and mortars.

7-56. The security subunit provides reconnaissance for early warning of approaching aggressor forces and prevents aggressor forces from reinforcing the assaulted position. The Russian commander may accept risk and employ a security subunit that can only provide early warning but is not strong enough to halt or repel aggressor response elements.

7-57. It is typically the first element to act in an assault. Security subunits move to a position to guard the main body. It denies the aggressor freedom of movement along any ground or air avenues of approach that can reinforce the objective or interfere with the mission of the main body. The security subunit can be directed to perform other tactical tasks to include—

- Ambush.
- Block.
- Canalize.
- Delay.
- Disrupt.

- Fix.
- Contain. (This task usually requires multiple subunits.)
- Isolate. (This task usually requires multiple subunits.)
- Destroy.

Obstacle Subunit

7-58. The obstacle subunit ensures the mobility of the assault group. It initially breaches prepared obstacles and marks the lane or lanes. It prepares and places explosive charges to breach the defensive barricades or structures of the defending unit. On direction from the assault group, it detonates those charges and immediately assesses whether a repeated demolition is necessary to breach the defensive fortifications. It also accompanies the assault group to provide aerosol screens to allow maneuver close to the objective or thermobaric munitions fire to disable defenders.

Reserve Subunit

7-59. If allocated, a reserve subunit consists of one or two squads or a platoon for a larger assault group. It strengthens either the assault or security subunits. It also may exploit the success of the assault or perform unexpected tasks.

AMBUSH

7-60. An ambush is a surprise attack from a concealed position directed against a moving or temporarily halted target. Ambushes are categorized as fire, reconnaissance, and false. The fire ambush is typically used as an offensive action to destroy, defeat, or deter an aggressor unit. A reconnaissance ambush gains information on aggressor plans or equipment. A false ambush delays, redirects, or distracts an aggressor as part of a deception plan.

7-61. In a fire ambush, aggressor action determines the time of attack, whereas the SV selects the location of attack. Ambush effects include but are not limited to—

- Gain information on aggressor units, equipment, and personnel.
- Destruction or capture of aggressor personnel and supplies.
- Demoralization and continued harassment of aggressor.
- Denial or blocking of aggressor maneuver and supplies.
- Canalizing aggressor units into kill boxes.

7-62. Key factors in an ambush are—

- Surprise.
- Control.
- Simplicity.
- Security.
- Coordinated fires.
- Withdrawal.

Organization for an Ambush

7-63. An SV combined arms unit or subunit conducting an ambush is typically organized into several subunits or groups: observer, capture, security, and control and fire support subgroups. There may be more than one of each of these types of subunits.

Observers

7-64. The observer subunit sets the outer security perimeter for the designated ambush site. Its mission is to observe and report on movement of aggressor forces. It communicates directly with the control subunit to provide information for a decision to launch the ambush. It does not engage aggressor forces unless discovered and forced to withdraw.

Capture

7-65. The capture subunit attacks to defeat or destroy aggressor forces in a kill zone. The capture group takes prisoners and gathers documents, weapons, and equipment. An ambush can be a primary or complementary action that prevents an aggressor from accomplishing its mission.

Security

7-66. The security subunit has the mission to prevent aggressor elements from responding to the ambush before completion of the capture subunit actions. The security subunit prevents the capture subunit from becoming decisively engaged and supports effective withdrawal of all subunits from the ambush site.

Support

7-67. The support subunit of an ambush has the same basic functions as that of an assault. Typically, the detachment commander exercises C2 from the support subunit.

ORGANIZATION FOR AN AMBUSH

7-68. Planning and preparation of an ambush prioritizes massing combat power into a kill zone. One or more kill zones can be employed depending on the terrain, expected size of the aggressor elements, and Russian combat systems coverage of the kill zone. Firing positions provide concealment, cover, and favorable fields of fire into the kill zone. Manmade obstacles reinforce the restrictions of natural obstacle and the terrain.

EXECUTING AN AMBUSH

7-69. At a C2 signal or terrain-oriented point, the capture subunit engages the aggressor forces in the kill zone. Security subunits engage any aggressor elements not in the kill zone as well as any quick reaction forces responding to the ambush. After the aggressor has been rendered combat ineffective, the capture subunits exploit the objective area and kill zone and withdraw to a rally point. Successful execution of an ambush focuses on the desired effects in the mission order. Effects to achieve can include gaining intelligence information, harassment, seizing prisoners, and annihilation of aggressor elements. See figure 7-3 for an example of ambush.

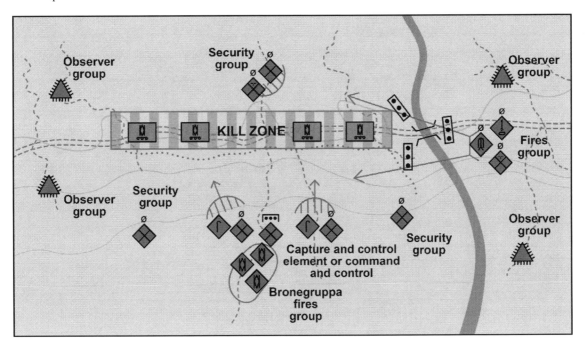

Figure 7-3. Ambush

RAID

7-70. A raid is an attack to temporarily seize key terrain or strike a stationary or moving target to capture or destroy personnel and equipment. Raids can also be tasked to secure selective information and deceive an aggressor by its actions. In the Russian system a raiding detachment can also be used to block aggressor reserves. The SV forward detachment can also conduct raids. See figure 7-4 for an example of raid.

7-71. Raids are characterized by actions to include but not limited to—

- Destroy or damage key systems or facilities.
- Secure designated aggressor materiel.
- Seize prisoners.
- Support IV objectives.
- Support operations that create a tactical opportunity for another Russian unit or subunit.

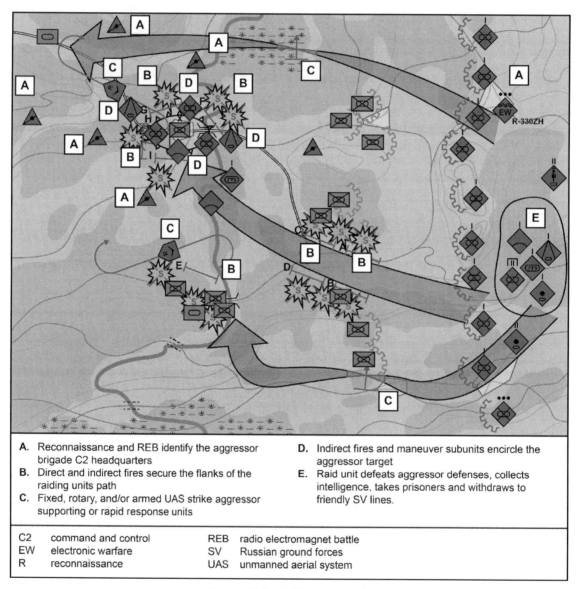

A. Reconnaissance and REB identify the aggressor brigade C2 headquarters
B. Direct and indirect fires secure the flanks of the raiding units path
C. Fixed, rotary, and/or armed UAS strike aggressor supporting or rapid response units

D. Indirect fires and maneuver subunits encircle the aggressor target
E. Raid unit defeats aggressor defenses, collects intelligence, takes prisoners and withdraws to friendly SV lines.

C2	command and control	REB	radio electromagnet battle
EW	electronic warfare	SV	Russian ground forces
R	reconnaissance	UAS	unmanned aerial system

Figure 7-4. Raid (example)

Organization for a Raid

7-72. The raiding subunit typically consists of multiple subunits and additional forces and means depending on the situation; this can include reconnaissance, observers, attack, destruction, capture, support, armored, and reserve. Other supporting units may be task-organized dependent on the mission such as rotary or fixed-wing ground support aircraft or long-range fires. The size of the raiding subunit depends upon its mission, the nature and location of the target, and the size and disposition of the aggressor. Typically, a Russian raiding detachment will consist of a reinforced battalion with allocated functional forces and means.

7-73. Reconnaissance units and subunits perform intelligence collection on the raid objective to determine critical information. Using ground, air, electromagnetic warfare methods, reconnaissance provides the raiding unit with the essential information on the raid objective. The reconnaissance determines—

- Specific objective location.
- Strength of aggressor units and subunits.
- Composition and weapons.
- Defensive and security organization.
- Covered or covert avenues of approach.
- Landing sites for insertion of raid groups.
- Aggressor reserves or response units and the likely routes they will use.

7-74. The composition of the reconnaissance group depends on the size and location of the raid objective. It may generally have a base of 1–2 reconnaissance companies to cover the entire perimeter of the raid objective. Initial reconnaissance will most likely be accomplished by UAVs or army aviation.

Raiding Subunit

7-75. The raiding subunit has functional groups that perform the attack, capture, and destruction of personnel, equipment, and facilities. The attack group is organized to conduct the assault to overcome the aggressor forces at the raid objective. It may be allocated sappers, flamethrowers, grenade launchers, and other direct fire supporting weapons. The capture group focuses on seizing documents, prisoners, or specified equipment. The demolition group prepares designated equipment and facilities for destruction.

Support Subunits

7-76. The support subunit uses stealth to occupy positions to fix aggressor security and response forces that could disrupt the raiding subunit in its tasks. Security tasks can include preventing aggressor escape from the objective. The raid commander generally accompanies the support subunit to coordinate the actions of the various raid subunits. The security subunit also protects the withdrawal as raiding subunits move to new locations.

7-77. The security subunit moves to a position to deny the aggressor freedom of movement along any ground or air avenues of approach that can reinforce the objective or interfere with the mission of the assault subunit. The security subunit can be directed to perform other tactical tasks to include—

- Ambush.
- Block.
- Canalize.
- Delay.
- Fix.
- Contain. (This task usually requires multiple subunits.)
- Isolate. (This task usually requires multiple subunits.)
- Destroy.

Armor and Reserve Subunits

7-78. Based on reconnaissance information the senior commander allocates armor units and sufficient maneuver reserves to defeat an aggressor counterattack. The armored group and reserve remain under the control of the raid commander.

EXECUTING A RAID

7-79. The reconnaissance group conducts preliminary information gathering on the raid objective and any supporting aggressor positions. The reconnaissance group identifies aggressor positions and unit dispositions via aviation and electromagnetic warfare capabilities. Ground reconnaissance subunits subsequently use identified covered routes and approaches to advance to the area of the raid objective to establish over watch. Advances are typically conducted during limited visibility and dismounted at a distance to allow covert approach to the raid objective.

7-80. Army aviation, fixed-wing air strikes or indirect fires target likely aggressor units or positions that could support the raid objective. The allocated fires are focused on defeating a coordinated response against the raid.

7-81. Multiple observer groups establish a perimeter around the raid objective. These groups report to the raid commander to provide constant information flow on the activities at the objective. They also report on any aggressor ground or aviation units responding to the raid.

7-82. The support group follows using covered or covert routes to establish blocking position around the objective. Its positions cover both the raid objective as well as potential avenues used by aggressor units responding to the raid.

7-83. The attack group conducts a covert approach to the target and conducts the initial assault to defeat aggressor defenders. Once the raid objective is secure the capture group moves to seize, secure, and evacuate designated personnel or equipment. The destruction group prepares equipment or facilities for demolition and then withdraws as part of the raid subunit under the cover of the support unit.

7-84. The armor group either supports the raiding subunit to assist in overcoming any aggressor maneuver forces or defends against responding aggressor armored units. Armored personnel carriers or tanks of the attack group my form the armored group as a bronegruppa.

TACTICAL OFFENSIVE ACTIONS

7-85. The types of tactical SV offensive actions guide decision making on how to best achieve a mission during large-scale war. An offensive mission typically includes subordinate units executing specified offensive and defensive actions within an overall offensive mission framework. In the SV tactical combat formations, both units and subunits are typically deployed in two echelons in both the offense and defense. On the offense, the second echelon is expected to take advantage of the success of the first echelon and, by maintaining the offensive, attain the subsequent objective of the parent organization.

ATTACK

7-86. An attack is an offensive action that destroys or defeats aggressor forces, seizes and secures terrain, or both. It seeks to achieve a tactical objective through primarily military means by defeating the aggressor's military power. This defeat does not necessarily result from the destruction of equipment but through the disruption, dislocation, and subsequent paralysis that occurs when combat forces are rendered irrelevant by the loss of the capability or will to continue the fight.

7-87. All SV attacks integrate offensive actions using combined arms to destroy the aggressor's will and ability to continue armed conflict. An integrated attack is often conducted when SV forces enjoy overmatch against an aggressor and focus significant aspects of combat power on an objective. It can also be directed against a more sophisticated and capable opponent when a tactical opportunity emerges or is created during an operation. See figure 7-5 on page 7-17 as an example of an integrated attack.

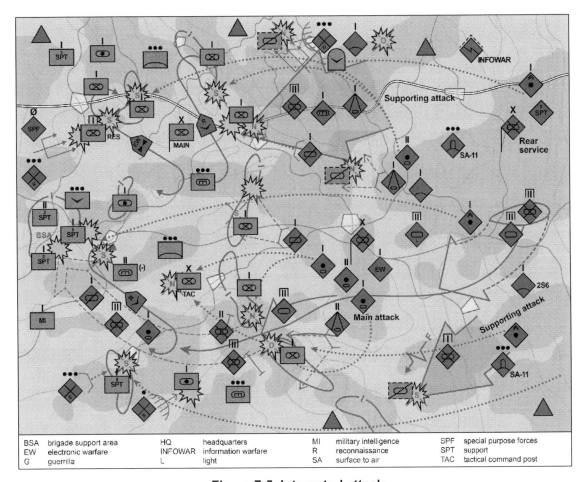

BSA	brigade support area	HQ	headquarters	MI	military intelligence	SPF	special purpose forces
EW	electronic warfare	INFOWAR	information warfare	R	reconnaissance	SPT	support
G	guerrilla	L	light	SA	surface to air	TAC	tactical command post

Figure 7-5. Integrated attack

7-88. The SV recognizes that modern militaries cannot continue without effective command and control or adequate logistics support. Successfully striking either one severely impacts an aggressor's ability and will to continue to fight. As such, an integrated SV attack locates the main groupings of the aggressor maneuver units and bypasses or fixes them with sufficient forces and means to allow the main body to strike weak points and attack into the C2 and logistics support areas.

7-89. The SV uses automated control and communications systems coupled with connected C2 points to manage forces and means and integrate their effects against an aggressor. The integrated network and organization provide rapid solutions to generate the desired impact on aggressor forces.

COMBINED ARMS ATTACK

7-90. Combined arms attacks are characterized by—

- Integrated management of forces and means using automated systems in combat with an aggressor.
- Targeting and focused attacks on aggressor logistics and C2.
- Degrading aggressor situational understanding with IV actions.
- Disrupting aggressor forces using reinforced complex terrain and irregular forces.
- Fixing designated aggressor maneuver forces.
- Isolating and striking targeted critical components of the aggressor combat system.
- Defeating aggressor forces with fires, creating the conditions for combined arms maneuver, and capitalizing on IV actions.

- Ultimately destroying the aggressor unit's will and resolve to continue armed conflict.

7-91. The SV prefer to conduct integrated attacks when most or all of the following conditions exist:

- Possess significant overmatch in combat power over aggressor forces.
- Operate in an operational environment with at least air parity in an AO against the aggressor. Key fire complexes are secured using maneuver units, air defenses, and electromagnetic warfare units.
- Degrade aggressor standoff reconnaissance and attack systems to acceptable levels of risk assessment as determined by the SV commander.

ORGANIZATION FOR A COMBINED ARMS ATTACK

7-92. A combined arms integrated attack employs all available types of forces and means to strike an aggressor at vulnerable points. The SV commander assigns designations to subordinate units that correspond to their intended roles in the attack. An integrated attack employs units and subunits to locate and report on aggressor activities, security or protection subunits, main body, and support forces.

7-93. The advance guard and forward security subunits prevent aggressor defending forces, reserves, and counterattack forces from interfering with the actions of the main body. The mission task for the advance guard and forward security units of a designated aggressor force can be time-related or when relieved of the task by the Russian commander.

7-94. The main body is charged with destroying a particular component of the aggressor's combat system or seizing key terrain. This action will permit another force to do the same.

7-95. A support force provides the assaulting detachment with one or more of the following but is not limited to—

- Material technical support.
- Supporting direct fire such as an antitank reserve.
- Supporting indirect fire.
- Mobility and countermobility support.
- Electromagnetic warfare.
- Security, isolation, and fixing functions.

7-96. The main body seeks to exploit the actions of a forward detachment and advance guard. This force must be capable of penetrating or avoiding aggressor defensive forces and destroying targeted critical components of the aggressor combat system. To accomplish the assigned immediate and subsequent objectives, the main body will typically possess a task-organized combination of subunits that provide both mobility and protection, as well as firepower.

7-97. Russian doctrine states that a successful modern offensive is not possible without strikes throughout the breadth and depth of an opposing aggressor's defense using continuous fires, extensive maneuver, and a constant build-up of combat forces to achieve overwhelming mass. The battlefield situation may dictate that the SV use an offensive that relies on dispersion of forces and IV effects to conduct tactical actions while overmatched by an aggressor. Depending on the battlefield situation it may be necessary for the SV to conduct an attack using multiple avenues of attack or the remote effects of dispersed forces and means. These types of offensive actions are particularly necessary when threatened by an aggressor that retains precision fire or aerospace strike capabilities. The primary objective of dispersed attack is to create tactical opportunities to destroy the aggressor's will and capability to continue armed conflict. To achieve this, the SV does not necessarily have to destroy the entire aggressor force, but simply destroy or degrade key components of the aggressor's combat system.

DIVERSIONARY ATTACK

7-98. The concept of a diversionary attack is to conduct recurring attacks throughout the battlefield, using varied timing, to degrade vulnerable aggressor capabilities. A diversionary attack can be used against peer forces when tactical opportunities emerge and support the gradual defeat of the aggressor combat system. Diversionary attacks by air inserted ground forces, reconnaissance, and spetsnaz throughout the battlefield integrate with the main attack as shown in figure 7-6 on page 7-19.

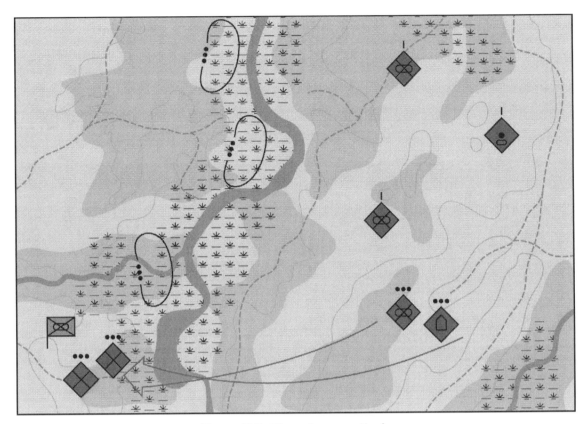

Figure 7-6. Diversionary attacks

7-99. Diversionary attacks are characterized by—

- Degrading aggressor situational understanding with IV.
- Targeted attacks on key components of the aggressor's combat system.
- The use of multiple exploitation forces such as reconnaissance, air assault, airborne, and spetsnaz.
- Disrupting aggressor forces with reinforced complex terrain and disruption forces.
- Fixing designated aggressor forces.
- Isolating targeted critical components of the aggressor combat system.
- Conducting recurring attacks on critical components of the aggressor combat system.
- Defeating aggressor will and resolve with IV.
- Destroying aggressor will and resolve to continue armed conflict.

7-100. To establish tactical conditions favorable for diversionary attacks, considerations include but are not limited to—

- Destroy aggressor ground reconnaissance.
- Deceive aggressor imagery and signals sensors.
- Create a vulnerable air defense environment.
- Deceive situational awareness and understanding by the aggressor.
- Optimize use of complex urban and rural terrain.

Diversionary Attack Organization

7-101. The mission of a diversionary attack is to disrupt or destroy a particular component of the aggressor's combat system or seize key positions to support the main attack. Such an assault can create favorable conditions for the exploitation force(s) to rapidly move from dispersed locations and penetrate or infiltrate aggressor defenses.

7-102.   A diversionary attack employs various types of forces to strike critical targets and divert aggressor forces from the main attack. The tactical group commander assigns subordinate unit designations that correspond to their intended roles in the attack; assigned designations include ambush, raids, air assaults, irregular forces strikes, or airborne assaults. A diversionary attack includes indirect fires to disrupt or destroy target defenses that facilitate attacks to complete the destruction of the immediate and subsequent defending aggressor units.

7-103.   The air assaults may use ground forces without combat platforms to allow insertion into the aggressor support areas. These air assaults may be conducted by a motorized rifle battalion up to 60 km into the aggressor support area and a company up to 40 km.

7-104.   Attacking numerous points throughout the battlefield, the diversionary attack strikes the aggressor to disrupt communication, C2, and reserve forces to facilitate the actions of the main body. The mission task of a diversionary unit may be to fix a designated aggressor force for a designated time or until relieved of the task by the Russian commander. Multiple diversionary units and subunits of various types may be employed during the attack.

7-105.   Combat support subunits throughout multiple dispersed sites in an area of operations manage and supply the diversionary attack. Support includes one or more of the following but is not limited to—
- Command and control (C2).
- MTO.
- Supporting tank and ATGM direct fire.
- Supporting indirect fire.
- Mobility support of engineer and NBC subunits.
- Information warfare support using psychological warfare and REB.
- Security, isolation and or fixing functions.

URBAN ASSAULT

7-106.   When conducting offensive actions in an AO that contains dense urban terrain the SV bypasses it if possible. The SV does so to continue taking advantage of the motorized rifle and tank unit and subunit mobility and maneuverability. If an assault on dense urban terrain is necessary as an objective the SV units and subunits use surprise and sudden rapid maneuver as much as possible to advance. The target urban area is encircled to prevent resupply or reinforcement of the aggressor garrison. Artillery suppresses and destroys aggressor strongpoints as the assault begins and continues fires to block reserves.

7-107.   Assault detachments are specially organized depending on the size of the defending aggressor unit and the amount of defensive preparation accomplished prior to the assault. These task-organized subunits have the offensive task of capturing strongpoints or a designated portion of the urban terrain, normally 2–3 blocks.

7-108.   Assault detachments are motorized rifle battalions and subunits based on motorized rifle companies task-organized as assault groups. A typical assault group often contains—
- 3 motorized rifle (airborne, air assault) platoons.
- 1 tank platoon.
- 1 flamethrower squad (three flamethrower operators).
- 1 ZSU (self-propelled air defense mount, Shilka or Tunguska).
- 1 engineer obstacle-clearing vehicle.
- 1 UR 77 (mine clearing vehicle).
- 1 combat engineer platoon.
- 1 medical team (physician and corpsmen).
- 1 technical support squad.

7-109.   The tanks and organic armored personnel carriers or BMPs follow the assault groups to provide supporting fires. Their heavier fires are used to engage and destroy aggressor strongpoints, to cover the flanks of the assault and repel any counterattacks. Tanks do not typically travel down contested streets because of the lack of maneuver space. The BMPs or armored personnel carriers may trail the assault groups to provide supporting fire once buildings on each side of a street are secured to avoid aggressor attacks from above.

7-110. The assault groups move to the target objective by advancing through buildings on each flank of a street or thoroughfare. The BMPs or armored personnel carriers take up positions behind the assault group and approximately 200 m from the target objective. If available, robotic devices perform reconnaissance, detection, or engagement of aggressors found along the route of advance.

7-111. Artillery subunits and army aviation helicopters support the assault with preliminary precision fires. Forward air controllers and artillery fire direction soldiers collocate with the assault command post to coordinate fires.

7-112. Using incendiaries, smoke, and aerosols the assault group launch simultaneous attacks on separate areas of the defending aggressor. Artillery in direct fire mode engages opposite corners of a structure to create breaches for the assault group to use in penetrating into the building. Engineers accompany the assault to expand the breaches and, if present, defuse mines or improvised explosives.

7-113. The assault group enters the building or facility and attacks to the top. Once at the top they clear from the top to any subterranean levels. This process continues until the urban area is cleared and the destruction of the aggressor garrison is complete. Once the assault is complete the assault detachment is immediately withdrawn and reconstituted for follow-on missions.

FORCING WATER BARRIERS

7-114. The SV anticipates that in almost any operating environment its units and subunits will be required to force a water obstacle whether rivers, lakes, canals, estuaries, reservoirs, flooded or marshy areas or other bodies of water. In the operating environment of Eastern and Central Europe, a 6 m wide obstacle is found every 20 km, rivers up to 100 m wide are found every 35–60 km, those that are 100–300 m wide every 100–150 km, and at 250–300 km are rivers that are 300 m wide. In offensive actions over this terrain the SV units and subunits would be required to force one medium sized river and several tributaries daily.

7-115. Recognizing this potential offensive requirement the SV equips its tanks, armored personnel carriers, IFVs and other supporting equipment with the ability to ford shallow bodies of water by using either an integrated snorkel or swim capabilities. In the event of deeper water obstacles, the SV uses engineer bridging subunits with armor-launched bridges, pontoon ferries, engineer temporary repair of damaged bridges, or deliberate bridge construction.

7-116. The SV conducts two types of assaults to force water barriers, unopposed and opposed. An unopposed river assault may be launched against light or unorganized defenses as shown in figure 7-7. An opposed assault normally involves an established aggressor defense based on the river as an obstacle and requires significant ground, artillery, engineer, army aviation, and NBC forces to successfully attack.

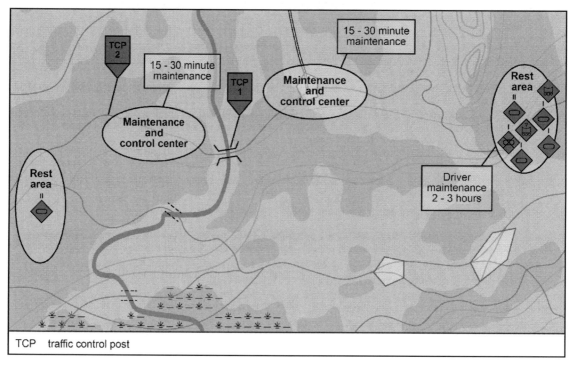

Figure 7-7. Unopposed river assault

PLANNING AN OPPOSED CROSSING OF A WATER BARRIER RIVER ASSAULT

7-117.   Opposed river assaults require deliberate planning and organization of the forces and means as opposed to forcing a hasty crossing using fording sites or the swim and snorkel capabilities of combined arms units and subunits. A successful crossing requires—

- Comprehensive reconnaissance of both the defending aggressor and the water barrier.
- Careful and thorough preparation to control movement to and crossing of the water barrier.
- Identification of covered approaches to the crossing site.
- Misdirection or deception to create surprise.
- Air defense of both the crossing and the march approaches.
- Annihilation fires against the defender positions, C2 positions, tank concentrations, and ATGMs.
- Positioning and deployment of ferries or bridging equipment supporting the crossing.

7-118.   The desired method of forcing a water barrier on the move is a rapid advance to the selected crossing site, heavy but brief indirect fires on the defending aggressor, crossing the water barrier on a wide front, and immediately launching a decisive attack on the defenders on the opposite bank. Once the advance units force the crossing, they continue the attack to prevent the defenders from re-establishing a defensive line or counterattacking.

7-119.   For an opposed crossing when in direct contact the planning and preparation are more deliberate and systematic. The commander conducts a thorough reconnaissance and analysis of both the near and far banks to identify a crossing site. The assessment also determines whether the threat of defender air defenses will allow an air assault to the far bank to block any counterattack force and to disrupt the defense.

7-120.   The supporting crossing elements composed of engineer bridging, pontoon ferries, NBC aerosol and smoke subunits, and crossing management teams assemble in protected sites close to the water barrier. Electromagnetic warfare and counterreconnaissance patrols cover the crossing unit to prevent aggressor early detection by electromagnetic or physical reconnaissance means. If possible, an air assault is landed to isolate the rear of the defensive positions and repel any attempt at reinforcement. An indirect fire bombardment of the defending position suppresses the defenders on the far bank as well as fires against supporting aggressor artillery. Tank and ATGM fires strike the defensive positions as the crossing unit begins its transit of the water barrier. The crossing unit navigates the water barrier and continues the attack to quickly destroy the aggressor strongpoints and continue to penetrate the depths of the defense as shown in the figure 7-8.

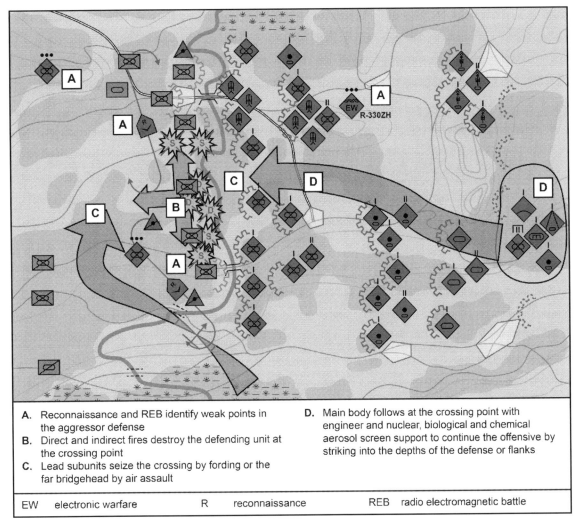

A. Reconnaissance and REB identify weak points in the aggressor defense
B. Direct and indirect fires destroy the defending unit at the crossing point
C. Lead subunits seize the crossing by fording or the far bridgehead by air assault

D. Main body follows at the crossing point with engineer and nuclear, biological and chemical aerosol screen support to continue the offensive by striking into the depths of the defense or flanks

EW	electronic warfare	R	reconnaissance	REB	radio electromagnetic battle

Figure 7-8. Opposed river assault

RECONNAISSANCE BY BATTLE

7-121. A reconnaissance by battle is a tactical offensive action to confirm situational understanding of an aggressor's location, disposition, and actions to fix, defeat, or destroy a designated aggressor. This offensive action can be used to gain specified information and intelligence on an aggressor's capabilities and intentions for Russian tactical advantage in a future mission.

7-122. The SV fights for information and resulting intelligence when necessary to retain or regain the initiative. Reconnaissance by battle integrates a complex set of mission tasks and can be employed when other reconnaissance means do not provide accurate situational understanding of an aggressor and an AO.

7-123. Key factors in employing a reconnaissance by battle, as a complement to continuous aggressive reconnaissance, security, and related offensive actions, include but are not limited to—

- Situational awareness requirements of an evolving aggressor presence and actions in an AO.
- Tempo of conditional developments to regain situational understanding and tactical initiative.

- Multiple attack routes or axes often characterize reconnaissance by battles. There may also be objective rally points and orientation objectives.

Reconnaissance by Battle Organization

7-124. The detachment commander typically organizes a reconnaissance by battle with reconnaissance, security, action, and support subunits. More than one subunit of each type is typical in this mission due to the several simultaneous requirements and actions occurring in multiple zones within an AO.

7-125. The reconnaissance by battle employs several reconnaissance subunits to confirm the location and actions of aggressor elements operating in the detachment's AO and conditions of the OE. If the mission purpose is to fix and destroy aggressor elements when located, reconnaissance subunits provide reconnaissance support to other subunits such as security and actions subunits.

7-126. Security subunits operate in conjunction with reconnaissance elements, but also conduct reconnaissance tasks during the security mission. Upon locating an aggressor element and on order of the detachment commander, actions by security subunits include but are not limited to—

- Fix or isolate designated aggressor elements.
- Block aggressor reinforcement avenues of approach.
- Ambush aggressor on withdrawal routes from a target or objective.
- Protect subunits during movements, maneuver, and follow-on mission tasks.

7-127. The action subunit or subunits obtain a mission descriptor that clearly identifies the primary action task. Actions can include mission tasks such as assault, ambush, or raid.

7-128. The detachment commander monitors initial reconnaissance and security actions that confirm the aggressor situation and then decides on actions to fix, isolate, defeat, or destroy a designated aggressor element. More than one action subunit is normal due to simultaneous actions occurring in multiple zones of action within an AO.

7-129. Support subunits are task-organized with particular capabilities and a priority of effort and support to designated elements in the reconnaissance by battle detachment. The detachment commander locates command and control nodes in an AO to most effectively receive and report timely reconnaissance and security indicators among the detachment subunits. An extended depth and width of an AO may require a detachment FCP well forward in an AO for reliable real-time information and intelligence for C2 situational understanding of the OE and the aggressor.

Executing Reconnaissance by Battle

7-130. Multiple subunits normally infiltrate or maneuver separately within an AO to find and report the current aggressor situation. Then, the detachment commander directs when to fix, and defeat or destroy the aggressor elements.

7-131. Initial supporting functions include multiple reconnaissance and security subunits operating within designated zones of action to confirm the aggressor situation. Other actions include reporting on an AO trafficability of routes and axes for follow-on movements and maneuver of the reconnaissance by battle. See figure 7-9 on page 7-25 as an example of reconnaissance by battle.

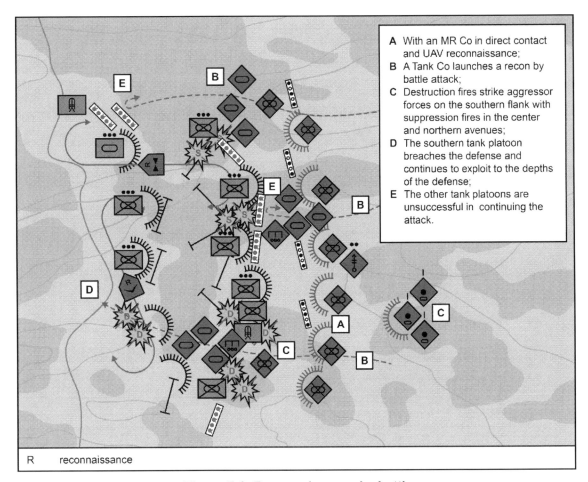

Figure 7-9. Reconnaissance by battle

Support of a Reconnaissance by Battle

7-132.   The SV uses multiple types of forces and means that collectively support the mission task of reconnaissance by battle. Support systems can include reconnaissance, security, direct and indirect fires support, aviation, radio-electromagnetic combat, air defense, engineer, logistics, and higher-level IV.

Fires

7-133.   Integrated indirect fires, air defense, and radio-electromagnetic combat provide responsive fires to all subunits prior to and during the reconnaissance by battle, and support the withdrawal of reconnaissance, security, action, or other support subunits after completion of the mission. Fires in a reconnaissance by battle strike planned or opportunity targets to—

- Protect reconnaissance and security subunits in their zones.
- Protect action and support subunits in maneuver or other offensive actions on aggressor locations and terrain-oriented objectives.
- Suppress, neutralize, or destroy designated targets in an area of operations.

Aerospace

7-134.   Army aviation elements can be task-organized and integrated into the fires support, or to reconnaissance and security subunits, and maneuver subunits. Aerospace forces also provide airlift of SV units and subunits to conduct air assaults to strike specified objectives for the reconnaissance by battle. The

MTO support requirements for the air assault units and subunits may be provided by army and aerospace forces until ground linkup with SV maneuver subunits is accomplished.

Engineer

7-135. Engineer support focuses initially on mobility tasks to assist SV movements and maneuver throughout an AO. This support is primarily to provide breaching manmade or natural obstacles. Engineer units are also task-organized to conduct countermobility actions in support of tasks such as block or isolate designated aggressor elements as integral to the reconnaissance by battle by emplacing obstacles and minefields on likely avenues of counterattack.

Material Technical Support

7-136. A reconnaissance by battle typically has dispersed subunits throughout an AO and often operates over extended time periods. The SV positions task organized MTO support with subunits and can conduct a system of logistics caches and mobile resupply points to sustain the subunits during the mission.

INFORMATION WARFARE

7-137. Information Warfare (IV) activities in a reconnaissance by battle are primarily executed to—
- Protect SV units from aggressor detection by technical means.
- Deceive aggressor units to reveal their actions and intentions.
- Assist in fixing or isolating aggressor elements.
- Degrade or disrupt C2 capabilities.
- Deny, defeat, and destroy aggressor communication networks.

DISRUPTIVE ATTACKS

7-138. A disruptive attack achieves results critical to a tactical operation by denying critical capabilities to the aggressor. The results of a disruptive attack typically support the overall success of Russian operations, preserve Russian combat power, and degrade aggressor capabilities. The primary objective of a disruptive attack is to degrade a particular aggressor capability, system, or group of systems, but can also disrupt the aggressor tempo of operations.

7-139. Disruptive attacks are characterized with actions to—
- Focus on disruption or destruction of a designated target or objective.
- Fix designated aggressor forces.
- Isolate targeted critical components of the aggressor combat system.
- Optimize use of systems warfare.
- Deny the aggressor a particular capability.

7-140. There are two types of tactical disruptive attack: spoiling attack and counterattack. These share some common characteristics but differ in tactical purpose. Disruptive attacks are conducted in battle or pre-battle formations. If in contact, the defending unit transitions directly into a battle formation. If not in contact, it moves from a position into a pre-battle, then battle formation.

COUNTERATTACK

7-141. A counterattack is an offensive action by a designated force against an aggressor attacking force with the primary aim of destroying an attacking aggressor unit. A counterattack unit may also recover lost positions and establish favorable positions for follow-on offensive actions. Typically, it is a mission task initiated from a SV defending force, it causes an aggressor offensive action to culminate and allows the SV to control the tempo of operations and retain or regain the tactical initiative.

7-142.   Counterattacks are characterized with actions to—
- A shifting in command and support relationships to assume an offensive posture for the counterattacking force.
- A proper identification that the aggressor is at or near culmination.
- The planned rapid transition of the remainder of the force to the offense.
- The possibility that a counterattack may open a window of opportunity for other combat actions.

7-143.   The SV seeks to set the following conditions for a counterattack:
- Locate and track aggressor reserve forces and cause them to be committed.
- Destroy aggressor reconnaissance forces that could observe counterattack preparations.

SPOILING ATTACK

7-144.   The purpose of a spoiling attack is to preempt or seriously disrupt an aggressor attack while the aggressor is in the process of planning, forming, assembling, or preparing to attack. A spoiling attack can also affect aggressor defensive operations by disrupting the tempo of related aggressor activities. The spoiling attack is designed to disrupt or deny aggressor actions favorable to conducting an aggressor attack.

7-145.   Spoiling attacks are characterized with actions that—
- Confirm intelligence of aggressor tactical plans and preparations.
- Identify a critical aggressor vulnerability.
- Indicate a timely and rapid action to counter aggressor plans and preparations.
- Retain or regain the tactical initiative.

7-146.   The SV shape the following conditions for a spoiling attack with—
- Reconnaissance, intelligence, and surveillance of aggressor attack preparations.
- Target acquisition of aggressor security, reserve, and response forces that could possibly disrupt the spoiling attack.
- Fix designated aggressor forces.
- Isolate targeted critical components of the aggressor combat system.

Organization for a Disruptive Attack

7-147.   Organization for a disruptive attack may appear similar to a combined arms integrated attack. However, the functions of forces differ in the tactical conditions. A disruptive attack could be ordered during offensive or defensive operations, while a counterattack would typically be ordered for execution out of a defensive operation. Disruptive attacks are characterized with actions to—
- Focus on disruption or destruction of a designated target or objective.
- Fix designated aggressor forces.
- Isolate targeted critical components of the aggressor combat system.
- Optimize use of systems warfare.
- Attack to deny the aggressor a particular capability or disrupt aggressor tempo.

7-148.   The most common type of action force in a disruptive attack is an assault force or exploitation force. The primary purpose of the mission task is the description assigned the action force.

7-149.   A counterattack often employs fixing, assault, and support forces. The disruption force was generally part of a previous Russian defensive posture.

7-150.   The fixing unit in a counterattack is that part of the force engaged in defensive action with the aggressor. These forces continue to fight from their current positions and seek to account for the key parts of the aggressor array and ensure they are not able to break contact and reposition. Additionally, the fixing force has the mission of contacting and destroying aggressor reconnaissance forces and any combat forces that may have penetrated the Russian defense.

7-151. The assault unit, an enabler when supporting an exploitation force, can be assigned tasks of forcing a penetration of aggressor forces, continuing the assault, causing commitment of aggressor reserves, and similar actions that fix aggressor forces and degrade aggressor reaction to an exploitation force.

7-152. A support unit provides task-organized material technical support and C2 functions. Other specialized support is mission dependent.

7-153. Attacks can include domains of land, maritime, air, space and cyber. Interdependent and coordinated actions by dispersed units/subunits attack throughout assigned areas of responsibility. Specific actions aim to destroy key components of an aggressor's combat system, degrade the resolve of an aggressor, and gradually defeat an aggressor's ability to continue a conflict with continuous IV actions.

OFFENSIVE TYPES

7-154. The SV continues to structure offensive actions based on three battlefield conditions relating to the state of the targeted aggressor unit. The primary distinction among types of offensive missions is the senior commander's purpose defined by the tactical objective in support of an operation. These include—
- The attack against an aggressor unit in either a hasty or prepared defense.
- The meeting battle against a maneuvering aggressor.
- The pursuit of a withdrawing aggressor.

7-155. The integration of ground and air reconnaissance, REB, and information from higher echelons all provided by automated C2 greatly aids the SV commanders in selecting the time and place of offensive actions. The senior commander directs and controls indirect strikes and fires using precision targeting provided by the automated complexes. The damage to the aggressor defenders and their positions allows the ground maneuver units and subunits to attack and complete the destruction of the target unit.

Attack Against a Defending Aggressor

7-156. The attack against a defending aggressor is the primary type of Russian offensive combat operations. There are two methods used to conduct this attack: attack from the depths out of direct contact, often termed an attack from the march, and attack from a position in direct contact with the aggressor.

7-157. An attack from the march is the favored mode of attack. A division, regiment, or brigade will launch the attack from a concentration area out of indirect fire range. The SV moves units and subunits to the source area using Russia's extensive rail network, heavy transporters, or aerospace aircraft. The source area allows the units and subunits to disperse sufficiently to protect against aggressor long-range and aerospace strikes. The senior commander directs the organization of the march from the source area, along designated routes, to the attack line.

7-158. The units and subunits of the attacking brigade or division conduct the march with synchronized indirect fires, air defense, REB, NBC, and higher-level strikes. The SV perceive the advantages of the attack from the march as follows:
- Unit is not committed prior to attack to allow rapid redirection or maneuver.
- Improved chance of surprise.
- Greater flexibility.
- Less vulnerability to indirect fire.
- Preparations for combat are made from aggressor contact.
- Increases momentum.

7-159. The attack from a position in direct contact with a defending aggressor is the less preferred manner of attack, although, the SV believes that it does have certain advantages. The SV units in contact with the aggressor defense synchronize their fires with those of the attacking units to suppress and destroy long-range ATGMs, tanks, and indirect fire platforms. Direct contact allows the SV to use the advantages of—
- More thorough reconnaissance for understanding of the terrain and aggressor defenses.
- Permits organization of the attack to focus on weak points or gaps in the defense.

● Improved coordination of fires to strike the selected breach point creating the conditions for rapid maneuver and attack through the first echelon aggressor defenses.

7-160. An attack against a defending aggressor can transpire in a variety of tactical situations. These actions include, encirclement battles, supporting attacks, breakthroughs, development of the attack into the depths, or exploitation. An attack against a defending aggressor is used when the aggressor is in hasty or prepared defensive positions.

Meeting Battle

7-161. The meeting battle is the second Russian offensive action. A typical meeting battle will occur when aggressor forces are deploying forward, or its attacking force runs into an aggressor counterattack. A meeting battle can also occur when friendly forces advance into the rear of the aggressor's tactical sector. A meeting battle can also come about during the pursuit. Meeting battles are a common expectation on the modern battlefield because of the introduction of sophisticated weapons systems with greater fire power, strike potential, mobility, and maneuverability. See figure 7-10.

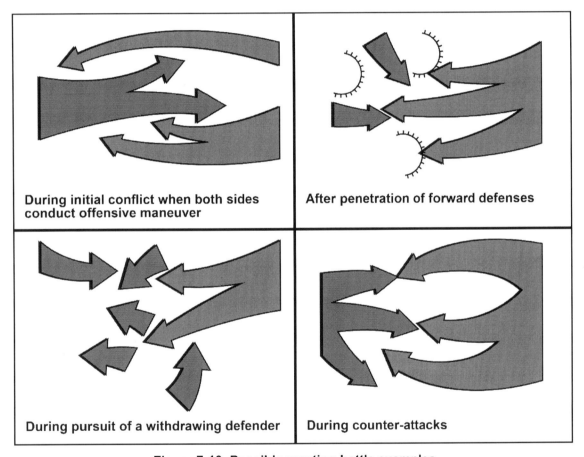

Figure 7-10. Possible meeting battle examples

7-162. The objective of the meeting battle is to annihilate the aggressor and to maintain offensive action as shown in the example in Figure 7-11. The SV believes the side who grasps and maintains the initiative will prove victorious, even when outnumbered by their opponent. Because of the nature of its assignment, forward detachments often play a substantial role in meeting battles. The forward detachment moves in advance of the brigade or army main body by 2 – 3 hours to secure key terrain and to fight the aggressor's covering force and cause it to commit without the SV main body being engaged.

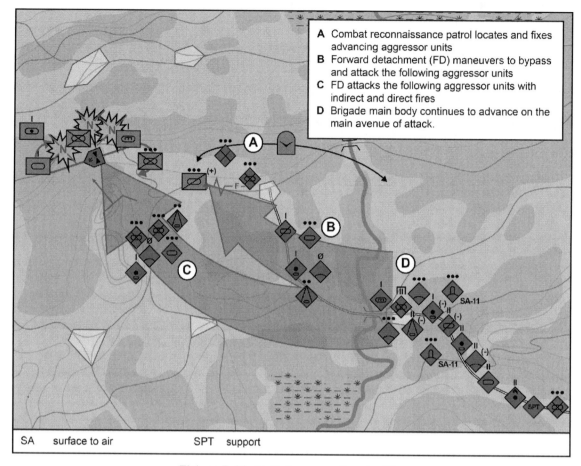

A Combat reconnaissance patrol locates and fixes advancing aggressor units
B Forward detachment (FD) maneuvers to bypass and attack the following aggressor units
C FD attacks the following aggressor units with indirect and direct fires
D Brigade main body continues to advance on the main avenue of attack.

SA   surface to air   SPT   support

Figure 7-11. Battalion meeting battle

7-163.   Russian military leaders stress the following thoughts on the meeting battle:

- Continuous and thorough reconnaissance to ensure success.
- Continuous and intense fires and combat to seize and maintain the initiative.
- Rapid troop deployment from march or pre-battle formation to battle formation.
- Situation uncertainty at the outset and throughout the battle.
- Rapid and sharp situation changes.
- Fluidity of operations.
- Developing in-depth operations along a wide front.
- Rapid decision making and bold action to allow an inferior force to defeat a superior force.
- Deployment and firing first may be the deciding factor.
- Exposed flanks and gaps in the forward line and great emphasis on maneuver make good flank and rear security critical.
- Initiative and creativity by battalion, company, and platoon commanders will be crucial.

7-164.   The SV states that the meeting battle is more than just a chance encounter. SV commanders are trained to foresee and plan for meeting battles. They quickly identify the likely point of contact, swiftly seize key terrain, and above all, seize the initiative through massed fires. The SV reasons that the side which violently seizes the advantage with fire and maneuver will prevail in a meeting battle.

7-165.   A meeting battle continues until the assigned mission objective is completed. It may last for a few minutes for a small security outpost to several hours or days for a brigade or division. Ultimately, its goal is to destroy the targeted aggressor and continue offensive action in the direction specified by the senior commander.

Pursuit

7-166. The pursuit is an attack upon a withdrawing aggressor, with the aim of destroying or preventing the aggressor from transitioning into an organized defense. Russian commanders are authorized to initiate the pursuit without waiting for orders from their higher headquarters. This allows the Russian commander to keep pressure on the aggressor, ensuring that it is unable to break contact and conduct a disciplined withdrawal. The SV considers pursuit the principal form of exploitation that allows the attack to be carried into the operational depths of the aggressor. There are three types of pursuit as shown in figure 7-12.

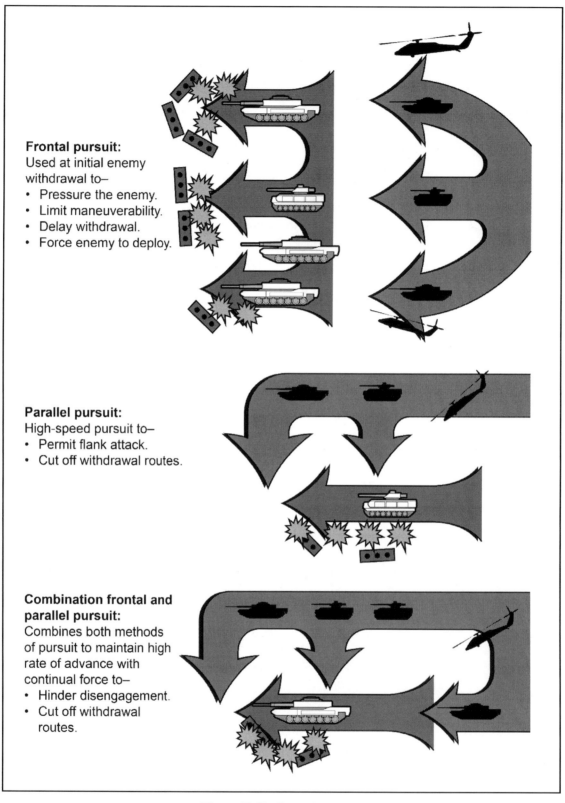

Frontal pursuit:
Used at initial enemy withdrawal to–
- Pressure the enemy.
- Limit maneuverability.
- Delay withdrawal.
- Force enemy to deploy.

Parallel pursuit:
High-speed pursuit to–
- Permit flank attack.
- Cut off withdrawal routes.

Combination frontal and parallel pursuit:
Combines both methods of pursuit to maintain high rate of advance with continual force to–
- Hinder disengagement.
- Cut off withdrawal routes.

Figure 7-12. Pursuit types

7-167. A frontal pursuit is an attack along the aggressor's withdrawal route. The parallel pursuit is designed to outdistance the aggressor and perform a close or deep envelopment intended to firmly block and attack the retreating aggressor. Used alone however, the parallel pursuit runs the risk of losing contact with the aggressor. To set conditions for success, the SV prefers a combined pursuit. Employing a combination of the frontal and parallel pursuit, the combined pursuit is designed to destroy the aggressor's covering force and apply constant pressure on its withdrawal. See figure 7-13 for an example of a combined pursuit. In all cases the pursuit continues to use all forces and means to close with and destroy the aggressor units.

7-168. A combined arms maneuver battalion typically fights as a brigade subunit during a pursuit, but it may conduct an independent pursuit of a smaller aggressor force if the tactical situation occurs. In an independent pursuit a platoon advance party moves to a blocking position in front of the withdrawing aggressor force. The remainder of the battalion conducts a secure march on a route parallel to the aggressor and deploys successive company subunits into pre-battle and then battle formations to attack the flanks of the withdrawing aggressor at favorable positions.

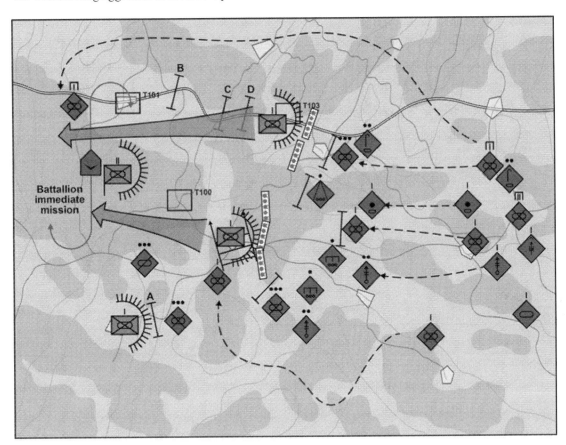

Figure 7-13. SV combined pursuit of a withdrawing aggressor

MARCH – PRE-BATTLE – BATTLE FORMATIONS

7-169. Motorized rifle and TDs, regiments, and brigades use three formations when moving towards an aggressor and conducting an attack. The SV uses march, pre-battle, and battle formations for combined arms attacks. The senior commander defines the sequence and transition points based on their understanding of the terrain, aggressor dispositions, the capabilities of their own units and subunits.

March

7-170. The SV conducts marches from concentration areas beyond the range of tactical aggressor artillery to attack defenses or to pursue withdrawing forces. The SV uses the march formation to allow rapid maneuver while retaining the capability to shift quickly from offense to defense or vice-versa. Normally the SV conducts a march at night to use the advantage of reduced visibility to decrease the chance of detection. The significant advantages U.S. and NATO forces have in night vision and radar systems increase the likelihood that the SV will conduct marches during daylight hours under the cover of organic and higher echelon air defenses, electromagnetic suppression of ISR, and smoke that degrades both visual and electromagnetic detection.

7-171.   To organize units and subunits the march begins from the concentration area 30–40 km from the front edge of the defending aggressor. While in the concentration area units and subunits are dispersed to mitigate damage from long-range precision engagements by an aggressor. The dispersion between units in a battalion may occupy 10 sq km or more depending on the terrain and ability of aggressor fires to strike the area. Under the same conditions a maneuver brigade may disperse over a 100 sq. km area. The example in figure 7-14 shows a possible laydown of units and subunits with at least 1.5 km between the companies of a battalion.

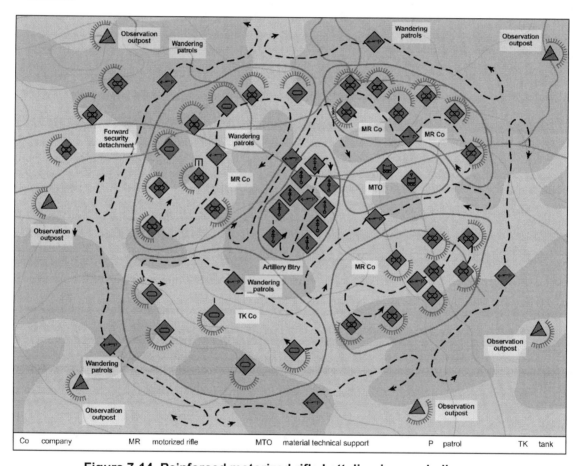

Figure 7-14. Reinforced motorized rifle battalion in marshaling area

7-172.   The senior commander defines positioning of units in concentration areas and the sequence of forces in the march to ensure the planned offensive maintains speed, maneuverability, and massing at a selected place and time. The march formation typically places reconnaissance, guard, and march support units and subunits forward to develop the situation, ensure rapid movement, and give advance information on the location and disposition of aggressor units as shown in figure 7-15 on page 7-35. In modernized brigades and divisions forward reconnaissance and security will include UAVs capable of flying out to 120 km from the main body to supply real-time information to the marching unit. Using automated C2 complexes the information transmitted by tactical UAVs as well as higher level intelligence is pushed to marching units and subunits.

7-173. The formations found in the march order of a brigade, regiment or higher tactical force conducting offensive maneuver are as follows:

- Reconnaissance detachment—As much as 60 km forward of the leading units of the main force.
- Forward detachment—Up to 50 km forward of the main force including allocated artillery. Attacking against a defending aggressor an army-level forward detachment is a reinforced battalion from the second echelon brigade and if from an attacking brigade then the forward detachment is a reinforced battalion or company from the brigade's second echelon.
- Advance guard—15–20 km forward of the main force to cover the route of the main body with the mission of destroying aggressor forward security, attack to breakthrough to the main aggressor unit, and maintain contact with the aggressor while aiding the deployment and attack of the SV main body.
- Movement support—Moving with the security element are engineer, NBC, or other support subunits required to ensure the routes for the main body are clear.
- Artillery subunits—Positioned between the security element and main body to conduct planned fires that breach the aggressor's defense from the forward edge to the depths of the defense.
- Air defense—Interspersed in the march formation from the security force through the main body to provide anti-air protection while on the move or during brief stops to engage threats.
- Main body—The threat from aggressor precision strikes causes the main body to increase its dispersion to 100–150 m between vehicles and up to 1 km or more between battalion march columns.
- MTO subunits—Typically trail the rear of the main body by at least 1–2 km. As required by a nonlinear battlefield rear march outposts normally composed of a reinforced platoon will cover the march route to guard against attack from the rear.
- March outposts—Each battalion posts detachments that guard the head, flanks, and rear of the march formation. The lead march security detachment (known as GPZ) is normally a reinforced platoon with the task of destroying small aggressor groups. The lead march security detachment employs patrol squads to move on the route of march to identify ambushes, mined, or other obstacle areas. The patrols rapidly advance under the cover of fire from the lead march security detachment's main body. If unable to overcome the aggressor, it deploys to place fires on the aggressor and aid in the deployment of the security subunit to complete the destruction. Lateral marching outposts and rear marching outposts are also deployed by the unit to guard the flanks and rear of the march formation.

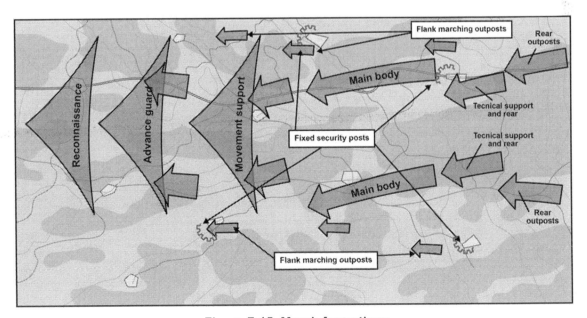

Figure 7-15. March formations

7-174.   The march plan defines the routes, rest or halt areas, as well as the concentration area for the attack. It defines the rate of advance between rests as well as the control lines to maintain synchronized movement. It also defines the areas of responsibility for flank guards and fixed positions during the passage of the main force. The designated march route uses the names of local objects or urban areas to indicate the start, checkpoints, and the final concentration area or line designating the transition to the pre-battle formation. As shown in figure 7-16, it directs the deployment from single columns to multiple columns in preparation for arrival at the concentration area.

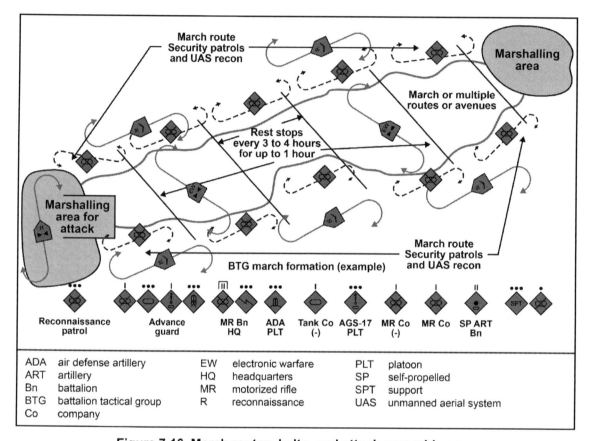

Figure 7-16. March routes, halts, and attack assembly area

Pre-Battle

7-175.   Pre-battle formation is used when transitioning from march formation to begin the offensive maneuver, to overcome chemically contaminated areas or manmade or natural obstacles. It is designed to facilitate rapid deployment into battle order requiring high rates of advance to reduce exposure and vulnerability to nuclear strikes or attacks by antitank, artillery, or air. The brigade or division commander allocates supporting forces and means to ensure the formations are covered by air defenses, REB, artillery, engineer, and smoke screens generated by NBC units.

7-176.   During pre-battle formation the subunits of divisions, regiments, and brigades break down into columns based on the plan and sequence of attack for maneuver towards the designated battle line. The reorganization into columns spreads the attacking units in both width and depth to disperse and reduce the effects of nuclear or precision fires.

7-177.   As shown in figure 7-17, as the unit closes with the defending aggressor's line the units and subunits split into multiple columns to disperse and make targeting more difficult for effective strikes. The line of safe distance from friendly artillery shifts forward as artillery strikes shift into the depths of the aggressor defense.

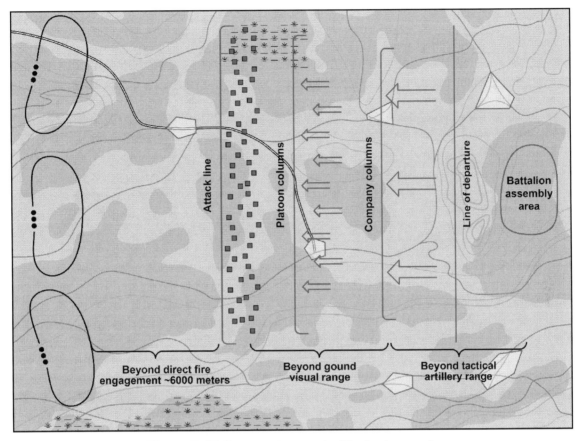

Figure 7-17. Successive pre-battle deployments

7-178.   The example in figure 7-17 should not be interpreted as a rigid deployment of units and subunits into a required formation at a specified distance from the aggressor defense. Pre-battle formations are designed and used by the SV to rapidly disperse and, if the situation requires it, to reassemble into march formation to maintain speed and protection as the unit moves to the attack position. Depending on the terrain and battlefield situation, SV units and subunits may shift between march and pre-battle formation at different times on different routes during the approach to the attack line.

Battle

7-179.   Based on their personal reconnaissance and information from Razvedka subunits, the commander plans the attack on a defending aggressor position and arrays the organic and allocated subunits into a final battle formation. The battle formation positions the main combat power against the weakest point of the defending aggressor to facilitate penetration and attack into the depths of the defense. The final battle line is the designated point prior to contact with the target aggressor unit where the units and subunits are assembled and ready to go on the attack.

7-180.   The formation consists of first echelon, second echelon or reserve, indirect fire, and reinforcing units remaining under the direct control of the senior commander. The final battle formation may include forward, special, flanking, raid, or assault detachments. Airborne assault forces may be included to bypass a natural or manmade obstacles, strike into the rear of the defense, or capture key terrain or facilities in the depth of the defense.

7-181.   The commander's plan integrates forces and means with the battle formation to ensure penetration of the defense and attack throughout its depth. These include helicopter fires, electromagnetic suppression, and artillery delivered mines to obstruct and compartmentalize maneuver by the defending force. A maneuver brigade or division allocates supporting subunits to motorized rifle or tank battalions to create greater independence during the attack. For the duration of the battle the allocated subunits are directly subordinate and respond to the battalion commander. The remaining parent units are subordinate to the senior commander but will also support the battalions based on the allocations specified in the senior commander's plan. See - figure 7-18.

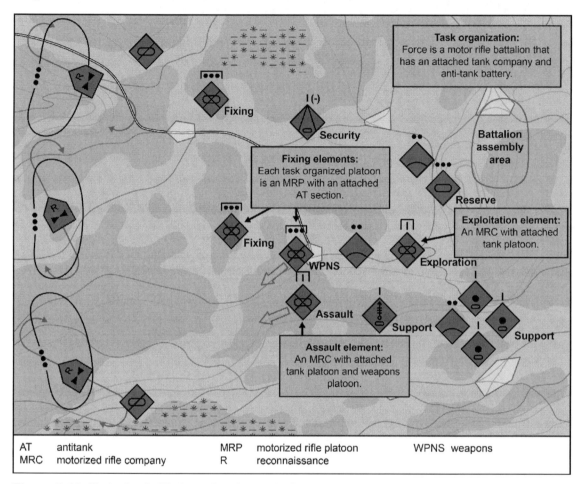

Figure 7-18. Motorized rifle battalion in battle formation, tanks allocated to the first echelon

TACTICAL MANEUVERS

7-182.   While the march, pre-battle, and battle formations are used by the SV as the methods to get offensive units and subunits to the attack, it is the use of tactical maneuvers that places the SV in position to conduct a decisive attack. There are several common tactical maneuvers the SV uses either singularly or together: close envelopment, deep envelopment, and double envelopment.

7-183.   Close and deep envelopments involve indirect fires placed on the defending aggressor force often in barrage lines or moving barrage lines. Based on the senior commander's specified level of damage or destruction the artillery barrages proceed the attacking ground force using successive lines or area fires as the attack progresses. A unit or subunit attacks the aggressor positions from the front while a close envelopment maneuvers to an open flank, penetrates to the depth of 3 – 5 km for a battalion or brigade depending on the depth of the aggressor defenses and attacks into the open flank. For a deep envelopment the process is much the same with the depth of the envelopment possibly 15 km or more, again, depending on the aggressor defenses.

7-184.　As shown in figure 7-19, a deep envelopment would penetrate to the depth of an aggressor battalion defense. The figure depicts a task-organized BTG conducting a double envelopment against a defending aggressor mechanized infantry company.

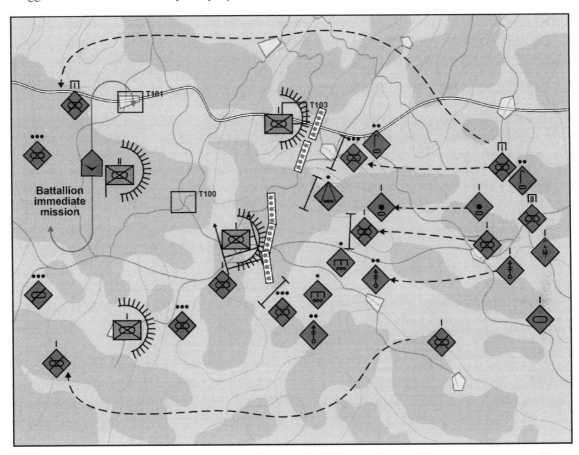

Figure 7-19. BTG deep double envelopment

7-185.　Double envelopments combine both close and deep envelopments. The attacking force once again applies indirect fires throughout the depth of the aggressor defense. Targets are identified by both ground and aerial reconnaissance or as part of the preplanned fires specified by the senior commander. The attacking force presses the frontal attack while the enveloping units or subunits maneuver on both flanks of the defense to penetrate and attack from the flank or rear of the defense.

LOCAL WARS AND ARMED CONFLICT

7-186.　Russian Federation doctrine describes LW/AC in two elements as separate types of conflict not included as part of large-scale war. First, local wars are conflicts waged for limited military or political goals conducted within the boundaries of the warring states. Second, armed conflicts or internal armed conflicts are limited conflicts between states or limited to the territory of one state. These type actions limit the scope of the SV to conflicts involving primarily tactical echelons with some forces and means from operational and strategic echelons short of total war mobilization. SV actions during LW/AC include all offense and defense tactics as well as those focused on targeting or using irregular or security forces of a target.

7-187.　LW/AC actions create conditions that enable the successful design and execution of SV actions in an OE short of large-scale combat. LW/AC actions compliment SV conduct of other regular and irregular offensive and defensive tasks to counter stability actions of an aggressor, supporting coalition partners and allies. Russia also views LW/AC as including those actions necessary to conduct counterterrorism. These type actions are a main reason behind Russia's development of new methods and forms of tactical actions.

7-188. These doctrinal views stem from the lessons learned during SV actions in the 1980s, 1990's, and beginning of the 21st century. The Russians based development of new tactics, techniques, and procedures on these lessons learned and characteristics of LW/AC. Russia's view of the changes in the world social order indicates that direct large-scale combat is decreasing in likelihood and that LW/AC will be predominant. These type conflicts will stem from interethnic and interreligious conflict. The main results from their analysis guiding their TTP development are as follows:

- LW/AC as a system of warfare includes either action against or inclusion of irregular or disguised regular formations. It will emphasize guerrilla TTPs, avoid direct force-on-force battles, and employ terror, sabotage, and intimidation against civil populations and organized resistance against security forces.
- Hostile actions involve a broad range of unconventional actors, units, and subunits. In tactical actions against atypical aggressors, it is necessary to conduct not only combined arms actions but also integrate other elements of national power.
- The establishment of the BTG is an effective unit formation for actions against irregular forces. It can also integrate and effectively support actions by friendly host-nation elements. The addition of new capabilities of equipment complexes such as unmanned aerial vehicles, REB, and precision fires provides a broad range of responses for LW/AC.
- Precision fires capabilities are more pervasive and necessary in conflict environments.
- Defensive formations required and received a "New Look" to enhance the capability to deter and stabilize a zone of action.
- The SV gained significant experience in the principles of combined arms combat actions.
- The means of combat management to control and direct units and subunits were greatly advanced. Organization of cooperation with friendly host-nation elements, the ability to train units and subunits, and to fully support combat actions all were significantly improved.

7-189. In the evolution of Russia's military forces and means based on their analysis they developed improved methods for fighting illegal groups and for integration of those type groups into their own actions. From this the SV developed a range of tactical tasks for LW/AC. These tasks include—

- Blokirovanie (see paragraph 4-25).
- Encircling and eliminating illegal armed groups, sabotage, and reconnaissance units.
- Security and defense of important facilities.
- Security of communications.
- Escort of columns.
- Maintaining an established regime.
- Enforcing curfews.
- Ensuring security and training of friendly host-nation elements.
- Rapid response to relieve trapped units, subunits, friendly elements or facilities.
- Conduct evacuation of the civilian population or critical property from the zone of conflict.

7-190. The SV views the BTG as an ideal force structure to conduct actions against threats posed by insurgents, irregular forces, and small armies during LW/AC. The BTG provides forces that are more flexible with the combat power and mobility to defeat smaller scale aggressor forces operating in OEs on Russia's periphery. Other security forces from the National Guard and internal security organizations will primarily have the lead in responding to internal threats and conventional SV units and subunits may support their actions as tasked.

7-191. LW/AC is an integral aspect of SV military actions that may have an impact that reaches beyond the tactical and operational effects of armed combat. Whether conducted by regular forces, irregular forces, combinations of regular and irregular forces, and willing or coerced civilians, the desired effects of LW/AC actions focus on disrupting major areas of potential stability in an OE. In support of tactical and operational missions, and probable support of strategic goals, the SV can plan, prepare, and execute LW/AC activities to—

- Discredit an aggressor's civil law enforcement and internal security forces.
- Deride an aggressor's judicial processes.

- Damage an aggressor's civilian infrastructure.
- Degrade an aggressor's civil governance.
- Dissuade relevant population by overt support to the aggressor.
- Disrupt coalition partner and allied support to the aggressor.
- Dislocate the aggressor from regional/global community and diaspora support.
- Defeat the aggressor's military and internal security actions.
- Destroy an aggressor's civilian and military resolve to resist the SV and other Russian forces.

Planning Local War and Armed Actions

7-192. The SV uses conditions of instability to enhance achieving its assigned missions that support Russia's goals and objectives. LW/AC actions can range from covert influence to overt violence and may be based on religious fundamentalism, global competition for resources, climate change, residual territorial claims, ideology, ethnic tension, elitism, greed, and the desire for power. They use these motivations to identify, target, and create conditions of instability, and establish conditions that promote a gradual acceptance of SV objectives by local and regional populations, and can even obtain an eventual acceptance and support from the regional and international communities.

7-193. Russian military forces, including SV units and subunits, plan actions to exceed an aggressor's capacity to exercise effective governance, maintain civil order and obedience, and ensure economic development. An overarching aim is to sustain recurring incidents in a relevant population, create disruptive conditions that threaten to collapse the aggressor's effective governance in an OE, and defeat the practical resolve of the aggressor's forces and the population it represents. Examples of instability sources that the SV can institute or co-opt include but are not limited to—

- Economic conditions that do not provide opportunities for individual work and family livelihood.
- Social and civil conditions that do not provide adequate systems for health programs and general welfare support to a relevant population.
- Degrade or make obsolete infrastructure that diminishes a relevant population's quality of life.
- Charismatic individuals and special interest groups that disrupt effective civil governance.
- Irreconcilable religious, ethnic, economic, or political differences among competing relevant populations.
- Natural and manmade disasters.
- Natural or manmade scarcity of a required commodity.
- Ineffective or corrupt host-nation law enforcement forces.
- Ineffective or corrupt host-nation security forces.
- Rampant criminal activities.
- Guerrillas operating in paramilitary actions.
- Insurgents operating an underground support system and self-proclaimed governance in a relevant population.

7-194. An integrated concept to the SVs conducting LW/AC tasks typically requires a long-term framework that expands and sustains unstable conditions in an OE until achieving the ability to achieve its plans and policies. The range of LW/AC tasks and missions can include support to military actions from small-scale military or paramilitary engagements to participation in major military actions. Related coercive activities in a civilian sector often include crime. Implementation at any point along this range of military, paramilitary, or nonmilitary civil activities can be coordinated by the SV to destabilize the actions of an aggressor and enhance the IV effects of the Russian agenda. LW/AC tasks can be initiated and sustained to discredit an aggressor in various OE conditions that can include but are not limited to—

- Military engagement missions in a region occupied by an aggressor that may or may not have partners or allies in the OE.
- Peace actions to keep and enforce international peace agreements in an aggressor state or aggressor region.

- Civil governance and social well-being activities by an aggressor host-nation or de facto government.
- Civil law enforcement and social justice activities by an aggressor host-nation or de facto government.
- Emergency humanitarian relief actions following a natural or manmade disaster in the region.
- Whole-of-government actions against SV irregular warfare in the aggressor host nation and region.
- Military combat actions against SV regular or irregular forces in a region.
- Post-conflict environments following the general cessation of organized hostilities in a region.

7-195. The SV recognize that decisions and actions by U.S. forces are compliant with international conventions and legal restrictions on conduct of war activities. U.S. forces act typically in a cooperative environment to host-nation laws and regulations when operating as part of a coalition or alliance in a region and conduct actions with rules of engagement that are typically more restrictive than actions demonstrated by the SV.

7-196. Mission planning of LW/AC actions apply combinations of offensive and defensive tasks. Key elements in planning LW/AC tasks include—

- Determine the goals and objectives of the SV.
- Define the time available for plans, actions, and mission completion.
- Discipline the amount of time allowed to plan and prepare for actions.
- Organize forces by function for missions.
- Coordinate IV activities in support of each mission.
- Incorporate recurring observations into refined plans and actions for success of SV goals and objectives.

7-197. LW/AC actions require detailed reconnaissance and surveillance to collect information, develop situational awareness, and determine situational understanding of OE conditions. This continuous intelligence preparation and production, often complemented with support of an indigenous population, provides an appreciation of how to conduct actions most effectively with available resources to achieve specified and implied tasks. Decisions for action will be either offensive or defensive in nature and execution. A conceptual cycle of planning, preparing, executing, and exploiting execution results is a continuum of assessment and evaluation. Learning from this cycle is integrated into performance and improved effects.

7-198. Tactical actions during LW/AC are focused on control of a target population as well as destruction of insurgent or irregular forces. The main actions, in addition to defense and offense, are those that control movement in the battle zone and elimination of the aggressor or target forces. Many are the same actions and tactics used by the SV during large-scale combat with slight variations. To accomplish strikes against aggressors during LW/AC the SV performs actions that are the same as offensive actions during large-scale war as well as some unique to LW/AC.

Blokirovanie

7-199. Blokirovanie (Blocking (блокировка - blokirovka) or screening (экранирование - ekranirovaniye) positions units and subunits to conduct a blocking action against small groups in the zone of responsibility. It positions a Blokirovanie group to cover all means of ingress or egress from a defined area to isolate the aggressor force as shown in the example in figure 7-20 on page 7-43. This group focuses on the designated Blokirovanie area to set the conditions that facilitate the capture or destruction of the aggressor force.

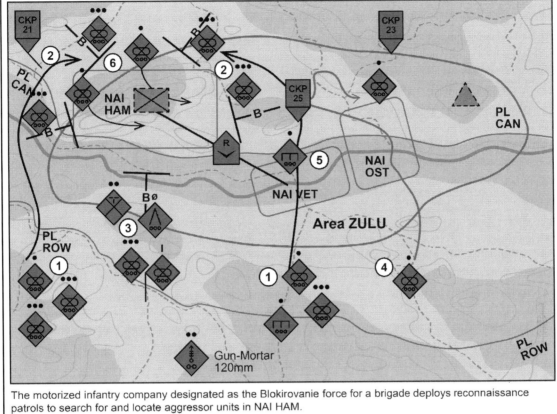

Figure 7-20. Blocking action

The motorized infantry company designated as the Blokirovanie force for a brigade deploys reconnaissance patrols to search for and locate aggressor units in NAI HAM.

Actions to move to and search NAI HAM are as follows:
1. Reconnaissance patrols and UAS move on routes to envelop NAI HAM.
2. PLTs follow and move to occupy blocking positions on all sides of NAI HAM.
3. Supporting mortar, antitank, and sniper subunits position to observe NAI HAM and report readiness.
4. Security element screens eastern flank.
5. Engineer reconnaissance moves to identify crossing sites in NAI VET and NAI OST
6. Reconnaissance patrols search NAI HAM for aggressor units.

| CKP | checkpoint (NATO) | NAI | named area of interest | R | reconnaissance |
| mm | millimeter | PL | phase line | | |

Reconnaissance-Search

7-200. Reconnaissance-search (Разведывательная-поиск - Razvedyvatel'naya-poisk) is often coupled with Blokirovanie as a method of specifically locating insurgent, irregular, or other aggressor forces in a designated Blokirovanie area. The reconnaissance-search enables either the capture or destruction of the targeted aggressor forces. The reconnaissance-search action by SV units and subunits uses all Razvedka assets from deployed motorized rifle platoons to special forces teams (spetsnaz or KSSO), unmanned aerial complexes and REB. The time allocated for the search depends on numerous factors to include subunit tasked, type terrain, urbanization, and fire support coverage among many. The rate of the reconnaissance-search varies based on type terrain:

- Open—up to 3 kph.
- Medium/broken—up to 2 kph, and mountainous.
- Forested or urbanized—1 kph or less.

Ambush

7-201. The SV emphasis on fires is evident in the tactic ambush (Пожарная засада - Pozharnaya zasada). A fire ambush is intended to defeat a target using fires from an unexpected direction or at an unexpected time. It employs preplanned direct fires, surprise short-range concentrated fires, and the use of mine and chemical obstacles. A motorized rifle or tank subunit will conduct a fire ambush and may be allocated snipers, flamethrowers, or sappers depending on the aggressor target.

Raids/Assaults

7-202. Raids/assaults (набег/нападение - nabeg/napadeniye) are used to either destroy an important aggressor unit or facility or to gather intelligence information. For intelligence collection the raid mission is conducted by the reconnaissance (combat reconnaissance) patrol according to the senior commander's plan. The raiding subunit is allocated the combined arms forces and means necessary for mission success.

Pursuit

7-203. Pursuit (преследование - presledovaniye) is an attack upon the withdrawing aggressor with the goals of completing their defeat and preventing them from conducting an organized transition to a defense along favorable axes in depth. For both large-scale combat and LW/AC the SV continues to emphasize the pursuit as an essential tactic for contemporary conflict actions.

Outpost

7-204. Normal missions for an outpost (movement control point) during LW/AC are to control movement to discover and destroy illegal armed formations. The outpost also provides area security to ensure that the approaches to a protected area are not mined. It can also assist ambush subunits with security.

7-205. In addition to typical offense and defense tactical actions the SV is including a new form of combat for LW/AC, a special action. It involves combat actions using a limited SV contingent conducting actions with the border service, internal troops, and security forces to engage either aggressor combat units or its irregular forces. The objectives of special actions are to destroy the aggressor or their irregular forces, their bases, create a zone of separation between warring factions, stabilize the situation, and create conditions for peaceful resolution of a conflict. To accomplish a special action mission, the SV will position its unit and subunits to use the tactical actions listed above.

Manipulation of the Relevant Population

7-206. Infiltrating governmental, intergovernmental, and nongovernmental organizations in an OE is a typical way for the SVs to disrupt aggressor actions and relationships among aggressor actors and institutions. Intergovernmental organizations and nongovernmental organizations are the primary sources of subject matter expertise in many essential services and governance responsibilities. They also are the primary provider of humanitarian, infrastructure, and essential services in immature OEs. Intergovernmental and nongovernmental organizations usually have experienced and detailed knowledge of the civil environment within which they operate. In this principally civilian context, a diverse array of noncombatants can be a significant resource to be manipulated by the SVs.

7-207. Population manipulation is typically the purview of IPb and as such is controlled and directed at the national, strategic, and operational levels of command. The integrated nature of SV C2 and battle management provides the ability of tactical-level units to exploit and complement the effects of the manipulation stratagems, but they are not controlled or directed by tactical level commands.

Preparing LW/AC Actions

7-208. In the preparation phase, the SVs focus on ways of applying all available resources and the full range of actions to place the aggressor in a vulnerable position. The SV takes action to prepare the OE and forces to achieve a mission purpose and considers mission requirements for branches and sequels to a designated LW/AC task. Aspects of camouflage, concealment, cover, and deception and complex terrain provide degrees of force protection and actions security to SV plans, preparations, and actions. As in typical offensive and defensive actions, key considerations include but are not limited to—

- Identify mission objective.
- Conduct reconnaissance (Razvedka).
- Coordinate functional support and logistics.
- Determine plans and actions.
- Rehearse critical actions and finalize mission order.
- Position forces and resources for execution of the mission.

Executing LW/AC Actions

7-209. Executing LW/AC actions may appear as discrete events; however, the SV typically plans and operates with a comprehensive approach to conducting actions to achieve unity of effort toward a primary objective. Cooperation and coordination use the capabilities of disparate actors to conduct a broad array of actions. Shared understanding and appreciation among actors may be a formal organization, long-term association, and temporary affiliation of forces and resources for mutual benefit.

7-210. SV leaders often acknowledge that actors are not compelled to work together toward one common goal but can often be convinced of mutual support and benefit for select activities or support of actions. Achieving a desirable end state can be crafted to accommodate the best interests and goals of diverse participating actors.

7-211. SV actors often use terms for cooperation or coordination that can be understood or misinterpreted depending on the expectations of a particular threat actor. Realistic, consistent, and achievable expectations for an actor in terms of goals, time, and resources can fortify the resolve of SV actors to work together and measure progress of expectations. Several terms that the threat uses with common agreement on definition include—

- Coordination is the process of organizing a complex enterprise in which numerous organizations are involved and bring their contributions together to form a coherent or efficient whole. It implies formal structures, relationships, and processes.
- Consensus is a general or collective agreement, accord, or position reached by a group as a whole. It implies a serious treatment of every group member's considered position.
- Cooperation is the process of acting together for a common purpose or mutual benefit. It involves working in harmony and implies an association between organizations. It is the alternative to working separately in competition. Cooperation with other agencies does not mean giving up authority, autonomy, or becoming subordinated to the direction of others.
- Collaboration is a process where organizations work together to attain common goals by sharing knowledge, learning, and building consensus. Some organizations attribute a negative meaning to the term collaboration as if referring to those who betray others by willingly assisting an aggressor of one's country, especially an occupying force.
- Compromise is a settlement of differences by mutual concessions without violation of core values. Compromise can also be understood to be an agreement reached by adjustment of conflicting or opposing positions, by reciprocal modification of an original position. Compromise should not be regarded in the context of win or lose.

7-212. The SV may desire to create legitimacy for its actions and typically seeks to establish control of a process, resources, or commodity with the acceptance of a relevant population. The manner in which SV actors conduct themselves in long-term actions can foster legitimacy or cause indirect and direct resistance to its actions. Consent or dissent is the extent to which a relevant population agrees with SV actions and complies with the declared authority of a SV mandate. Consent or resistance in a relevant population is typically based on how the SV provides a positive way to improve OE conditions and livelihood of the relevant population.

7-213. SV actions often concentrate on convincing a relevant population that the contemporary actions of the population's established governmental organizations are dysfunctional and corrupt, and that a mandate proclaimed by the governmental organization offers an improved lifestyle. To improve the posture and support of SV goals and objectives in an OE, the SV conducts actions to destabilize aggressor civil and military organizational performance and disrupt support to the aggressor by coalition partners and allies, and defeat aggressor military actions. The threat often replaces the destabilized systems of its aggressor with demonstrated support system capabilities as one of several ways to obtain the active or passive acceptance of a relevant population.

7-214.   In addition to offensive and defensive actions by military forces in an OE, acts of crime can be applied to increase the types and amount of recurring destabilizing incidents that an aggressor must confront.

Appendix A

Fires

This appendix addresses doctrinal capabilities and application of the missile and artillery troops (known as RV&A) as a branch of SV. It provides an overview of equipment and capabilities and limitations of indirect fire units in combined arms operations. These forces employ conventional, chemical, and nuclear fires to destroy aggressor forces.

FIRES COMPLEX

A-1. The Russian military expects a significant threat from U.S. and NATO air power and precision weapons. While having a significant air force and air defenses for protection from those threats it continues to rely heavily on indirect fires rather than fixed or rotary-wing air support. The SV remains an army centered on artillery, missiles, and rockets used to create the conditions for maneuver actions. It continues to use fires to fix and destroy aggressor targets to set the conditions for successful combined arms maneuver tactical actions. Indirect fire complexes coupled with improved precision target acquisition, automated C2, and extended artillery and missile ranges deliver fires either according to the commander's plan or as the battlefield situation requires.

A-2. The SV allocates missile and artillery troops units and subunits from army and corps levels to division and brigade. Division and brigade tactical-level units organize and reorganize artillery units into groups that conduct fires to execute the commander's plan. As the communications and data networks of automated C2 complexes evolve these formations become less necessary. With current fire control capabilities, the SV artillery batteries are capable of split-battery missions and can evolve to the level of single gun missions.

A-3. In addition to these groups that provide planned fires there are strategic-operational and operational-tactical level fires complexes created that link reconnaissance, automated C2, and dedicated artillery and missile units to strike high-value targets. The reconnaissance-strike and reconnaissance-fires complexes target aggressor high-value targets at the strategic-operational and operational-tactical levels respectively. Army and higher retains control of surface-to-surface missiles but will use them to strike high-value targets with these precision weapons.

A-4. At the tactical level artillery complexes consist of the following types:
- Cannons.
- Howitzers.
- Cannon-howitzers.
- MRLs.
- Mountain guns.
- Mortars.
- Antitank guns.

A-5. These complexes are further characterized by size and means of movement:
- Small.
- Medium.
- Large.
- Towed.
- Self-propelled.
- Man-portable.

FIRES EQUIPMENT OVERVIEW

A-6. The speed and ranges on the modern battlefield emphasize the need for rapid movement, establishment of firing positions, and maneuverability in the likely area of operations. These factors influence the fielding of mainly self-propelled artillery in the SV divisions and brigades. Towed artillery remains in some units but is more effective in prepared defensive positions that don't require extensive maneuver for tactical actions. Antitank, guns, and howitzers with direct fire capability are normally positioned on a likely aggressor armored approach while mortars and rocket artillery are in areas that will slow or prevent maneuver by armored threats. See table A-1.

Table A-1. Self-propelled artillery

Characteristic	2S9 Howitzer "Nona"	2S1 Howitzer "Gvozdika"	2S3 Gun "Akatsiya"	2S5 Gun "Goatskins-S"	2S19 Howitzer "Msta-S"	2S7 Howitzer "Pion"	2A35 "Koalitsiya-SV"
Caliber (mm)	120	122	152	152	152	203	152
Max Range (km)	12.8	15.2	17.3–20	28.4–33	29	47.5	70
Rate of Fire (rpm)	8–10	4–5	3–4	5–6	7–8	1.5	12–16
Shell Weight (kg)	17.3	14.1–21.8	43.6	46	42.9–43.6	110	43
System Weight (kg)	8,000	15,700	27,500	28,200	42,000	46,000	49,895
Crew	4	4	4	5	5	7	3
Chassis	BTR-D	MT-LB	Object 123	Object 123	T-80/T-72	T-80	T-90
Ammo Load	40	40	45	30	50	4	65
Set Up Time	-	.3	.5	3	2–2.5	5–6	1.5
Unit of Fire (rds)	80	80	60	60	50	?	60
kg kilogram		mm millimeter		rds rounds		rpm rounds per minute	

CAPABILITIES AND LIMITATIONS OF FIRES

A-7. Russia continues modernization of the SV with a constant emphasis on maintaining its indirect fire capabilities. Improving the flow of information to support target acquisition and transmission of firing data directly to designated artillery or missile units or subunits is a key component of Russia's modernization. Automated command complexes allow SV indirect fire units and subunits to fire on preplanned targets as well as targets of opportunity identified by ground, UAV, or REB sensors.

A-8. Cannons, howitzers, and guns that have a direct fire capability are used in that role to engage and destroy armored targets and prepared defensive positions. These platforms have the necessary sighting systems and crew training to operate effectively.

A-9. Integrated fires in the SV are more reliant on precise target identification and acquisition as well as rapid transmission of target data using automated communications networks. The SV plans to create and operate in a contested electromagnetic environment so their equipment is designed with this in mind. Once the integrated allocation and control of fires is interrupted fires will revert to massed fires required to produce the level of damage defined by nomogram calculations. The reconnaissance complexes supporting target acquisition at the tactical level are shown in figure A-1.

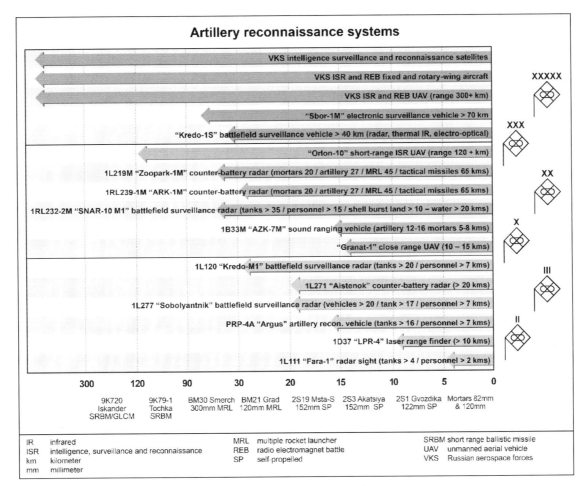

Figure A-1. Artillery reconnaissance

A-10. The necessity of rapid relocation to avoid counterfire creates a vulnerability for missile and artillery troops. While more precise fires is a growing capability in the SV, the continued use and reliance on massed fires creates a high demand for ammunition. The Material Technical Support Operations (known MTSO) plans ammunition resupply based on the normative calculations used to develop the maneuver commander's plan. These calculations determine the quantities, types, and locations of ammunition dumps based on battle plan. Interdiction or destruction of the ammunition transport or storage sites will quickly restrict the plans and actions of tactical forces.

This page intentionally left blank.

Appendix B
Ground Forces Maneuver

The SV contains approximately forty active and reserve maneuver brigades and eight maneuver divisions. Composed of roughly 350,000 personnel, the ground forces are the largest component of the Russian Federation armed forces. Underfunded compared to other branches of the Russian Federation armed forces, the SV relies heavily on Soviet-era equipment stockpiles. By modernizing Soviet-era platforms like the T-72, BMP-2, and BTR-80/82 the SV managed to modernize its maneuver forces at a significantly lower cost. However, the SV is fielding new platforms such as the BMD-4M Airborne Combat Vehicle, BTR-MDM Armored Personnel Carrier, and the Koalitsiya-SV 155-millimeter self-propelled gun. This is considered a hybrid approach, relying on older inventory, while at the same time fielding new systems. Using this amalgam, the SV has greatly expanded its tank forces as well as the size and proficiency of its ground maneuver forces.

GROUND FORCES EQUIPMENT OVERVIEW

B-1.   SV maneuver forces can be broken into two separate spheres. The first, combined arms ground combat, embraces forces involved in large-scale, high intensity ground operations and includes tank and motorized rifle units. Other SV maneuver forces include rapidly deployable Special Operations Forces (known as MTR) which will be covered in Appendix K.

B-2.   The "New Look" reforms which did away with the four-tiered command structure of the military district-army-division-regiment and replaced it with a three-tiered command structure of military district-army-brigade is now a relic of the past. Lessons learned from the conflict in Ukraine provided eye-opening examples of high intensity combat, leading, according to some analysis, to the re-establishment of divisions.

B-3.   The conflicts in Ukraine and Syria have provided the SV with unique testing and training opportunities, particularly in the realm of high intensity combat involving tanks and IFVs. Many SV systems have been tested in combat against current anti-armor guns and missiles.

Note. The equipment overview provided in this appendix is not intended to be exhaustive, but rather to introduce the most widely employed variants of major equipment types used by the SV. For more detailed equipment information, consult the Worldwide Equipment Guide (https://odin.tradoc.army.mil/WEG).

B-4.   What follows are descriptions of equipment divided into three categories: tanks, BMPs and BTRs, and airborne vehicles.

TANKS

B-5.   The SV contains a vast number of tanks. Tank soldiers can be found in tank brigades, regiments and divisions, as well as tank battalions of motorized rifle brigades. Typically, a motorized rifle brigade will have one tank battalion of 31 tanks. However, some motorized rifle brigades contain four companies of 41 tanks. Tank brigades and tank regiments will normally contain three tank battalions.

B-6.   Since the fall of the Soviet Union, Russia has developed three new tanks, two of which, the T-90 and T-14 have been fielded in limited numbers. The modernized T-72 series of tanks remains the mainstay within the SV.

B-7.   The T-14 Armata tank built on the Armata chassis was introduced in 2015, it represents a divergence from historical Soviet/Russian tank production, which stressed uncomplicated mass fabrication. The T-14 is an expensive, technologically advanced tank with adjustable suspension, composite multilayered passive armor protection, and a 125mm smoothbore cannon which can fire numerous types of munitions. Plans are in the works for an upgraded 152mm gun. Powered by a Chelyabinsk A-85-3A X diesel engine which can produce 1500hp, the T-14 also contains a technologically advanced Tank Information Control System (known as TICS) which monitors the tanks internal workings. The T-14 Armata also utilizes the Afganit active protection complex, which can intercept shaped-charged grenades, antitank missiles, and sub caliber projectiles. Plans are also in the works to provide the T-14 with a tethered UAV. The SVs goal of building 2,300 vehicles on the Armata chassis by 2025 appears unrealistic based on high cost and current state of the Russian economy.

B-8.   The T-90 first entered service in 1992. Over the years it has undergone several upgrades. In 2020 an upgraded version, the T-90M was received by a motorized rifle division in the Western Region of Russia. This division is part of a guard's TA. Plans are in the works to upgrade 350–400 T-90s to the T-90M. The high cost of the T-14 Armata was a key factor in this decision. The T-90M incorporates some of the new technology found in the T-14 Armata. As an example, the improved 125mm stabilized cannon was borrowed directly from the T-14 Armata. This cannon fires new kinetic rounds designed to penetrate denser armor. Interestingly, the T-90M is also designed to use the complete range of older ammunition. Also, borrowed from the T-14 Armata is the Kalina automatic target tracker, which allows the gunner to identify the target, lock on to it, and automatically fire while moving. A host of add-on armor attachments were also created for the T-90M based on significant losses to T-72 tanks during the Syrian Civil War from antitank guided missiles and rocket-propelled grenades.

B-9.   The T-80 main battle tank was first produced in the late 1970s. The current variant the T-80U is equipped with the 9M119 Refleks antitank guided missile system. Fired from the main gun it has a range of 4,000 m and is designed to defeat explosive reactive armor. The system can also engage helicopters at a range of 5 km. The T-80Us main gun is a 125mm automatic smoothbore gun with thermal sleeve that can fire up to 8 rounds a minute. The main gun can fire a host of rounds including armored piercing, high-explosive antitank and high-explosive fragmentation.

B-10. The T-72 is the real workhorse of the SV armored force. Approximately 50,000 T-72 tanks have been built since 1972. When assessing SV armored forces, the modernized T-72 and not the T-14 should be the focal point. The modernized T-72 will remain the mainstay of SV maneuver forces for the foreseeable future. The current upgraded versions of the T-72 include the T-72B3 or T-72B3M/T-72B4. This massive refurbishment program for the T-72 has produced what is basically a new tank, with more in common with the T-90 than with earlier versions of the T-72. It is estimated that at least 1,300 older model T-72s have been upgraded to T-72B3 versions. Current upgraded versions of the T-72 include a radio system for encrypted digital voice and data transfer, a snorkel system for fording operations, and a built-in blade for self-entrenching. The T-72B3M is equipped with the 2A46M5 smoothbore gun and can fire a wide range of ammunition as well as the 9M119 Refleks guided antitank missiles. Both the projectiles and missiles are loaded by an autoloader. Indeed, the T-72B3M can rival the most advanced tanks in the world.

B-11. The BMPT tank support vehicle nicknamed the "Terminator" is constructed on a T-72 or T-90S tank chassis and is designed to maneuver with tanks. It weighs 47 tons and contains a crew of five. The vehicle has a low-profile turret and laminated reactive armor. The BMPT contains a 30mm automatic cannon and a coaxial grenade launcher, as well as an AT-14 Kornet ATGM, and a 7.62mm Machine gun. A new version of the BMPT is now being field tested. Called a Combat Fire Support Vehicle (known as BMOP) and dubbed "Terminator-2" it performs the same mission as the BMPT, although the Combat Fire Support Vehicle with its dual 2A42 30mm automatic cannons has the capability to successfully engage light armored vehicles, tanks, IFVs, fortified structures, and low flying aircraft.

BMPs and BTRs

B-12. Motorized riflemen of the SV are typically carried into combat by the wheeled BTR-80/BTR-82 or the tracked BMP-3. In the artic areas the MT-LB is often used.

B-13. There are currently 4,000 BMPs in the SVs regular formations and 8,500 in depots. Introduced in 1990, the current mainstay of motorized rifle troops is the BMP-3. The BMP-3 is an amphibious tracked IFV intended to operate in independent units or in unison with main battle tanks. It is equipped with the 2A70 100mm rifled gun. The rifled gun can fire conventional shells and the 9M117 ATGMs (AT-10 Stabber). The BMP-3 is also equipped with a 2A72 30mm and a 7.62mm PKT machine gun. The vehicle also contains two 7.62mm bow machine guns. The BMP-3 has a crew of three and can hold seven dismounts. With the 9K116-3 "Basnya" ATGM weapons system the BMP-3 can engage targets out to 6,000 meters. The top speed of the vehicle is 45 mph with a combat radius of 370 miles. The BMP-3M is the new upgraded version of this vehicle. The BMP-3M has upgraded combat sights and upgraded night-fighting capabilities. Experts in the field believe that most of the BMP-3Ms have been enhanced to the BMP-3M specifications.

B-14. A new IFV, the Kurganets-25, designed to replace the large fleet of BMPs has been indefinitely delayed due the budget restraints. In its place, the SV plans to upgrade current BMP-3s with a variant christened the Manul. The Manul would be a "transitional" IFV with a more powerful engine mounted in the front of the hull for better crew protection. The Manul would also carry eight dismounts and would include a rear door ramp. The Manul would also have an unmanned turret. The BMP-3s 100mm rifled gun has been removed while features developed for the Kurganets-25, like remote-control systems and sensors have been incorporated into the Manul. It is unlikely that any of these vehicles have been fielded.

B-15. The BTR-80 is an 8x8 wheeled amphibious armored personnel carrier which entered the SV inventory in 1986. The BTR-80 has a crew of two and can hold a motorized rifle squad of eight soldiers. The vehicle employs a turret mounted KPVT 14.5x114mm heavy machine gun and a coaxial 7.62-54mm PKT machine gun. The BTR-80 also has seven side firing ports which allow the motorized rifle squad to fire from inside the vehicle. The BTR-80 has a top speed of 50 mph and a combat radius of 375 miles. There are no rear doors on the BTR-80. Crews dismount through the roof hatches or through two side doors. Certain variants of the BTR-80 mount a 30mm 2A72 automatic cannon.

B-16. The BTR-82 is an improved version of the BTR-80. The BTR-82 entered the SV inventory in 2011 and is used by the SV, Naval Infantry, and Airborne forces. The BTR-82 has a more powerful engine than the BTR-80, and enhanced features which provide better protection to the crew from mines and small-arms fire. A special spall liner also provides greater protection from other weapons systems. Experts believe the new enhancements give the BTR-82 a twenty percent higher survival rate than the BTR-80. The BTR-82 is also equipped with air conditioning, digitally encrypted R-168 radios, and a topographic navigation system. While a new BTR, the Bumerang, is in the works, it has not yet been fielded.

B-17. The MT-LB was initially designed as an armored, amphibious artillery tractor. Because of its good performance on wetlands and snow it has become the preferred vehicle for units serving in northern regions of Russia. The MT-LB has a crew of two and can carry 11 dismounts. The MT-LB is sometimes equipped with the 12.7x108mm NSVT heavy machine gun which has a maximum effective range of 1500 m.

AIRBORNE VEHICLES

B-18. The SVs concept of "deep battle" requires high levels of mobility, and this applies to its airborne and special operations forces. To be both airmobile and mechanized lighter vehicles are required.

B-19. The BMD-4M is the most recent IFV employed by airborne and special operations forces. The BMD-4M is an upgraded version of the BMD-4. In 2018, 132 BMD-4Ms were ordered by the SV for delivery to airborne and special operations forces in 2018-2020. The vehicle has a crew of two and can hold six soldiers. Firing ports were removed to increase armored protection. While the BMD-4M is lightly armored due to weight limits, it does possess extremely powerful weapons systems designed to engage aggressor armored vehicles. The BMD-4M is armed with a 100mm gun and a 30mm automatic cannon. The 100mm gun uses an automatic loading system with a maximum rate of fire of ten to 15 rounds per minute. The 100mm gun can also fire the Bastion laser-guided anti-tank missile. With a range of 5.5km, the Bastion can successfully engage helicopters as well as tanks. The BMD-4M also contains a new digital fire control system.

B-20. The BTR-MDM is a tracked airborne-multipurpose amphibious armored personnel carrier. The vehicle is also used by naval infantry. The BTR-MDM was designed for the transportation of soldiers, fuel, ammunition, spare parts, and lubricants. The BTR-MDM can also be used as a command post and medical vehicle. Armaments on the BTR-MDM include a roof-mounted autonomous fire control turret which can be armed with a 7.62mm or 12.7mm machine gun. The carrier also has two smoke grenade dischargers. The BTR-MDMs hull offers protection against small arms fire and shell fragments.

B-21. The 2S25 Sprut-SD was designed for use by airborne forces and naval infantry. The amphibious vehicle is a 125mm tank turret mounted on a BMD chassis. The Sprut-SD has a three-man crew. The gun system can fire a host of rounds and is equipped with an autoloader. The Sprut-SD can also fire ATGMs. New versions of this light tank are in the works. The new Sprut (Sprut-SDM1) will purportedly be placed on a BMD-4M chassis and will be outfitted with new electromagnetics, targeting, and fire control resources. According to experts in the field, the upgrades will give the Sprut almost the same firepower as a T-90 tank.

CAPABILITIES AND LIMITATIONS

B-22. Recruiting professional soldiers has increased over the last ten to fifteen years, along with upgrading heavy artillery, missile artillery, and electronic warfare units. Ostensibly, Russia has prioritized reconnaissance, communication, and the creation of permanently ready units at full staffing levels. Ground forces emphasize mobility and are increasingly capable of conducting short but complex, high-tempo operations.

B-23. However, SV still heavily rely on conscription and variations of similar equipment yet fall short in personnel and unit numbers. Russia's most advanced capabilities are in the Western Military District, and the Southern Military District appears to have the most competent units. Even with a focus on permanent readiness, however, only a few subunits can be considered deployable.

B-24. Conscription is unpopular and, at 12 months, considered too short by the Russian military to effectively train new conscripts. Most conscripts occupy secondary support roles, although in most maneuver units conscripts comprise up to one-third of personnel. The Russian military's experiences in Ukraine and Syria have reaffirmed for it the importance of massed artillery, rocket fire, and armored forces. However, ground forces have been a relatively low funding priority in Russia's modernization; most of these efforts went into upgrading existing platforms, which decreased standardization across units and increased maintenance costs.

Appendix C
Aerospace Support

With the current reorganization of its aerospace forces (VKS), Russia consolidates all space operations, medium to high level air defense, fixed and rotary-wing aircraft, and transport under one service branch. The integrated VKS supports the SV during strategic, operational, and tactical actions. Fixed and rotary-wing aircraft conduct transport, anti-air, as well as air-to-ground attack in support of SV tactical actions. Army aviation units with rotary-wing aircraft are part of the VKS but primarily support SV ground maneuver. The SV retains organic UASs which primarily support reconnaissance, although air-to-ground attack plays an increasingly significant role.

ELECTROMAGNETIC FIGHTER AVIATION

C-1. Electromagnetic fighter aviation consists of fighter regiments working in close coordination with anti-aircraft units to provide integrated air defense for the SV. The integrated air defense's main purpose is to defeat attacks by aggressor aircraft and cruise missiles as well as prevent or degrade reconnaissance. Front-line aviation fighter regiments are composed of command, combat, and support units located at main and alternate airfields prepared to fully support combat aircraft. Regiments typically consist of two squadrons with four aircraft in each squadron.

C-2. Strike aviation units are the main bomber and assault force of front-line aviation. Units can launch strikes against targets at operational depths of 250 - 400 km. It also provides direct support to tactical level SV units. Its main tasks are destruction of aggressor mass destruction weapons and launch systems, defeat of reserves, C2, air assaults, and support for ground maneuver. Strikes require detailed coordination and integration between the strike aviation, army aviation, missile, rocket, and artillery, as well as electromagnetic warfare (REB) units.

C-3. Reconnaissance aviation uses manned and unmanned aircraft to obtain data on aggressor units, terrain, and weather. Many reconnaissance aircraft have dual capability to both collect data as well as attack high priority targets located during reconnaissance. The main tasks of reconnaissance aviation are collecting information on aggressor units and battlefield conditions to include—
- Locating weapons of mass destruction and launch systems.
- Identifying unit locations, defensive lines and facilities.
- Identifying lines of communication and support.
- Locating airfields and launch facilities.
- Identification of air defense units and coverage.
- Precision target acquisition prior to strikes.
- Nuclear, chemical, and biological conditions.
- Determining the result of missile and aviation strikes on targets.

C-4. Military transport performs not only movement of soldiers and equipment but also has the capability to conduct strikes, REB, and support of special operations units. The main tasks of transport aviation are—
- Transport and air landing or air drop of troops and equipment.
- Air drops of ammunition, equipment, and other supplies.
- Location of sick or wounded personnel by search and air rescue and evacuation.
- Infiltration and supply of special operations forces.
- Air refueling.
- Airborne C2 and REB.

C-5. Heavy bomber aviation is primarily a strategic force but under certain conditions may be used to support tactical actions. Capabilities include precision strikes with guided and unguided bombs, launching long-, medium-, and short-range cruise missiles and REB attacks.

C-6. Bases and airfields for aviation supporting the SV are generally defined by the type of aviation unit. Front-line aviation typically locates no closer than 50–70 km from the battle zone. Long-range bombers and military transport aviation units conduct operations from the interior of Russia. Army aviation bases or airfields typically locate 20–30 km from the supported SV units to allow quick response and recovery after strikes.

C-7. In addition to direct cover and defense of the SV maneuver force, the VKS provides support using both fixed and rotary-wing aircraft in the following areas:

- Ground attack—Engages aggressor ground—and sometimes air—targets using air-to-ground missiles, cruise missiles, anti-radiation missiles, guided bombs, direct fire rockets, cannons, and heavy machine guns.
- Aerial reconnaissance—As a high priority task it collects and analyzes aggressor air and ground forces, terrain, and the area of operations.
- Transport—Movement of personnel, equipment, and material for delivery by air-landing or air-drops.
- Electromagnetic warfare—Identifies and monitors the EMS to collect, analyze, and summarize data to degrade, disorganize, or disrupt aggressor C2, precision weapons, equipment, reconnaissance, and electromagnetic warfare. Simultaneously, electromagnetic warfare supports the stability of SV communications, C2, and automated weapons control.
- Navigation support—Measures to achieve high accuracy of ground attacks, reconnaissance, and electromagnetic warfare.
- Communications—Use of radio, satellites, radio relay, tropospheric, wire, and optoelectromagnetic means to provide voice, telegraph, facsimile, and data transmissions.
- Tactical disguise—Conducting concealment, imitation, demonstrations, and misinformation to protect aerospace units and actions.
- RHBZ protection—Identification and assessment of the use of RHBZ weapons by an aggressor, destruction of aggressor RHBZ complexes, and stability of aerospace operations in an RHBZ environment.
- Nuclear support—Maintains the readiness of nuclear munitions and capability to accurately deliver those munitions for designated strikes.
- Topographic and geodetic support—Data collection to support the analysis of terrain to support decision making, use of weapons, supplying maps, terrain photos, and terrain changes.
- Meteorological support—Collection of data to support analysis of meteorological conditions and impacts on flight operations and the effects on weapons of mass destruction.
- Engineering—Supports the survivability and operational capability of air actions from bases, airfields, and covert locations.
- Search and rescue—Conduct timely location and recovery of air crews forced to abandon aircraft over both aggressor and friendly territory.
- Psychological struggle—Preparation and delivery of electromagnetic media or printed materials of an information-psychological impact on a target population or aggressor military units.

EQUIPMENT OVERVIEW

C-8. The following equipment tables cover fixed wing aircraft, rotary wing aircraft, and unmanned aerial vehicles.

Note. The equipment overview provided in this appendix is not intended to be exhaustive, but rather to introduce the most widely employed variants of major equipment types used by the SV. For more detailed equipment information, consult the Worldwide Equipment Guide (https://odin.tradoc.army.mil/WEG).

FIXED WING

C-9. While the VKS provides defense against aggressor air and cruise missile attacks, it also serves as a strike component of Russian joint strategic, operational, and tactical actions. For tactical-level strikes the VKS uses fixed wing aircraft to conduct electromagnetic suppression of aggressor air defenses as well as direct attacks against high-priority mobile targets.

C-10. In recent years, the modernization of its aircraft has been one of Russia's main priorities. Roughly 75 percent of the former Soviet aircraft have either been replaced or modernized with precision navigation, digital flight controls, missile guidance, improved sensors and self-defense capabilities. Aircraft modernization allows the VKS and SV to conduct integrated combat actions with improved coordination, responsiveness, and accuracy of aerospace support. The Russian VKS aircraft capable of supporting SV ground actions follow in table C-1.

Table C-1. Fixed-wing aircraft

Type	Role	NATO Codenames	Crew	Range	Service Ceiling
Tu-22M3M	Regional Bomber	Backfire-C	4	6,800 km	2,300 m
Tu-95MSM	Strategic/Tactical Bomber	Bear	6–7	15,000 km	13,716 m
Tu-160M	Strategic/Tactical Bomber	Blackjack	4	12,300 km	16,000 m
Su-35	Multi-Role Fighter	Flanker-E	1	3,600 km	18,000 m
Su-30	Multi-Role Fighter	Flanker-C/G/H	2	3,000 km	17,300 m
Su-34	Multi-Role Fighter-Bomber	Fullback	2	2,200 km	17,000 m
MiG-31	Fighter Interceptor	Foxhound	1	3,000 km	25,000 m
Su-27	Multi-Role Fighter	Flanker	2	3,530 km	19,000 m
Yak-130	Light Attack Fighter/Trainer	Mitten	1	2,100 km	12,500 m
MiG-29	Multi-Role Fighter	Fulcrum	1	1,430 km	18,000 m
Su-25	Ground Attack	Frogfoot	1	1,000 km	7,000 m
Su-24	Ground Attack	Fencer	2	2,775 km	11,000 m
An-30	Reconnaissance	Clank	7	2,630 km	8,300 m
A-50	Early warning & control	Mainstay	15	7,500 km	12,000 m
Il-78	Refueling	Midas	6	7,300 km	12,000 m
An-12BK	Transport	Cub	5	5,700 km	10,200 m
Tu-134	Transport	Crusty	3–5	3,000 km	12,100 m
Tu-154	Transport	Careless	5	3,900 km	12,100 m
Il-76MD	Transport	Candid	5	4,400 km	13,000 m
km	kilometer	m		meter	

ROTARY WING

C-11. Rotary-wing aircraft are part of the aerospace forces but typically support SV operational and tactical actions. Support includes airlift of soldiers and equipment, support of defensive and offensive actions with direct fire, and air-to-air engagements of aggressor rotary, unmanned, and fixed-wing low level aircraft. Ground support fires are primarily from rotary-wing aircraft with limited support provided by fixed-wing aircraft such as the Su-25 Frogfoot or other platforms.

C-12. The characteristics and typical mission of the various rotary-wing support aircraft follow in table C-2.

Table C-2. Rotary-wing aircraft characteristics

Aircraft	Missions	Weapon	Speed	Weight	Payload	Ceiling	Range	Personnel
Ka-226T	Recon Target Acq. BDA Transport	N/A	250 km/h	3,800 kg	1,050 kg internal 1,100 kg sling	6,200 m	600 km	1–2 crew 7 pax.
Mi-8 / Mi-17	Recon Fires CSAR MEDEVAC NBC Mining Jamming Airborne Air Assault Transport	Rockets Cannon-23mm Machine-guns 7.62x54	250 km/h	11,100 kg	3,629 kg internal 2,721 km external	5,000 m	960 km	3 crew 24 pax. 12-MEDEVAC
Mi-26	Transport MEDEVAC Airborne Air Assault	N/A	295 km/h	49,600 kg	20,000 kg	4,600 m	1,952 km	5 crew 90 pax. 60-MEDEVAC
Mi-28NE	Day/Night Ground Attack Escort Airborne Air Assault Low-speed & Low-level aircraft	Cannon 30mm — Ataka-V air-to-surface missiles – 16ea — SA-24 air-to-air missiles — Rockets 80mm – 40ea 130mm – 10 ea.	320 km/h	10,700 kg	N/A	5,700 m	1,100 km	2 crew
Mi-24 / Mi-35	Day/Night Ground Attack Airborne Air Assault MEDEVAC	Cannon 23mm — Rockets 80mm – 80ea — ATGM Strum – 8ea	335 km/h	8,500 kg	1,500 kg internal 2,400 sling	4,900 m	450 km	2 crew 5 Pax. 4 MEDEVAC
Ka-52	Day/Night Ground Attack	Cannon 30mm — ATGM - 12ea	310 km/h	7,700 kg	N/A	5,500 m	545 km	2 crew
ATGM ea kg	anti-tank guided missile each kilogram	km km/h MEDEVAC	kilometer kilometer per hour medical evacuation		m mm N/A	meter millimeter not applicable		

UNMANNED AERIAL SYSTEMS

C-13. In the realm of development and integration of UAS to support combat actions, Russia has not kept pace with innovation and emerging technology. To remedy this gap in capability it is rapidly adopting UASs from foreign sources as well as prioritizing national development programs to enhance its reconnaissance and target acquisition capabilities. Likewise, it is working to develop direct attack UAS platforms as well as loitering munitions. The SV linked the precision target acquisition capabilities of UAS with its indirect fire platforms via automated C2 to create reconnaissance strike and reconnaissance fire complexes. See table C-3 for more information on indirect fires platforms. See figure C-1 on page C-6 for information about ground support unmanned aerial vehicles.

Table C-3. Indirect fires platforms

UAV	Weight (max. Takeoff)	Service Ceiling	Range	Endurance	Simultaneous Operations (Yes/No)
Dozor-100	720 kg	7,100 m	3,700 km	24 hours	No
Eleron-3SV	4.9 kg	3,500 m	20 km	90 min	Yes, 2 per GCS
Gorizont Air S-100	200 kg	5,500 m	180 km	6 hours	No
Orlan-10	16.5 kg	5,000 m	150 km	16 hours	Yes, 4 per GCS
Orlan-30	27 kg	5,000 m	500 km	8 hours	Yes, 4 per GCS
Orlan-50	50 kg	5,000 m	500 km	8 hours	Assessed Yes, 4 per GCS
Pchela-1T /Shmel-1T	138 kg	2,500 m	INA	2 hours	No
Tu-143 (Strike)	1,410 kg	3,000 m	190 km	INA	No
Zala 421-08	2.55 kg	3,600 m	10 km	1 hour	No
Zala 421-20	2.0 kg	1,000 m	5 km	35 min	No
Lancet-3/5	3.0 kg	INA	40 km	40 min	INA
GCS ground control station INA information not available kg kilogram km kilometer m meter					

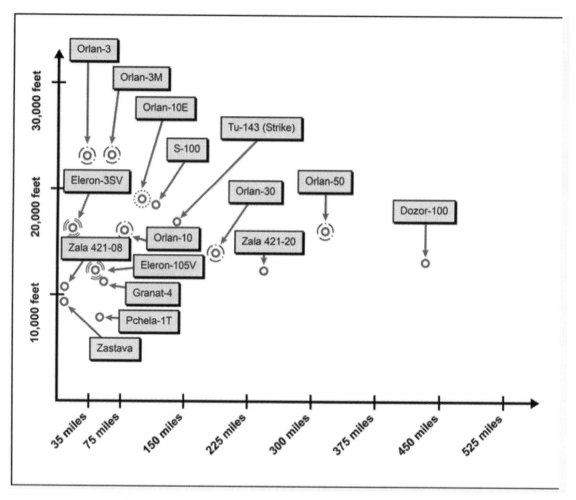

Figure C-1. Ground support unmanned aerial vehicles

AIR DEFENSE

C-14. Operational-level air defense forces of the VKS use both fixed-wing aircraft and ground missile and gun platforms to provide an integrated air defense envelope for the SV ground forces. The air defense units combine collected battlefield data to create a common operational picture of the aggressor airborne threat. They position ground air defense units to provide sufficient coverage of the SV based on the senior commander's plan.

C-15. High- and mid-level air defense complexes integrate the coverage of air defense platforms to engage likely corridors of aggressor attacks. Fixed-wing aircraft plan to fill any gaps in the coverage provided by ground-based air defenses.

C-16. Integrated air defenses have a wide range of tasks with the priority being to repulse aggressor reconnaissance from space and airborne platforms. The priority targets for air defense engagements are for protection of priority nuclear delivery complexes, C2 centers, ground maneuver forces, and industrial and economic centers from aggressor air and missile attacks.

C-17. Air defense target categories span from ground level to an altitude of 100 km. Low level engagements are described as small (0 up to 1,000 m), medium (1,000 to 4,000 m), large (4,000 to 12,000 m), and into the stratosphere at 12,000 m and beyond. Ground complexes are categorized by their maximum weapons range with short range up to 30km, medium range to 100 km, and long range more than 100 km.

CAPABILITIES AND LIMITATIONS

C-18. Many of the aircraft models in the VKS have been operational since the end of the Soviet era. While the airframes and components continue to be modified, they are still older designs. Resources continue to dictate that the Russian military maintain sufficient capability to support the SV and ground action, but dedicated ground support aircraft are not currently in development.

C-19. Most of the role of direct ground support by the VKS is expected to be assumed by combat UAVs that are now in development. These platforms will offer a high degree of stealth, extended loiter times over the battlefield, and the capability to attack and re-attack if necessary.

C-20. The majority of the VKS ground attack capability currently exists in the rotary-wing units. These aircraft offer good duration over the target, precision direct engagement capability with guided missiles, rockets, and guns. Some of the VKS rotary-wing aircraft are specifically designed for night or limited visibility conditions that allows the VKS to provide continuous support day and night. The rotary-wing aircraft of the VKS are also designed and equipped to conduct air-to-air strikes against aggressor low and slow flying aircraft.

EMPLOYMENT IN SUPPORT OF COMBINED ARMS

C-21. In the past, the SV relied more on missile and artillery indirect fires at the tactical level than it did on the capabilities of the VKS. The character of the modern battlefield involving nonlinear actions emphasizes the role of the VKS to provide strikes and fires to secure the flanks of maneuver units and as covering force support.

C-22. Fixed and rotary-wing aviation provide precision fires against mobile high-priority targets that massed indirect fires cannot target in a timely manner. Reconnaissance strike complexes typically support strategic-operational level attacks while reconnaissance fire complexes support operational-tactical level attacks. Fixed and rotary-wing attacks integrate into the reconnaissance strike or fire complex to provide a responsive means of attacking designated aggressor targets.

C-23. For SV maneuver units conducting a maneuver or positional defense the VKS performs four types of support actions. These actions are mainly performed by army aviation rotary-wing aircraft:

- Containing actions provide support to maneuver forces to hold prepared defensive positions.
- Maneuver support provides rapid response to aggressor air assault, flanking, or envelopment attacks.
- Raid support requires reconnaissance and strike aircraft to support the rapid movement of the maneuver force to strike the aggressor target and then return or advance to a designated position.
- Flanking action support provides reconnaissance and aerial fires to secure the flanks of the maneuver force.

C-24. For SV offensive actions the VKS first targets aggressor air defense weapons to gain local air supremacy. Strike aircraft approach targeted air defense at low or extremely low altitude using the masking properties of terrain and simultaneous electromagnetic suppression by either airborne or ground REB. Attacks are short using either a shallow dive or a pitch up and attack from level flight.

C-25. Once aggressor air defenses are neutralized then the VKS supports SV offensive action with air strikes. Typically, VKS aircraft will not fly over SV ground formations because of the difficulty of coordinating friendly air defense weapons tight or hold status. Also, with mortar and artillery units and subunits located well forward, overflights would cause interruption of fires to avoid fratricide. Following this approach allows both artillery and aircraft fires to hit aggressor targets simultaneously.

C-26. To ensure coordination of air strikes the VKS deploys command posts to collocate with the SV. The control of the strike formation is transferred from the airbase control to the forward control point at predetermined distances from the target. Guidance to the target is then carried out by aircraft controllers collocated with the maneuver commander using VHF radios.

This page intentionally left blank.

Appendix D

Air Defense Support

Russian IADS has historically been a critical asset and likely will continue to be so in the future. An IADS is a key component of the integrated fires and C2 system that provides early warning and vectors of approaching aggressor aircraft. Air defense systems span the numerous low altitude MANPADS, as well as the use of other unit weaponry, in each SV maneuver unit and subordinate units. Mobile air defense gun and low-to-medium altitude/range missile systems, and other mobile surface-to-air missile systems are typically positioned in a maneuver unit's defensive zone to provide overlapping air defense coverage. Air defense systems at higher headquarters provide additional overlapping air defense to counter medium-to-high altitude aggressor targets. The combination of artillery, rockets, and air defense as an integrated fires and C2 system supports an expectation of minimal aggressor aircraft influence in the maneuver brigade's tactical mission.

D-1. While Russia's Aerospace Defense Forces long-range, operational and strategic resources have been heavily examined and analyzed, the bulk of Russian air defense weapons are located with the SV's Air Defense Troops. Russia has always placed a high priority on countering aggressor airplanes and helicopters and recently expanded this mission to cover cruise missiles and UAVs. While dedicated SV air defense brigades provide both medium- and short-range coverage, maneuver brigades and divisions have their own ensemble of short-range air defense systems. There are typically two air defense battalions in a motorized rifle or tank brigade.

D-2. The SV brigade commander is responsible for all assets within their brigade conducting intelligence, surveillance, and reconnaissance functions, consequently they are responsible for the placement of the air defense battalions' radars.

D-3. A SV brigade in the defense will be bolstered by its organic anti-aircraft and missile systems. The air defense system is intended to shield the brigade from air attack and cruise missile strikes. The air defense missile battalion armed with the "Tor-M1" is responsible for zonal coverage designed to protect the brigade's subunits and command post from air attack. A battery of 2K22 "Tunguska" (SA-19s) typically protects the first echelon of the brigade. Customarily, two platoons of the "Strela-10" missile battery will furnish protection to the BrAG. The brigade's first echelon will also be protected by two platoons outfitted with "Igla" MANPADS, while the third platoon defends the brigade command post.

ORGANIZATION OF AIR DEFENSE IN THE SV BRIGADE

> *Note.* The equipment overview provided in this appendix is not intended to be exhaustive, but rather to introduce the most widely employed variants of major equipment types used by the SV. For more detailed equipment information, consult the Worldwide Equipment Guide (https://odin.tradoc.army.mil/WEG).

D-4. The 9K330 Tor (SA-15 Gauntlet) is an all-weather low-to-medium altitude, short-range surface-to-air missile system. It is intended to engage aircraft, helicopters, cruise missiles, precision guided munitions, and UAVs. The launch platform is the 9A331 combat vehicle. The system has 8 ready to fire 9M330 missiles with an engagement range of 12km. There are 12 launcher vehicles in in an SA-15 Battalion. They are located within the batteries of the air defense missile battalion. There have been numerous variants to the combat vehicle, to include the Tor-M2DT designed to operate in arctic regions. The Tor is currently being replaced by the Tor-M2 which will be equipped with 16 missiles with an improved flight ceiling. The system will be able to engage 4 targets at the same time and fire on the move.

D-5.   The 2k22 Tunguska (SA-19 Grison) is a tracked, self-propelled anti-aircraft weapon equipped with a surface-to-air gun and missile system. The vehicle holds eight missiles with a secondary armament of two 30mm 2A38 cannons. Intended to provide both day and night protection to SV brigades and regiments the system was designed to target low flying aircraft, helicopters, and cruise missiles regardless of weather conditions. Designed as a replacement for the ZSU-23-4, the Tunguska was first developed in 1970. Improved versions entered service in 1990, 2003, and 2007. The new versions include the 2K22M/2S6M and the Tunguska-M1 or 2K22M1. The 9M311-M1 missile used with the Tunguska-M1 has an improved capability against cruise missiles and a range of 10km.

D-6.   The 9K35 Strela-10 (SA-13 Gopher) is a short-range missile system most commonly found on the MT-LB chassis. The Strela-10 is a visually sighted missile. The system contains four close-range missiles with the ability to engage targets up to 5 km away and has a flight ceiling of 3.5 km. The system is considered less susceptible to electromagnetic warfare countermeasures. Each battery within the air defense missile battalion normally has six launcher vehicles. There are several missile variants including the 9M31M, 9M37, 9M37M and 9M333.

D-7.   The 9K310 Igla (SA-18 Grouse) is a very short-range MANPADS. The system can engage targets at a distance of up to 5 km and has a flight ceiling of 3.5 km. Normally each brigade will have 27 MANPADS. These are located within the battery of the air defense missile-artillery battalion. The 9K333 Verba is currently being manufactured as a replacement for the Igla. It is believed that the Verba contains an improved guidance system and will be better equipped to evade countermeasures.

CAPABILITIES AND LIMITATIONS

D-8.   While Russia's Aerospace Defense Forces contain a vast array of operational and strategic air defense assets, the bulk of short and medium range air defense resources are situated with the Air Defense Troops of the SV. Indeed, medium and short-range air defense assets can be found in dedicated SV air defense brigades while SV maneuver units contain an abundance of organic short range air defense resources. This three-tier or layered system allows for the creation of anti-access area-denial zones which could prove challenging to aggressor aircraft, cruise missiles, and UAVs. However, recent conflicts in Syria and Libya have shown that many of the exported Russian air defense systems proved ineffective in countering drones and low flying missiles. The Israeli Air Force also has been extremely successful in defeating Russian air defense systems using combinations of electromagnetic warfare (REB), anti-radiation missiles, and precision guided munitions. These limitations for export versions are at least partly due to inadequate operator training and lack of dedicated maintenance. These limitations will have reduced impact on the effectiveness in the SV. Although Russian Aerospace Forces and the SV have certainly made great strides in building an integrated air defense system, major challenges remain in the realm of acquisitions, training, and operational viability.

D-9.   In addition to direct cover and defense of the SV maneuver force, the VKS provides support using both fixed and rotary-wing aircraft in the following areas:

- Ground attack—Engages aggressor ground and air targets using air-to-ground missiles, cruise missiles, anti-radiation missiles, guided bombs, direct fire rockets, cannons, and heavy machine guns.
- Aerial reconnaissance—As a high priority task it collects and analyzes aggressor air and ground forces, terrain, and the area of operations.
- Transport—Movement of personnel, equipment, and material for delivery by air-landing or air-drops.
- Electromagnetic warfare—Identifies and monitors the EMS to collect, analyze, and summarize data to degrade, disorganize, or disrupt aggressor C2, precision weapons, equipment, reconnaissance, and electromagnetic warfare. Simultaneously, electromagnetic warfare supports the stability of SV communications, C2, and automated weapons control.
- Navigation support—Measures to achieve high accuracy of ground attacks, reconnaissance, and electromagnetic warfare.

- Communications—Use of radio, satellites, radio relay, tropospheric, wire, and optoelectromagnetic means to provide voice, telegraph, facsimile, and data transmissions.
- Tactical disguise—Conducting concealment, imitation, demonstrations, and misinformation to protect aerospace units and actions.
- CBRN protection—Identification and assessment of the use of CBRN weapons by an aggressor, destruction of aggressor CBRN complexes, and stability of aerospace operations in an CBRN environment.
- Nuclear support—Maintains the readiness of nuclear munitions and capability to accurately deliver those munitions for designated strikes.
- Topographic and geodetic support—Data collection to support the analysis of terrain to support decision making, use of weapons, supplying maps, terrain photos, and terrain changes.
- Meteorological support—Collection of data to support analysis of meteorological conditions and impacts on flight operations and the effects on weapons of mass destruction.
- Engineering—Supports the survivability and operational capability of air actions from bases, airfields, and covert locations.
- Search and rescue—Conduct timely location and recovery of air crews forced to abandon aircraft over both aggressor and friendly territory.
- Psychological struggle—Preparation and delivery of electromagnetic media or printed materials of an information-psychological impact on a target population or aggressor military units.

This page intentionally left blank.

Appendix E

Antitank Support

Antitank fires within the SV serve the primary function of securing high-speed avenues of approach against aggressor armor forces. Antitank systems include antitank grenade launchers, ATGMs, guns (ATG), and direct-fire artillery platforms. Antitank functions range from the capability of specific weapon platforms to purpose-formed antitank units. This appendix, in conjunction with the other appendixes and chapters of this publication, provides a doctrinal appreciation for antitank support.

EQUIPMENT OVERVIEW

E-1. The following tables (E-1 and E-2 on page E-2) provide important parametric data for the included equipment.

> *Note.* The equipment overview provided in this appendix is not intended to be exhaustive, but rather to introduce the most widely employed variants of major equipment types used by the SV. For more detailed equipment information, consult the Worldwide Equipment Guide (https://odin.tradoc.army.mil/WEG).

Table E-1. Barrel-launched antitank missiles

	AT-10 "Kastet"	9K116-1 "Bastion"	9K116-2 "Sheksna"	9K116-3 "Basnya"	9K119 "Svir"	9K119M "Refleks"
Caliber (mm)	100	100	115	100	125	125
Maximum range (m)	5,500	5,500	5,500	5,500	5,000	5,000
Armor penetration (mm)	500–550	500–550	500–550	500–550	900	900
Guidance	Laser	Laser	Laser	Laser	Laser	Laser
Platform	MT-12	T-55	T-62	BMP-3	T-72/72S/ 2A45	T-80B /80U/ T90/ T-72B3
m meter mm millimeter						

Table E-2. Towed antitank guns

	2A19 "MT-12 Rapira"	2A18 "D-30"	2A65 "Msta-B"	2A36 "Giatsint-B"
Caliber (mm)	100	122	152.4	152.4
Maximum range (km)	3	15.3	8.1	28.3
Direct fire range (m)	1850	870	2130	1530
Rate of fire (rpm)	7	8	6	6
Unit of fire (rds)	60	80	80	60
Crew	6	6	6	8

km	kilometer	mm	millimeter	rpm	rounds per minute
m	meter	rds	rounds		

Appendix F

Electromagnetic Warfare (REB)

The focus in this appendix is the REB complexes found at the tactical level. To gain a full appreciation of the REB capabilities of the SV it is necessary to study the integrated capabilities at the strategic and operational levels as well. The SV integrates all REB complexes to create a networked capability that collects, analyzes, and engages EMS targets at any given time prior to or during large-scale war.

F-1.   The SV incorporates REB capabilities at the tactical echelon to enhance use of the EMS in support of its combined arms actions. It uses integration of REB, fires, air defense, aviation, and maneuver forces and means to support the objective of restricting aggressor ability to strike SV units and subunits. The SV's REB capabilities allow it to disrupt, degrade, and disorganize aggressor C2, communication, and precision weapons.

F-2.   Using the EMS, SV REB—

- Jams radio communication and disrupts command links to degrade C2 networks.
- Degrades or spoofs GPS telemetry.
- Degrades electromagnetic fuses including artillery, antitank, and missiles.
- Provides target acquisition information for indirect fire attacks on aggressor command, control, communications, computers, intelligence, surveillance, and reconnaissance platforms.
- Transmits psychological operations to target aggressor troop morale and unit effectiveness.
- Counters and disrupts artillery and aviation targeting.

F-3.   As a result of the reorganization of the SV, each maneuver brigade or regiment has an electromagnetic warfare company. The REB complexes of the company produce a 50km spherical footprint to target aggressor systems and protect brigade units and subunits. These REB complexes are adequate to cover the units of a brigade or regiment as they conduct defensive or offensive actions.

F-4.   In addition to the REB companies, the SV uses complexes found in five REB brigades in each military district to enhance the EMS coverage in support of maneuver units. These complexes have extended range capabilities that allow collection of EMS signatures and transmissions. Current trends indicate that the ability to link and share data collected from the EMS is a growing capability of Russia's REB units.

F-5.   The VKS aerospace forces supporting the SV include both airborne and ground-based REB units and subunits. REB battalions are included in VKS air defense armies. They are designed to protect and support the air defense divisions of the armies. Army aviation units include dedicated REB helicopters, and the transport regiment provides fixed-wing REB.

CAPABILITIES AND LIMITATIONS

F-6.   The Russian military continues to make modernization of its REB capabilities a priority. The SV modernized many older REB complexes while continuing to develop and field new REB complexes. Table F-1 shows some of the various REB complexes found in the SV and their general function. The capability of REB complexes is a constantly changing field that requires detailed study to develop a full understanding of what the SV may use in support of tactical actions.

F-7.   Note. The equipment overview provided in this appendix in table F-1 on page F-2, is not intended to be exhaustive, but rather to introduce the most widely employed variants of major equipment types used by the SV. For more detailed equipment information, consult the Worldwide Equipment Guide (https://odin.tradoc.army.mil/WEG).

Table F-1. Electromagnetic capabilities

REB Complex Name/Designation	Function
RB-531B (Infauna)	Jams communications, radio-proximity fuses, and remote detonators. It also incorporates electro-optical sensors to detect the flash of launches and automatically trigger a covering smoke screen.
RB-341V (Leer-3)	GSM communications jamming using a command post and up to three Orlan-10 UAVs to collect and transmit SMS messages to 3 and 4G networks.
RB-301B (Borisoglebsk-2)	Tactical SIGINT, automated jamming system (detection, direction finding, analysis and suppression of HF/VHF radio communication). Includes R-330KMV (Mandat) command post and several jamming stations mounted on MT-LBs.
R-934UM	Radio jamming station (detection, direction-finding, analysis and suppression of VHF/UHF radio communications). Part of R-3301P Diabazol automated jamming system.
Pole-21	Disruption of UAV and precision weapon control systems by jamming Global Positioning System (GPS) and radio control signals. It provides coverage in a 50km radius in support of tactical actions.
R-330Zh (Zhitel)	SATCOM/GPS/GSM jamming station (detection, direction finding, analysis, and suppression of UHF radio signals). Part of 330M1P Diabazol automated jamming system.
Shipovnik-Aero	UAV interception system for suppression of aggressor intelligence, surveillance, and reconnaissance (ISR) platforms.
Torn	Automated SIGINT complex mounted on two KamAZ-5350 trucks. It is capable of real-time detection, analysis, and transmission of target information for signal emanation in the 1.5 – 3,000 MHz frequencies. Conducts direction finding at ranges up to 70km for HF, VHF, and UHF frequencies.
Rtut-BM	Radio proximity fuse jamming station (protecting personnel and equipment from munitions using proximity fuses). Covers .5 sq km for up to 6 hours of continuous operation.
RB-636AM2	Monitors airwaves and tracks various radio emitting sources.
R-318T	COMINT system. Includes command post and several stations operating in HF/VHF/UHF frequencies
MKTK-1A (Djudist)	Radio control and information protection system (detection, direction finding, and analysis of radio signals). Intended to assist with emission control
Palantin	Designed to jam communications systems that use software defined radio (SDR) technology. Also conducts SIGINT to identify and locate transmissions from current and future radio systems. Jams 3,000-30,000 kHz and 30 – 300 MHz
Moskva-1	A passive SIGINT collection complex that reportedly covers all frequency ranges. Capable of passively detecting aircraft or missiles in a 400km coverage area.
Krasuka-2	SIGINT collector that jams radars and returns false target information to misdirect aggressor attack aircraft and radar-directed missiles. Jams S-band radar used by (airborne warning and control systems) AWACS.
Krasuka-S4	Detects and jams X and Ku-band radars used by fighter-bomber aircraft.
Rychag-AB	Jamming station on an MI-8MITPR-1 REB helicopter used to protect flights of Army Aviation helicopters by jamming aggressor aircraft radars and air-to-air missile systems.
RB-109A (Bylina)	SIGINT collector that deploys on five trucks to control and direct REB complexes to attack aggressor communications and C2 networks. It also contains its own self-protection countermeasures integrated into its capabilities.

AWAC	Airborne Warning and Control System	MT-LB	multipurpose tracked armored vehicle
C2	command and control	MHz	megahertz
COMINT	communications intelligence	REB	radio electromagnet
HF	high frequency	SIGINT	signal intelligence

EMPLOYMENT AND INTEGRATION IN COMBINED ARMS

F-8.   The Russian military and the SV conduct integrated REB actions during all phases leading up to large-scale war, competition, crisis, and conflict. During competition REB complexes collect EMS signals, intelligence, and emanations against all potential aggressors as they conduct training or operations. The SV uses those signatures to identify and track aggressor units in preparation for any transition to conflict.

F-9.   The SV uses the resulting intelligence data to plan and execute disruption and degradation of C2 networks near and far, from 1 to 8,000km. To protect SV units and subunits the REB not only targets aggressor C2 but it also degrades aggressor intelligence gathering and weapons targeting systems. REB units also protect the SV by identifying and controlling EMS emanations from its own platforms.

F-10. Russia is designing its new REB complexes to include limited artificial intelligence capable of autonomously directing actions. As an example, the Bylina complex autonomously collects EMS emanations for real-time analysis, selects the optimal REB platform under its control, and then directs the attack of the target.

F-11. The SV employs ad hoc networks that organize REB fires along the same lines as the strike and fire complexes of the missile troops and artillery (RViA). The REB ad hoc networks integrate reconnaissance, guidance, C2, and means of electromagnetic fires. The REB networked subsystems are labeled as the reconnaissance-electromagnetic strike and fires complexes. As part of combined arms actions these networks exist for the period of the combat action to complete the electromagnetic destruction and suppression of aggressor electromagnetic networks and system. REB brigades field separate battalions in each military district and the organic REB companies in each maneuver brigade provide the necessary units and complexes to generate the electromagnetic reconnaissance and fires that engage acquired targets.

This page intentionally left blank.

Appendix G
Engineer Support

The SV employs a robust combat engineer capability throughout its maneuver formations, underpinning the consistent focus on obstacles, entrenchments, fortifications, and mobility. Engineer units and subunits in the SV are a specialty branch supporting combined arms operations with special trained soldiers and engineer equipment.

Engineer formations facilitate the following support actions:

- Engineer reconnaissance.
- Combat engineering.
- Obstacle clearing.
- Construction.
- Breaching.
- Bridging.
- Camouflage.
- Water supply.
- Deception.

Note. The equipment overview provided in this appendix is not intended to be exhaustive, but rather to introduce the most widely employed variants of major equipment types used by the SV. For more detailed equipment information, consult the Worldwide Equipment Guide (https://odin.tradoc.army.mil/WEG).

ENGINEER SUPPORT EQUIPMENT OVERVIEW

G-1. The BAT-2 combat engineer vehicle is part of the SV engineer formations route construction and clearing section at every echelon. It is used for road and track clearing and grading. There are four BAT-2s in the battalion. The vehicle is almost always a part of the movement support detachment (known as OOD) for each column. The movement support detachment will often move behind the advance guard or forward detachment conducting engineer reconnaissance and improving roadways. The vehicle is an armored tracked bulldozer with an adjustable width dozer blade and a two-ton crane with a maximum 7.3-meter boom reach. The BAT-2 can ford up to 1.3 meters of water and can winch 25 tons. Operated by a two-man crew, the vehicle has a fully enclosed cab and can carry a squad of eight combat engineers. The cab provides NBC protection, and a storage unit behind the cab can carry a large assortment of combat engineer supplies. The BAT-2 contains no defensive armaments.

G-2. The DZ-180A wheeled road grader/scraper is typically part of the engineer battalion's route construction team. The vehicle will normally move with the movement support detachment. Each engineer battalion will have two DZ-180As. The DZ-180A is used for excavation and blading in road construction and maintenance. The vehicle can also be used for creating embankments, leveling, and creating ditches. The DZ-180A is also often used in snow and ice removal.

G-3. The KRAZ-257B wheeled crane is also part of the engineer battalion's route construction team and is normally a part of the movement support detachment. There are two KRAZ-257Bs in each engineer battalion.

G-4. The TMM-3 truck-launched bridge sets are almost always attached to the movement support detachment. There are four TMM-3 truck-launched bridge sets in each engineer battalion. Each bridge set can position a 10-meter bridge span. Bridge spans can also be connected. Used together, the vehicles can construct a 42-meter bridge that is 3.8 meters wide.

G-5. The GMZ tracked mine layer is assigned to engineer regiments (military district level assets) and engineer brigades (army-level assets). The system can place a 1,200 m, three-row minefield comprising 624 mines in 26 minutes. There are three GMZ-3 tracked mine layers in each SV obstacle platoon. The SV also employs the UMZ remote mine delivery system. This system is used to deploy antipersonnel mines and antitank mines. The system consists of six firing modules which are attached to the back of the ZiL-131 truck. Each module has thirty firing tubes for a total of 180 firing tubes. The UMZ can place from 180 to 11,520 mines without a reload dependent on mines/cassettes employed. One UMZ can position a minefield 150 to 1,500 m long subject to the type of mine used. The UMZ can propel the minefield 30–60 m from the ZiL-131 truck while the vehicle is moving at from 10 to 40 km per hour.

G-6. The URAN-6 is a self-propelled, tracked, remote controlled UGV designed for countermine operations. The operator can control the UGV at up to 1000 m. The device has four cameras that provide a 360-degree view. The Uran-6 detects, identifies, and destroys any type of explosive device if the blasting power does not exceed 60 kilograms (or equivalent) of TNT. The UGV can be equipped with five different interchangeable tools such as a bulldozer blade and grappling hooks. The maximum speed of the Uran-6 is three km/h while conducting demining operations. The system is a license-built copy of the Croatian MV-4 robotic flail.

G-7. The IRM is a fully amphibious, tracked, engineer reconnaissance vehicle based on the BMP-1 chassis. The IRM collects information on depths of water obstacles, determines angles of slope, and detects buried landmines. The IRM is equipped with two retractable propellers in ring covers for swimming and steering and two cases with 16 9M39 solid engines (each has a thrust of 312 kg and weighs 6.3 kg), for getting out of mud. Special reconnaissance equipment consists of two R-147 radios; one PIR-451 periscope; TNPO-160, TNP-370, and TNV-25M periscopic observation devices; an AGI-1s horizon indicator; a DSP-30 portable periscopic rangefinder, a PAB-2M portable aiming circle; one TNA-3 gyroscopic navigational device; an EIR echo depth finder with automatic recorder and three sonar transducers; a RShM-2 river-type wide-span mine detector; RVM-2M and IMP-2 portable mine detectors; a PR-1 portable penetrometer used to analyze soil for crossability; and an ice drill with ice stake.

G-8. The PMP ribbon bridge set consists of 32 center pontoons and 4 ramp pontoons, the normal bridge unit consists of a half-set (one complete bridge) made up of 16 center and 2 ramp pontoons. Each 4-section is launched from the KRAZ-255B. It automatically unfolds upon entering the water. The sections then lock in place to form a bridge unit 6.75 m long and 8 m wide. Normally, all the units are launched simultaneously. They join together parallel to the near shore to form a continuous roadway. The roadway then swings across the water obstacle; powerboats (6 per half-set) hold it in place on the designated center-line. Engineers can use the full 36- pontoon set to construct 227 m of bridge. They may also configure it as 40- to 170-ton rafts. A half-set gives the capability to construct 119 m of 60-ton bridge, 191 m of 20-ton bridge, or rafts. Under ideal conditions assembly speeds of 7 m of bridge per minute can result.

G-9. The MTU-72 armored bridge layer is a combat engineering vehicle, designed to launch an assault bridge for tanks and other military vehicles across trenches and water obstacles. The MTU-72 bridge layer is based on a modified T-72 main battle tank chassis. A number of the Soviet T-72B or T-72M1 tanks were converted to an armored bridge layer by removing the turret and replacing it with a bridge-launching system.

G-10. The IMR-3M was created on the basis of the T-90A tank and is equipped with a KMT-R3 track width mine plough with an EMT electromagnetic detachable device for trawling mines with rod-type and noncontact magnetic fuses. The vehicle is capable of lifting loads up to 2 tons. The IMR-3M is armed with the 12.7mm remote-controlled machine-gun mount. It can fire at ground, low-speed air targets, and explosive objects openly lying on the ground.

G-11. The BTM-3 is designed to dig defensive and communication trenches in soils of up to IV type. The BTM consists of the basis vehicle and digging equipment. A heavy artillery prime-mover was used as the vehicle basis. When the vehicle is moving in transport mode, the gear box provides five gears for forward movement and one for backward.

DEFENSIVE AND OFFENSIVE ENGINEERING TASKS

G-12. Time and resources will determine SV engineer efforts in the defense. Engineer support for the defense focuses on reconnaissance, countermobility support, and survivability support. The general aims of engineer support for the defense include—

- Controlling access and tempo by delaying, disaggregating, and canalizing aggressor forces.
- Establishing conditions necessary for organizing the defense.
- Preparing deception positions.

G-13. The priority field construction tasks for engineers in the defense include—

- The security zone or forward positions.
- Command post.
- Artillery firing positions.
- Artillery ammunition storage.
- Artillery transport.
- Communication trenches.

G-14. In the security zone or forward positions, the goals of SV engineer support are to hold up the aggressor advance. Within the conflict zone, engineer support facilitates organized withdrawal, maneuver, or counterattack by SV forces. Defensive planning measures ensure extensive use of obstacles, integrated with preplanned direct and indirect fires, to affect the aggressor's advance and facilitate its destruction.

G-15. During preparation for the offense, the SV engineers focus on four major activities:

- Preparing routes for the advance and employment of combat forces.
- Providing survivability support to units in assembly areas.
- Establishing passages in obstacles and minefields.
- Establishing and maintaining crossings over water obstacles.

G-16. During the offense, SV engineers' primary mission is to support the attack and assist in maintaining a high tempo of combat. Once the attack has started, engineer troops continue to perform tasks contributing to the high rate of advance. Occasionally, the POZ will create obstacles to protect the flanks, disrupt counterattacks, and block aggressor reinforcements. Ongoing engineer reconnaissance is performed independently or in conjunction with other reconnaissance elements.

G-17. The SV views the commitment of exploitation forces or reserves as one of the most critical and vulnerable periods of combat. Engineer troops play a vital role in ensuring its success. They ensure the force's timely arrival and provide support for its deployment and protection against flank attacks.

G-18. Offensive tactical missions requiring SV engineer support include—

- Movement forward, deployment, and transition to the offense.
- Preparation of assembly areas.
- Crossing water obstacles.
- Repelling counterattacks.
- Penetration of aggressor defenses.
- Conduct of the battle.
- Commitment of exploitation force or reserve.
- Reinforcing captured positions.

EMPLOYMENT AND INTEGRATION IN COMBINED ARMS

G-19. SV engineer troops are a specialty branch and conduct highly complex engineering tasks in support of combined arms operations. They are organized into formations, units, and subunits to perform myriad specialized missions in support of combined arms operations. SV engineers are also charged with countering aggressor intelligence systems and targeting by aggressor weapons systems. To do this, SV engineers will often design various deceptions (camouflage) as to the location of SV units and subunits as well as facilities.

G-20. All SV maneuver brigades contain an organic engineer battalion. Its purpose is to support the mobility of SV forces and to thwart the mobility of aggressor forces. This is accomplished by a multitude of engineering task, ranging from engineer reconnaissance to water crossing support to obstacle construction and preparation of defenses. Without doubt, SV engineering troops play a vital role in the integration of combined arms.

Appendix H
Material Technical Support

Material Technical Support Материально Техницеское Обеспецение - Material'no-tekhnicheskoye obespecheniye - MTO) services and support units of the SV critically address supply issues for Russian forces. This equipment overview contains general information on the basic capabilities of MTO technical support means. Capabilities and limitations describe the level of support provided by MTO forces and any limiting factors. The employment and integration section describes how the MTO supports combined arms actions.

H-1. The MTO mission is to provide the means to supply forces in a timely manner with all necessary resources supporting reliable battlefield actions and the rapid restoration of weapons and military equipment. MTO maintains not only the units but also the infrastructure for storage, transport, and technical support. MTO also provides for soldier health, well-being, and readiness with transport, consumer services, and sanitary and veterinary services.

H-2. The SV holds the bulk of supplies and transport services at the military district and army levels. This allows rapid shifts in priority of support as dictated by the flow and pace of defensive or offensive actions. This system directs the flow of support to the units that are critical for success of the commander's plan. MTO units move equipment, supplies, and services from warehouses and depots to designated points using ground transport, rail, pipelines, and in limited cases, air. In some cases, certain support functions can be shifted to contract support from commercial providers to free MTO units for direct support to maneuver units and subunits.

H-3. The military districts may have a single or multiple logistic complexes depending on the number of armies in the district. These complexes are a mix of Soviet-era warehouses and ammunition dumps and modernized mobilization and support facilities. The modernized facilities, labeled transshipment and logistic complexes (Perevalochno-Logisticheskie Kompleksy - Perevalochno-logisticheskiye kompleksy (PLK)), serve as transshipment and logistics complexes in areas considered by the General Staff to be threatened by aggressor actions.

H-4. Each PLK contains pre-positioned brigade equipment sets that include heavy weapons ranging from tanks to wheeled vehicles. For each brigade set of equipment it also packages and stores 2.5 times the full combat ammunition loads. Deploying SV units will leave their normal equipment at home base, move by air transport and fall-in on the sets available to the PLK. Complicating this process is the fact that SV units do not have standardized equipment sets which may result in personnel being unfamiliar with the equipment set at the PLK.

H-5. A limited high-speed road network requires Russia to rely heavily on rail and barge transport to move units and equipment forward from the PLKs or home installations. Also, with limited heavy-airlift capability, even the VDV relies on ground and rail transport to move heavy equipment such as tanks for air assault missions.

H-6. The importance of railway transport in the Russian military is emphasized by the fact that it fields railway Troops within the MTO, dedicated to operation and maintenance of military rail. These units, consist of ten brigades, at an approximate strength of 29,000 soldiers, as well as independent battalions which are allocated to each military district. Deployment of the SV during large-scale war relies on transport by rail of most personnel, equipment, and supporting supplies railway troops not only perform operation of the railway but also repair rail lines, perform bridge building and repair, and conduct concealment as part of rail-based logistics support.

H-7. Units and subunits typically stock three to five days of supply on organic vehicles. Units that are not the priority may not receive support and rely on organic stocks or forage for required supplies. Forward positioned support units prioritize returning lightly injured soldiers to their units and lightly damaged equipment to battle readiness. Heavily damaged units are consolidated into smaller units or combined with other units to create combat-ready forces.

H-8. The MTO commander determines the support requirements for a brigade or division based on several factors:

- The unit's mission as directed by the army commander's plan.
- Brigade task organization including the various types of units and subunits.
- Established consumption rates or norms for missions, equipment, and supplies.
- Required reserves at the end of planned offensive or defensive actions.
- Expected losses due to aggressor actions.
- Terrain and weather conditions.

H-9. Types of material and technical support include—

- Artillery and rockets.
- Tank and automotive.
- Transportation and route maintenance.
- Communication and automated command and control complexes.
- Radiological, chemical, and biological.
- Material supplies.
- Meteorological services.
- Veterinary services.
- Housing and financial services.

H-10. MTO units and services for each level are—

- Military district:
  - Repair-evacuation regiments, supply depots, warehouses, and PLKs generally located in the deep interior of the districts.
- Army:
  - MTO brigades fall under the command of military districts in peacetime but can be subordinated under wartime conditions or during periods of armed conflict. For offensive actions the delivery of ammunition and fuel is typically carried out by the MTO brigade rather than divisional or brigade material support battalion.
  - A MTO battalion is either a single modernized combined battalion or two battalions that perform logistics and maintenance. Subordinate companies positioned to support the lead maneuver forces for offensive or defensive actions.
- Brigade:
  - Separate material support battalion is most likely a single modernized combined battalion performing logistics and maintenance. For the defense, the battalion typically positions behind the second echelon maneuver battalions away from the expected aggressor avenue of attack. For offensive actions the MTO battalion follows the second echelon on one or two designated routes according to the commander's plan.
  - Material support companies are located within the defensive position of the maneuver battalions for the defense. For offensive actions the MTO companies are integrated into the march formation for offensive actions and follow the main force column at a distance of 2–3km.

H-11. Provisioning of supplies such as ammunition; petroleum, oils, and lubricants; technical and nontechnical supplies; and rations are prioritized based on the assigned mission for a unit. A unit of fire is the supply label for the quantities of ammunition allocated to a unit and for petroleum, oils, and lubricants it is a refill.

H-12. A unit of fire varies by type weapon, as examples, for a combat rifle it is 400 rounds, mortars are 80 rounds, a tank main gun is 40 rounds, and an artillery howitzer is based on the caliber of the gun system. The standard unit of fire for artillery is 80 rounds for 120 mm systems, 60 rounds for 152 mm systems, and 20–40 rounds for 203 mm and 240 mm systems. The unit of fire for multiple rocket launchers is three loads of rockets per system. Based on the assigned mission a unit may receive multiple units of fire to achieve the number of rounds necessary to calculated desired level of damage or destruction on a target.

H-13. A refill is the amount of petroleum, oil, and lubricants required for brigade vehicles to travel 500km. Each combined arms brigade stocks three to five days of supplies on weapons platforms and organic transport.

H-14. Maneuver units are fueled by battle formations at designated fuel points while artillery and special vehicles such as REB are fueled at its designated positions. The combined arms reserve is also fueled at its battle position.

MATERIAL TECHNICAL SUPPORT EQUIPMENT OVERVIEW

H-15. The MTO equipment of the SV is designed specifically to work well in the geographic region and borders of the Russian Federation. For large-scale war the SV expects to have interior lines of supply and communications for MTO and to rely on the extensive rail network within the country.

H-16. At the tactical level MTO equipment are those platforms that move supplies, materials, and recover or maintain combat systems. The MTO Battalion has approximately 408 transport vehicles and trailers capable of hauling 1,870 tons of cargo. Trucks used by the SV for MTO support functions come in many varieties with a range of capabilities (see table H-1) for parametric date of included logistic vehicles.

Note. The equipment overview provided in this appendix is not intended to be exhaustive, but rather to introduce the most widely employed variants of major equipment types used by the SV. For more detailed equipment information, consult the Worldwide Equipment Guide (https://odin.tradoc.army.mil/WEG).

Table H-1. Logistic vehicles

Designation	Zil 131	GAZ 66	URAL 43206	URAL 4320-31	URAL 5323	KamAZ 4350	KamAZ 5350	KamAZ 6350
Crew and Personnel	3 15 (est.)	2 21	3 24	3 27	3 39	3 30	3 30	3 39
Chassis	6x6	4x4	4x4	6x6	8x8	4x4	6x6	8x8
Weight (GVW kg)	10,425	5,440	12,300	15,550	22,260	11,900	15,850	22,600
Cargo (kg)	5,000	2,000	4,200	6,500	10,000	4,100	6,650	10,500
Fuel	Petrol	Diesel	Diesel	Diesel	Diesel	Diesel	Diesel	Diesel
Engine (hp)	150	115	180	240	300	240	260	360
Max speed (kph)	80	95	85	85	85	100	100	95
Range (km +/-)	650	875	1000	1000	1000	1000	1000	1000
Gradient (%)	58	67	58	62	58	68	68	68
Fording (m)	1.4	.8	1.75	1.75	1.2	1.75	1.75	1.75
GVW gross vehicle weight hp horsepower kg kilogram		kph m	kilometer per hour Meter					

H-17. The MTO units use tracked and wheeled recovery vehicles as well as wheeled maintenance trucks to provide the required support. A variety of wheeled transport trucks and trailers haul dry cargo, fuel, water, and other liquids to supported units. Wheeled field kitchens and trailers prepare hot meals and bake bread to support SV soldiers.

CAPABILITIES AND LIMITATIONS

H-18. Combined arms maneuver battalions have few organic support units, normally only a platoon that performs maintenance and transport. The SV relies heavily on the detached support companies from the MTO battalion. Support platoons with transport and maintenance capabilities move supplies forward to the maneuver units, conduct limited maintenance support, and evacuate damaged equipment.

H-19. Fuel points have from 10 to 20 filling points and can dispense 1,000 to 2,600 liters per minute. A fully prepared refueling point using fuel tanker trucks or bladders can fuel a motorized rifle company in 10 minutes, a battalion in 30 minutes, and a maneuver brigade in 2 to 2.5 hours. Transport of fuel forward is performed by pipeline, train tank car, or truck and trailer transport.

H-20. Food is prepared three times daily when conditions allow. If in march formation meals are issued at the beginning and during the second half of the 24-hour march day. Soldiers are issued dry rations for the interval between meals. If conditions do not permit preparation of and issue of hot meals, then combat field rations are issued per the direction of the senior commander.

EMPLOYMENT AND INTEGRATION IN COMBINED ARMS

H-21. MTO support focuses on maintaining the combat readiness of fire and maneuver units and subunits. It collects required supplies from designated supply warehouses and delivers them to the forward deployed units. It also evacuates wounded or sick soldiers as well as damaged or faulty equipment to care or repair points respectively. It delivers food, water, ammunition, fuel, and maintenance support based on the timing and direction of the senior commander's plan.

H-22. The SV uses established norms to calculate the supplies and support required for both defensive and offensive actions. Combined arms units at the brigade level and above have organic MTO units that provide the level of supplies and support required by the senior commander's plan down to subordinate subunits.

H-23. At the tactical level the SV typically relies on push logistics support to accomplish the senior commander's plan for offensive actions. If the higher echelon does not have the resources to transport supplies to subordinate subunits, then the subunits will pull the allocated supplies using organic transport vehicles. Units and subunits may also pull supplies from higher levels during a defense or preparing for offensive action.

H-24. Each maneuver battalion receives support from an organic MTO platoon that is subordinate to a MTO company. The platoon moves with the battalion during defensive and offensive actions. The platoon evacuates damaged or inoperable vehicles, transports rations, supplies, and provides other soldier life support functions. During a defense the MTO companies move forward to the rear of the fire and maneuver battalions to decrease the amount of time required to provide logistics support.

H-25. A medical platoon is also organic to the maneuver battalion. It also moves with the maneuver battalions during offensive and defensive actions. The medical platoon moves to the combat area to treat and prepare soldiers for evacuation to medical facilities by helicopters or ground transport. The medical platoon is focused on returning lightly injured soldiers to their units as quickly as possible.

H-26. The ultimate goal of MTO is to ensure the readiness of designated units and subunits at the required place and time to accomplish the tasked mission.

Appendix I

Nuclear, Chemical, and Biological Operations

This appendix presents the SV unit and subunit capabilities of the RHBZ troops. It begins with a functional overview of RHBZ forces, presents the equipment used, the capabilities and limitations, followed by how the RHBZ is integrated into SV combat actions at the tactical level.

I-1. RHBZ units support integrated combined arms actions to maintain SV combat power. In addition to tactical support missions during large-scale war, the RHBZ also supports the Russian Federation in the event of peacetime industrial accidents involving nuclear, chemical, or biological agents. The stated purpose of RHBZ forces is to eliminate or mitigate the loss of Russian Federation forces, formations, or populace, caused by radioactive, chemical, and biological contamination. Unlike NATO CBRN forces, RHBZ forces also possess an offensive CBRN capability and can deliver flame (thermobaric) weapons and smoke.

I-2. The SV organization generally has RHBZ units and subunits at every level of its maneuver forces. See table I-1 for more information.

Table I-1. RHBZ Units

Combined arms units	RHBZ
Military district	Brigade
Combined arms and tank armies	Regiment
Motorized rifle and tank divisions	Battalion
Motorized rifle and tank brigades	Company
Motorized rifle and tank regiments	Platoon
Artillery brigades and regiments	Platoon

I-3. The SV expects and is prepared to conduct operations in a nuclear, chemical, and biological environment. The SV includes chemical weapons use and the resulting effects in many of its maneuver exercises. The objective is to ensure that SV units and subunits are prepared and capable of conducting tactical actions under contaminated conditions.

I-4. At the tactical level, a RHBZ company typically supports a motorized rifle or tank brigade. The company has four platoons with unique functions and equipment, but this may change depending on the supported unit:

- Reconnaissance—RHkM-6 (13 each), RAG-3U (1 each), and KRPP-U (1 each).
- Decontamination—DKB-1K (2 each) and ARS-14KM (8 each).
- Aerosol—TDA-2K (5 each).
- Flame—TOS-1/1a/2 (3 each) and BMO-T (3 each).

I-5. The SV RHBZ reconnaissance and decontamination platoons have some of the same capabilities as Western CBRN forces. The tactical support missions of the RHBZ include reconnaissance to identify CBRN hazards; mitigation of radiological, chemical, and biological effects; employment of smoke to protect against precision fires; and flame weapons to kill enemy personnel and destroy enemy systems.

I-6. Detection of contamination during reconnaissance is the first of five main objectives for RHBZ units and subunits, which are to locate and identify the radiological, chemical, and biological hazards. The RHBZ units and subunits integrate with maneuver reconnaissance to identify contaminated areas and transmit data concerning the level of the threat, boundaries of contaminated areas, and clean or less contaminated routes.

I-7. The capabilities of the RHBZ reconnaissance platoon of a motorized rifle or tank brigade include—

- Reconnoiter an area up to 60 sq. km. or one route of up to 30 km in a radioactive or chemical contaminated zone. For biological contamination the area covered is reduced to 10 sq. km.
- Identify the boundaries of contaminated areas and report the level of radiation or chemical contamination.
- Identify and monitor one nuclear or one chemical strike in the zone of action.
- Test and monitor for contamination of personnel, weapons, equipment, or material.
- Use remote chemical sensors to conduct surveillance of an area with a radius of 5 km.

I-8. The second main objective for RHBZ units and subunits is protection of SV units and subunits from contamination. All SV units and subunits have personal protective equipment, and many combat vehicles have organic collective protective equipment that removes contaminants from the air before it enters the crew compartment. The protection of SV units by the RHBZ involves mitigation measures to reduce or eliminate contamination using decontamination equipment and processes. Operations include the decontamination of contaminated personnel and equipment at wash stations and the transfer for burial of contaminated human remains.

I-9. The decontamination platoon performs the following tasks:
- Decontamination of troops and personal equipment.
- Decontamination of equipment and devices.
- Decontamination of terrain areas.
- Decontamination of military facilities and structures.
- Generation of foam coatings to protect equipment and facilities.
- Aerosol cloud generation to counter aggressor reconnaissance and precision weapons.

I-10. The other three tasks are accomplished by the aerosol and flame platoons. The aerosol platoon creates aerosol clouds to obscure and hide SV formations from aggressor precision attack means. The aerosol platoon also uses cloud generators and smoke grenades to create obscuring smoke that obstruct aggressor reconnaissance and targeting. The flame platoon delivers thermobaric weapons and conducts liquidation of the consequences of actions (destructions) at radiological, chemical, and biological facilities.

NUCLEAR, CHEMICAL, AND BIOLOGICAL EQUIPMENT OVERVIEW

I-11. The following tables display parametric data for reconnaissance and detection platforms utilized by SV (See table I-2):

Note. The equipment overview provided in this appendix is not intended to be exhaustive, but rather to introduce the most widely employed variants of major equipment types used by the SV. For more detailed equipment information, consult the Worldwide Equipment Guide (https://odin.tradoc.army.mil/WEG).

Table I-2. Nuclear, chemical, and biological reconnaissance complexes

Designation	KDKhR-1n	RHkM-4-01	RHkM-6	RAG-3U
Detection	Radiation Chemical	Radiation Chemical	Radiation Chemical	Calculation & Analytical Center
Time to plot (s)	10	INA	Real-time	Initial - 10 min Plot effects of 10-20 nuclear and 1-10 chemical strike – 1 hr.
Range (km)	75		6	N/A
Radiological	-	30	50	N/A
Chemical	-	10	10	N/A
Operational duration (h)	130	24	24	N/A
Prime mover	MT-LB	BTR-80	BTR-80	KAMA3-4350
Prime mover range (km)	500 land	200–600 land 12 water	200–600 land 12 water	1,000 (+)
Speed (km/h)	61 highway 30 off-road 6 water	80 highway 20–40 off-road 9 water	80 highway 20–40 off-road 9 water	100 highway
Weapons	N/A	1x14.5mm 1x7.62mm	1x14.5mm 1x7.62mm	N/A
Range (m)	N/A	2,000 1,500	2,000 1,500	N/A
Crew	3	3	3	4
h hour km/h kilometer per hour s seconds km kilometer mm millimeter m meter RAG Regiment artillery group				

I-12.   The following table provides parametric data for protection and decontamination platforms utilized by SV (see table I-3 on page I-4):

Table I-3. Nuclear, chemical, and biological protection complexes

Designation	KRPP-U	ARS-14K/15M	TMS-65M	Protektor-N
Mission	Radiological /Chemical Analysis	Decontamination Aerosol	Decontamination Aerosol	Decontamination Aerosol
Complex	Field laboratory	Tank, pump, and multiple spray array	Tanks and turbo-fan engine	Tanks and turbo-fan engine
Capacity (units/hr)	N/A	8 / 12	10 – 40	40
Capacity total (units)	N/A	187 / 175	UNK	UNK
Station	N/A	8/12	1	1
Ground decon.	N/A	1,400 / 1,200 (m)	1.5 – 2.5 (ha/hr.)	1.2 (ha/hr.)
Deployment (min.)	30–60	15 / 30	10 - 12	10 - 12
Primary mover	ZIL 131	KAMAZ-43114	URAL-4320	KrAZ-260
Primary mover range (km)	350–435	930	1,100	1,000
Station weight (kg)	13,500	15,000	13,425	22,000
Crew	UNK	3	2	2
h hour kg kilogram km/h kilometer per hour min minute ha/hr hectares km kilometer m meter				

I-13. Table I-4 provides parametric data for nuclear, biological, and chemical aerosol generators.

Table I-4. Nuclear, chemical, and biological aerosol generators

Designation	TDK-2K	Multipurpose Generator
Mission	Aerosol clouds	Decontamination Aerosol clouds
Cloud length (m)	1,000	1,000
Operation duration (hr)	5	5 (est.)
Mobile cloud generating speed (kph)	15–40	N/A
Deployment (m)	1–1.5	UNK
Prime mover	KAMAZ-43114	UNK
Prime mover range (km)	930	UNK
Speed (kph)	60 highway 40 roads	UNK
Weight (kg)	15,300	UNK
Crew	2	UNK
est. estimate kph kilometers per hour UNK unknown hr hour m meter km kilometer N/A not applicable		

I-14. This following table provides parametric data for flame weapon platforms utilized by the SV (see table I-5):

Table I-5. Nuclear, chemical, and biological fire complexes

Designation	TOS-1	TOS-1A	TOS-2	RPO– A/D/Z	MRO-A/D/Z
Caliber (mm)	220	220	220	90–93	72.5
Maximum range	3.5 km	6.0 km	10.0 km	600–1700 m	400–450 m
Minimum range (m)	400	400	400	20	90
Rate of fire (sec.)	15	6–12	6–12	-	-
Damage area (m^2)	40,000	40,000	40,000	50–150	50–80
Combat load (rds)	30	24	18	2	2
Crew	3	3	3	1	1
Munition	Incendiary Thermobaric	Incendiary Thermobaric	Incendiary Thermobaric	(A)Thermobaric (D)Smoke (Z)Incendiary	(A)Thermobaric (D)Smoke (Z)Incendiary
Prime mover	T-72 Chassis	T-72 Chassis	URAL-6376	Man-portable BMO-T/BMP-2	Man-portable BMO-T/BMP-2
Prime mover range (km)	550	550	1,000	600 (+/-)	600 (+/-)
System weight (kg)	42,000	46,000	34,500	12	4.7
Set up time (min.)	1.5	1.5	TBD *AI enhanced	.15	.15

kg	kilogram	km/h	kilometer per hour	min	minute	sec	seconds
km	kilometer	m	meter	rds	rounds		

CAPABILITIES AND LIMITATIONS

I-15. The SV maintains the most current and modernized capabilities in its RHBZ units based on its assessment of modern battlefield conditions. The capabilities of the RHBZ units and subunits are necessary to identify, mitigate, and recover on a contaminated battlefield. The RHBZ generates aerosol screens to obstruct observation and targeting of SV forces with indirect and precision fires.

I-16. The ability to use flame weapons is considered an important asset available to SV commanders for both the physical as well as psychological effects against aggressor threats. Heavy flame weapons in the form of TOS-1, 1A, and 2 complexes are generally found in a 9-launcher battalion at military district level. There is also an RHBZ company of 3 launchers in the RHBZ Regiment of combined-arms and tank armies.

I-17. The TOS complexes are typically integrated with combined-arms units to protect them from direct fires of the aggressor force. With limited armor protection, the TOS launchers are vulnerable to fire that can hit the rockets prior to launch causing premature detonation. The addition of artificial intelligence enhancements in the TOS-2 launchers will allow a faster cycle of emplacement, target calculation, launch, and withdrawal to avoid counter fires.

I-18. The TOS complexes will most likely be integrated with direct or indirect fire complexes to launch an attack. Because of the limited range of the rockets, the launchers must maneuver close to the forward edge of the battle to launch a strike. Once the TOS launchers are in position, direct or artillery fires will pin the target aggressor units to allow the TOS to strike the area occupied by the target unit. Combined-arms maneuver units and subunits will then exploit the resulting gap in aggressor forces.

I-19. RHBZ troops also integrate with combined-arms subunits to support tactical actions using man-portable flame weapons such as the RPO or MRO launchers. These launchers are particularly effective against bunkers, fortified positions, or defended buildings in urban terrain. Variants of each type launcher can create thermobaric, flame, or smoke strikes against selected targets.

I-20. Motorized rifle troops do have thermobaric grenades for their rocket propelled grenade (RPG) launchers but RHBZ flamethrower troops generally employ the RPO or MRO launchers. The composition of a flamethrower platoon is three 7-man squads with a basic load of two launchers per man. Transport for each squad is a modified BMP-2 or a T-72 variant labeled a BMO-T.

EMPLOYMENT AND INTEGRATION IN COMBINED ARMS

I-21. Because the SV expects to conduct actions on a contaminated battlefield, it assigns RHBZ units at all echelons. RHBZ understand the criticality of supporting maneuver forces by executing operations to locate and mark contaminated routes and areas, mitigate contamination effects, degrade enemy observation and targeting, and employ flame weapons.

I-22. The RHBZ reconnaissance data is integrated into the SV automated command and control complexes. Information on contamination is automatically passed to the command network to the attention of the commander at each level.

I-23. Protection from contamination starts at the lowest level with soldier RHBZ kits that include over-garments, boots, gloves, and masks. Many combat vehicles have integrated overpressure systems that remove radioactive or chemical contamination from the air before it enters the crew compartment. These capabilities are reinforced through training at all echelons. The SV units and subunits are practiced and familiar with tactical actions on a contaminated battlefield. RHBZ decontamination augment these capabilities by providing decontamination support.

I-24. The SV also trains to use flame weapons at echelon during offensive and defensive actions. Soldiers are trained to use thermobaric grenades and specially designed launchers. Heavy flame weapons support from RHBZ units provides enhanced capabilities during offensive and defensive actions. Thermobaric weapons also create impact on enemy forces.

Appendix J

Automated Command and Communication Complexes

This appendix provides an overview of Russian automated command and control complexes and communication networks. In particular, it addresses the transition by the SV to automated command and control systems (автоматизированных системах управления войсками – АСУВ) and the trend toward autonomous system engagement. It also discusses the communications systems used for tactical actions.

FUNCTIONAL OVERVIEW

J-1.   In its quest to reform and modernize, the Russian military continues to make significant strides in the development and integration of automated command and control systems (АСУВ). These systems are intended to allow higher headquarters and senior commanders to synchronize maneuvers and receive information from a wide variety of multifaceted military groupings, covering the spectrum from individual ground combat vehicles, artillery, REB, air defense, aircraft, and naval vessels.

J-2.   A component of АСУВ capabilities at the national level includes the Unified Tactical-level Command and Control System (YeSU TZ). The YeSU TZ complex collects, transmits, and conducts analysis of battlefield information to support the commander's decision process. It also transmits decisions and control instructions to units and subunits at the army, division, and brigade levels. In short, YeSU TZ automates the calculations and use of normative tables that Soviet-era commanders and staffs used to plan battles and campaigns. The guiding principles of the АСУВ are to—

- Integrate computerized control in all strategic, operational, and tactical headquarters.
- Support the decision process with automated planning and troop control.
- Establish a communication network that rapidly and accurately collects and transmits all battlefield data.

J-3.   By creating a system that integrates command, control, communications, computers, intelligence, surveillance, and reconnaissance within the SV, Russia will be capable of network-centric warfare. This evolution includes the capability of the SV to control tactical battlefield maneuvers incorporating satellite communications, photo and optical electromagnetic reconnaissance, near real-time intelligence, precision navigation, radio-electromagnetic suppression, and automation of C2.

J-4.   The SV places great emphasis on gaining and maintaining information dominance on the battlefield. Communication is the critical network that transmits the collected battlefield information for delivery to the commander and ground maneuver units. The SVs extensive use of electromagnetic warfare systems necessitates communication systems that are shielded against interference or include modes of operation that mitigate the impact of electromagnetic warfare strikes.

J-5.   The modernization of C2 and supporting communications networks also incorporates the introduction and expansion of robotic systems and artificial intelligence. These capabilities seek to increase the speed of effective decision making, transmission of C2 instructions, and engagement by all forces and means of the Russian military. This aspect of net-centric warfare may equal the SV's version of a human-in-the-loop to control automated complexes. Instructions issued from the headquarters may place weapons platforms such as air defense in an autonomous mode to automatically engage targets that meet the defined parameters without crew interaction.

ORGANIZATION

J-6.   The National Defense Command Center (Natsionalnyj tsentr upravlenija oboronoj - NTsUO) serves as a point of integration for military-civil coordination and control of strategic actions. Using the YeSU TZ network and other systems, it collects, analyzes, and delivers information to senior Russian leaders. It also transmits and monitors compliance with the senior leader decisions by both civilian and military elements. At subordinate levels down to brigade the Akveduk stations receive and retransmit command and control instructions to the battalion level. The YeSU TZ complex maintains continuous operation and connectivity to all military districts and regions of Russia.

J-7.   All Russian military branches including the SV are modernizing their C2 and communications networks to rapidly take advantage of modern technology. The YeSU TZ integrates C2 and those ACYB complexes used by subordinate units and subunits specifically designed for the requirements of assigned missions. The armed forces integrate the following representative complexes to form a system of systems and create network-centric capabilities.

COMMAND AND CONTROL

J-8.   Akatsiya-M is essentially the backbone C2 automation complex for the SV that integrates troop control and logistics from the National Defense Command Center down to individual brigades. As a modular C2 system it is possible to rapidly assemble in support of a headquarters. Within 20 minutes of arriving at a position it is configured and operational and it may be rapidly returned to march configuration in 30 minutes. It is flexible and may be installed in a variety of configurations: staff vehicles, vans, containers and field positions such as tents or bunkers.

AIRBORNE

J-9.   The integration of the Andromeda-D complex provides a near real-time plot of the battlefield situation to coordinate the actions of airborne forces. The capabilities of the Andromeda-D are very similar to those of the Strelets or Compass soldier terminals to automate control of units and subunits. While tested by Russian airborne units, it is not strictly limited to those type forces and is also used an ACYB complex with tank and other maneuver units.

AIR DEFENSE

J-10. The Akatsiya-E is a two-van complex that supports automated C2 of aviation and air defense units. It creates the integrated air defense view of the air battlespace for operational-tactical forces down to individual subunits. Multiple brigade level ACYB complexes integrate with the Akatsiya-E such as the Baikal-1ME, Universal-1E, Fundament-E, and Polyana-D4M1. The integration of these various complexes creates a common operational picture of the air threat and integrates the acquisition and engagement of aggressor air threats.

ANTITANK

J-11. The automated C2 complex, Командирша-E, integrates antitank missile fire with other SV weapons fires. It creates an integrated common battlefield situation map to be used by the antitank unit to engage designated tanks, IFVs, armored personnel carriers, and defensive positions. Using reconnaissance feeds from its own targeting systems in conjunction with the feed from higher headquarters it identifies and engages priority targets. It is capable of selecting and engaging targets at 6km, day-night or in limited visibility using the Kornet-E, Metis-M1, or Konkurs-M antitank missiles.

ARTILLERY AND ROCKETS

J-12. The ASUNO-S (1V168) supports automated target engagements by artillery and multiple rocket launcher weapon platforms. These platforms currently include the 2S19, BM-21, and BM-30. Its integrated GPS supports automatic registration of the firing platform, use of digital maps and collection of local topographic data, automatic download of target information and calculation of fire solutions, as well as, maintaining a real-time situational graphic for C2. As an example, ASUNO capabilities reportedly allow a

BM-30 MRL to launch a strike 120 seconds after receiving target data to the maximum 90 km range of its rockets in a 40-second volley.

MANEUVER

J-13. Strelets complexes provide individual soldiers with integrated terminals capable of voice, data, and video transmission. They are capable of precision navigation, linking to weapon sights, and other electro-optical attachments such as a laser rangefinder. Operating in the VHF band it links to company level communications networks with a battery life of 12-14 hours. A C3 variant allows distribution of targeting information to linked terminals. It is found at the squad through company levels.

REB

J-14. Organic to the REB brigade is a complex of five trucks that creates the Bylina (RB-109A) ACYB that provides an integrated view of the battlefield EMS. The Bylina uses artificial intelligence to identify EMS targets, select the REB unit or subunit to best engage the target, and engage those aggressor targets at the designated time.

Integrated ACYB Complexes

J-15. Integrated ACYB complexes are becoming more ubiquitous throughout the Russian military. The complexes support planning and communications at the national command levels down to tactical-level units and subunits. Communications platforms span the range from satellites down to individual man-portable radios. The integrations of automated C2, on-board planning, and secure communications creates a network-centric capability within SV units and combat platforms.

J-16. The SV continues to expand and enhance the tactical level communication and control complexes far beyond those found in the Soviet-era ground forces. Soviet-era ground forces relied on limited radio communication and used direction by visual signals or physical messages. While those capabilities still exist, the modernizing SV now employs radios down to the soldier level. It integrates ACYB equipment and networks into modernized tanks, armored personnel carriers, IFVs, artillery, air defense, REB, and many other maneuver and support vehicles.

J-17. Networking the expanded ACYB complexes relies on radios that provide voice, data, and telegraph transmissions. Table J-1 on page J-4, lists the terminals, radios, and retransmission equipment included to create automated C2 capabilities.

J-18. Russia clearly plans to conduct large scale war in a contested EMS environment. As such, the automated C2 and communications complexes have built-in capabilities to mitigate the effects of EMS targeting by aggressor forces. Training exercises include an EMS-challenged environment to develop the skills and knowledge necessary for operational and tactical actions.

Table J-1. Radio designations and specifications

Radio	Frequency	Capabilities (Freq. Hop - FH)	Maximum Range (km)	Mount
R-142NMR	30-108 MHz (VHF) 1.5-30 MHz (HF)	FH Voice + Data center	350	Vehicle
R-149MA1	30-108 MHz (VHF) 1.5-30 MHz (HF)	FH Voice + Data center	350	Vehicle
R-168-MRAE	1.5-1.75 GHz (UHF)	Voice + Data	20	Vehicle
R-168-MRDE	1.5-1.75 GHz (UHF)	Voice + Digital data network	1	Vehicle
R-168-0.1UE	44-56 MHz (VHF)	Voice	1	Portable
R-168-0.1U (M)E	44-56 MHz (VHF)	Voice + Data	1	Portable
R-168-0.1U(M)1	44-56 MHz (VHF)	Voice + Data	3	Portable
R-168-0.5ME	30-80 MHz (VHF)	FH Voice + telegraph	3	Vehicle
R-168-0.5UE	30-108 MHz (VHF)	Voice	5	Portable
R-168-0.5U(D)E	390-440 MHz (UHF)	Voice + Data	1.6	Portable
R-168-0.5U(M)E	30-88 MHz (VHF)	Voice + Data	2	Portable
R-168-0.5U(R)E	30-88 MHz (VHF)	Retrans for R-168-0.5UM	5	Portable
R-168-0.5USE	94-100 MHz (VHF)	Voice + Data	2.2	Portable
R-168-1KE	1.5-10 MHz (HF)	Voice	300	Portable
R-168-5KNE	1.5-30 MHz (HF)	FH Voice + telegraph	40	Manpack
R-168-5KVE	1.5-30 MHz (HF)	Voice + telegraph	300	Vehicle
R-168-5UNE	0-108 MHz (VHF)	FH Voice + Data retrans	20	Manpack
R-168-5UNE	30-108 MHz (VHF)	FH Voice + Data retrans	25	Manpack/Vehicle
R-168-5UN(1)E	30-88 MHz (VHF)	FH Voice + Data	10	Manpack/Vehicle
R-168-5UTE	30-108 MHz (VHF)	FH Voice	12	Manpack/Vehicle
R-168-5UVE	30-108 MHz (VHF)	FH Voice + Data retrans	35	Vehicle
R-168-25UE	30-108 MHz (VHF)	FH Voice + Data retrans	40	Vehicle
R-168-100KAE	1.5-30 MHz (HF)	FH Voice + Data telegraph retrans	350	Vehicle
R-168-100KBE	1.5-30 MHz (HF)	FH Voice + Data telegraph	350	Vehicle
R-168-100UE	30-108 MHz (VHF)	FH Voice + Data retrans	60	Vehicle
R-169-1	39-48.5 MHz (VHF) 146-174 MHz (	FH Voice + Data		Manpack
R-173	30-76 MHz (VHF/FM)	FH Voice + Data	50	Vehicle

GHz gigahertz	MHz megahertz	UHF ultrahigh frequency	VHF very high frequency	
HF high frequency				

EMPLOYMENT AND INTEGRATION IN COMBINED ARMS

J-19. The ACYB complexes and communications networks are designed and integrated to enhance the command of the military during competition and conflict. It is focused on increasing the stability, continuity, speed, and security of command-and-control actions. It supports the commander's ability to quickly assess the battlefield situation, supports rapid decision making, and transmits those decisions to tasked units and subunits.

J-20. Integration of ACYB coordinates the actions of units and subunits on the main avenue of attack in the offense and the likely avenues of attack by aggressor units in the defense. By using the ACYB, the SV seeks to synchronize the actions of combined arms units including but not limited to indirect fires, maneuver, aviation, and other supporting forces and means. The ACYB complex shares battlefield information to create near real-time situational awareness, direct strikes and fires against priority targets, and direct maneuver forces to exploit the advantages created.

J-21. The Russian military and SV certainly recognize the advantages offered by network-centric warfare. Its capabilities allow the SV to use strikes and fires by direct, indirect, electromagnetic, and computer attack complexes to attack aggressor information systems. These attacks disrupt, destabilize, and destroy aggressor C2 systems to reduce or eliminate their ability to synchronize battlefield actions.

This page intentionally left blank.

Appendix K
Special Operations Forces

This appendix provides a doctrinal appreciation for Russian Federation special operations forces and the different categories of special purpose forces. The SV tactical-level units do not control these forces but do use the intelligence they generate in support of tactical actions. This includes using the reconnaissance and target acquisition for action by tactical-level units and subunits, integrated fires, and higher echelon forces.

K-1. In 2009 the Russian General Staff launched a reorganization of its military forces. It also began a reorganization of its special operations forces after study of Western special forces organizations, training, and employment. The military special forces of the Soviet era, commonly labeled Spetsnaz, were subordinate to the GRU. The GRU Spetsnaz were principally tasked with intelligence collection; direct actions against aggressor forces were not a primary capability.

Note. Spetsnaz is a general term used in the Russian military to indicate that a designated unit or subunit has a narrow area of specialization. The label may apply to engineer, signal, reconnaissance, or other type units. It does not equate to the Western concept of special operations forces. The creation, organization, and training of the new special operation forces (SSO) focuses on providing highly trained contract personnel with the capability to conduct direct action missions.

K-2. The reorganization of the special operations forces created the Command for Special Operations Forces (KSSO) and a 1,000-man force. These units are directly subordinate to the chief of the General Staff of the Russian Federation Armed Forces. The KSSO directs actions of SSO during local wars and armed conflicts. During large scale war the GRU Spetsnaz and SSO will conduct reconnaissance and intelligence collection to support situational awareness and precision targeting of priority targets. The SSO and the VDV will conduct the preponderance of strategic and operational level direct action missions.

K-3. The New Generation Warfare construct states that there are no clear distinctions between peace and war, and that employment of all elements of national power are essential to accomplish national goals and objectives throughout the spectrum of competition to conflict. The KSSO, VDV, and GRU Spetsnaz forces support Russian national objectives both prior to, during, and after combat actions.

K-4. For the new KSSO, its forces, and the established GRU Spetsnaz this translates to employment throughout the spectrum of competition to conflict and return to competition. Missions range from peacekeeping to military training and support of friendly nations, as well as support of full military conflict with an aggressor military. This approach translates to employment of the SSO and GRU Spetsnaz to train and support proxy forces that perform the actual fighting against an aggressor.

K-5. Spetsnaz forces of the Russian military are trained and equipped to conduct specialized missions associated with their type of unit. They will often conduct missions where Western militaries would use elite special forces teams. The VDV airborne units and subunits are considered the most elite maneuver units in the Russian military. The GRU Spetsnaz missions have been to conduct deep reconnaissance; destroy command posts and nuclear weapons delivery platforms; disrupt communications; disrupt power supply; and disrupt local and national government functions.

K-6. The KSSO forces, subordinate directly to the chief of the General Staff, will most likely be tasked with strategic missions: destruction of high-level command posts, kidnapping, or assassination of local or national leaders, and destruction of strategic-level nuclear platforms or critical command, communications, and control networks. The projected missions for the SSO units are to engage in specialized combat where GRU Spetsnaz teams are now tasked with intelligence, espionage, and subversion. The SSO will be task-organized for each mission with the necessary number of soldiers, tanks, IFVs, artillery, and aviation support.

ORGANIZATION

K-7. The GRU Spetsnaz brigades remain subordinate to the Main Intelligence Directorate (GRU) of the General Staff until deployed in support of the SV. There are seven regular brigades and one regiment with an approximate total of 19 battalions available for SV actions. Four independent special purpose naval reconnaissance units support the Navy. The VDV conducts both airborne and air landing (десантные войска - Desant) actions with units specifically trained for each type. The VDV also has one independent special purpose regiment that conducts reconnaissance for VDV missions. In addition, there are three separate Spetsnaz elements: one regiment and two brigades directly assigned mission tasks for special events or in selected regions.

K-8. The reorganization of the SV resulted in some of the military Spetsnaz forces being recruited under the new KSSO. The SSO units are reportedly manned strictly by contract soldiers. There are some conscripts in the MTR that are personnel with specialized skills or high levels of athletic training. The trend towards an increasing number of contract soldiers in the MTR continues.

K-9. The KSSO now directs allocation of SSO for missions supporting strategic actions both during competition and conflict. The SSO is expected to operate independently and has its own aviation support allocated for operations.

K-10. At the tactical level, the GRU Spetsnaz and SV reconnaissance units focus primarily on reconnaissance to identify and provide targeting information on critical aggressor units and installations. These teams remain covert unless there are no fires platforms to engage the identified targets in an essential time window. In that event they take direct action to destroy or cripple C2, network and communications nodes, and nuclear delivery systems of the aggressor.

K-11. Table K-1 provides details on Russian MTR types and units supporting Russian military actions focused on the SV.

Note. The equipment overview provided in this appendix is not intended to be exhaustive, but rather to introduce the most widely employed variants of major equipment types used by the SV. For more detailed equipment information, consult the Worldwide Equipment Guide (https://odin.tradoc.army.mil/WEG).

Table K-1. Russian MTR types and units supporting Russian military actions.

Type	Division	Brigades	Regiments	Battalions	Companies	Strength Estimate
Airborne (VDV)	4	5				45,000
Special Operations (SSO)			2 (est.)	UNK		1,000
GRU (Spetsnaz)						15,000–17,000
Ground Forces (SV)		3		12	50	13,000–14,000
est estimate		UNK unknown				

K-12. The GRU teams generally consist of a 12-man subunit introduced to the area of operations prior to open conflict. The teams seek out friendly host-nation forces to gain the advantage of local knowledge and available manpower to undertake reconnaissance, direct action, and other specialized missions.

CAPABILITIES AND LIMITATIONS

K-13. The GRU Spetsnaz are now primarily an information and intelligence collection force. They may conduct limited direct action missions involving sabotage, demolition, assassination, sniper, or other low-level attacks. The SSO are envisioned as a more robust fighting specialized force. They may conduct several different strategic and operational level missions: airborne insertion to seize key strategic and operational positions; covert infiltration to attack critical support facilities, and attacks on high-value aggressor units or host-nation government facilities or other strategic and operational targets. A mission typically not performed by Western special operations is counteraction. The SSO may be assigned mission tasks that include counteraction to locate and destroy those specialized aggressor units.

K-14. Team equipment depends on the assigned mission. The basic kit includes the following mix of small arms, machine guns, and crew-served weapons that may be used by the GRU Spetsnaz or SSO subunits:

- Pistols
  - PYa pistol
  - Glock 34
  - Glock 22
- Submachine gun
  - SR-2 "Veresk"
  - MP5
  - APS
- Rifles
  - AK-74M
  - AK-105
  - VSS
  - VSK-94
  - Steyr-Mannlicher SSG 08
  - Sako TRG
  - Orisis T-5000M
- Machine Gun
  - PKM
  - Pecheneg
- Grenade launchers
  - GP-25
  - GM-94
  - AGS-17
  - RPG RShG-2
- Specialized
  - Shotgun - Saiga-12S
  - Rocket flamethrower - RPO PDM-A
  - ATGM - 9K111 Fagot
  - AP mine - MON-50

K-15. Vehicles are typically specialized for actions in the mission task environment:
- ATV - Yamaha Grizzly 700
- Armored car - Iveco LMV Lynx
- Helicopter Mi-8MTV-5
- Transport aircraft - AN-26
- Watercraft - Jet ski SEA-DOO GTX LTD & RTX-215
- GAZ-2330 Tiger

- UAZ-3132 Gusar
- BTR-82a
- All terrain buggy - Cheetah
- KamAZ-5350 Mustang

K-16. The organization and capabilities of the VDV are similar to other combined arms units and subunits. The special capabilities of the VDV are its airborne and air landing of soldiers and equipment based on the requirements of an assigned mission task. The VDV units provide heavier fires and maneuver forces projected against critical targets. The VDV units and subunits are reliant on aerial resupply until ground linkup with other SV maneuver units and subunits. The material technical support aspect limits the amount of time the VDV can continue actions without material technical support.

K-17. Equipment of the VDV units and subunits is in the process of transitioning from Soviet era to modernized platforms. The older equipment consists of BMD-2s, BTR-Ds, and only attached tank units instead of organic subunits. Once the modernization is completed the VDV will be capable of deploying 1,500x BMD-4M IFVs, 2,500x BTR-MDM armored personnel carriers, and an estimated 60x T-72B3 tanks. In addition, the VDV units and subunits also use the 2S9 Nona-S self-propelled 120mm mortar and the BTR-ZD anti-aircraft gun.

EMPLOYMENT AND INTEGRATION IN COMBINED ARMS

K-18. As previously noted, both the KSSO and GRU Spetsnaz receive mission tasks from the strategic level of the Russian military. Both types of MTR forces perform mission tasks that are integrated with the combined arms maneuver of the SV at the strategic and operational levels. Likewise, the General Staff assigns the VDV mission tasks involving airborne assaults or air landing of assault units and subunits.

K-19. Missions at the tactical level where Western militaries would use special forces teams are often assigned to SV high-readiness maneuver units or subunits. The BTG is one example in which a task-organized battalion could be assigned mission tasks of a raid, ambush, or assault to seize critical terrain or facilities, reconnaissance by battle, or another high-priority target.

Glossary

The glossary lists acronyms and definitions. Acronyms appearing in ATP 7-100.1 that are not Army or joint are marked with an asterisk (*). The proponent publication is listed in parentheses after the definition.

SECTION I – ACRONYMS AND ABBREVIATIONS

*AAG	army artillery group
*AC	army corps
AO	area of operations
ADP	Army Doctrine Publication
AR	Army Regulation
*ATGM	antitank guided missile
ATP	Army techniques publication
*Blokirovanie	blocking action
*BMP	infantry combat vehicles
*BRAV	coastal missile and artillery troops
*BrAG	brigade artillery group
*BTG	battalion tactical group
C2	command and control
CAA	combined arms army
*COFM	correlation of forces and means
COP	command observation post
*CRP	combat reconnaissance patrol
*CSOP	combat security outpost
*CTG	company tactical group
*DAG	division artillery group
DOD	Department of Defense
EMS	electromagnetic spectrum
*FCP	forward command post
FM	field manual
*GRU	General Staff Main Intelligence Directorate
HF	high frequency
IED	improvised explosive device
IFV	infantry fighting vehicle
*IV	information warfare
*IPb	Information Confrontation
JP	joint publication

km	kilometer
*KRUS	reconnaissance, command and control, and communications system
*KSSO	Special Operations Forces Command
kt	kiloton
LOA	limit of advance
LW/AC	local war and armed conflict
m	meter
MANPADS	man-portable air defense system
MCP	main command post
mm	millimeter
*MP	naval infantry
mph	miles per hour
*MRB	motorized rifle brigade
*MRD	motorized rifle division.
*MRL	multiple rocket launcher
*MTB	motorized tank brigade
*MTO	materiel technical support
*MTO CP	material technical support command post
*MTR	Special Operations Forces
NBC	nuclear, biological, and chemical
*NG	Russian National Guard
*NTsUO	National Defense Management Center
OE	operational environment
OP	observation post
*OSK	Joint Strategic Commands
*Pb	reconnaissance brigade
PLs	phase lines
*PLK	transshipment and logistical complex
PMCs	private military companies
PMESII-PT	political, military, economic, social, information, infrastructure, physical environment, and time
*PO	reconnaissance detachment
*PRO	forward detachment
*RAG	regiment artillery group
*RFC	reconnaissance – fire complex
*RP	reconnaissance patrol
*SV	Russian ground forces
*TA	tank army
*TD	tank division
UAS	unmanned aircraft system
UAV	unmanned aerial vehicle

*UGV	unmanned ground vehicle
UHF	ultrahigh frequency
*VDV	airborne troops
VHF	very high frequency
*VKS	Air-Space Force
*VVS	military air forces
*ZOR	zone of responsibility

SECTION II – TERMS

This section contains no entries.

This page intentionally left blank.

References

All websites accessed on 20 December 2023.

REQUIRED PUBLICATIONS

These documents must be available to the intended user of this publication.

DOD Dictionary of Military and Associated Terms. September 2023.

FM 1-02.1. *Operational Terms*. 09 March 2021.

FM 1-02.2. *Military Symbols*. 18 May 2022.

RELATED PUBLICATIONS

These sources contain relevant supplemental information.

JOINT PUBLICATIONS

Most joint doctrinal publications are available online at the Joint Electronic Library (JEL) at https://www.jcs.mil/Doctrine/Joint-Doctine-Pubs/.

This section contains no entries.

ARMY PUBLICATIONS

Army doctrine and training publications are available at https://armypubs.army.mil/.

AR 350-2. *Operational Environment and Opposing Force Program*. 19 May 2015.

FM 3-0. *Operations*. 01 October 2022.

FM 6-27/MCTP 11-10C. *The Commander's Handbook on the Law of Land Warfare*. 7 August 2019.

AIR FORCE PUBLICATIONS

Air Force Future Operating Concept: A View of the Air Force in 2035. September 2015. Available at https://www.af.mil/Portals/1/images/airpower/AFFOC.pdf.

OTHER PUBLICATIONS

MIL STD 2525D, *Common Warfighting Symbology*. 10 June 2014.

WEBSITES

TRADOC G-2 Russia Landing Zone page: https://oe.tradoc.army.mil/how-russia-fights/.

World Wide Equipment Guide: https://odin.tradoc.army.mil/WEG.

PRESCRIBED FORMS

This section contains no entries.

REFERENCED FORMS

Unless otherwise indicated, DA forms are available on the Army Publishing Directorate website at https://armypubs.army.mil.

DA Form 2028. Recommended Changes to Publications and Blank Forms.

RECOMMENDED READINGS

ADP 3-0. *Operations*. 31 July 2019.

JP 3-0. *Joint Campaigns and Operations*. 18 June 2022.

JP 3-85. *Joint Electromagnetic Spectrum Operations (JEMSO)*. 22 May 2020.

JP 5-0. *Joint Planning*. 01 December 2020.

Defense Intelligence Agency. *Russia Military Power: Building A Military to Support Great Power Aspirations*. 2017. Available at: https://www.dia.mil/Portals/110/Images/News/Military_Powers_Publications/Russia_Military _Power_Report_2017.pdf.

Foreign Military Studies Office. Charles Bartles and Lester W. Grau. *Russia's View of Mission Command of Battalion Tactical Groups in the Era of Hybrid War*. 12 June 2018. https://community.apan.org/wg/tradoc-g2/fmso/m/fmso-monographs/233611.

Foreign Military Studies Office. Dr. Lester W. Grau and Charles K. Bartles. *The Russian Way of War: Force Structure, Tactics, and Modernization of the Russian Ground Forces*. Army University Press, 2017. Available at https://www.armyupress.army.mil/portals/7/hot%20spots/documents/russia/2017-07-the-russian-way-of-war-grau-bartles.pdf.

Foreign Military Studies Office. Timothy Thomas. *Thinking Like A Russian Officer: Basic Factors and Contemporary Thinking On the Nature of War*. April 2016. Available at https://www.armyupress.army.mil/Portals/7/Hot%20Spots/Documents/Russia/Thomas-Russian-Officer.pdf.

Lester W. Grau and Charles K. Bartles. The Russian Reconnaissance Fire Complex Comes of Age. University of Oxford, Changing Character of War Centre. 30 May 2018. Available at: https://community.apan.org/cfs-file/__key/telligent-evolution-components-attachments/13-14863-00-00-00-24-27-09/2018_2D00_05_2D00_01-The-Russian-Reconnaissance-Fire-Complex-Comes-of-Age-_2800_Grau_2D00_Bartles_2900_.pdf?forcedownload=true.

Lt. Col Timothy Thomas, U. S. Army, Retired. *Russia's Forms and Methods of Military Operations: The Implementors of Concepts*. Military Review (May–June 2018). Available at: https://www.armyupress.army.mil/Military-Review/.

Military Intelligence. Major Charles K. Bartles. *Recommendations for Intelligence Staffs Concerning Russian New Generation Warfare*. October-December 2017. Available at: https://mipb.army.mil/archive/oct-dec-2017#lg=1&slide=0.

Russian Strategic Initiative (RSI). Russian Military Doctrine RSI Primer. 2022. Available at: https://oe.tradoc.army.mil/wp-content/uploads/2022/06/RSI-Russian-Military-Doctrine-Primer-Final-single-page-04282022.pdf.

Index

Entries are by paragraph number.

Entries are by paragraph number.

Entries are by paragraph number.

Entries are by paragraph number.

Entries are by paragraph number.

Made in the USA
Columbia, SC
29 July 2024

39580373R00148